D0897846

Microbial ecology
organisms · habitats · activities

CAMBRIDGE STUDIES IN ECOLOGY

EDITORS

R. S. K. Barnes *Department of Zoology, University of Cambridge UK*
H. J. B. Birks *Botanical Institute, University of Bergen, Norway*
E. F. Connor *Department of Environmental Sciences,*
University of Virginia, USA
J. L. Harper *School of Plant Biology, University of North Wales,*
Bangor, U.K.
R. T. Paine *Department of Zoology, University of Washington, Seattle*

ALSO IN THE SERIES

H. G. Gauch, Jr *Multivariate Analysis in Community Ecology*
Robert Henry Peters *The Ecological Implications of Body Size*
C. S. Reynolds *The Ecology of Freshwater Phytoplankton*
K. A. Kershaw *Physiological Ecology of Lichens*
Robert P. McIntosh *The Background of Ecology: Concept and Theory*
Andrew J. Beattie *The Evolutionary Ecology of Ant–Plant Interactions*
F. I. Woodward *Climate and Plant Distribution*
Jeremy J. Burdon *Diseases and Plant Population Biology*
N. G. Hairston *Community Ecology and Salamander Guilds*
Janet I. Sprent *The Ecology of the Nitrogen Cycle*

Microbial ecology
organisms · habitats · activities

HEINZ STOLP

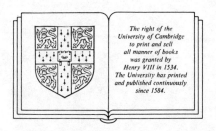

The right of the
University of Cambridge
to print and sell
all manner of books
was granted by
Henry VIII in 1534.
The University has printed
and published continuously
since 1584.

CAMBRIDGE UNIVERSITY PRESS

Cambridge
New York   New Rochelle   Melbourne   Sydney

Published by the Press Syndicate of the University of Cambridge
The Pitt Building, Trumpington Street, Cambridge CB2 1RP
32 East 57th Street, New York, NY 10022, USA
10 Stamford Road, Oakleigh, Melbourne 3166, Australia

First published 1988

Printed in Great Britain at
the University Press, Cambridge

British Library cataloguing in publication data
Stolp, Heinz
Microbial ecology · Organisms · habitats
activities – (Cambridge studies in ecology).
1. Microorganisms
I. Title
576   QR41.2

Library of Congress cataloguing in publication data
Stolp, Heinz
Microbial ecology.
(Cambridge studies in ecology)
Includes bibliographies.
1. Microbial ecology. I. Title. II. Series.
QR100.S76   1988   576'.15   87–34213

ISBN 0 521 25657 7 hard covers
ISBN 0 521 27636 5 paperback

PN

Contents

List of Figures   *page* xi
Preface   xiii

1   Introduction   1

2   The microbial world: A brief introductory review   4
The prokaryotic and eukaryotic microorganisms   5
The prokaryotic microorganisms   10
The eukaryotic microorganisms   12
Taxonomy   13

Chemical composition of microbial cells   16

Nutrition and growth   16
Nutritional requirements   16
Nutritional types   18
Physiology of growth   19
Growth under aerobic and anaerobic conditions   22

Microbial metabolism and regulation   24
Energy-yielding processes   24
Energy-consuming processes   42
Fixation of molecular N_2 44
Metabolic regulation   46

Isolation, cultivation, identification   49
Pure culture   49
Direct isolation   51
Isolation following enrichment   52
Media, cultivation   54
Preservation   56
Identification   56
Books   56
Articles   58

3   **Characterization and occurrence of the major groups of
     microorganisms**   61
     Prokaryotic microorganisms   61
     The phototrophic prokaryotes   61
     Cyanobacteria   61
     Phototrophic bacteria   64
     The chemotrophic prokaryotes   68
     The gliding bacteria   68
     The sheathed bacteria   70
     The budding and/or appendaged bacteria   71
     The spirochetes   75
     Some helical and curved bacteria   77
     The pseudomonads and related bacteria   79
     Some dinitrogen-fixing bacteria   80
     Physiologically defined assemblages of bacteria   81
     Obligately chemolithotrophic bacteria   84
     Aerobic, Gram-negative bacteria of medical importance   87
     Enterobacteriaceae and Vibrionaceae   88
     Facultatively anaerobic, Gram-negative, rod-shaped
       bacteria   92
     Anaerobic, Gram-negative, rod-shaped bacteria   94
     Gram-negative cocci and related bacteria   95
     Gram-positive cocci   96
     Gram-positive, asporogenous, rod-shaped bacteria   98
     Endospore-forming bacteria   99
     The coryneform bacteria   101
     The actinomycetes   102
     Some obligately symbiotic bacteria   103
     Cell wall-deficient bacteria   104
     The archaebacteria   105

     Eukaryotic microorganisms   106
     Fungi   106
     The microalgae   107
     The protozoa   108
   Books   110
   Articles   111

4 The natural environments of microorganisms 114
The terrestrial environment 116
Composition and structure of the soil 116
Physico-chemical conditions affecting microorganisms 119
Substrates for microbial growth 120
Energy flow 120
Abundance, distribution, and survival of microorganisms 123
Macro- and microhabitats 126
Surfaces and gradients as habitats 127

The aquatic environment 129
Physico-chemical conditions affecting microorganisms 129
Substrates for microbial growth 131
Energy flow 131
Abundance, distribution, and survival of microorganisms 132
Growth at interfaces and gradients 136

Extreme environments 137
Microbes at low water potential 138
Microbes at extreme temperatures 140
Microbes at extreme pH values 142
Microbes at low nutrient concentration 144
Microbes at extreme hydrostatic pressure 145
Books 146
Articles 147

**5 Structure, behaviour and growth of microorganisms
as related to the environment** 152
Cell structure and environment 152
Size and shape 152
Rigidity, flexibility 152
Spores, cysts, storage materials 153

Cell behaviour and environment 154
Motility 154
Buoyancy 155
Attachment to surfaces 156

Microbial growth as affected by environmental factors   158
Water regime   158
Range of temperature   163
Range of pH   165
Osmotic conditions   165
Atmospheric conditions   166
Oxidation–reduction potential   167
Light and radiation   167
Books   168
Articles   169

6 **Dispersal of microorganisms and development of microbial populations**   172
Dispersal   174

Development of microbial populations   175
Colonization and successions   175
Population growth   176
Natural selection   177
Adaptation   180
Books   180
Articles   180

7 **Interactions**   182
Types of interactions   182

Microbe–microbe interactions   184
Metabolic associations   184
Antagonisms   187

Interactions between microorganisms and plants   191
The phyllosphere   191
The rhizosphere   191
Mycorrhiza   192
Root nodule systems   194
Plant pathogens   197

Interactions between microorganisms and animals   198
Microbes as symbionts   200
Microbes as pathogens   204
Books   210
Articles   211

8 Microbial activities of ecological significance 215
The role of microorganisms in the cycling of bioelements 215
The carbon cycle 217
General aspects of carbon cycling 217
Degradation of organic matter 220
Degradation of fossil fuels 229
The nitrogen cycle 232
General aspects of nitrogen cycling 232
Ammonification 234
Nitrification 235
Denitrification 236
Dinitrogen fixation 239
The sulphur cycle 241
The phosphorus cycle 247
Transformations of other ions 249
Iron and manganese 249
Calcium 250
Silicon and other elements 251

The role of microorganisms in the degradation
of man-made compounds 252
Pesticides 254
Synthetic polymers 259
Other recalcitrant chemicals 260
Books 262
Articles 262

9 Methods used for the study of microorganisms in their
natural environments: a guide to pertinent literature 269
Types, numbers, and distribution of microorganisms 271
Books and articles 272

Microbial biomass 273
Books and articles 274

Growth rates and activities 276
Books and articles 278

Epilogue 282

Index 284

List of figures

Fig. 2.1   Section of a DNA molecule   7
Fig. 2.2   Building blocks and structure of murein   8
Fig. 2.3   Structure of teichoic acids   9
Fig. 2.4   The chemical structure of ATP   25
Fig. 2.5   The chemical structure of NAD^+/NADH (nicotinamide
           adenine dinucleotide)   26
Fig. 2.6   The Calvin cycle   28
Fig. 2.7   Electron transport chain and (re)generation of ATP by the
           proton motive force   30
Fig. 2.8   Terminal electron acceptors in aerobic and anaerobic
           respiration   32
Fig. 2.9   Dissimilatory nitrate reduction (nitrate respiration)   33
Fig. 2.10 Dissimilatory sulphate reduction (sulphate respiration)   34
Fig. 2.11 Substrate-level phosphorylation by oxidation of
           glyceraldehyde phosphate to 3-phosphoglycerate   35
Fig. 2.12 The major pathways of glucose catabolism   38
Fig. 2.13 Conversion of pyruvate into fermentation products   39
Fig. 2.14 The pyruvate dehydrogenase complex   40
Fig. 2.15 The tricarboxylic acid cycle (TCC)   41/42
Fig. 2.16 Activation of ribose-5-phosphate   44
Fig. 2.17 N_2-fixation   45
Fig. 2.18 Feedback inhibition of threonine deaminase by
           isoleucine   47
Fig. 2.19 Regulation of phosphofructokinase   48
Fig. 3.1   Schematic representation of some representative
           cyanobacteria   62
Fig. 3.2   Schematic representation of some phototrophic bacteria   65/66
Fig. 3.3   Development cycle of *Caulobacter* and *Hyphomicrobium*   72
Fig. 3.4   Morphology of a spirochete cell (a schematic diagram)   75
Fig. 4.1   Vertical soil profile   118
Fig. 4.2   Diagrammatic representation of microbial colonization
           on soil particles   119

Fig. 4.3   Food chain and energy flow through an ecosystem
           (simplified representation)   121
Fig. 4.4   Vertical profile of a stratified lake   133
Fig. 5.1   Minimum water potential for growth of bacteria and fungi   161
Fig. 5.2   Minimum water potential for growth of selected bacteria   161
Fig. 5.3   A. Cardinal growth temperatures   164
           B. Ranges of growth temperature and optimum growth
               temperatures of some thermophilic bacteria   164
Fig. 6.1   Winogradsky Column for enrichment of phototrophic
           bacteria   179
Fig. 7.1   Development cycle of *Bdellovibrio*   189
Fig. 7.2   Mycorrhizae   193
Fig. 7.3   The legume–*Rhizobium* symbiosis   195
Fig. 7.4   The ruminant symbiosis   201
Fig. 8.1   The carbon cycle (biological reactions)   218
Fig. 8.2   The structure of cellulose (β-1,4-linked glucan)   221
Fig. 8.3   Components of xylans (hemicelluloses)   222
Fig. 8.4   Structure of amylose (α-1,4-linked glucan)   223
Fig. 8.5   Structure of pectin (poly α-1,4-galacturonic acid)   224
Fig. 8.6   Some components of lignin   225
Fig. 8.7   Structure of chitin (β-1,4-linked N-acetylglucosamine)   226
Fig. 8.8   The nitrogen cycle (biological reactions)   233
Fig. 8.9   The sulphur cycle (biological reactions)   242
Fig. 8.10 Chemical structure of some herbicides   255
Fig. 8.11 Chemical structure of some insecticides   256
Fig. 8.12 Chemical structure of some fungicides   257
Fig. 8.13 Chemical structure of dioxin   258
Fig. 8.14 The chemical basis of some synthetic polymers   259
Fig. 8.15 The chemical structure of alkylbenzyl sulphonates   260
Fig. 8.16 The chemical structure of some recalcitrant polycyclic
           aromatics   261

Preface

An interest in ecology, dealing with the interrelationships of organisms and the relationships between organisms and their environment, was formerly more or less confined to the scientific community. This has changed during the past two decades. Growing environmental problems have created a public awareness of the ecological disturbances and dangers related to excessive industrial expansion and the way of life in 'disposable societies'. As a consequence of the perceived importance of ecology, research in this field has developed rapidly. Although ecological studies have largely concentrated on plants and animals, microbial ecology has also gained increasing attention during the past few years. Besides numerous original papers and many review articles, a number of books on microbial ecology have also been published. In view of this situation one may question the need for another book on this subject. In the author's opinion there is a lack of concise textbooks which cover the many aspects of microbial ecology but which are not off-putting to students because of voluminous comprehensiveness.

This book on microbial ecology focusses on the microorganisms, their habitats and their activities in nature and addresses itself primarily to microbiology students who already have a basic knowledge of science and of general microbiology, as far as the major groups of organisms, their morphology, structure, physiology and metabolism are concerned. It may also be of value to students majoring in other fields, such as plant ecology, zooecology, phytopathology, agronomy, forestry or environmental science.

The book has been divided into nine main chapters. Each ends with an extensive bibliography comprising books and articles relevant to the treated subject. For the sake of better readability I decided not to include literature citations in the text but instead added an appropriate and comprehensive list of references to each chapter. The inclusion of the full titles will facilitate access to specific pertinent literature. I gratefully acknowledge the many publications from which data, information and ideas have been supplied, but which have not been cited in the text. The reader will notice that some chapters have been treated more thoroughly than others. I do not deny my own background and bias for bacteriology and concede that the microscopic fungi, microalgae and protozoa maybe deserved more consideration.

I am greatly indebted to Professor Dennis D. Focht (University of California, Riverside) for reading and criticizing the first draft of the manuscript. His constructive criticism, comments and suggestions from afar were most valuable for improving the concept and the text. I also wish to express my appreciation to Professor Erwin Beck (University of Bayreuth) for valuable suggestions to improve the manuscript. As a co-editor of 'Cambridge Studies in Ecology', he invited me to write the text and patiently encouraged me to get the manuscript finished. I also wish to thank Cambridge University Press for their generous assistance. It goes without saying that despite the given support I alone bear the responsibility for all imperfections of this book.

Finally I would like to ask the reader to make allowances for my lack of linguistic proficiency considering that English is not my mother tongue.

October 1986   *Heinz Stolp*

1

Introduction

Microbial ecology is an interdisciplinary science closely related to both microbiology and ecology. It deals with the interrelationships among microorganisms, with the relationships between micro- and macro-organisms, and with the relationships to the environment. Since the early days of microbiology several organism-oriented and habitat-oriented disciplines have emerged from the study of the microbial world. Bacteriology, mycology, protozoology and algology (of microalgae) have developed into separate organism-oriented branches of microbiology. Virology has deliberately not been listed because of the non-organismic nature of viruses. The habitat-oriented fields comprise soil microbiology, aquatic microbiology (limnology, oceanography), medical microbiology, plant pathology, food microbiology and related disciplines. As an inter-disciplinary science microbial ecology is characterized by many connections not only to the special fields of microbiology but also to botany, zoology, soil science, hydrology and related fields.

Microbial ecology aims at unravelling the properties and activities of microorganisms in their natural environments. Because of the unusually large numbers of different microorganisms living together, the complexity of their relationships to other microbes, plants and animals, and because of the multiplicity of their activities, the study of microbial ecology was not attractive to most microbiologists while the trends were towards biochemistry of microorganisms and molecular biology. The situation has changed with the increase of societal interest in environmental problems and the broader support of ecological research programmes. Today, microbial ecology is quite a respectable science.

Microorganisms occur in any natural habitat where higher forms of life exist, but also in extreme environments devoid of plants and animals. The term 'natural habitat' as used in this book is not restricted to an environment free of man-made influences (that with few exceptions no longer exists), but refers to any habitat in nature. As coinhabitants of this planet microorganisms play a prominent role in global ecology. Together with the green plants they participate in the primary production, both under aerobic (cyanobacteria) and anaerobic conditions (phototrophic sulphur bacteria), and secure the continuity of appropriate living conditions on earth by mineralization of the organic matter and cycling of the bio-elements. The world we live in has, to a large extent, been shaped by microorganisms causing biogeochemical changes. Another important aspect of microbial ecology is the role of microorganisms as symbionts and pathogens.

There are different ways to deal with microbial ecology. Autecology is concerned with individual species in their relation to biotic and abiotic environmental factors. This analytical approach is opposed by syne-cology, an integrated research field concerned with the manifold mutual relations between the different species of organisms and with their relation to the abiotic environment. Synecology aims at understanding the entirety of microbial interactions and activities as they occur in nature.

Autecological studies, as a rule, are performed in the laboratory with representatives of defined species in axenic culture under the influence of varying physical and chemical factors. It must be emphasized that our present knowledge of morphology, structure, physiological properties, metabolic activities and genetics of microorganisms comes essentially from such laboratory experiments. In principle, autecological field studies are also possible. These are based on the inoculation of a defined organism into a natural environment and the following of its fate for a period of time. Experiments of this kind have gained interest, for instance, in connection with field inoculation of azospirillae or the release of genetically manipulated bacteria.

Because of the spatial and temporal heterogeneity and the complex network of processes in nature, synecological studies in the field are more difficult to perform than autecological studies in the laboratory. The methods and tools presently available are not yet adequate and allow direct measurement of only very few microbial activities. Because of the fundamental difficulties encountered in field studies, laboratory experi-ments have been designed which approach natural conditions by gradu-ally increasing the complexity of the experimental system. This can approximately be achieved by operating a chemostat with mixed cultures. Although experiments of this kind cannot fully mimic natural conditions, the chemostat has proved to be a valuable tool in ecophysiological studies. Contrary to batch experiments, the chemostat also allows studies under conditions of extremely low nutrient concentrations (starvation) as they commonly occur in natural habitats.

Since extrapolation of laboratory data to natural conditions is not possible or requires at least strongest reservation, and technical difficulties limit the realization of informative field experiments, progress in microbial ecology largely depends on progress in methodology. Because of the complementary function of laboratory and field studies, both approaches are indispensable for the elucidation of complex microbial processes in nature.

In ecological studies related to plants and animals the role of microorganisms has often been neglected or not taken into consideration at all. In view of the direct or indirect influences of microbial activities on macroorganisms it is necessary and profitable to also consider the role of microorganisms in macroecological studies.

2

The microbial world:
A brief introductory review

Macroorganisms, represented by the higher developed plants and animals, differ from microorganisms in many respects. The microbial world comprises organisms that in comparison to animals and plants have but a minor morphological differentiation. Most microorganisms are unicellular. Based on their cellular structure microscopically small organisms belong to two different groups: the eukaryotic and the prokaryotic microorganisms. Algae, fungi and protozoa are eukaryotic while the bacteria comprising cyanobacteria, eubacteria, and archaebacteria are prokaryotic microorganisms. The basic difference between prokaryotes and eukaryotes is the organization of the nuclear material, which is reflected in the vernacular names prokaryotes and eukaryotes derived from the Greek.

Compared to botany and zoology the field of microbiology is a relatively young scientific discipline. Despite the discovery of bacteria by Antonie van Leeuwenhoek in 1676, two hundred years passed before the scientific study of the microbes began in earnest. Mankind has, however, made use of microbial activities for thousands of years in the production of wine, beer, milk products, and in the conservation of foods.

The prokaryotic microorganisms developed long before the atmosphere of the planet earth became aerobic and before carbohydrates became the dominating primary organic material. During their evolution, the prokaryotes learnt to exploit a multitude of compounds as sources of energy, which is reflected by the metabolic versatility of the present-day microbes. Apart from morphological differences, some of the most outstanding features of the prokaryotes – in contrast to eukaryotes – are the existence of life under obligately anaerobic conditions, the use of inorganic e-donors for growth, the ability to fix molecular dinitrogen, and the utilization of C_1-compounds such as methane. The small size of microorganisms has considerable impact on their metabolic activity, their physiological flexibility, and their distribution in nature. The size of bacteria is in the range of 1 μm, that of yeast cells up to 10 μm. In relation to their volume, bacteria have a relatively large surface. This is easily exemplified by a comparison of the surface/volume ratio of a cube of 1 cm^3 and the bacterial mass corresponding to the same volume. A cube of a volume of 1 cm^3 has a surface area of 6 cm^2. A bacterium (idealized) of a volume of 1 μm^3 has a surface area of 6 μm^2. The volume of 1 cm^3 equals the volume of 10^{12} bacteria having a surface area of 6 $\times$ 10^{12} μm^2 (equivalent to 6 $\times$ 10^4 cm^2). As shown by this calculation, bacteria have a surface area 10 000 times that of the cube with the same volume. The consequence of this enormously increased surface/volume ratio is an enlargement of the exchange processes of bacteria when compared to larger cells allowing intensive metabolism. The situation is mirrored by the high specific respiration rate ($Q_{O_2} = \mu l O_2/$mg dry weight/h) of microorganisms as compared to the tissues of higher organisms. The Q_{O_2} values of bacteria are normally between 1000 and 2000, whereas root materials and plant leaves have values less than 5. Directly related to the intensive metabolism is the short generation time of microorganisms. Under optimal conditions, *E. coli* divides every 15 minutes. Under such conditions, it is feasible to produce any wanted amount of microbial biomass (or microbial protein) within a relatively short time.

In connection with their small size, the bacteria have evolved a high capacity of adaptation to environmental – particularly nutritional – conditions. Since a bacterial cell can only harbour a restricted number of protein molecules (some 100 000), the organism does not produce all the enzymes required but only those necessary under given conditions. Mechanisms for regulation of enzyme production, therefore, are more important in microorganisms. Another consequence of the small size and great numbers of microorganisms is their ubiquitous distribution in nature.

The prokaryotic and eukaryotic microorganisms

Compared to the size of the prokaryotic cells, which usually measure about 1μm in diameter and a few μm in length, the size of the eukaryotic cells is considerably larger. Most of the eukaryotic microorganisms have dimensions between 2 and 20 μm. A plant cell measures around 100 μm, but can be as long as 50 cm and more.

The prokaryotes have a rather simple morphology. Their shape is described as coccus, rod or curved rod (vibrio, spirillum). The morphological uniformity of the prokaryotes contrasts with their physiological versatility. Microorganisms even occur in extreme environments where eukaryotes have no chance of surviving. Compared with higher

organisms that generally depend on oxygen, the prokaryotic microorganisms comprise metabolic types that either live aerobically or
anaerobically. A number of bacteria can use both ways of life. They can
generate their energy by respiration in the presence of oxygen or by
fermentation in the absence of oxygen. Photosynthesis in eukaryotes
occurs principally under oxic conditions. The prokaryotic phototrophs,
on the other hand, comprise organisms with oxic photosynthesis
(cyanobacteria) and others with anoxic photosynthesis (phototrophic
bacteria).

The main differences between the structure of the prokaryotic and the
eukaryotic cell relate to the organization of the genetic material, the
structure of the ribosomes, the composition of the cell walls, the nature of
organelles for motility, and the presence or absence of chloroplasts and
mitochondria.

Genetic material

The prokaryotes have one circular DNA molecule of 0.25 to 3 mm in
length ('nucleoid', bacterial chromosome). The genetic material is not
surrounded by a membrane, and its division is non-mitotic. The DNA
molecule of *E. coli* consists of 4×10^6 pairs of nucleotides and has a mass
of 2.8×10^9 daltons. A section of the DNA molecule is shown in Fig. 2.1.
Many bacteria possess extrachromosomal DNA (plasmids). In
eukaryotes, the nucleus is surrounded by a porous membrane, and
division of the chromosomes occurs by mitosis and meiosis.

Ribosomes

The ribosomes of a prokaryotic cell have a size of 16×18 nm and a
molecular weight of 2.7×10^6. The number of ribosomes varies with the
size of the cell; in *E. coli* the number is around 10 000. The ribosomes of
prokaryotes belong to the 70S type and are composed of two subunits of
50S and 30S, respectively. The eukaryotes, on the other hand, have
ribosomes of the 80S sedimentation type.

Cell wall

With the exception of the archaebacteria the prokaryotic microorganisms
possess a unique cell-wall structure, the murein (Fig. 2.2). This is a
heteropolymer of N-acetylglucosamine and N-acetylmuramic acid in
alternating sequence. The heteropolymeric chains are connected by
peptide chains, thus forming the murein sacculus. This structure confers

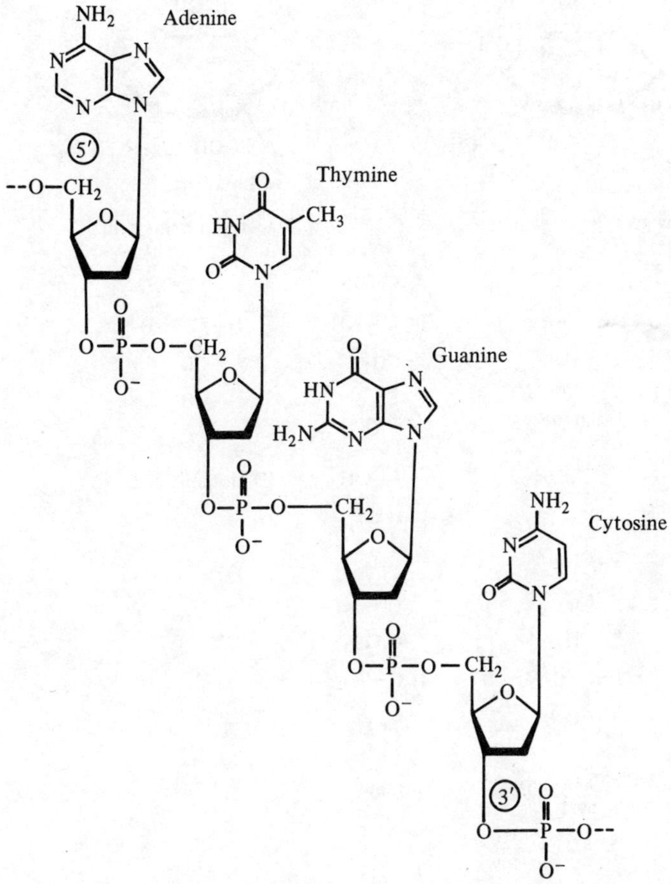

Fig. 2.1 Section of a DNA molecule

shape and rigidity to the cell. The murein of the cell wall is associated with other constituents. In Gram-positive bacteria the cell wall is mainly composed of murein (30–70%, several to many layers) and, in addition, contains teichoic acids (Fig. 2.3). The Gram-negative bacteria have a monolayer network of murein which is associated with larger amounts of lipoproteins, lipopolysaccharides and lipids. The archaebacteria do not possess the typical murein but a so-called pseudomurein. The cell walls of eukaryotes, if present, are different in composition. The major component of plant cells is cellulose, that of most fungi chitin. Diatoms have in their cell walls an inorganic polymer of siliceous nature.

A

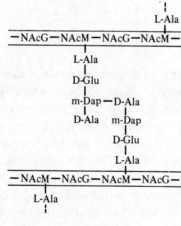

N-acetylglucosamine

N-acetylmuramic acid

L-alanine

D-alanine

D-glutamic acid

L, L-α, ε-diaminopimelic acid

L-lysine

B

```
                                      L-Ala
                                        |
   —NAcG—NAcM—NAcG—NAcM—
            |
          L-Ala
            |
          D-Glu
            |
        m-Dap—D-Ala
          |        |
        D-Ala    m-Dap
                   |
                 D-Glu
                   |
                 L-Ala
                   |
   —NAcM—NAcG—NAcM—NAcG—
     |
   L-Ala
```

NAcG: N-acetylglucosamine
NAcM: N-acetylmuramic acid
L-Ala: L-alanine
D-Glu: D-glutamic acid
m-Dap: L, L-α, ε-diaminopimelic acid

Fig. 2.2 A Building blocks
        B Structure of murein

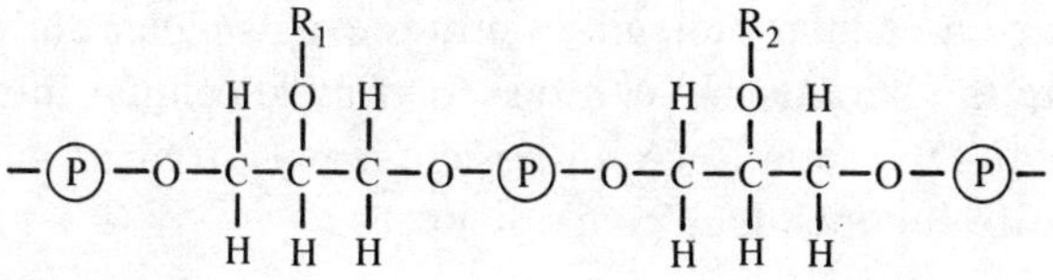

$$R_1 \qquad\qquad\qquad R_2$$

$$-\!\!\overset{}{\text{(P)}}\!-\!O\!-\!\underset{\underset{H}{|}}{\overset{\overset{H}{|}}{C}}\!-\!\underset{\underset{H}{|}}{\overset{\overset{O}{|}}{C}}\!-\!\underset{\underset{H}{|}}{\overset{\overset{H}{|}}{C}}\!-\!O\!-\!\text{(P)}\!-\!O\!-\!\underset{\underset{H}{|}}{\overset{\overset{H}{|}}{C}}\!-\!\underset{\underset{H}{|}}{\overset{\overset{O}{|}}{C}}\!-\!\underset{\underset{H}{|}}{\overset{\overset{H}{|}}{C}}\!-\!O\!-\!\text{(P)}\!-$$

Glycerol teichoic acid

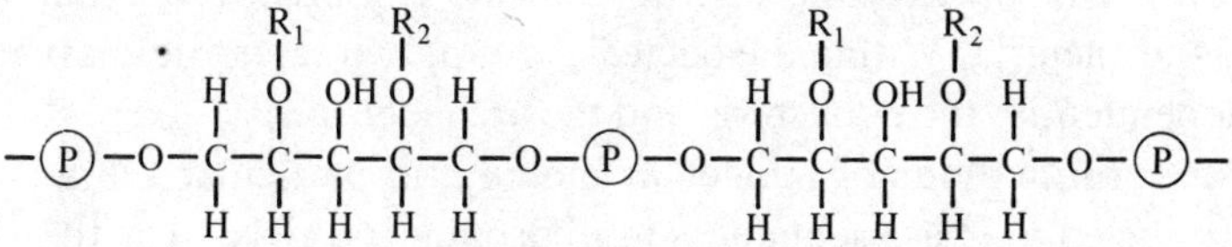

$$R_1 \quad R_2 \qquad\qquad\qquad R_1 \quad R_2$$

$$-\text{(P)}-O-\underset{H}{\overset{H}{C}}-\underset{H}{\overset{O}{C}}-\underset{H}{\overset{OH}{C}}-\underset{H}{\overset{O}{C}}-\underset{H}{\overset{H}{C}}-O-\text{(P)}-O-\underset{H}{\overset{H}{C}}-\underset{H}{\overset{O}{C}}-\underset{H}{\overset{OH}{C}}-\underset{H}{\overset{O}{C}}-\underset{H}{\overset{H}{C}}-O-\text{(P)}-$$

Ribitol teichoic acid

R: residues of D-alanine (R_1)
   or sugars (R_2)
(P): phosphate group

Fig. 2.3 Structure of teichoic acids

Flagella

The bacterial flagella are 12–18 nm in diameter and have one or several fibrils in helical arrangement. In eukaryotic microorganisms, such as algae, protozoa and spermatozoa, the flagella or cilia have a regular pattern of two central and 9×2 peripheral filaments.

Mitochondria, chloroplasts

In eukaryotes, mitochondria are the site of respiration and energy generation, and, in algae and in green plants, chloroplasts are the site of photosynthesis. Both structures are absent in the prokaryotes, and in fact are the same size as the prokaryotic cell. In connection with the symbiont theory of mitochondria and chloroplasts, it is interesting to note that the ribosomes of these structures belong to the 70S type characteristic for the prokaryotic cell.

Although viruses do not have the attributes of living cells and are of a non-cellular nature, some distinctions between viruses and cellular microorganisms may be briefly listed.

Viruses are non-cellular biological entities possessing either DNA or RNA. They are composed of a nucleic acid core and a protein capsid and depend on a cellular organism as the host and the machinery of cellular metabolism in order to multiply within cells. They possess one or a few enzymes. Non-cellular biological entities even smaller and simpler than viruses are the 'viroids'. In contrast to viruses, cellular microorganisms possess both DNA and RNA, dispose of many enzymes, and are usually metabolically independent from other cells.

The prokaryotic microorganisms

The prokaryotic microorganisms comprise the cyanobacteria and the bacteria. Within the bacteria group, two categories have evolved independently, the eubacteria and the archaebacteria.

Modern methods of molecular biology, in particular the analysis of oligonucleotide base sequences in ribosomal 16S rRNA (or 18S rRNA), have revealed that there are three kingdoms of organisms which have evolved from a progenote, the hypothetical ancestor of all living creatures: the archaebacteria, the eubacteria, and the eukaryotes. These three groups of organisms started their independent development at about the same time, several billion years ago. The three groupings that have emerged are equivalent in hierarchical rank. Most of the archaebacteria as such were already known before their unique nature was discovered. Up to then, however, they had been regarded as special groups of the eubacteria. The archaebacteria comprise the methanogens, the extreme halophiles, and certain thermoacidophilic bacteria. They differ fundamentally from the eubacteria and the eukaryotes in a number of features:

(a)   The cell wall does not contain murein (peptidoglycan),

(b)   the membranes contain diether-linked lipids (diglycerol-tetra-ethers),

(c)   the tRNA starter-amino acid is methionine (instead of formyl-methionine),

(d)   the transfer RNAs are devoid of ribothymidine in the TC-loop,

(e)   the elongation factor reacts with diphtheria-toxin, coenzyme M is a cofactor in C_1 transfer reactions, and

(f)   they are insensitive to chloramphenicol.

The present-day archaebacteria have retained properties that were probably very common in the early microorganisms.

Cyanobacteria

The cyanobacteria (formerly known as blue-green algae) are prokaryotic organisms that live in oxic environments and evolve O_2 during photosynthesis. They contain chlorophyll a as do the higher plants. Compared to the algae, however, they lack chloroplasts and other eukaryotic traits.

The cyanobacteria occur in fresh water, brackish, or marine habitats. Some are the dominating species in water blooms. Terrestrial forms are found on moist soils, and as symbionts or as epiphytic associates with higher plants. In some lichens, certain cyanobacteria occur as phycobionts. A number of cyanobacteria are capable of dinitrogen fixation. They grow as unicellular organisms or form trichomes (chains of cells). The cell wall contains peptidoglycan. Many species exhibit a gliding motility. Most cyanobacteria are obligate phototrophs and only grow in the presence of light. Some are capable of photoheterotrophic growth and assimilate a number of organic compounds in a light-dependent process. Unicellular species divide by binary fission. Trichomes grow by division of the intercalary cells. Heterocysts are the site of N_2 fixation under aerobic conditions.

Eubacteria

The eubacteria comprise a variety of phototrophic, chemolithotrophic, and chemoorganotrophic organisms. The phototrophic bacteria are capable of photosynthesis in anoxic environments, some can also photoassimilate substrates such as acetate. The bacterial phototrophs do not evolve oxygen. The chemolithotrophic bacteria obtain their energy from the oxidation of reduced inorganic electron donors. In general, they are also capable of fixing CO_2. The chemoorganotrophic bacteria obtain their energy from oxidation–reduction reactions and make use of organic compounds as electron donors.

The bacteria are the smallest cellular prokaryotic organisms. The normal size of a few selected bacteria is given below:
(a)   Some smaller cells:
       Bacteroides pneumosintes, 0.1 × 0.15 to 0.3 μm;
       Bdellovibrio bacteriovorus (swarmers), 0.25 to 0.4 × 0.8 to 1.2 μm;
       Mycoplasma spp., 0.1 × 0.25 μm;
       Treponema pallidum, 0.13 to 0.15 × 10 to 13 μm;
(b)   Some larger cells:
       Achromatium oxaliferum, 5 × 100 μm;
       Azotobacter chroococcum, 2 × 5 μm;
       Cristispira pectinis, 1.5 × 36 to 72 μm;
       Thiovolum majus, 5 × 25 μm.
Differences in morphology exist in cellular size and shape, rigidity or flexibility of the cell, life cycle, production of endospores or cysts, cell division by binary fission, budding or fragmentation, cytoplasmic inclu-

sions, differences in number and insertion of flagella, presence of prosthecae or other cellular appendages, production of holdfasts and other
adhesive structures, and presence of sheaths and capsules. The relatively
small overt morphological diversity is contrasted by an immense array of
physiological differences with respect to nutrition, relation to O_2, energy
conversion, catabolic diversity, motility, tactic movement, luminescence,
and effects of temperature, pH, barophilic, halophilic conditions, etc.

Archaebacteria.
The archaebacteria comprise organisms of the genera *Methanococcus,*
Methanosarcina, Methanobacterium, Methanomicrobium, Halococcus,
Halobacterium, Sulfolobus, and *Thermoplasma.* They will be described
in Chapter 3.

The eukaryotic microorganisms
Fungi
The fungi are chemoorganotrophic organisms living mainly
under aerobic conditions and generating energy by the oxidation of
organic materials. The vegetative structure of a fungus is a thallus which
consists of filaments having a diameter of around 5 μm. The filaments are
normally branched. A single filament or hypha consists of the cytoplasm
with its cellular elements and the cell wall. The conglomerate of hyphae is
called a mycelium. In the lower fungi, the hyphae have no cross-walls
(septae). The cells of septate hyphae are connected by a central pore in
the septum allowing cytoplasmic movement from cell to cell within the
hypha.
Classification of the fungi is mainly based on the structure of hyphae
(septate or non-septate), the formation of asexual or sexual spores, the
production of fruiting bodies, the development cycle, and the chemical
nature of the cell wall (chitin, cellulose, or other glucans). The characteristics of the main taxonomic groups are given in Chapter 3.

Microalgae
The algae are photosynthetic eukaryotes containing chlorophyll a, and in
some groups also other chlorophylls (b, c, d, e). Many species are of
microscopic size and thus classified as microorganisms. Some algae
forming seaweeds grow to considerable length. All algae produce spores
or gametes within unicellular structures. Some algae are motile by means
of flagella, others by gliding.
The algae use H_2O as an electron donor in photosynthesis and evolve

O_2. Most are obligate phototrophs and do not grow in the dark at the expense of organic compounds. Others are facultative phototrophs that assimilate sugars or organic acids (e.g. acetate) in the absence of light. Some algae can also photoassimilate simple organic compounds.

The algae are the major primary producers in aquatic environments. Their classification is primarily based on morphological features, nature of pigments, and reserve materials synthesized during photosynthesis. The characteristics of the main taxonomic groups are given in Chapter 3.

Protozoa

According to a more general and broad definition, the protozoa are regarded as unicellular small animals. Since, in some groups, there are close links between protozoa and algae or slime moulds, the lines for separation of protozoa from other eukaryotes are not distinct. A typical protozoan cell lacks the cell wall and feeds phagotrophically. Many protozoa are predators on other microorganisms, and some are parasitic in animals. The major protozoal groups have briefly been characterized in Chapter 3.

Taxonomy

Taxonomy is the practice of classification. The principle of any classification is to unite identical and/or similar organisms in basal categories and to arrange such basal categories in a system of superior (higher) taxa. Thus, taxonomy is a pragmatic science dealing with classification, nomenclature, and identification of organisms. Systematics is not identical with taxonomy: it aims at the development of a system reflecting phylogenetic relationships (natural relationships) among organisms. Phylogenetic taxonomy is opposed by phenetic taxonomy.

In bacteriology the basic category is the strain (i.e. a pure culture, a population descending from clonal development). Several strains are united in one species, several species combined in a genus. The 'species' concept in bacteria has a different meaning from that in higher organisms. The potential crossing of populations within one species as requested in the speciation of higher organisms cannot be applied to bacteria. Bacterial species have to be regarded as populations with a high degree of phenotypic similarity. Therefore the species of bacteria are at best taxospecies comprising organisms of a well-defined taxon. They usually cannot be viewed as genospecies based on the existence of gene transfer among the members of a particular species. Often a bacterial species is merely a nomenspecies, i.e. an organism that has been given a name. Because of the taxonomic difficulties and limitations, bacterial species have always been designated more or less arbitrarily.

For decades the taxonomy was largely based on data from morphology and physiology. During the past few years, information from genetics and molecular biology have gained increasing importance in bacterial taxonomy.

Since the bacteria have very little morphological differentiation, non-morphological traits have always had more importance in the taxonomy of bacteria than in the taxonomy of other biological disciplines. Among the morphological and ultrastructural characters, the following features have taxonomic value: cell shape, cell size, cellular motility, sporulation, cellular inclusions, pigments, and colonal morphology. Likewise the topography of cell-wall layers, the arrangement of intracytoplasmic membrane systems, the presence of special organelles and other fine structural characters are important for the taxonomic grouping. The same is true for the staining properties of cells (Gram-positive, Gram-negative, acid-fast). The catalogue for the physiological characterization of bacteria is broad and refers to nutritional requirements, attribution to a nutritional type, temperature relationships, aerobic/anaerobic metabolism, pH, degradation of starch, gelatin, casein, and other polymers, ability of dissimilatory nitrate reduction, nature of fermentation products, production of indole, presence of lysine-decarboxylase, arginine-dihydrolase, lipolytic activity, catalase, cyt c oxidase, and many other properties. Also pigment production, pathogenicity, immunological properties, the capacity of N_2-fixation, and symbiotic or parasitic relationships are important for characterization and classification of bacteria. In the eighth edition of Bergey's *Manual of Determinative Bacteriology* (1974) the bacteria have been classified in 19 parts. Because of the steadily accumulating knowledge of the features and the behaviour of bacteria, their classification has always been, and will be, subject to rearrangements and alterations. The first of a series of four volumes of the new Bergey's *Manual of Systematic Bacteriology* has recently (1984) been published.

Numerical taxonomy (computer taxonomy) aims at the quantification of similarities or differences among bacteria. This method is based on the Adansonian principle giving all characters the same weight, thus preventing bias of particular characters. A cluster of strains with a high degree of similarity is called a phenon. The degree of similarity is expressed in so-called S-values (S for similarity). In principle, numerical taxonomy is comparable with the classical methods based on morphological, physiological, biochemical, serological, and cultural methods.

Although the basis of the taxonomic hierarchy is the species, sub-division has been introduced for the differentiation of special types within an established species. For the differentiation at the subspecies level several terms have been introduced, such as biovar (biotype, physiological type), chemovar (refers to production of a particular chemical), cultivar (refers to special cultivation properties), morphovar (morphotype), pathovar (pathotype), serovar (serotype), phagovar (phagotype), and forma specialis (indicating a special form).

The advances in genetic, biochemical and immunological methods have given new insights into the evolutionary relationships among bacteria. Studies at the genetic level include the G + C mol% of DNA, hybridization of nucleic acids, and nucleotide sequence of 16S and 5S rRNA. At the epigenetic level the homology of proteins, the cell-wall composition, the nature of lipids, and patterns of regulation have been used as taxonomic determinants. The principle underlying the evaluation of genotypic relatedness of nucleic acids is as follows: double-stranded DNA is submitted to thermal separation, and followed by reassociation with DNA (or rRNA) from a reference strain (isotopically labelled). The reassociation is a very specific reaction requiring a high degree of nucleotide base sequence complementarity. Related DNA will result in reassociation, unrelated DNA will not. Because of the higher degree of conservation of rRNAs during evolution, the hybridization of DNA/rRNA is more useful in the evaluation of relatedness.

The comparison of nucleotide sequences in nucleic acids has revealed phylogenetic relationships among bacteria that had not been thought of before. The 16S rRNA (1580 nucleotides in *E. coli*) is a highly conservative macromolecule and can be regarded as a 'living fossil'. The similarity of identical sequences is established by comparison of identical hexamers and larger oligomers of the rRNA (partial sequencing). The degree of relatedness is expressed by a similarity coefficient, the so-called S_{AB}-value. On the basis of S_{AB}-values, the uniqueness of archaebacteria has been discovered. The data have also given new insights into the origin of the living matter. If life started some 3.5×10^9 years ago, the development of the three independent kingdoms (eubacteria, archaebacteria, eukaryotes) occurred 2.5×10^9 years ago, and all three independent kingdoms must have developed from one hypothetical 'progenote'. According to S_{AB}-values, the phototrophs are more related to Gram-negative eubacteria than to cyanobacteria. *Chromatium*, for instance, is more related to *E. coli* than to *Rhodopseudomonas*. The chemoorganotrophic Gram-negatives must be regarded as descendants of the phototrophic bacteria. Since 16S rRNA from chloroplasts and 16S rRNA from cyanobacteria have been proved to be closely related, the symbiont theory of the plant chloroplast has obtained new substantial support. Recently, total nucleotide sequencing of 5S rRNA (120 nucleotides) has revealed additional informations on the phylogenetic relationships between organisms of the different categories.

The progress in molecular biology has opened a new era of bacterial taxonomy. Nucleotide sequencing of the rRNAs, nucleic acid homology, amino acid sequences of functionally identical enzymes, and studies on gene transfer may finally result in a phylogenetic taxonomy reflecting evolutionary relationships.

Chemical composition of microbial cells

The biomass of microorganisms can be measured by determining the fresh weight or the dry weight. The fresh weight contains between 70 and 85% water; thus, the dry matter of microbial biomass is between 15 and 30% of the fresh weight. The dry matter of cells is composed of 50% proteins, 10–20% cell-wall materials, 10% lipids, 10–20% RNA, and 3–4% DNA. On the basis of the bioelements, the composition of the cells is as follows: 50% C, 20% O, 14% N, 8% H, 3% P, 1% S, 1% K, 0.5% Ca, 0.5% Mg, 0.2% Fe. Organisms growing in sea water have a N and P content that is usually 10^5 times that of the sea. Other elements become less concentrated (Ca 10 times, K 100 times), still others are less concentrated in the organisms than in their environment (e.g. Mg 1/10, Na 1/100, Cl 1/100). N and P are often the limiting factors in biomass production in terrestrial and aquatic habitats.

Nutrition and growth

The presence of nutrients is essential for growth and multiplication, and is a prerequisite for generation of energy and biosynthesis of cellular materials both in natural habitats and in the laboratory. Basically, the cell must be supplied with all the elements required for the production of cellular materials.

Nutritional requirements

The composition of the cell reflects the elemental requirements. Those elements needed in relatively high concentrations are called macroelements, those needed in minor concentrations are called microelements. The ten macroelements are carbon, oxygen, hydrogen, nitrogen, sulphur, phosphorus, potassium, calcium, iron, and magnesium (C,

O, H, N, S, P, K, Ca, Fe, Mg). The first six elements represent about 95% of the dry matter of many microorganisms. The microelements (or trace elements) comprise manganese, cobalt, copper, molybdenum, zinc, vanadium, nickel, chlorine, sodium, boron, selenium, silicon, and tungsten (Mn, Co, Cu, Mo, Zn, Va, Ni, Cl, Na, B, Se, Si, W). Apart from certain marine cyanobacteria and anaerobic phototrophs, sodium (Na) is not usually required by bacteria. Many, however, need Zn, Cu, Co, Mn, Mo, and Ni. The trace elements function in enzymes or coenzymes. Selenium and tungsten, for instance, stimulate growth of *Methanococcus vannielli* on formate.

Among the bacteria, there are basic differences as to carbon requirements. The chemolithotrophic and photolithotrophic bacteria use CO_2 as the principal source of cellular carbon (C autotrophy). In these organisms, energy source and carbon source are separated. The chemoorganotrophic bacteria, on the other hand, use the same organic compound both for generation of energy and for biosynthetic needs. Bacteria may differ considerably in the number of carbon compounds they can use. Some, like the pseudomonads, are versatile and are capable of metabolizing more than a hundred carbon compounds (carbohydrates, sugar acids, polyalcohols, fatty acids, dicarboxylic acids, other organic acids, primary alcohols, amino acids, aromatic compounds, etc.). Other bacteria are restricted in their activity to metabolizing carbon compounds and only use a limited number of substrates, e.g. the obligate methylotrophs, which use CH_4 and related C_1-compounds. CO_2 is not only required by autotrophic organisms but also by heterotrophs (chemoorganotrophs) for the synthesis of fatty acids and in 'heterotrophic CO_2-fixation'. Since CO_2 is produced during catabolism it usually does not become a limiting factor. Some bacteria require up to 10% of CO_2 in the atmosphere for good growth in organic media.

In addition to minerals, carbon, and an energy source, many bacteria also need specific growth factors. These are organic compounds, constituents or precursors of cellular components, which are needed but which cannot be synthesized by these bacteria. There are three main classes of growth factors: (a) amino acids, the building blocks of proteins, (b) purines and pyrimidines, which represent building blocks for synthesis of nucleic acids and coenzymes, and (c) vitamins which are part of coenzymes or prosthetic groups in certain enzymes. These growth factors are required in very low concentration (ppm). The lactic acid bacteria have complex growth factor requirements. Representatives of this group are, therefore, used in vitamin assay procedures. Also compounds such as porphyrin are needed by certain organisms (e.g. *Haemophilus influenzae*). This requirement is met by the addition of red blood cells containing porphyrin in the haemoglobin to a nutrient medium. Some rumen bacteria require short-branched or straight-chain fatty acids, and most mycoplasmas are known to require cholesterol.

In the cellular components, nitrogen and sulphur occur mainly in the reduced form as amino and sulphhydrylic groups. Only some bacteria depend on the supply of reduced compounds such as NH_4^+-salts, NH_2-groups containing compounds, or compounds containing SH-groups. Most are capable of assimilating the oxidized form and of reducing nitrate and sulphate by assimilatory nitrate and sulphate reduction. Some fastidious bacteria need polypeptides, peptones or even genuine proteins whereas others are capable of fixing elementary dinitrogen. If both ammonium and nitrate are present, the organism usually uses ammonium first, i.e. the substance which requires the least amount of energy to become incorporated into the cellular components.

Nutritional types

In order to characterize the mode of nutrition of plants and animals, the terms 'autotrophic' and 'heterotrophic' have been introduced. These terms refer to the nature of the carbon source. Autotrophy involves assimilation of CO_2 and life at the expense of inorganic nutrients only. Heterotrophy, on the other hand, refers to the dependency on preformed organic materials. Since these terms do not cover the broad variety of nutritional types, the characterization of microorganisms in terms of energy source and hydrogen donor has come into use. With respect to the type of energy source, two basically different microbial groups exist, the phototrophs and the chemotrophs. Organisms capable of utilizing radiation energy (light) are called phototrophs (photosynthetic organisms). There exist two large groups of phototrophs: (a) the anaerobic phototrophic bacteria which perform an anoxic photosynthesis, and (b) the aerobic phototrophic cyanobacteria which produce oxygen during photosynthesis, as do algae and green plants. The term chemotroph (chemosynthetic) refers to the generation of energy by oxidation–reduction reactions which organic nutrients undergo during metabolism. This applies both for respiration and for fermentation.

With respect to the nature of the H-donor, the terms 'organotrophic' and 'lithotrophic' have been introduced. An organism using organic compounds as H-donor is termed organotrophic, whereas lithotrophic refers to the capability of using reduced inorganic compounds as H-donors. According to this classification scheme, the nitrifiers are chemolithoautotrophs. While the anaerobic phototrophic bacteria, the cyanobacteria, and the green plants, have to be regarded as photolithotrophs, most microorganisms and the animals are chemoorganotrophs. With reference to microorganisms, the term autotroph describes the situation where the cell carbon is almost exclusively derived from CO_2, whereas the term heterotroph is used if the cell carbon is derived from organic compounds. Microorganisms that have simple requirements with respect to carbon and energy source are called prototrophs. If they depend on the supply of growth factors, they are called auxotrophs.

Physiology of growth
Growth in batch culture
After inoculation of bacteria into liquid media, growth occurs until a nutritional factor becomes limiting or until it is inhibited by accumulation of toxic products. If additional nutrients are not supplied and metabolic products are not removed during growth in a 'closed system', this system is called a static culture or batch culture. Growth in batch culture is characterized by the following sequence of growth phases: lag phase, log (exponential) phase, stationary phase, and death phase. The length of the lag phase depends on the preculture conditions and the age and number of the inoculated cells. The adaptation to the new environment is accompanied by an increased synthesis of RNA, ribosomes, and enzymes. Growth of a population is exponential as the consequence of binary fission; at each division period the total population is doubled. During exponential growth, the generation time (doubling time) is constant. The organisms are in a state of balanced growth, and the increase of biomass is proportional to the increase of cellular components (proteins, nucleic acids, lipids, etc.). The rates of exponential growth vary among organisms under optimum conditions. The generation time of *E. coli* may be as short as 15 min, and in some thermophilic bacteria it is even shorter. The majority of bacteria have generation times lasting from one to several hours. During stationary growth, there is no further increase in cell density. Growth is limited by lack of nutrients and accumulation of toxic metabolic products. Compared to exponential phase cells the stationary phase cells differ in composition because of the unbalanced growth. The cell mass present in the stationary phase is the maximum crop. During the death phase, a portion of the population dies. The number of viable cells often decreases exponentially, and the cellular death is accompanied by autolysis due to cellular enzymes. Batch cultures

are operated in culture vessels such as tubes or Erlenmeyer flasks. Growth in static cultures is usually characterized by data on yield coefficients, growth rate, maximum cell crop, and duration of the lag phase.

Growth in continuous culture

While exponential growth in a batch culture is limited to a short period, growth in a system of continuous cultivation is constantly exponential. This can be achieved by continuous supply of the growing culture with nutrient solution. Continuous cultivation is possible in a chemostat or a turbidostat.

A chemostat is run by continuous addition and simultaneous removal of culture medium from the system. By aeration and mechanical agitation, the oxygen supply and the immediate distribution of the added nutrients is kept optimal. The flow rate and the growth rate are directly related. Growth is controlled by limiting one nutritional factor (C, N, S, P, or other). Under such conditions, the growth rate is externally controlled by the substrate. The population density is constant and the culture is in 'steady state'. Continuous cultivation in a turbidostat is monitored by turbidity. The nutrients are supplied in excess and growth occurs at maximum growth rate under the given nutritional and environmental conditions. A photoelectric cell that monitors cell density regulates the flow rate of the nutrient solution in such a way that turbidity remains constant. Since the growth rate itself regulates the flow rate of nutrients, the turbidostat has an internal regulation.

Growth parameters

Growth of microorganisms is related to increase in numbers and increase in biomass. The increase in cell number and cell mass in batch culture is not necessarily proportional during all phases of growth. It is, therefore, necessary to differentiate between cell number and cell mass when characterizing population growth.

The division rate (k) is defined as the number of cell divisions (n) per unit of time $(k = n/t)$. The reciprocal value of the division rate is the generation time $(g = 1/k = t/n)$. It is equivalent to the doubling time.

If during exponential growth the increase in cell number is determined it is possible to calculate the number of cell divisions which allows calculation of g and k.

After n cell divisions the total number of bacteria is

$$N_t = N_0 \cdot 2^n$$

N_0: number of bacteria at time 0.
N_t: number of bacteria at time t.

The number of cell divisions (n) is given by

$$n = \frac{\log N_t - \log N_0}{\log 2}$$

It follows that the number of cell divisions per hour (h) is

$$\frac{n}{t(\text{h})} = \frac{\log N_t - \log N_0}{\log 2 \, (t - t_0)}$$

The growth rate (μ) and the doubling time (t_d) describe the increase of the bacterial mass.

During exponential growth

$$\mu = \frac{1}{x} \cdot \frac{dx}{dt}$$

x: bacterial density measured as dry weight per ml. It follows by integration that

$$x = x_0 \cdot e^{\mu \cdot t}$$

Doubling of the cell mass is then represented by

$$x = 2x_0; \, t = t_d, \quad \text{thus}$$
$$2x_0 = x_0 \cdot e^{\mu \cdot t_d}$$

Consequently,

$$t_d = \frac{\ln 2}{\mu} \quad (\ln 2 = 0.693)$$

and

$$\mu = \frac{\ln 2}{t_d}$$

Under conditions of identical increase in cell number and cell mass ($t_d = g$ in standardized cells)

$$\mu = k \cdot \ln 2$$

In addition to growth rate and duration of lag phase the yield is often used as a parameter characterizing growth in a static culture. The growth yield (Y) is defined as the ratio of produced biomass and used substrate. The molar yield coefficient Y_m describes the yield (in dry weight of cells) per mole of substrate used. If the amount of energy derived from degradation of 1 mole of substrate is known, the energy growth yield coefficient (gram cells per mole ATP) can be calculated. In anaerobic bacteria that gain their energy by fermentation, Y_{ATP} is rather constant. A cell mass of 12–14 g are produced per mole of ATP. Unusually high Y_{ATP} values of up to 26 have been reported for periplasmic growth of the bacterial parasite *Bdellovibrio bacteriovorus*. By direct utilization of nucleoside monophosphates from the host and the direct incorporation of fatty acids from the host into fatty acids of the parasite the energy requirements are considerably reduced.

Growth under aerobic and anaerobic conditions
Obligate aerobes

Oxygen is a universal constituent of microbial cells and is available from water, from many organic compounds and from carbon dioxide. A great number of microorganisms require molecular oxygen. Among the obligate aerobes are many bacteria, most fungi, algae, and protozoa. The strictly aerobic bacteria obligately depend on O_2. Molecular oxygen is mainly required for respiration and serves as the terminal e-acceptor. In addition to respiration, molecular O_2 is also required for the biosynthesis of unsaturated fatty acids and sterols and for the catabolism of alkanes and aromatic compounds. High concentrations of O_2 are toxic not only for anaerobic but also for aerobic bacteria. Many organisms prefer reduced oxygen concentrations. The microaerophilic bacteria do not tolerate the partial pressure of air (0.2 bar) but prefer partial pressures from 0.01 to 0.03 bar. Growth of aerobic organisms in water is often limited by the lack of oxygen. This is related to the extremely low diffusion of air in water which is only 1/100 000 compared to that in air. One litre of water contains 6.2 ml O_2 (equivalent to 0.28 mmole O_2) in the dissolved state (20 °C, 1 atm). This amount of oxygen allows complete oxidation of only 8.3 mg glucose. Since laboratory media usually contain 1000 times the amount of glucose that can be metabolized by the dissolved oxygen, it is obvious that the organisms must be supplied with additional O_2. Aeration procedures, therefore, play an important role in the methodology of growing aerobic bacteria.

Obligate and facultative anaerobes

Organisms capable of growing in the absence of molecular oxygen are termed anaerobes. Anaerobic bacteria can be grouped into obligate and facultative anaerobes. For obligately anaerobic bacteria, molecular oxygen is toxic. The facultatively anaerobic bacteria, on the other hand, can grow both in the presence and in the absence of molecular oxygen. Strict anaerobes, moderate anaerobes, and oxygen-tolerant anaerobes are differentiated on the basis of O_2-tolerance. Strict anaerobic bacteria belong to the genera *Bacteroides, Butyrivibrio, Fusobacterium, Megasphaera, Peptococcus, Ruminococcus, Selenomonas, Succinivibrio, Methanobacterium, Methanococcus, Methanospirillum, Methanosarcina.* Among the clostridia are moderately oxygen-tolerant forms such as *C. tetani* and *C. sporogenes*, and highly oxygen-tolerant forms such as *C. acetobutylicum* and *C. perfringens*. The lactic acid bacteria are fully oxygen tolerant. They tolerate O_2 but do not use it.

Because of the low solubility of O_2 in water, the deeper layers in stagnant water, rice paddies, swamps, and ponds become anaerobic by microbial activities. Both phototrophs and chemotrophs can live under anaerobic conditions. In addition to the obligate anaerobic bacteria characterized by fermentative metabolism and lack of the respiratory electron transport chain, there is a variety of bacteria that under anaerobic conditions use nitrate, sulphate, sulphur, carbon dioxide, iron(III) ions, or fumarate as the terminal electron acceptors in the respiratory process. While nitrate respiration is an alternative to O_2 respiration, sulphate respiration is strictly anaerobic. The fermenting anaerobes generate ATP by substrate-level phosphorylation. However, e-transport phosphorylation is also present in nitrate, sulphate, and sulphur-reducing bacteria. It probably also occurs in methanogens. Anaerobes generating ATP by e-transport phosphorylation generally have a somewhat lower yield than aerobic bacteria using molecular O_2. The anaerobic breakdown of organic material either ends with the production of CO_2 and CH_4 or CO_2 and H_2S, and depends largely on the sulphate concentration in the environment. The end products are determined by the use of SO_4^{2-} or CO_2 as the terminal e-acceptors.

Indefinite growth under anaerobic conditions is confined to prokaryotic organisms. In most eukaryotes, energy conversion under anaerobic conditions is only a transient process which occurs at hypoxic conditions. A number of eukaryotic microorganisms is known to occur in anaerobic habitats. Thus, special types of protozoa live in the rumen, and representatives of *Entamoeba, Diplomonas,* and *Trichomonas* are capable of strict anaerobic growth. Facultative anaerobes are known among the helminths such as *Trichinella spiralis*. Fungi are usually not encountered in typically anaerobic habitats. Some fungi, however, are capable of growing anaerobically, e.g. the fermenting yeasts.

Oxygen toxicity

In aerobic organisms molecular O_2 functions as the terminal e-acceptor during respiration, resulting in reduction of O_2 to H_2O. Certain enzymes such as flavoproteins, however, also react with O_2 producing H_2O_2. This toxic compound is detoxified by a peroxidase (catalase)

$$2\,H_2O_2 \rightarrow 2\,H_2O + O_2$$

Since O_2 can also be reduced by single electron steps, O_2^- radicals (superoxide anion radicals) occur in aerobic metabolism. In the presence of superoxide dismutase the accumulation of O_2^- radicals is prevented by the reaction

$$2\,O_2^- + 2\,H^+ \rightarrow O_2 + H_2O_2.$$

The aerobic and aerotolerant anaerobic bacteria, as a rule, possess superoxide dismutase and catalase. Lactic acid bacteria are an exception to this rule; they decompose H_2O_2 by means of peroxidases. Since the strict anaerobic bacteria do not possess catalase and superoxide dismutase they are inhibited by molecular O_2. Therefore, only anoxic environments are appropriate locations for strictly anaerobic bacteria. Since the anaerobes must be protected from the toxic products of O_2 metabolism, special laboratory techniques have been developed for the cultivation of anaerobes. Since traces of O_2 are already inhibitory for strict anaerobes, inoculations and transfer of such bacteria require conditions of complete exclusion of O_2 by handling the organisms in a stream of N_2 or CO_2 gas. Some obligate anaerobes contain superoxide dismutase while others are completely intolerant of O_2. The methanogens belong to the latter group.

Another type of O_2 toxicity is related to the growth of N_2-fixing aerobic bacteria. While *Azotobacter* has developed a protective mechanism against O_2 and can fix N_2 in the presence of air, other bacteria such as *Xanthobacter autotrophicus* and *Azospirillum* only fix molecular nitrogen and grow at reduced pO_2.

Microbial metabolism and regulation

Energy-yielding processes

All organisms require energy for growth and maintenance. It is a fundamental property of all living systems to generate the necessary energy by specific processes. The energy sources are light (phototrophs), organic substrates (organotrophs), and reduced inorganic substrates (lithotrophs). With respect to energy in metabolism, there are two categories of reactions, (1) energy-yielding and (2) energy-consuming

$$\text{NH}_2$$

(chemical structure diagram)

ATP | ADP | AMP | Adenosine

Adenosine-5′-monophosphate

Adenosine-5′-diphosphate

Adenosine-5′-triphosphate

~ Energy-rich bond

Fig. 2.4 The chemical structure of ATP

processes. The energy-yielding reactions (catabolic reactions) are coupled to the degradation of organic nutrients leading to CO_2 and H_2O as the end products. During catabolism, compounds of higher molecular weight are degraded to compounds of lower molecular weight. The conversion of an organic compound (carbon and energy source) serves two functions: (1) production of energy (ATP; Fig. 2.4) for biosynthesis and other energy requiring processes; (2) production of precursors for the synthesis of macromolecules. The energy-consuming reactions (anabolic reactions) are related to the biosynthesis of monomers such as sugars, amino acids, fatty acids, purine, and pyrimidine bases, and to the synthesis of polymers such as polysaccharides, proteins, nucleic acids, murein, and reserve materials. The degradation of organic compounds occurs via specific metabolic pathways which are restricted in number and are almost identical in all living organisms. The identity of the main metabolic pathways indicates that all organisms on earth have evolved from common ancestors. This idea is supported by some other facts: The cell constituents are more or less uniform, ATP is the elementary quantum of biological energy, the genetic code is universal, the respiratory chain is of the same nature, and identical mechanisms of energy conversion are present. The original biochemical set-up was anaerobic in

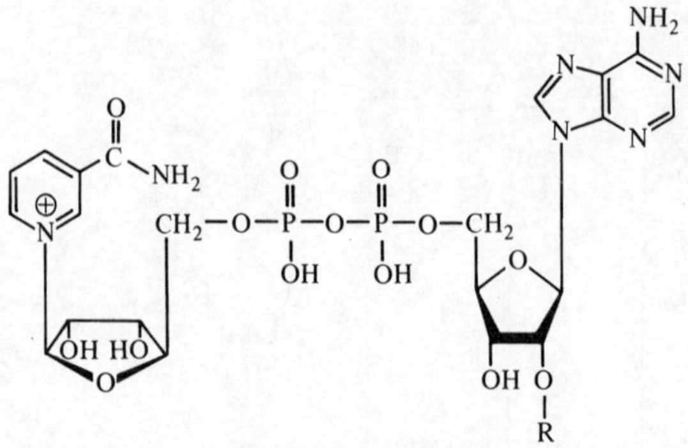

R = H in NAD⁺ : PO₃H₂ in NADP⁺

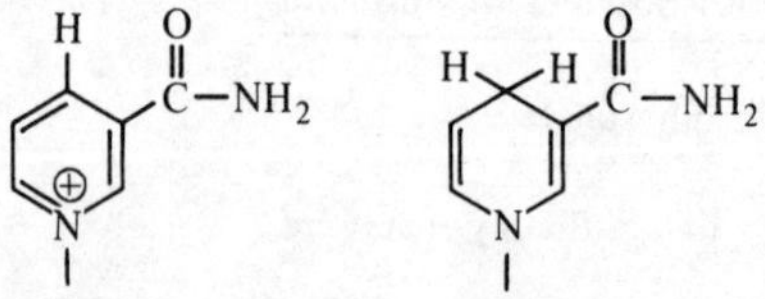

NAD⁺   NADH
(Oxidized)   (Reduced)

Fig. 2.5 The chemical structure of NAD⁺/NADH (nicotinamide adenine dinucleotide)

nature, and the respiratory chain developed after oxygen became available in the biosphere.

Catabolic and anabolic processes are intimately connected. The energy metabolism is directed towards the continuous regeneration of the cellular pool of ATP. The energy charge (EC) is an indicator of the proportions of the adenylates (ATP, ADP, AMP) in the cell. It is defined as the ratio of the number of energy-rich bonds and the concentration of the total adenylates according to the following equation:

$$EC = \frac{[ATP] + \frac{1}{2}[ADP]}{[ATP] + [ADP] + [AMP]}.$$

In exponentially growing cells, the EC is around 0.8. In metabolically inactive cells the EC drops to 0.5 or less.

Regeneration of ATP (by phosphorylation of ADP) occurs by photophosphorylation (in phototrophs), by substrate phosphorylation, or oxidative phosphorylation (in chemotrophs). Besides the production of ATP, the function of energy yielding processes involves the production of reduced pyridine nucleotide (NADH; Fig. 2.5) which is a potential energy carrier and allows generation of ATP in the respiratory electron transport chain by oxidative phosphorylation. In addition, reduced pyridine nucleotide (NADPH) is used as the reducing power in biosynthetic processes.

Phototrophs

There are three groups of microorganisms capable of converting the energy from the sun's radiation into biochemically useful energy (ATP): the phototrophic bacteria, the cyanobacteria, the halobacteria.

The phototrophic bacteria perform an anoxic photosynthesis. They do not 'split water' and, therefore, do not produce O_2. Instead, the anaerobic phototrophic bacteria use H_2S, S^0, or S_2O_3 as the external H-donor. Many are also capable of using molecular H_2. All photoautotrophs are capable of fixing CO_2 using the Calvin cycle (Fig. 2.6). The various purple and green phototrophs exhibit differences with respect to the H-donors and to the assimilation of carbon. While all types can grow anaerobically in the light, the non-sulphur-purple bacteria and the green bacteria of the genus *Chloroflexus* can also live aerobically in the dark performing aerobic respiration. Bacterial photosynthesis depends on the presence of reduced substrates in the environment. The light reaction creates a proton potential which allows the generation of ATP. The photosynthetic complex acts as a light-driven proton pump, and the proton potential is a prerequisite for the energy conversion in photophosphorylation. Anoxic photosynthesis is generated by a single light reaction supporting a cyclic electron transport. This light reaction is, in many respects, analogous to the first light reaction of the green plant. The reaction centre consists of a protein complex which contains bacteriochlorophyll a, bacteriophaeophytin, carotenoid, ubichinon, and FeS-proteins. As in green plants, the primary photochemical event is the absorption of a photon of light by the chlorophyll molecule. Secondary pigments such as carotenoids transmit the energy they absorb to the reaction centre of the chlorophyll molecule. NADH is produced by an ATP-driven reversed electron transport.

As algae and green plants, the cyanobacteria dispose of two light reactions. The e-donor is water, and O_2 is released during photolysis of water. Light energy produces a proton gradient over the thylakoid membrane. The generation of ATP is the consequence of the proton potential. In this respect, photophosphorylation during photosynthetic electron transport is comparable to oxidative phosphorylation during respiratory electron transport.

A

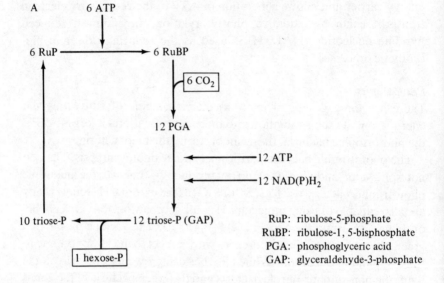

RuP: ribulose-5-phosphate
RuBP: ribulose-1, 5-bisphosphate
PGA: phosphoglyceric acid
GAP: glyceraldehyde-3-phosphate

B

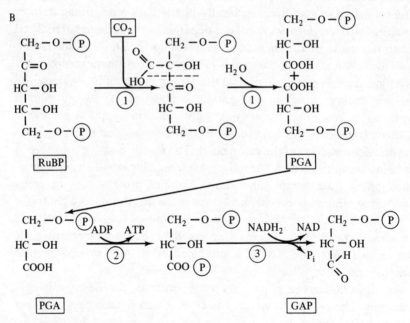

Enzymes involved:

① ribulose-1, 5-bisphosphate carboxylase
② phosphoglycerate kinase
③ glyceraldehyde-3-phosphate dehydrogenase

Halobacterium halobium is an aerobic chemoorganotrophic halophilic bacterium. This organism is capable of performing a special type of photophosphorylation in a so-called purple membrane. The purple membrane contains the pigment bacteriorhodopsin which during illumination produces a proton gradient across the membrane. The electrochemical membrane potential is coupled to the generation of ATP. Although this organism generates energy primarily by aerobic substrate oxidation, it is capable of producing additional ATP from photophosphorylation, which is important during growth at decreased pO_2.

Chemotrophs

The chemoorganotrophs generate their energy during respiration or fermentation. Compared to fermentation of organic substrates under anaerobic conditions, the aerobic respiration of organic materials is much more efficient with respect to generation of ATP.

In aerobic respiration, the oxidation of substrates is coupled to the reduction of O_2. The respiring organisms dispose of a respiratory chain (electron transport chain) and the enzyme ATP-synthase (Fig. 2.7). With this special equipment, they generate ATP by oxidative phosphorylation whereas the anaerobically living organisms derive their energy from substrate phosphorylation. In the prokaryotes, the apparatus for generation of energy (e-transport chain and oxidative phosphorylation) is located in the cytoplasmic membrane whereas in the eukaryotes, energy generation occurs in the membranes of mitochondria. During aerobic respiration, the oxidation of the substrates is coupled to the reduction of molecular O_2. The electron transport chain is the site of the 'oxygen–hydrogen reaction'. Compared to the chemical oxygen–hydrogen reaction the biochemical reaction allows the conservation of a considerable part of the free energy in the form of ATP, and only a small part of the energy is lost as heat.

The overall reaction is

$$4[H] + O_2 \rightarrow 2\,H_2O + 2 \times 57 \text{ kcal } (2 \times 238.3 \text{ kJ})$$

(where [H] stands for substrate–hydrogen). In respiring organisms about 3×8 kcal (3×33.45 kJ) are conserved in the form of 3 ATP. The electron transport chain contains four groups of components: flavo-

---

Fig. 2.6 The Calvin cycle
A Synthesis of hexose phosphate from CO_2 (simplified)
B Conversion of RuBP into GAP

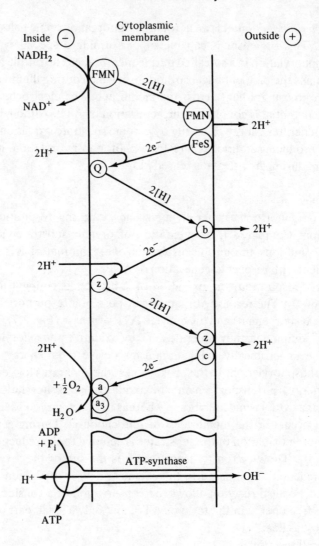

FMN: flavin mononucleotide
FeS: Fe-S-protein
Q: coenzyme Q
z: H-transmitter
b, c, a, a_3: cytochromes

Fig. 2.7 Electron transport chain and (re)generation of ATP by the proton motive force

proteins, chinons, cytochromes, Fe-S proteins. The components of the electron transport chain are typical redox systems. The flow of H and electrons is accompanied by an oscillation between oxidation and reduction of the components.

The flavoproteins of the respiratory chain are enzymes containing FMN or FAD (flavin adenine dinucleotide) as prosthetic groups. They transfer hydrogen. The iron–sulphur proteins transfer electrons. The chinones, especially ubichinone, are lipophilic components that transfer hydrogen or electrons. The cytochromes only transport electrons. In the cytochromes, haem is the prosthetic group. The central iron atom of the haemine ring system is involved in the electron transfer. There exist several types of cytochromes (a, a3, b, c, o, etc.), and the different categories of aerobic organisms may dispose of different sets of cytochromes. Cyt c is present in almost all organisms. The transfer of electrons to oxygen is mediated by cytochrome oxidase (the complex of cyt a and a3). Some flavoproteins also have the property of transmitting electrons directly to molecular oxygen, as explained in the preceding chapter on oxygen toxicity.

The oxidation of organic substrates by substrate dehydrogenases is coupled to the production of NADH. The hydrogen of NADH is transferred by means of NADH dehydrogenase into the electron transport chain. During the H(e)-transfer to molecular oxygen, three molecules of ATP are produced. Thus, respiration of 1 mole of glucose is coupled to the production of 38 moles of ATP. According to the chemiosmotic hypothesis (Mitchell), the energy conservation in the electron transport chain is related to the proton motive force. The enzyme ATP-synthase which is involved in the energy conversion is located in the membrane associated with the electron transport chain. The proton potential is the force that keeps phosphorylation of ADP proceeding to ATP (Fig. 2.7).

Aerobic respiration is also performed in the chemolithotrophic bacteria. These organisms are capable of utilizing reduced inorganic compounds as e-donors (S^{2-}, S^0, SO_3^{2-}, NH_3, NO_2^-, Fe^{2+}). By oxidation of such reduced H-donors the organisms generate reducing power and energy for their biosynthetic processes. Generation of energy is coupled to the reduction of oxygen as the terminal e-acceptor. Some of these lithotrophs can also use nitrate, sulphate, or CO_2 as the ultimate e-acceptor under anaerobic conditions. Most of the chemolithotrophs are capable of utilizing CO_2 as the sole carbon source. The chemolithoautotrophic bacteria assimilate CO_2 via the ribulose-bisphosphate cycle (Calvin cycle). CO_2-fixation is catalysed by ribulose–bisphosphate–carboxylase.

e⁻ Acceptor	Product	Type of respiration	Organisms
O_2	H_2O	Aerobic respiration	All strict or facultative aerobic organisms
NO_3^-	NO_2^- N_2O N_2	Nitrate respiration	Various aerobic and facultative anaerobic bacteria
SO_4^{2-}	S^{2-}	Sulphate respiration	Various obligately anaerobic bacteria
S^0	S^{2-}	Sulphur respiration	A few facultative and obligate anaerobic bacteria
CO_2 HCO_3^-	CH_4	Carbonate respiration	Methanogens
CO_2 HCO_3^-	$CH_3 \cdot COOH$	Carbonate respiration	Acetogenic bacteria
Fumarate	Succinate	Fumarate respiration	Succinogenic bacteria

Fig. 2.8 Terminal electron acceptors in aerobic and anaerobic respiration

The synthesis of 1 mole of hexose from 6 moles of CO_2 requires 18 moles of ATP and 12 moles of NAD(P)H (Fig. 2.6).

A variety of bacteria are capable of anaerobic respiration. These organisms dispose of an electron transport chain which allows energy generation as during aerobic respiration with oxygen. In anaerobic respiration, however, molecular oxygen is replaced by other terminal e-acceptors. The most important anaerobic respiratory processes are nitrate respiration, sulphate respiration, and carbonate respiration (Fig. 2.8).

Nitrate respiration (dissimilatory nitrate reduction) by common usage refers to the reduction of nitrate to nitrite under anaerobic conditions. Denitrification, on the other hand, is associated with the generation of the gaseous compounds N_2O and N_2 (Fig. 2.9). Nitrate respiration is carried out by facultative aerobes (e.g. *Rhizobium* and many pseudomonads), facultative anaerobes (e.g. enterics) and strict anaerobes (e.g. *Clostridium*). Denitrification is only known in facultative aerobes; obligate anaerobic denitrifiers are unknown. Nitrate and nitrite reductase are only produced in the absence of molecular oxygen. In the presence of oxygen, these systems are repressed. The reduction of nitrate and nitrite is coupled to the respiratory chain. During nitrate respiration the efficiency

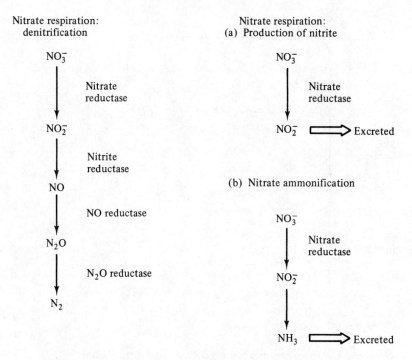

Fig. 2.9 Dissimilatory nitrate reduction (nitrate respiration)

of energy generation is about $\frac{1}{2}$ to $\frac{2}{3}$ compared to aerobic respiration on an electron basis.

In contrast to the nitrate respiring bacteria the sulphate respiring bacteria are obligate anaerobes. The product of sulphate respiration (dissimilatory sulphate reduction) is H_2S (Fig. 2.10). Most of the H_2S found in nature is produced by sulphate respiration. The most important sulphate reducers belong to the genera *Desulfovibrio* and *Desulfotomaculum*. These organisms are characterized by incomplete oxidation of the H-donors, primarily organic acids. The main end product of their metabolism is acetate. Recently a great variety of desulphurizing bacteria has been discovered capable of oxidizing acetate or higher fatty acids (*Desulfotomaculum acetoxidans, Desulfobacter, Desulfococcus, Desulfosarcina, Desulfonema*).

A few bacteria are capable of anaerobic sulphur respiration. *Desulfuromonas acetoxidans* uses sulphur as terminal e-acceptor during acetate oxidation and lives in syntrophic association with phototrophic green sulphur bacteria that oxidize H_2S and produce S^0.

Carbonate respiration is performed by methanogenic bacteria. The

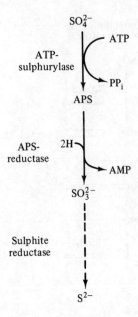

APS: adenosine-5′-phosphosulphate

Fig. 2.10 Dissimilatory sulphate reduction (sulphate respiration)

methanogens are capable of activation of hydrogen and couple the oxidation of molecular hydrogen to the reduction of CO_2.

Another type of carbonate respiration is the production of acetate from CO_2 by acetogenic bacteria such as *Clostridium aceticum*.

Electron transport phosphorylation is also known under anaerobic conditions in organisms that use fumarate as the terminal e-acceptor. Fumarate respiration is widespread among anaerobic chemoorganotrophs. In anaerobic processes leading to the production of succinate, fumarate reductase probably is involved and thus allows additional generation of ATP. Fumarate respiration has also been found in other strict aerobic organisms (lower animals) allowing generation of energy during transient anoxic conditions.

While in aerobic and anaerobic respiration, hydrogen (e), produced during oxidation of organic or reduced inorganic substrates is oxidized in the respiratory chain leading to production of ATP, the hydrogen derived from organic substrates during fermentation is transferred to organic hydrogen acceptors. Fermentation is a partial oxidation. Part of the energy is conserved during substrate phosphorylation, while the rest leaves in the fermentation products. Generation of energy during

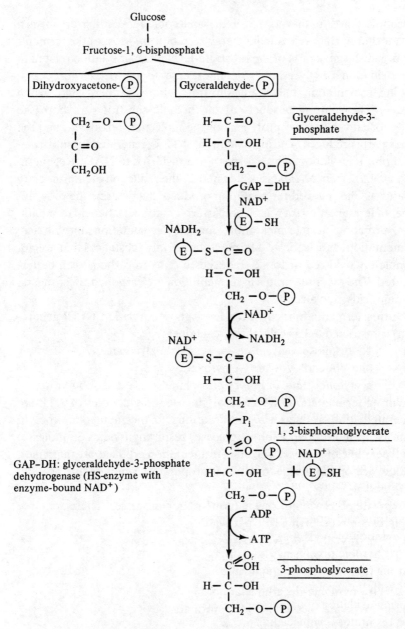

Fig. 2.11 Substrate-level phosphorylation by oxidation of glyceraldehyde phosphate to 3-phosphoglycerate

glycolysis (EMP-pathway) is, for the anaerobic fermenting organisms, the most important reaction in energy metabolism. Most of the fermenting organisms make use of the substrate-level phosphorylation related to the oxidation of glyceraldehyde phosphate to pyruvate (Fig. 2.11). During fermentation, the organic substrate is both the energy and carbon source. The splitting products of the organic substrate are both the H-donor and the H-acceptor. Part of the molecule is oxidized, and the other part is reduced. During oxidation, ATP is generated by substrate-level phosphorylation. The hydrogen is transferred to NAD. Regeneration of NAD from NADH is performed by the reduction of intermediary products. The reduced fermentation products characterize the different types of fermentation such as alcoholic fermentation, lactic acid fermentation, propionic acid fermentation, formate fermentation, butyric acid fermentation, and acetic acid fermentation. Only substances that are not completely oxidized or totally reduced (e.g. hydrocarbons) can be fermented. The main substrates in fermentation are carbohydrates, sugars, organic acids, and alcohols.

During fermentation, substrate-level phosphorylation (ATP-generation) is restricted to basically three reactions:

(1)   1,3-bisphosphoglycerate $\rightarrow$ 3-phosphoglycerate
(2)   phosphoenolpyruvate $\rightarrow$ pyruvate
(3)   acetylphosphate or butyrylphosphate $\rightarrow$ acetate or butyrate.

During fermentation of 1 mole of glucose, only 2 moles of ATP are generated, the products varying according to the metabolic type. In contrast to the fermentation of glucose, respiration yields 38 moles of ATP per mole of glucose. The main fermentation products are methanol, lactate, acetone, butyrate, butanol, 2-propanol, 2,3-butanediol, acetate, CO_2, and H_2.

Pyruvate plays a major role in fermentation processes. There are three main reactions occurring with pyruvate:

(1)   pyruvate $\rightarrow$ acetyl-CoA
       by pyruvate-dehydrogenation
(2)   pyruvate $\rightarrow$ acetaldehyde
       by pyruvate-decarboxylation
(3)   pyruvate $\rightarrow$ acetyl-CoA + formate
       by pyruvate–formate–lyase.

Formate (HCOOH) in some organisms is split into CO_2 and H_2 by formate–hydrogen–lyase. In most anaerobic bacteria, the NADH produced during oxidation is transferred to organic H-acceptors. Certain bacteria also have the ability of transferring the hydrogen of NADH to

ferredoxin by a NADH: ferredoxin oxidoreductase. From reduced ferredoxin H_2 is released by a hydrogenase.

In clostridia and other anaerobic bacteria, pyruvate can also be
oxidized according to the reaction

$$\text{pyruvate} + \text{CoA} + 2\ \text{Fd} \rightarrow \text{acetyl-CoA} + 2\ \text{FdH} + CO_2.$$

The reduction of ferredoxin is catalysed by pyruvate: ferredoxin
oxidoreductase. From reduced ferredoxin, molecular hydrogen is
released by a specific hydrogenase, the ferredoxin: H_2 oxidoreductase
according to the reaction

$$2\ \text{FdH} \xrightarrow{\text{hydrogenase}} 2\ \text{Fd} + H_2\ .$$

The release of molecular hydrogen in fermentation is of advantage to the
cell because it need not synthesize H-acceptor molecules.

Since many of the fermenting bacteria do not possess catalase and
superoxide dismutase, they are damaged in the presence of molecular
oxygen by the production of H_2O_2 or O_2^- radicals.

Major pathways of catabolism
Since carbohydrates are the most abundant products of primary production of green plants (photosynthesis), the majority of macro- and microorganisms are capable of degrading sugars. The central pathways in
catabolism are similar or identical in all living systems. Glucose and other
hexoses are metabolized in initial catabolic reactions yielding C_3-com-
pounds and energy from substrate-level phosphorylation. Pyruvate is the
most important intermediate which is subject to further reactions resulting in the production of intermediary compounds needed for biosyntheses
and the generation of energy. During oxidation of sugar to CO_2 and H_2O,
microorganisms capable of aerobic or anaerobic respiration generate
considerably more energy than fermenting microorganisms.

The major pathways of catabolism in bacteria are presented in Fig.
2.12: (A) the EMP-pathway (Embden–Meyerhof–Parnas pathway, fruc-
tose-1,6-bisphosphate pathway, glycolysis); (B) the oxidative pentose
phosphate pathway (Warburg–Dickens–Horecker pathway); and (C)
the KDPG-pathway (2-keto-3-deoxy-6-phospho-gluconate pathway,
Entner–Doudoroff pathway). During glycolysis, glucose is converted
into fructose-1,6-bisphosphate which is split into C_3 compounds (di-
hydroxy-acetone phosphate and glyceraldehyde phosphate) by an
aldolase reaction. Oxidation of glyceraldehyde phosphate to pyruvate via
several intermediates yields two moles of ATP per mole of GAP.

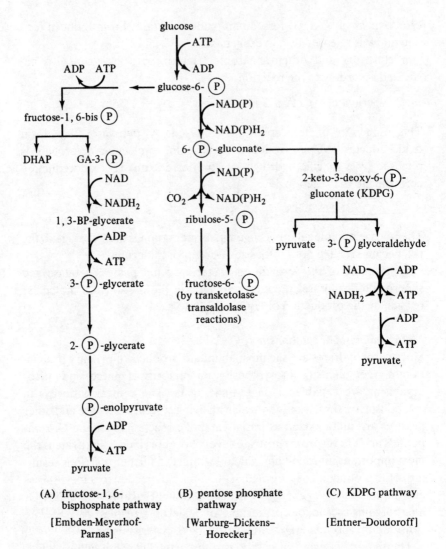

(A) fructose-1, 6-
     bisphosphate pathway

     [Embden–Meyerhof-
     Parnas]

(B) pentose phosphate
     pathway

     [Warburg–Dickens–
     Horecker]

(C) KDPG pathway

     [Entner–Doudoroff]

DHAP: dihydroxyacetone phosphate
GA-3-(P) : glyceraldehyde-3-phosphate

Fig. 2.12 The major pathways of glucose catabolism

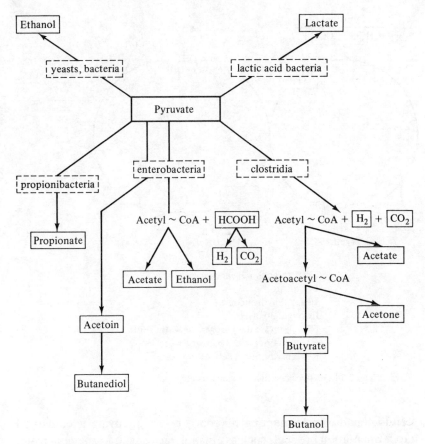

Fig. 2.13 Conversion of pyruvate into fermentation products

Breakdown of glucose via the pentose phosphate pathway results in the production of ribulose-5-phosphate and $2 NAD(P)H_2$. The importance of this pathway is related to the supply of essential intermediates (pentose phosphate, erythrose phosphate, glyceraldehyde phosphate) and reducing power $NAD(P)H_2$ for biosynthetic processes. Pentose phosphates are precursors in synthesis of nucleic acids. Erythrose phosphate is used in the synthesis of the aromatic amino acids. By a combined action of transketolases and transaldolases, pentose phosphate is transformed into fructose phosphate. The pentose phosphate pathway is thus also important for the conversion of pentose to hexose and vice versa.

Degradation of glucose via the KDPG-pathway yields 2 pyruvate, $1 NAD(P)H_2$, $1 NADH_2$, 1 ATP. This pathway is shared by a variety of bacteria and represents the major catabolic pathway in the

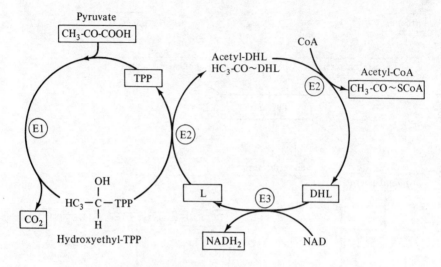

TPP: thiamin pyrophosphate
L: lipoate
DHL: dihydrolipoate
Enzymes involved
E1: pyruvate dehydrogenase (with TPP)
E2: dihydrolipoic transacetylase
E3: dihydrolipoic dehydrogenase

Fig. 2.14 The pyruvate dehydrogenase complex

pseudomonads. In fermenting microorganisms, pyruvate is converted into fermentation products such as ethanol, lactic acid, formate, acetate, butyrate, propionate, butanol, acetone, and others (Fig. 2.13). Aerobic organisms degrade pyruvate by a 'pyruvate dehydrogenase multienzyme complex' yielding acetyl-CoA, $NADH_2$ and CO_2 (Fig. 2.14). Acetyl-CoA is oxidized in the tricarboxylic acid cycle (TCC, Krebs cycle). The oxidation of acetate yields CO_2 and reducing power ($NADH_2$, $NADH(P)H_2$, $FADH_2$) which finally is oxidized in the respiratory chain and converted into ATP by e-transport phosphorylation. The starting reaction of the TCC (Fig. 2.15) is the production of citrate from acetyl-CoA and oxaloacetate by citrate synthase. During this reaction coenzyme A is regenerated. The total oxidation of acetate yields $2 CO_2$, $2 NADH_2$, $1 NAD(P)H_2$, $1 FADH_2$, and 1 ATP (adenosine triphosphate). The primary function of the TCC is the terminal oxidation of nutrients resulting in the production of reduced pyridine nucleotides ($NADH_2$, $NAD(P)H_2$) which are potential energy carriers. In addition, the TCC supplies the cell with intermediates needed in biosyntheses (e.g. 2-oxo-

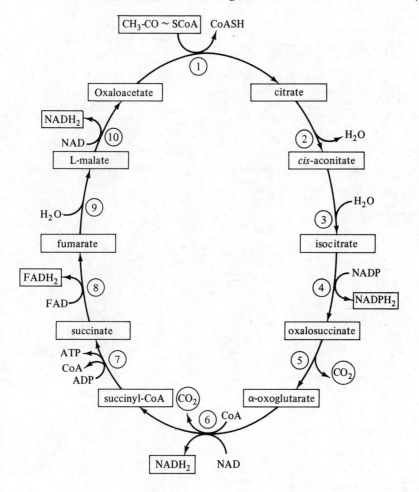

Fig. 2.15 The tricarboxylic cycle (TCC)
Enzymes involved

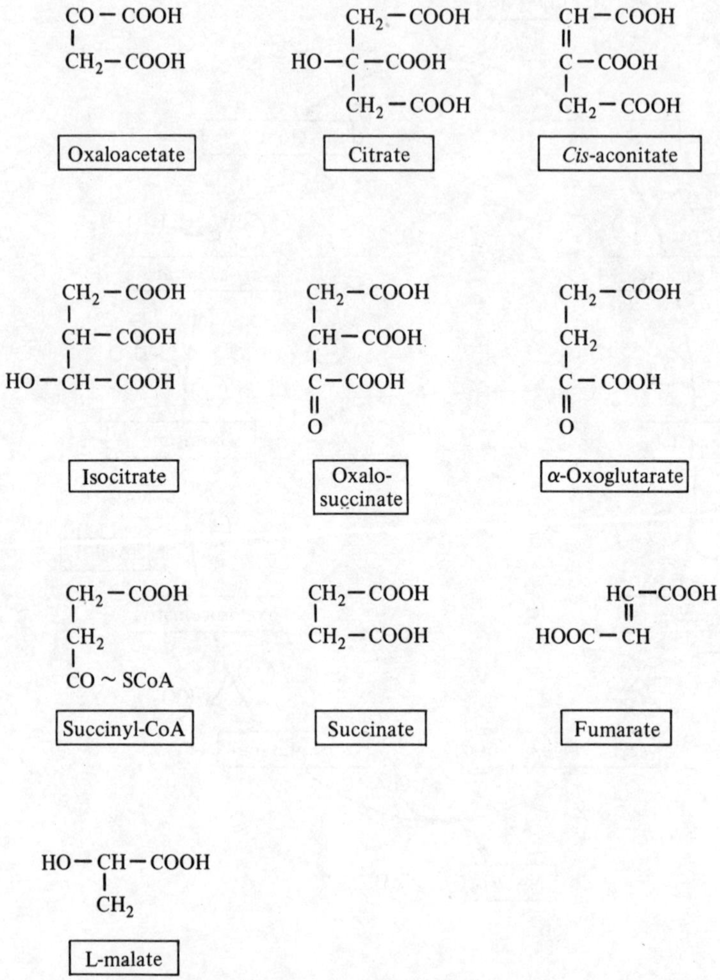

$$CO-COOH$$
$$|$$
$$CH_2-COOH$$

| Oxaloacetate |

$$CH_2-COOH$$
$$|$$
$$HO-C-COOH$$
$$|$$
$$CH_2-COOH$$

| Citrate |

$$CH-COOH$$
$$||$$
$$C-COOH$$
$$|$$
$$CH_2-COOH$$

| *Cis*-aconitate |

$$CH_2-COOH$$
$$|$$
$$CH-COOH$$
$$|$$
$$HO-CH-COOH$$

| Isocitrate |

$$CH_2-COOH$$
$$|$$
$$CH-COOH$$
$$|$$
$$C-COOH$$
$$||$$
$$O$$

| Oxalo-succinate |

$$CH_2-COOH$$
$$|$$
$$CH_2$$
$$|$$
$$C-COOH$$
$$||$$
$$O$$

| α-Oxoglutarate |

$$CH_2-COOH$$
$$|$$
$$CH_2$$
$$|$$
$$CO \sim SCoA$$

| Succinyl-CoA |

$$CH_2-COOH$$
$$|$$
$$CH_2-COOH$$

| Succinate |

$$HC-COOH$$
$$||$$
$$HOOC-CH$$

| Fumarate |

$$HO-CH-COOH$$
$$|$$
$$CH_2$$

| L-malate |

Fig. 2.15 The tricarboxylic cycle (TCC)
Intermediates

glutarate, oxaloacetate, succinate, malate). The removal of carbon compounds from the cycle is compensated by so-called anaplerotic reactions. These catalyse the production of C_4 compounds by carboxylation of C_3 compounds, e.g. carboxylation of pyruvate or phosphoenolpyruvate to oxaloacetate.

Energy-consuming processes
Catabolic (energy-yielding) and anabolic (energy-consuming) processes are intimately connected. Energy is required for maintenance

and biosynthetic processes. Growth and multiplication of cells depend on the availability of nutrients and energy. The cell has to produce all compounds represented in the biomass. Monomers such as sugars, amino acids, and nucleotides must either be incorporated or synthesized. With these monomers the cell synthesizes the polymers which are the major components of an organism. The polymeric macromolecules comprise polysaccharides, proteins, and polynucleotides (nucleic acids). For the synthesis of the various polymers, about 70 different precursors are needed: 4 r-nucleotides, 4 d-nucleotides, 20 amino acids, *c.* 15 monosaccharides, and *c.* 20 building blocks used for lipid production. When the synthesis of the monomers starts from glucose, the energy budget is balanced: 1 mole of glucose yields 1 mole of monomers without significant energy consumption. The synthesis of the macromolecules which represent about 95% of the bacterial cell mass, however, is a process requiring major amounts of energy that have to be generated by the cell. Apart from biosyntheses, the autotrophic CO_2-fixation by the anaerobic phototrophs and the aerobic chemolithoautotrophs is a process consuming considerable amounts of energy.

Autotrophic CO_2-fixation
In addition to the green plants, phototrophic bacteria, cyanobacteria, and chemolithoautotrophic bacteria are capable of fixing CO_2 via the Calvin-cycle (ribulosebisphosphate cycle, Fig. 2.6). Two key enzymes are involved in this process, phosphoribulokinase and ribulosebisphosphate carboxylase. After carboxylation, ribulose-1,5-bisphosphate yields 2 molecules of phosphoglycerate. This intermediate is reduced to glyceraldehyde phosphate and then converted into sugar phosphate. For the synthesis of 1 mole of hexose from 6 moles of CO_2, 18 moles of ATP and 12 moles of $NAD(P)H_2$ are required. The reaction follows the equation

$$6\,CO_2 + 18\,ATP + 12\,NAD(P)H_2 \rightarrow$$
$$\text{fructose-6-P} + 18\,ADP + 12\,NAD(P) + 18\,P_i$$

Biosyntheses
Most microorganisms have the capacity to synthesize the amino acids needed for protein synthesis. The same is true for the synthesis of other monomers required for the production of polysaccharides and polynucleotides. Organisms incapable of synthesizing the necessary building blocks are called 'auxotrophic' and depend on the external supply of such compounds. The activation of the monomers used for polymerization is an energy-consuming process:

glucose + ATP → glucose-P + ADP
amino acid + ATP → aminoacyl-AMP + PP
fatty acid + ATP → acyl-AMP + PP.

The activation of ribose-5-phosphate, a compound required for synthesis of nucleic acids, occurs according to

ribose-5-phosphate + ATP → phosphoribosyl pyrophosphate + AMP (Fig. 2.16).

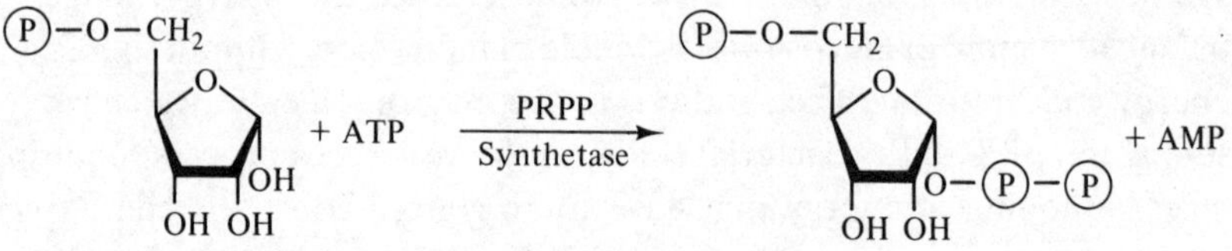

Ribose-5-phosphate

5-Phosphoribosyl-1-pyrophosphate (PRPP)

Fig. 2.16 Activation of ribose-5-phosphate

For the synthesis of nucleoside monophosphates (starting from glucose), four times the amount of energy is needed compared to the polymerization of nucleoside-monophosphates into polynucleotides.

Fixation of molecular N_2

The ability to fix atmospheric nitrogen (N_2) is restricted to the prokaryotes. The ability is distributed in a number of bacteria, namely (a) oxygenic and anoxygenic phototrophs, (b) chemoautotrophs, and (c) chemoorganotrophs. Dinitrogen fixing organisms exist in aerobic and anaerobic bacteria of all major physiological groups including methanogens, desulphurizing bacteria, and methylotrophs. Some live in symbiotic association with leguminous and non-leguminous plants, others are free-living. Among the aerobes and facultative anaerobes, *Azotobacter*, cyanobacteria, *Klebsiella*, and *Azospirillum*, and among the anaerobes, the clostridia and a number of anoxic phototrophs are capable of fixing nitrogen.

N_2-fixation is a reductive process mediated by the enzyme nitrogenase (Fig. 2.17). It is composed of two proteins which act in combination. One is a Fe–Mo-protein of two dissimilar pairs of sub-units with an overall molecular weight of 220 000 to 240 000. The other sub-unit is an Fe-

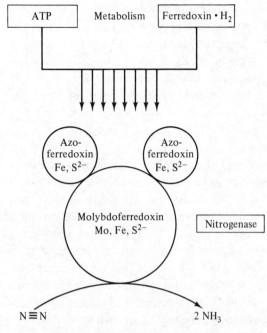

Fig. 2.17 N_2-fixation

protein of two identical sub-units with a MW of 60 000–65 000. Reduction of N_2 requires ATP and reducing power (reduced ferredoxin, flavodoxin). NH_3 is the first stable product which is incorporated into organic compounds of the cell. Under conditions of low NH_4^+ concentration, glutamine synthetase and glutamate synthase are involved in its incorporation. At high levels of ammonia, the production of glutamine synthetase and nitrogenase is repressed. Nitrogenase does not specifically react with N_2, but also reduces acetylene, azide, HCN, and N_2O. This enzyme also possesses an ATP-dependent hydrogenase activity and reduces protons to molecular hydrogen. An acetylene reduction test is now used as a routine technique for the demonstration of N_2-fixation. The ethylene produced is measured by gas chromatography. Since nitrogenase is highly sensitive to oxygen, symbiotic and free-living bacteria have developed special mechanisms to protect nitrogenase from the deleterious effect of a high pO_2. Before the introduction of the acetylene reduction technique, nitrogen fixation was measured by uptake of tracer ^{15}N (a stable isotope), which can be detected by mass spectrometry.

In some bacteria, the nitrogen-fixing ability is located on a plasmid. The *nif* gene region has successfully been transferred to other bacteria. For the global nitrogen balance and cycling of nitrogen, the N_2-fixing bacteria play an important role. In association with legumes, rhizobia fix up to 300 kg N ha^{-1} year^{-1}. The corresponding value for free-living nitrogen-fixers has been estimated to be in the range from 1–3 kg. The cyanobacterium *Anabaena azollae* living in symbiosis with water fern (*Azolla*) in rice paddies likewise produces 300 kg N ha^{-1} year^{-1}. Only 30–50 kg N ha^{-1} year^{-1} have been estimated as the result of free-living cyanobacteria in rice fields.

Metabolic regulation

The metabolic processes of a microbial cell are directed towards the generation of biochemically utilizable energy and the production of building blocks (monomers) necessary for synthesis of the macromolecules. In order to secure optimal growth conditions, the metabolic processes require perfect coordination. During evolution, specific regulatory mechanisms have evolved which coordinate the enzymatic activities in an ingenious and economic way in order to prevent over-production of enzymes and metabolites, thus saving energy and nutrients. Under conditions of an exogenous supply of a chemical compound needed for biomass production, the cell stops its own synthesis of the corresponding compound. As a rule, the cell also avoids excretion of those metabolites which can be utilized.

Regulation of metabolism occurs at two levels, (a) by control of enzyme synthesis, and (b) by control of enzyme activity. The various metabolic pathways are usually regulated at the level of enzyme production. The rate of synthesis of particular enzymes is controlled in relation to the rate of the total protein synthesis. Certain enzymes are constitutive, others are induced when necessary. By enzyme induction, the production of the catabolic enzymes is regulated. It is economic that the cell starts production of a specific enzyme only if it is needed under the actual nutritional conditions. A well-known example of enzyme induction is the production of β-glucosidase in the presence of lactose and its absence in the presence of glucose. The enzyme level may increase by a factor of a thousand.

Enzyme repression operates when the end product of an anabolic pathway is abundant (end product repression). Catabolite repression refers to the repression of particular enzymes in the presence of several substrates. If a cell is supplied with two substrates it prefers the one which allows fastest growth. Enzymes necessary for degradation of the second substrate are repressed and only produced after exhaustion of the first substrate. This phenomenon is referred to as diauxic growth. If *E. coli* is grown in the presence of glucose and sorbitol there is no simultaneous

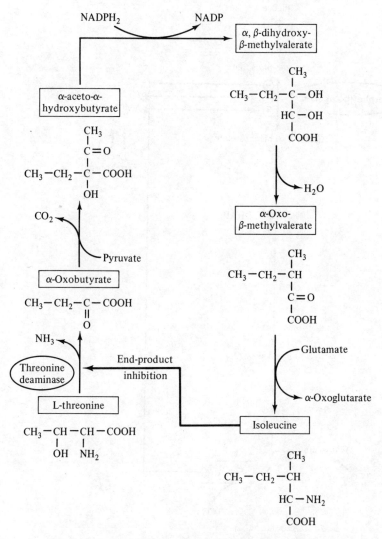

Fig. 2.18 Feedback inhibition of threonine deaminase by isoleucine

consumption. The cell has a preference for glucose and only takes up sorbitol after glucose is exhausted. During the degradation of glucose, the enzymes required for breakdown of sorbitol are repressed. Regulation of enzyme synthesis occurs at the molecular level of transcription of the genes which code for the structure of the polypeptide.

Regulation of enzyme activity usually effects the key enzymes of metabolism. The catalytic activity of an allosteric enzyme is enhanced by

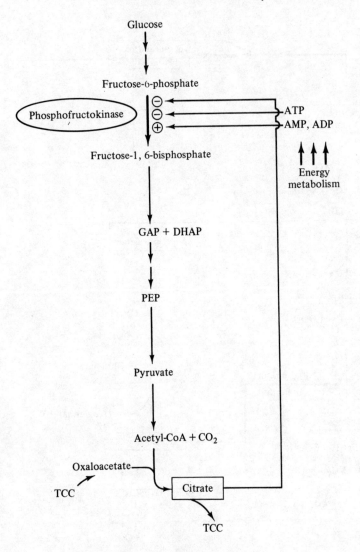

Glucose

Fructose-6-phosphate

Phosphofructokinase

⊖ ← ATP
⊖ ← ATP
⊕ ← AMP, ADP

Energy
metabolism

Fructose-1, 6-bisphosphate

GAP + DHAP

PEP

Pyruvate

Acetyl-CoA + CO_2

Oxaloacetate

TCC

Citrate

TCC

⊕ Activator   ⊖ Inhibitor

DHAP: Dihydroxyacetone phosphate
GAP : Glyceraldehyde-3-phosphate
TCC : Tricarboxylic acid cycle
PEP : Phospho-enol pyruvate

Fig. 2.19 Regulation of phosphofructokinase

a positive effector or reduced by a negative effector. Contrary to regulation of enzyme synthesis by induction or repression, which operates slowly, the change of enzyme activity is a spontaneous and fast effect. Accumulation of an end product in a sequence of metabolic steps causes 'feedback inhibition' by lowering or inhibiting the activity of the first enzyme in the reaction chain. An example of this type of regulation is the feedback inhibition of threonine deaminase by isoleucine (Fig. 2.18). The Pasteur effect, which describes the inhibition of glycolysis by respiration in yeast, is based on the regulation of phosphofructokinase (Fig. 2.19). ATP (and citrate) are the main negative effectors, AMP (in some organisms ADP) and P the main positive effectors. The flow of substrate is thus regulated by the energy status of the cell. If the O_2 supply is reduced in an aerobically growing yeast culture, the generation of energy likewise is reduced and causes a decrease of the ratio of ATP to AMP. A high AMP concentration causes activation of the phosphofructokinase which in turn accelerates the substrate flow and thus allows generation of ATP by substrate level phosphorylation (fermentation). Since fixation of CO_2 by the Calvin cycle (carboxylation of ribulose-1,5-bisphosphate) is extremely energy consuming, this cycle only operates at full speed if there is no lack of energy. Therefore, phosphoribulokinase is inhibited by higher concentrations of AMP.

Isolation, cultivation, identification
Pure culture

A pure culture of microorganisms represents a population (clone, strain) derived from an individual cell. A pure culture must be axenic (from Greek *xenic*: stranger), i.e. free of contaminating organisms. Pure cultures are the basis for laboratory studies with respect to morphology, physiology, metabolism, genetics, etc. This applies to bacteria, fungi, protozoa, microscopic algae, and also cell lines (tissue cells). When studying the properties of 'a bacterium', this normally does not refer to individual cells but to populations (clones). A pure culture, conventionally grown on an agar slant, contains around 10^{10} individuals which are not completely identical in the genetic sense. Population changes may occur, due to spontaneous mutation and selection of the mutants, thus causing heterogeneity of the population. This genetic heterogeneity is allowed in the concept of a pure (axenic) bacterial culture.

Large organisms can generally be studied individually. With small organisms such as bacteria, the study of individuals causes insuperable difficulties. Characterization of a definite organism, therefore, refers to the features and behaviour of a population. For this reason, pure cultures are indispensable for the study of microbes.

Although a microorganism in pure culture may differ considerably from the same organism in its natural environment, with respect to morphology and metabolic activities, pure culture studies are an essential requisite also in ecological research. It is true that pure cultures, as Winogradsky stated in 1949, cannot tell us much about microbial activities in nature. Nevertheless, pure cultures are also a necessity in microbial ecology because such studies give us information concerning the reactions under different environmental conditions and the metabolic potential of an organism. Because of the heterogeneous situation in most natural habitats, it is a practical impossibility to study *in situ* the physiological and biochemical activities of one particular organism living in close association with a great number of other organisms.

In nature, the occurrence of pure cultures is rare. In algal blooms developing in lakes one organism may prevail to such an extent that the situation resembles a pure culture. Under highly selective environmental conditions the usually complex microbial flora tend to become restricted to a small number of species so that, under extreme conditions, pure cultures of one particular organism may be encountered. Quasi-pure cultures may develop in diseased tissues of plants and animals. Special environmental conditions likewise may induce the mass development of a particular organism. An example of this type is the development of *Bifidobacterium bifidum* in the intestines of infants. Also on soil crumbs, discrete microcolonies possibly representing microbial pure cultures have been observed. As in pure cultures grown in the laboratory, micro-organisms in nature are subject to physiological variations caused by environmental factors and to genetic variations due to mutation and selection.

The preparation of pure cultures is based on the separation and immobilization of individual cells. This is possible in, or on, solidified media or in liquid media inoculated with appropriate dilutions of a mixture of microorganisms. In principle, an organism is removed from its natural environment where it lives in a complex community and is placed under sterile conditions allowing axenic development. The various techniques for preparing pure cultures comprise pour plates, spread plates, streak plates, dilution shake cultures, serial dilution in liquid media, and also single cell isolation under microscopic control. The microscopic methods are based on the use of microdroplets or a micro-manipulator. The aseptic conditions required for the preparation and handling of pure cultures are secured by the sterilization techniques including the autoclave and sterile filtration procedures. Certain bacteria and particular pathogens cannot yet be cultivated under laboratory conditions. Such obligate pathogens usually have unknown growth requirements. As soon as it becomes possible to imitate the natural environment in the laboratory for a hitherto obligate pathogen, the organism has to be classified as a facultative pathogen. Although pure cultures may differ in ecologically significant factors, pure culture studies are essential. Therefore, field studies should always be accompanied or combined with laboratory observations.

Direct isolation

Isolation of bacteria is possible in a direct way or following selective enrichment. The isolation of a particular organism in axenic culture requires knowledge of the precise conditions appropriate for its cultivation. For successful isolation the nutritional and physicochemical conditions required by the organism must be met. Difficulties in isolation arise whenever the conditions for growth are unknown or inappropriate. From microscopic observations of natural materials a number of micro-organisms are known that have not yet been isolated and propagated in the state of pure cultures. Examples are *Thiovolum*, *Achromatium*, *Blastocaulis-Planctomyces*, *Brachyarcus*, *Chlamydia*, *Mycobacterium leprae*, *Rickettsia*, and some treponemes. Direct electron microscopy of soil samples has revealed the existence of small cellular organisms which so far have not been cultivated.

During a century of experimental microbiology, a vast number of culture techniques for growing pure cultures have been developed. Our present knowledge of the prokaryotes is largely based on the development and progress of the cultural techniques. Despite the refinement of such cultural methods, entirely new types of bacteria are still being discovered.

In natural habitats, many different kinds of organisms live side by side. They coexist because each partner has its own function and occupies an ecological niche. Since microorganisms differ in their nutritional require-ments there is no culture medium that would allow growth of all bacteria existing in a given habitat. Any medium supporting the growth of microorganisms is, to some extent, selective. Inoculation of a mixture of bacteria into any such medium will allow growth of some organisms and exclude others. Selective media have the property of favouring (selecting) the desired organism and disfavouring (counterselecting) the accompany-ing organisms. The basis of selectivity can be nutritional, toxicological, or both.

Many bacteria can be isolated directly from natural materials by the use of selective agar media. Depending on the nature of the substrate, the types of bacteria developing on the plate will vary. Bacteria with special physiological traits and metabolic activities can easily be recognized during growth on specific media. There are many examples for the direct isolation of metabolic specialists such as casein-digesting bacteria, lipolytic bacteria, esterase-active bacteria, phosphatase-producing bacteria, or urease-producing bacteria. Direct isolation by use of selective media is usually based on nutrition allowing the development of the desired organism and avoiding growth of the undesired organisms. Besides the nutritional and toxicological conditions, physical factors may also determine the selectivity of media. This becomes obvious in the procedures used for isolation of thermophilic, psychrophilic, or halophilic bacteria. Direct isolation is often facilitated by the addition of selective agents such as dyes, antibiotics, or other growth inhibiting substances. During the years, numerous selective media have been introduced, not only for direct isolation of bacteria but also of fungi and other microorganisms. As an example, the highly selective medium for isolation of *Verticillium alboatrum* from soil may be mentioned. It is based on specific nutritional conditions and the addition of pentachloro-nitrobenzene, oxgall, and streptomycin.

Isolation following enrichment

The isolation of a particular organism from a mixed microbial population is difficult if the organism under investigation occurs only as a small fraction of the total population. The chances for direct isolation can be improved by increasing the number of the organism in question. The enrichment technique introduced by Winogradsky and Beijerinck has led to the discovery of many metabolic types of bacteria and has greatly influenced the development of microbiology. A great number of enrichment media exist for the isolation of phototrophs, chemolithotrophs, and chemoorganotrophs. For almost every bacterial group, enrichment procedures have been developed. A prerequisite of any enrichment culture is the selective advantage the medium provides for growth and multiplication of a particular organism from a mixed population. The possibilities for alteration of the enrichment conditions are enormous comprising nutritional, chemical, and physical conditions. In order to design favourable enrichment culture conditions it is necessary to understand the ecological niche of the organism to be enriched. The type best adapted to the chosen conditions has a selective advantage and finally may come to predominance, facilitating its direct isolation. For successful competition within a population of different species, the specific properties of the organism to be enriched must be considered. In many enrichment cultures the selective advantage is obvious, as noted by the example of *Azotobacter* being favoured in an environment containing hexose as the energy source but no combined nitrogen. Under such conditions the N_2-fixing organism is selectively enriched. In other organisms, the selective advantage is less obvious, e.g. in the isolation of Chlorobiaceae. These organisms compete successfully at low light intensities, but are overgrown at high light intensities by purple sulphur bacteria. The enrichment technique is often combined with counterselection by the addition of selective agents. It is basically possible to construct a highly specific 'selective pressure' for the deliberate isolation of a known bacterium from nature. It is even feasible to construct conditions for the isolation of so far unknown types of bacteria and isolate such 'new' organisms if they do exist.

Enrichment of bacteria is possible in closed and in open systems. In a closed system (batch culture) the liquid substrate is inoculated with natural materials and incubated under aerobic or anaerobic conditions. If the environment offers a selective advantage to the desired organism it may easily be isolated after selective growth by plating and separation from the other organisms. The disadvantage of a closed system is the continuous change of conditions by progressive consumption of nutrients and excretion of metabolic products. By such changes, successive enrichments of different types of microorganisms may occur. Such alterations may be caused by changes in the nutrient concentration and also in pH. In open systems, resembling natural ecosystems, the disadvantages caused by nutritional changes do not occur because the conditions remain constant. Under such conditions the selection depends largely on the growth rate of the members of the mixed population. The organism that grows best at the given dilution becomes dominant while others are washed out. By this procedure a population change is induced resulting in specific enrichment of a former minority population of a mixed flora.

Specific enrichment is not usually achieved in complex (rich) media but requires defined mineral media supplied with a definite carbon source, nitrogen source, and growth factors if necessary. Sterilization of the enrichment medium is often unnecessary because of the inoculation with natural materials containing a great variety of microorganisms.

Chemostat studies with mixed populations at different dilution rates have revealed the importance of the substrate affinity. At high dilution rates the substrate is in excess, and the fast-growing bacteria are favoured. At low dilution rates the organisms with the highest substrate affinity are favoured.

Enrichment procedures are usually directed towards the increase in number of a particular organism compared to the total number of associated organisms. A special type of enrichment is the so-called 'relative enrichment'. This technique is applicable to spore-forming bacteria. By pretreatment with heat (5 min, 80 °C) of a mixture of vegetative bacteria and spores, the ratio of spores to vegetative cells is increased and thus facilitates isolation of spore-forming bacteria. The same effect is also observed after treatment with ethanol. Vegetative cells are eliminated within one hour and thus favour the recovery of the aerobic bacilli or the anaerobic clostridia. A great number of selective media for direct isolation or enrichment of pathogens are being used in medical bacteriology. Since direct isolation is more rapid, continuous efforts are taken to construct new media with high selectivity.

Besides nutrition, some environmental factors greatly influence the enrichment conditions. Aerobic bacteria require O_2-supply (aeration of liquid culture). A variety of bacteria are selectively enriched under reduced pO_2. Anaerobic bacteria need complete exclusion of molecular O_2. Temperature has a drastic effect on the selection. Light is an important factor for enrichment of the phototrophs. By changing light intensities and wavelengths, particular phototrophs can be selected. It is logical that the isolation of an organism can be expected to be successful only in habitats where the organism to be enriched is present. There are more microorganisms present in nature than presently known and cultivable, and the instruments of enrichment culture are a powerful tool for the isolation of hitherto unknown organisms.

Media, cultivation

For the cultivation of microorganisms under laboratory conditions, culture media are an essential prerequisite. In order to achieve good growth, appropriate media must be used. Their preparation requires knowledge of the nutritional requirements and the growth conditions. The medium must contain essentially all the elements of the biomass of the organism to be cultivated. The concentration and the proportions of the individual nutrients require balanced conditions. At high concentrations, fatty acids, amino acids, and sugars may have inhibitory effects. The nutritional requirements of microorganisms reflect the natural habitats in which they live. The bacteria have extremely diverse nutritional requirements reflecting the diversity of their physiological properties. Because of the immense nutritional diversity, the number of culture media is essentially unlimited.

For cultivation of bacteria, synthetic or complex media are used. Synthetic media are chemically defined with respect to minerals, carbon, nitrogen, and other components. A great many synthetic media have been introduced for the cultivation of chemoorganotrophs, chemolithotrophs, and phototrophs. A minimal medium is defined as a synthetic medium containing only minerals and a carbon and energy source. Organisms growing on such minimal media do not require additional compounds such as vitamins or other growth factors. For routine cultivation of bacteria, complex media play a major role. Such complex media are partly undefined with respect to their chemical composition. The basis of complex media are extracts from animal tissues or plant materials. In addition, they often contain yeast extract which serves as a supplementation for vitamins, amino acids, peptides, purines, pyrimidines, carbohydrates, and other organic compounds. The use of highly complex media is necessary if the precise nutritional requirements of an organism are unknown. Many complex and special media are commercially available in the form of dehydrated media. Two main types of media are used in laboratory practice: liquid and solidified media. Selective media allow favoured development of particular organisms. Differential media are used for differentiation of bacteria by addition of specific compounds. Assay media are used for quantitative determination of vitamins, amino acids, and other growth factors. Maintenance media serve the preservation of stock cultures (stabs, slants). The criterion of a suitable maintenance medium is the viability of the organism during storage.

Cultivation of aerobic bacteria
On solid media, the O_2 supply is optimal. Cultivation on solid media is usually performed in covered glass or plastic dishes (petri dishes). Growth of aerobic bacteria in liquid media is largely influenced by the oxygen available for respiration. The amount of oxygen dissolved in a nutrient solution usually is insufficient to meet the respiratory potential of a growing population. Therefore, aeration is necessary to achieve good growth.

Cultivation of anaerobic bacteria
With respect to the tolerance towards molecular oxygen, there are two types of anaerobes. Moderate anaerobes tolerate transient exposure to air whereas strict anaerobes are unable to tolerate oxygen and are killed by oxygen contact. The nature of O_2 toxicity has been explained in a previous chapter. The methods for cultivation of anaerobic bacteria are specifically directed towards the exclusion of molecular oxygen. Several

techniques have been developed to achieve oxygen-free conditions. (1) removal of O_2 by catalysis; (2) removal of O_2 by alkaline pyrogallol solution (Wright–Burri closure); (3) removal of O_2 by growing anaerobic and aerobic organisms side by side (Fortner–Plate); (4) replacement of O_2 by N_2, Ar, H_2; (5) addition of reducing agents (e.g. ascorbate, thioglycolate, cysteine) to lower the oxidation–reduction potential required for the initiation of anaerobic growth and to protect the cell from the deleterious effect of O_2; (6) growth of moderate anaerobes in semi-solid media (0.02–0.2% agar) to retard diffusion of O_2.

Preservation

In order to keep cultures alive and growing, they must be maintained on appropriate media. This is usually done by periodic transfer of bacteria to fresh media. Some organisms require subculturing after days, others stay alive for months or years. Working cultures usually are transferred as agar slants, agar stabs, or broth cultures. Stock cultures required to possess a prolonged viability are often kept at low temperature (-20 to $-30\,°C$). Long-term maintenance of bacteria is achieved by freeze-drying (lyophilization) or storage in liquid nitrogen (ultrafreezing at $-196\,°C$). A variety of other preservation methods have been recommended: (1) overlaying of agar slants with mineral oil; (2) drying of bacteria in gelatin discs and storage at 0–$5\,°C$; (3) storage in 1% NaCl suspension; (4) storage in distilled water at extremely low bacterial concentration. Pathogenic bacteria, such as *Borrelia*, that cannot be cultivated on artificial media can be preserved in their vectors (lice, ticks) and successfully stored at $-70\,°C$.

Identification

The identification of a bacterium requires a number of data which allow recognition of the organism as a member of an already known taxon. The characterization refers to data from morphology, ecology, physiology, biochemistry, molecular biology, and genetics of the organism. If correspondence with an already known taxon is proven the organism can be identified and classified.

Further reading

Books
General microbiology
Brock, T. D., Smith, D. W. & Madigan, M. T. (1984). *Biology of Microorganisms*, 4th edn Englewood Cliffs, N. J.: Prentice-Hall.

Pelczar, M. J. jr, Reid, R. D. & Chan, E. C. S. (1977). *Microbiology*, 4th edn New York: McGraw-Hill.
Schlegel, H. G. (1985). *Allgemeine Mikrobiologie*, 6th edn Stuttgart: Thieme.
Stanier, R. T., Adelberg, E. A., Ingraham, J. L. & Wheelis, M. L. (1979). *Introduction to the Microbial World*. Englewood Cliffs, N.J.: Prentice-Hall.
Wilkinson, J. F. (1975). *Introduction to Microbiology*, 2nd edn Basic Microbiology Vol. I. Oxford: Blackwell Scientific Publications.

Taxonomy and identification

Buchanan, R. E. & Gibbons, N. E. (eds) (1974). *Bergey's Manual of Determinative Bacteriology*. 8th edn Baltimore: Williams & Wilkins.
Buchanan, R. E., Holt, J. G. & Lessel, E. F. jr. (1966). *Index Bergeyana*. Baltimore: Williams & Wilkins.
Gibbs, B. M. & Shapton, D. A. (eds) (1968). *Identification Methods for Microbiologists*, part B. London: Academic Press.
Gibbs, B. M. & Skinner, F. A. (eds) (1966). *Identification Methods for Microbiologists*, part A. London: Academic Press.
Goodfellow, M. & Board, R. G. (1980). *Microbial Classification and Identification*. London: Academic Press.
Krieg, N. R. & Holt, J. G. (eds) (1984). *Bergey's Manual of Systematic Bacteriology*, Vol. I. Baltimore, MD: Williams & Wilkins.

Contents of Vol. I: Gram-negative bacteria of medical and commercial importance: spirochetes, spiral and curved bacteria, Gram-negative aerobic and facultatively aerobic rods, Gram-negative obligate anaerobes, Gram-negative aerobic and anaerobic cocci, rickettsias, mycoplasmas.

The subsequent volumes will be arranged as follows:

Vol. II: Gram-positive bacteria of medical and commercial importance: Gram-positive cocci, Gram-positive endospore-forming and nonsporing rods, and the nonfilamentous actinomycetes.

Vol. III: Remaining Gram-negative bacteria: phototrophic, gliding, sheathed, and appendaged bacteria, cyanobacteria, lithotrophic bacteria, and the archaebacteria (methanogens, extreme halophiles, and the thermoacidophiles).

Vol. IV: Filamentous actinomycetes and related bacteria.

Lapage, S. P., Sneath, P. H. A., Lessel, E. F., Skerman, V. B. D., Seeliger, H. P. R. & Clark, W. A. (1975). *International Code of Nomenclature of Bacteria*. Washington, D.C.: American Society for Microbiology.
Skerman, V. B. D. (1967). *A Guide to the Identification of the Genera of Bacteria*. Baltimore: Williams & Wilkins.
Sneath, P. H. A. & Sokal, R. R. (1973). *Numerical Taxonomy. The Principles and Practice of Numerical Classification*. San Francisco: Freeman.

Structure and function of the cell

Fawcett, D. W. (1981). *The Cell*. Philadelphia: Saunders.
Lehninger, A. L. (1975). *Biochemistry, the Molecular Basis of Cell Structure and Function*, 2nd edn New York: Worth Publ.
Levinson, H., Sonenshein, A. L. & Tipper, D. J. (eds) (1981). *Sporulation and Germination*. Washington, D.C.: American Society for Microbiology.
Rogers, H. J., Perkins, H. R. & Ward, J. B. (1981). *Microbial Cell Walls and Membranes*. New York: Chapman & Hall/Methuen.

58   *The microbial world: an introductory review*

Stanier, R. Y., Rogers, H. J. & Ward, B. J. (eds) (1978). *Relation between Structure and Function in the Prokaryotic Cell.* Symposium 28 of the Soc. Gen. Microbiol. London: Cambridge University Press.

Nutrition and growth
Ingraham, J. L., Maaløe & Neidhardt, F. C. (1983). *Growth of the Bacterial Cell.* Sunderland, Mass: Sinauer Associates, Inc.

Basic physiology and metabolism
Gottschalk, G. (1986). *Bacterial metabolism*, 2nd edn New York: Springer-Verlag.
Jungermann, K. & Möhler, H. (1980). *Biochemie.* Berlin: Springer-Verlag.
Moat, A. G. (1979). *Microbial Physiology.* New York: John Wiley & Sons.
Nichols, D. G. (1982). *Bioenergetics: An Introduction to the Chemiosmotic Theory.* New York: Academic Press.
Rosen, B. P. (1978). *Bacterial Transport.* New York: Marcel Dekker.
Veldkamp, H. (1976). *Continuous Culture in Microbial Physiology and Ecology.* Durham: Meadowfield Press.

Respiration and fermentation
Payne, W. J. (1981). *Denitrification.* New York: Wiley Interscience.
Postgate, J. R. (1979). *The Sulphate Reducing Bacteria.* Cambridge: Cambridge University Press.

N₂-Fixation
Hardy, R. W. F., Bottomley, F. & Burns, R. C. (eds) (1979). *A Treatise on Dinitrogen Fixation.* New York: John Wiley.
Sprent, J. I. (1979). *The Biology of Nitrogen-fixing Organisms.* London: McGraw-Hill.
Stewart, W. D. P. & Gallon, J. R. (1980). *Nitrogen Fixation.* Phytochemical Society, Symposium Series 18. London: Academic Press.
Subba Rao, N. S. (ed.) (1980). *Recent Advances in Biological Nitrogen Fixation.* London: Edward Arnold.

Genetics
Lewin, B. (1983). *Genes.* New York: John Wiley.

Applied microbiology
Lenette, E. H., Spaulding, E. H. & Truant, J. (1974). *Manual of Clinical Microbiology*, 2nd ed. Washington, D.C.: American Society for Microbiology.

Articles
General microbiology
Stolp, H. & Starr, M. P. (1981). Principles of isolation, cultivation, and conservation of bacteria. In *The Prokaryotes, a Handbook of Habitats, Isolation, and Identification of Bacteria*, eds. M. P. Starr, H. Stolp, H. G. Trüper, A. Balows & H. G. Schlegel, pp. 135–75. New York: Springer-Verlag.

Taxonomy and identification
Schleifer, K. H. & Kandler, O. (1972). Peptidoglycan types of bacterial cell walls and their taxonomic implications. *Bacteriological Reviews*, **36**, 407–77.
Schleifer, K. H. & Stackebrandt, E. (1983). Molecular systematics of prokaryotes. *Annual Review of Microbiology*, **37**, 143–87.

Skerman, V. B. D., McGowan, V. & Sneath, P. H. A. (eds) (1980). Approved lists of bacterial names. *International Journal of Systematic Bacteriology*, **30**, 225–420.
Trüper, H. G. & Kramer, J. (1981). Principles of characterization and identification of prokaryotes. In *The Prokaryotes, a Handbook of Habitats, Isolation, and Identification of Bacteria*, eds. M. P. Starr, H. Stolp, H. G. Trüper, A. Balows & H. G. Schlegel, pp. 176–93. New York: Springer-Verlag.

Structure and function of the cell
Costerton, J. W. (1979). The role of the electron microscope in the elucidation of bacterial structure and function. *Annual Review of Microbiology*, **33**, 459–79.
Singer, S. J. (1974). The molecular organization of membranes. *Annual Review of Biochemistry*, **43**, 805–33.
Ward, J. B. (1981). Teichoic and teichuronic acids. *Microbiological Reviews*, **45**, 211–43.

Nutrition and growth
Matin, A. (1978). Organic nutrition of chemolithotrophic bacteria. *Annual Review of Microbiology*, **32**, 433–68.

Basic physiology and metabolism
Dills, S. S., Apperson, A., Schmidt, M. R. & Saier, M. H. jr (1980). Carbohydrate transport in bacteria. *Microbiological Reviews*, **44**, 385–418.
Khan, S. & Macnab, R. M. (1980). Protein chemical potential, proton electrical potential and bacterial motility. *Journal of Molecular Biology*, **138**, 599–614.
Lanyi, J. K. (1978). Light energy conversion in *Halobacterium halobium*. *Microbiological Reviews*, **42**, 682–706.
Magasanik, B. (1982). Control of nitrogen assimilation in bacteria. *Annual Review of Genetics*, **16**, 135–68.
Quayle, J. R. & Ferenci, T. (1978). Evolutionary aspects of autotrophy. *Microbiological Reviews*, **42**, 251–73.
Schlegel, H. G. (1975). Mechanisms of chemo-autotrophy. In *Marine Ecology, a Comprehensive, Integrated Treatise on Life in Oceans and Coastal Waters*, vol. II: Physiological Mechanism, part 1, pp. 9–60, London: John Wiley.
Smith, A. J. & Hoare, D. S. (1977). Specialist phototrophs, lithotrophs, and methylotrophs: A unity among a diversity of procaryotes? *Bacteriological Reviews*, **41**, 419–48.
Sutherland, I. W. (1982). Biosynthesis of microbial exopolysaccharides. *Advances in Microbial Physiology*, **23**, 79–150.
Umbarger, H. E. (1978). Amino acid biosynthesis and its regulation. *Annual Review of Biochemistry*, **47**, 533–606.
Whittenbury, R. & D. P. Kelly (1977). Autotrophy: a conceptual phoenix. In *Microbial Energetics*, 27th symposium, Society for General Microbiology, eds B. A. Haddock & W. A. Hamilton, pp. 121–50. New York: Cambridge University Press.

Respiration and fermentation
Aleem, M. I. H. (1977). Coupling of energy with electron transfer reactions in chemolithotrophic bacteria. In *Microbial Energetics*, eds B. A. Haddock & W. A. Hamilton, pp. 351–81. Cambridge: Cambridge University Press.
Boogerd, F. C. & Van Versefeld, H. W. (1982). The bioenergetics of denitrification. *Antonie van Leeuwenhoek*, **48**, 545–53.
Fillingname, R. H. (1980). The proton-translocating pumps of oxidative phosphorylation. *Annual Review of Biochemistry*, **49**, 1079–113.

Gottschalk, G. & Andreesen, J. R. (1979). Energy metabolism in anaerobes. In *International Review of Biochemistry*, vol. 21: Microbial Biochemistry, ed. J. R. Quayle, pp. 85–105, Baltimore: University Park.
Hamilton, W. A. (1979). Microbial energetics and metabolism. In *Microbial Ecology: A Conceptual Approach*, eds J. M. Lynch & N. J. Poole, pp. 22–44. Oxford, London, Edinburgh, Melbourne: Blackwell Scientific Publications.
Thauer, R. K., Jungermann, K. & Decker, K. (1977). Energy conservation in chemotrophic anaerobic bacteria. *Bacteriological Reviews*, **41**, 100–80.

N_2-fixation
Roberts, G. P. & Brill, W. J. (1981). Genetics and regulation of nitrogen fixation. *Annual Review of Microbiology*, **35**, 207–35.
Robson, R. L. & Postgate, J. R. (1980). Oxygen and hydrogen in biological nitrogen fixation. *Annual Review of Microbiology*, **34**, 183–208.

Genetics
Brill, W. J. (1979). Nitrogen fixation: basic to applied. *American Scientist*, **67**, 458–66.

3

Characterization and occurrence of the major groups of microorganisms

The general features of the prokaryotic and eukaryotic microorganisms have been explained in Chapter 2. Here, the major groups, their special features and their occurrence in the natural environment are discussed.

Prokaryotic microorganisms
The phototrophic prokaryotes
Cyanobacteria

On the basis of their size, cell structure, presence of murein, 70S ribosomes, and other features, the cyanobacteria are prokaryotes. They comprise a large group of morphologically different organisms that use water as the hydrogen donor and perform oxic photosynthesis. Some are capable of living in extreme environments, others have the capacity to fix molecular nitrogen. They occur as unicellular, colonial or filamentous organisms. Some are motile by gliding on solid surfaces. The fine structure of the cyanobacteria is comparable to that of the Gram-negative bacteria. Many species exude polysaccharides surrounding single cells as capsules or chains of cells (trichomes, filaments) as sheaths. The apparatus for photosynthesis is localized in flat, membranous vesicles, the thylakoids. The membranes of the thylakoids contain chlorophyll a, β-carotene, oxocarotenoids, and phycobiliproteins. Most species are obligate phototrophs. The intracellular storage product is glycogen deposited as granula. Some species are capable of photoheterotrophic growth; they assimilate organic compounds in a light-dependent process. The relative proportions of the various pigments determine the colour of the organism, blue-green, yellow-green, purple, red, or black. The cyanobacteria produce different kinds of specialized cells. Heterocysts possess thick cell walls and are the site of N_2-fixation. Akinetes are resting spores resistant to desiccation. Hormogonia represent short motile segments of a trichome that have separated from the parental organism. Many cyanobacteria possess gas vacuoles which are involved in floating. Unicellular species are reproduced by binary fission; trichomes grow by division

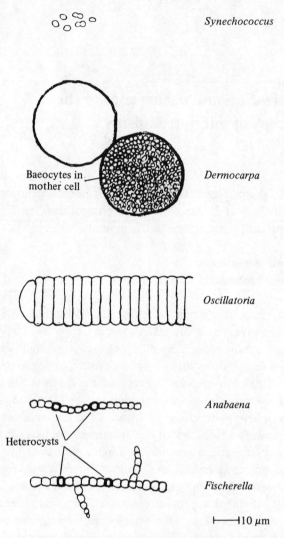

Synechococcus

Baeocytes in
mother cell

Dermocarpa

Oscillatoria

Anabaena

Heterocysts

Fischerella

⊢————⊣10 μm

Fig. 3.1 Schematic representation of some representative cyanobacteria

of intercalary cells. On the basis of morphological features several groups
of cyanobacteria can be differentiated (Fig. 3.1):

(1)   Unicellular cyanobacteria. They occur as single cells or as cell
       aggregates and multiply by binary fission or budding. Represen-
       tatives: *Synechococcus, Gloeocapsa, Gloeobacter.*

(2)   Unicellular types that also propagate by multiple fission of a large
       mother cell surrounded by a thick layer of polysaccharides. The

small progeny cells are known as baeocytes. Representatives: *Pleurocapsa, Dermocarpa.*

(3)   Filamentous cyanobacteria (trichomes) not producing heterocysts. The trichomes are composed of vegetative cells that divide in one plane. Representatives: *Spirulina, Oscillatoria, Lyngbya, Phormidium, Plectonema.*

(4)   Filamentous cyanobacteria producing heterocysts. Trichomes developing in the absence of nitrogen (HN_4^+, NO_3^-) produce nitrogenase containing heterocysts. The division of cells mostly occurs in one plane. Representatives: *Anabaena, Nostoc, Cylindrospermum, Calothrix.* In some species, cell division occurs in more than one plane, causing a branched appearance. Representative: *Fischerella.*

The cyanobacteria are mainly distributed in aquatic habitats but also occur in the upper layers of soils, and on rocks of the tidal zones. Blooms in fresh water and marine habitats are common. In eutrophic lakes, the blue-green *Anabaena* or the red *Oscillatoria rubescens* are often the cause of blooms. Some cyanobacteria have been found in water layers that contain fairly high amounts of H_2S. Under such conditions, anoxic photosynthesis – comparable to that of the purple sulphur bacteria – has been shown to occur. Certain species live as symbionts or in epiphytic association with higher plants. Some species such as *Nostoc* are phycosymbionts in lichens. As the cyanobacteria are independent of organic substrates and possess the capability of fixing both CO_2 and N_2, they are pioneers of poor habitats such as sea sand. Cyanobacteria are also found in extreme environments, such as hot springs, saline lakes, and deserts.

The cyanobacteria are particularly important in marine habitats. According to fossil records, these bacteria were probably the dominant photosynthetic organisms during the precambrian period. In distinct habitats such as intertidal zones, coral reefs, salt marshes, or open oceans, a characteristic flora of cyanobacteria is encountered. *Trichodesmium*, an oscillatorian cyanobacterium, is capable of forming dense blooms which cover vast areas of the open ocean in tropical and subtropical regions. *Synechococcus* has a wide distribution in the open oceans and reaches high cell densities (more than 10^5/ml) in the euphotic zone. It has been suggested that this organism may be responsible for as much as 10% of the total primary production of the oceans. Cyanobacteria also exist in hypersaline habitats such as salt lakes and salt evaporation ponds. Certain strains tolerate up to 16% of NaCl in their environment.

Various cyanobacteria that exhibit optimum growth at temperatures above 45 °C have been isolated from thermal habitats of geothermal, solar, or manufactured origin. *Chlorogloeopsis* sp. exists in hot springs in many parts of the world. Another thermophilic cyanobacterium is *Synechococcus lividus*. As with other bacteria, there is a continuum of overlapping temperature ranges and temperature optima. As temperature increases the number of species generally decreases.

Phototrophic bacteria

The phototrophic bacteria (purple and green bacteria) do not use H_2O as H-donor as do the cyanobacteria and green plants but perform photosynthesis with other electron donors (H_2S, H_2, or organic compounds). Consequently, they do not produce O_2 during photosynthesis. In contrast to the eukaryotic green plants and the cyanobacteria, the anaerobic phototrophs do not possess chlorophyll a but bacteriochlorophylls (bchl a to e). The anoxic phototrophs are divided into two large categories: (1) the purple bacteria and (2) the green bacteria. Differences between these groups are mainly due to physiological properties and pigments. The purple bacteria comprise the Chromatiaceae (purple sulphur bacteria) and the Rhodospirillaceae (non-sulphur purple bacteria); the green bacteria are divided into the Chlorobiaceae (green sulphur bacteria) and the Chloroflexaceae. The morphological diversity of the phototrophic bacteria is shown in Fig. 3.2 (A, B, C).

The Chromatiaceae can easily be recognized by the deposition of sulphur within their cells. Members of the genus *Ectothiorhodospira* deposit sulphur outside the cell. Some sulphur purple bacteria are extremely large, such as *Chromatium okenii* (5 × 20μm) or *Thiospirillum jenense* (3 × 50 μm). The bigger Chromatiae are kidney-shaped, while the smaller are rod-shaped.

Most Rhodospirillaceae are combined in two genera: *Rhodopseudomonas* and *Rhodospirillum*. Morphologically distinct is *Rhodomicrobium vannielii* producing buds connected to the parental cell by stalks. *Rhodocyclus purpureus* is a non-motile representative. The non-sulphur purple bacteria do not utilize H_2S. They photoassimilate simple organic compounds (acetate, alcohol) under anaerobic conditions and are able to grow chemotrophically under aerobic conditions in the dark.

The Chlorobiaceae are unicellular organisms (*Chlorobium*) which occur in star-like aggregations or produce net arrangements (*Pelodictyon*).

The Chloroflexaceae are photosynthetic flexibacteria. *Chloroflexus*

A: Chromatiaceae

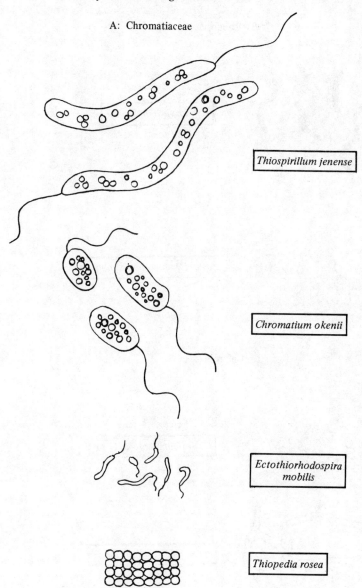

Thiospirillum jenense

Chromatium okenii

Ectothiorhodospira
mobilis

Thiopedia rosea

Fig. 3.2 Schematic representation of some phototrophic bacteria

B: Rhodospirillaceae

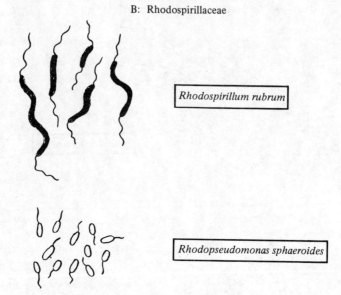

C: Chlorobiaceae

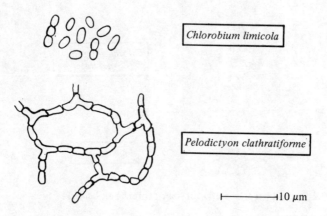

⊢————⊣10 µm

Fig. 3.2 Schematic representation of some phototrophic bacteria

resembles the green bacteria in cell structure and chlorophyll pigments but is similar to the non-sulphur purple bacteria with respect to the phototrophic and catabolic metabolism. Members of this group exhibit a slow gliding motility. The rod-like bacteria measure 0.6–0.7 × 2–6 μm.

The green and purple sulphur bacteria occur under similar environmental conditions in fresh water, estuarine, and marine habitats. Mass accumulations of pink to purple red sulphur bacteria occur in the water and on the mud of fresh-water ponds and lakes. Abundant development has also been observed in seawater pools of salt marshes and estuaries.

In many lakes and lagoons 'red water', caused by growth of phototrophs, has been reported. Mass development of phototrophs occurs in a wide range of aquatic habitats wherever H_2S and light are present. In stratified lakes the purple sulphur and marine bacteria develop 'bacterial plates' in the hypolimnion, below the thermocline. Species with gas vacuoles of the genera *Lamprocystis*, *Thiodictyon*, and *Pelodictyon* prevail. The primary production by anoxic photosynthesis in such habitats is of considerable importance. In contrast to estuarine habitats the oxygenated waters of the open sea do not contain phototrophic sulphur bacteria. *Chromatium* and *Ectothiorhodospira* have also been isolated from extremely saline and highly alkaline lakes. *Ectothiorhodospira halophila* and *E. halochloris* are adapted to extreme saline environments with salinities of 20–30%. *Chloroflexus* occurs in hot springs with temperatures up to 65 °C. The temperature optimum is 52–60 °C; mesophilic strains also exist. *Chloroflexus aurantiacus* is present in alkaline hot springs in most regions of the globe.

Non-sulphur purple bacteria (Rhodospirillaceae) do not occur in the open sea but are chiefly found in water bodies of intertidal flats, salt marshes, and harbour basins. As with other chemoorganotrophic bacteria, they are stimulated by pollution. Some marine strains seem to be selt dependent. This group of phototrophs has a great variety of species occurring in mud and water of ponds, ditches, and shores of eutrophic lakes. In mud, densities of 5 × 10^6 cells/ml have been observed.

A new type of phototrophic organism that combines traits of prokaryotes and characters of algae has recently been isolated. The organism named *Prochloron* possesses chlorophyll a and b and evolves O_2 when illuminated. It can be distinguished from the algae by the absence of a nucleus and plastids, and differs from the cyanobacteria by possessing both chlorophyll a and b but lacking phycobiliproteins. The organism occurs in extracellular symbiosis with marine invertebrates. One species (*Prochloron didemni*) has been described but has not yet been cultivated in pure culture. The bacteria grow on, or within, the colonies of ascidia in tropical coastal waters. Their coccoid cells (diameters of 6 to 25 μm) seem to be obligate associates and occur in locations where the light intensity is low (less than 500 lux). The host possibly profits from the oxygen released by the phototrophic bacterium.

The chemotrophic prokaryotes
The gliding bacteria

Gliding motility is found in several groups of bacteria. They live attached to solid surfaces and move under relatively dry conditions. In terrestrial habitats they are found on soil particles, in decaying plant materials, on dung of herbivores, or on the bark of living and dead trees. Some gliding bacteria also occur in aquatic habitats where they live on the surface of algae or animals and inhabit the bottom sediments. Most gliding bacteria are strictly aerobic and are generally found in well-aerated surface layers, yet some are known to live as facultative anaerobes. The gliding bacteria have the capability of decomposing polymeric compounds such as cellulose, agar, chitin, pectin, and proteins. Some also are able to decompose bacteria and yeast cells. Gliding bacteria are found in all climatic zones. Close associations with higher organisms are rare. Some (*Simonsiella, Alysiella*) live in the mouth and the intestinal tract of certain warm-blooded animals. The genus *Cytophaga* also includes fish pathogens.

   Gliding is known in

(1)   bacteria that deposit intracellular sulphur granules such as the filamentous *Beggiatoa* and the unicellular *Achromatium*,
(2)   filamentous bacteria that do not deposit sulphur such as *Leucothrix* and *Simonsiella*,
(3)   unicellular rod-shaped myxobacteria, the cytophaga-group and the filamentous flexibacteria.

The gliding *Chloroflexus* has been mentioned with the phototrophs.

   Beggiatoa is a genus of colourless sulphur bacteria forming trichomes (chains of cells, filaments). The diameter of the filaments varies from 1 to more than 25 μm. It occurs in the presence of H_2S but also requires at least traces of oxygen. While studying *Beggiatoa*, Winogradsky demonstrated that the organism could oxidize H_2S to SO_4^{2-}. On the basis of this observation he formulated in 1888 the concept of chemolithoautotrophy, i.e. the production of energy by the oxidation of reduced inorganic compounds, combined with autotrophic CO_2 fixation. In *Beggiatoa*, strict autotrophic growth has not been demonstrated. Pure cultures of *Beggiatoa* always grow heterotrophically with organic compounds such as acetate and glucose. Even in the presence of H_2S the bacteria require organic substances for growth. Obviously, *Beggiatoa* cannot use CO_2 as the sole carbon source but gains energy from the oxidation of H_2S. This organism is widespread in nature and is found in freshwater localities as well as in brackish waters and marine habitats. *Beggiatoa* is a characteristic organism in habitats where H_2S is present, and the O_2 concentration is low. In submerged rice paddies *Beggiatoa* lives in community with *Desulfovibrio*.

Thiothrix and *Leucothrix* are filamentous organisms that have the same life cycle. By means of a holdfast they attach to surfaces. *Thiothrix* is a chemolithotrophic bacterium that oxidizes H_2S. It is probably chemolithoautotrophic, although this property has not been shown with pure cultures. *Leucothrix* does not oxidize H_2S. It is the chemoorganotrophic counterpart of *Thiothrix*. The organism is capable of growing on glutamate as the sole C and N source. The life cycle involves production of gonidia (cells involved in asexual reproduction) and rosette formation of the multicellular filaments. These are large in diameter (2–3 μm) and may reach a length of 0.1–0.5 cm. *Leucothrix* is widespread and grows as an epiphyte on marine algae. It is obligately aerobic and thus prevails in aerated habitats. As a strictly marine organism it requires NaCl for growth.

Toxothrix trichogenes occurs in cold iron springs. It also forms trichomes and has not yet been grown in pure culture.

Another group of gliding bacteria are the Pelonemataceae. These are colourless bacteria with multicellular filaments (trichomes) and occur in lakes and ponds of sulphur springs. Like *Toxothrix*, *Pelonema* has not yet been obtained in pure culture.

Simonsiella and *Alysiella* are chemoorganotrophic bacteria that live exclusively in the oral cavities of warm-blooded vertebrates. *Simonsiella* filaments are as wide as 10 μm and as long as 90 μm. The incidence of *Simonsiella* in healthy human populations ranges from 30 to 40%, and approaches 100% in dogs and cats. Despite its predominance, the specific role of *Simonsiella* in the oral cavity is not yet known.

The fruiting myxobacteria have the most complex life cycles of the prokaryotic organisms. The vegetative cells are Gram-negative, rod-shaped bacteria (0.6–1.0 × 2.5–7 μm) that have the capability of gliding on solid surfaces. The outstanding traits are the ability to form fruiting bodies (smaller than 1 mm) and myxospores. The fruiting bodies are produced by a coordinated action of a great number of swarm cells. The induction of fruiting body formation is controlled by environmental conditions. The developmental cycle may be completed within 12 to 24 hours. The resting cells or 'myxospores' are resistant to desiccation. The temperature resistance is low (60 °C for 10–60 min) compared to endospores of bacilli. By the production of myxospores the bacteria survive under unfavourable environmental conditions, in particular dryness and starvation. The organisms are strictly aerobic and capable of degrading a variety of macromolecules by excreted enzymes. They obtain their nutrients mainly by lysis of other bacteria. The habitats of the myxobacteria are soil, dung, decaying plant materials, and barks of trees. They are widespread in neutral or slightly alkaline soils and have not been isolated from acid soils. The bacteria are abundant in cool and humid environments. Dung of herbivores such as rabbit, hare, deer, sheep, and goat is a good source for the isolation of myxobacteria. It is, however, not their primary habitat. They appear to originate from the surrounding soil and inhabit the dung after it has been dropped. Typical dung organisms are *Myxococcus fulvus, Cystobacter fuscus,* and *Stigmatella erecta.* The myxobacteria are rare in water; marine myxos are unknown.

The Cytophagales comprise a variety of unicellular gliding bacteria of the genera *Cytophaga, Sporocytophaga, Flexibacter, Sphaerocytophaga, Microscilla,* and *Lysobacter.* Members of the genus *Cytophaga* are flexible rods (thickness less than 1 μm, length up to 30 μm). These organisms decompose natural polymers such as cellulose, chitin, pectin, keratin, and agar. The organisms are aerobic, but facultative anaerobic species are known. They occur in organic materials, soils, decaying plant residues, and dung of herbivores. In marine environments, they are abundant near the shores, on seaweeds, and on decaying sea animals. It is not known whether they also occur in the open sea. The primary habitats are soil and fresh water. Many isolates from marine environments prefer lower temperatures (18–24 °C); also psychrophilic strains have been described. One representative, *Cytophaga columnaris,* is a fish pathogen.

The sheathed bacteria
Sheaths are produced in a number of filamentous aquatic bacteria, comprising the following genera: *Sphaerotilus, Leptothrix, Lieskeella Phragmidiothrix, Crenothrix,* and *Clonothrix.* The organisms are primarily found in flowing waters. *Sphaerotilus* consists of long filaments enclosed in a sheath. The individual bacteria within the sheath measure 1–2 × 2–10 μm and divide by binary fission. At the tip of the sheaths motile swarmers are released and start a new developmental cycle. *Sphaerotilus natans* is abundant in fresh water (rivers) with high organic

contents. Because of the fungus-like filamentous slime produced on surfaces, the organism is called the 'sewage fungus'.

The sheaths of the organisms of the *Sphaerotilus–Leptothrix* group often are coated with ironIII hydroxide ($Fe(OH)_3$) or manganeseIV oxide (MnO_2). Organisms that contain precipitated iron and/or manganese in the sheath are members of the genus *Leptothrix*, while bacteria without precipitated manganese are representatives of the genus *Sphaerotilus*. Although the bacteria of the *Sphaerotilus–Leptothrix* group are able to cause precipitation of ironIII hydroxide or manganeseIV oxide in the presence of Fe^{2+} and Mn^{2+}, they are not chemolithotrophs but chemoorganotrophs. The organisms are obligatorily aerobic and capable of growing at very low pO_2 which is prohibiting growth of most other aerobes. Thus they can successfully compete in habitats where the O_2 supply is restricted. The presence of a sheath has ecological consequences for the organism. By attaching to solid surfaces, growth is favoured in slowly running waters of low nutrient content. The attachment occurs by so-called holdfasts, i.e. sticky substances that harden. *Sphaerotilus natans* attaches to submerged stones, plants and other solid materials. *Leptothrix ochracea* occurs in slowly running unpolluted waters with high iron content. Possibly, *Sphaerotilus* and *Leptothrix* are the same organism that occur as habitat-variants, *Leptothrix* growing in iron-containing waters.

Sheathed bacteria of the genera *Lieskeella*, *Phragmidiothrix*, *Crenothrix*, and *Clonothrix* have not yet been grown in pure culture, and their nutritional requirements are unknown.

The budding and/or appendaged bacteria

The budding and appendaged bacteria differ in their morphology from the typical shape of the common bacteria. These are unicellular microorganisms producing buds or appendages (prosthecae). The organisms are mainly chemoorganotrophs. Representatives are *Caulobacter*, *Asticcacaulis*, *Hyphomicrobium*, *Planctomyces*, *Gallionella*, and *Metallogenium*. Morphologically similar organisms occur in phototrophs (*Rhodomicrobium*, *Rhodopseudomonas*) and in chemoautotrophs (*Seliberia*). By direct electron microscopy of soil samples multiple-appendaged bacteria have been discovered that so far have not been cultured.

A rare prosthecate bacterium is *Stella*. The shape of this non-motile organism is a flat star with six triangular prosthecae (diameter 0.7–2.0 μm). It is mainly found in soil and aquatic habitats under low nutrient conditions.

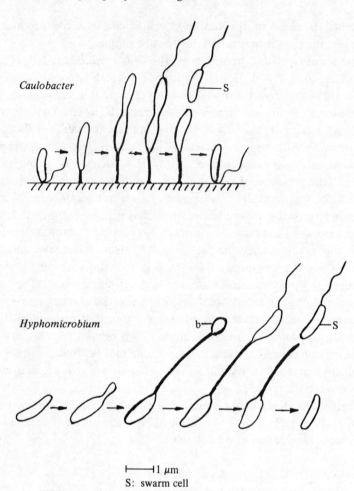

H——⊢1 μm
S: swarm cell
b: bud

Fig. 3.3 Development cycle of *Caulobacter* and *Hyphomicrobium*

Caulobacter and *Asticcacaulis* divide by asymmetric binary fission. These are obligate aerobic chemoorganotrophs. *Caulobacter* has a bimorphic life cycle (Fig. 3.3). A swarm cell produced by a sessile cell attaches to a surface due to an adhesive holdfast which is produced at the pole of the flagellum. *Caulobacter* and *Asticcacaulis* occur in fresh water with low concentration of organic nutrients. Although they seem to prefer habitats with low nutrient contents, they are also present in sewage and polluted streams. *Caulobacter* has been found in both terrestrial and marine habitats, while no marine isolates of *Asticcacaulis* have been reported.

The ecological advantage of the prosthecae, as in *Asticcacaulis*, may be enhanced by buoyancy. For obligate aerobic bacteria, the ability to resist sedimentation may be a survival advantage. In dilute surroundings, the large surface area of prosthecate bacteria may be another advantage. Thus, these bacteria can successfully compete in environments where the nutrients are scarce.

Prosthecobacter is an organism possessing one polar prostheca. It differs from *Caulobacter* with respect to the life cycle. The daughter cell of *Prosthecobacter* is not a motile swarmer but is already fully differentiated as the mother cell.

Hyphomicrobium, *Pedomicrobium*, and *Hyphomonas* are budding bacteria. The bud develops into a motile swarmer (Fig. 3.3). Many hypomicrobia have the ability to oxidize methanol under anaerobic conditions in the presence of nitrate. In such a specialized ecological niche *Hypomicrobium* can successfully compete with other organisms. In the presence of Fe^{2+} and Mn^{2+} *Hyphomicrobium* and *Pedomicrobium* become coated with a deposit of oxidized Fe or Mn salts. The nature of this process, which is not necessary for growth, is still unknown. The budding bacteria occur in soil, sea water, brackish water, fresh water and sewage. They are particularly present in habitats of low nutrient concentration (oligotrophic environment). Some strains attach to solid surfaces. Little is known on the distribution and ecology of *Hyphomonas*.

Thiodendron is a stalked sulphur bacterium. It belongs to a group of iron–sulphur bacteria discovered in 1961 and is related to *Hyphomicrobium*. The organism has been found in brackish and other interstitial waters with high salinity and high contents of H_2S. *Thiodendron latens* usually occurs as a bluish film on the surface of mud.

Another budding bacterium of aquatic habitats is *Pasteuria*. The organism has already been described by Metchnikoff in 1888 but was isolated not earlier than 1973 by Staley. The organism is commonly found attached to particulate material in aquatic habitats and occurs as an epiphyte of ensheathed cyanobacteria and diatoms.

Blastobacter is a Gram-negative aerobic chemoorganotrophic, mesophilic bacterium with rod-shaped cells and ovoid buds. Pure cultures have been isolated from forest ponds and lakes.

The *Blastocaulis–Planctomyces* group comprises budding and appendaged bacteria that have acellular (non-prosthecate) appendages. The group is a heterogeneous assemblage of aquatic bacteria. Some strains have been isolated in axenic culture. The majority of the strains behave as oligotrophs. The organisms have been isolated from aquatic habitats such as eutrophic fresh waters, oligotrophic fresh waters, and brackish and marine environments. Following algal blooms, these bacteria often reach significant cell densities. They are not rare in nature and are worldwide in distribution.

Planctomyces occurs in the plankton of aquatic habi'ats. The stalks of *Planctomyces* are commonly encrusted with iron c .ide. Pure culture studies have revealed that the organism is a typical prokaryote in structure. Besides the freshwater forms, brackish and marine types have been isolated.

Gallionella belongs to the so-called 'iron bacteria'. The organism possesses a stalk and has a sessile way of life. The stalk is not a part of the cell but is excreted from the cell surface. The twisted stalk contains iron hydroxide. *Gallionella* occurs in pure, iron-bearing waters that contain only traces of organic material. Therefore, they are mainly found in ferruginous mineral springs, water works, wells, and drainages. The organism may have practical significance by clogging drains, water pipes, and wells with deposits of iron oxide compounds. By mass development the organism may also participate in the sedimentary formation of iron ore.

Seliberia forms starlike aggregates (radial clusters) of rod-shaped cells. The rod-shaped daughter cells released from the aggregate are motile by a flagellum and attach to a substrate by means of a holdfast. The organism occurs in water with low organic concentrations. *Seliberia* is a strict oligotroph.

Nevskia is characterized by the formation of a laterally excreted slime stalk. The physiology of this bacterium is still unknown. It is aerobic, oligocarbophilic, chemoorganotrophic and widely distributed in shallow aquatic habitats. It is a typical neuston organism (i.e. the habitat is the surface film of a water body) and so far has not been isolated from soil.

Metallogenium is an aerobic, organotrophic, mycoplasma-like bacterium that oxidizes manganese. The organism is coccoid and does not possess a typical cell wall. In pure culture, it grows like mycoplasms. The oxidation of Mn has no significance as an energy source but has been thought to serve to detoxify the agent. *Metallogenium* is found in places of manganese redeposition, especially in oligotrophic lakes. Organisms similar to *Metallogenium* are *Caulococcus* and *Kusnezovia* which occur in mud. These are rare bacteria which have not yet been extensively studied. Because of the lack of axenic cultures, the understanding of the nature of these organisms is incomplete. Possibly, the latter genera are merely growth forms of *Metallogenium* in a special environment.

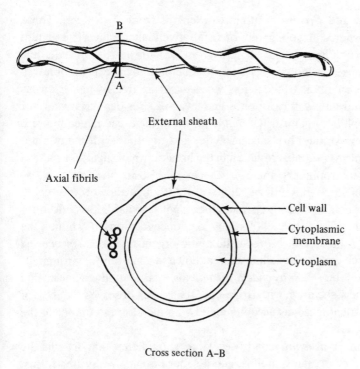

Cross section A–B

Fig. 3.4 Morphology of a spirochete cell (a schematic diagram)

The spirochetes

The spirochetes have a unique morphology (Fig. 3.4) and motility. The helical cells are rather slim with a diameter of 0.1–0.6 μm. The length of the cell may vary considerably and measure from 5–500 μm. The flexible, axial filament (fibrils) is responsible for locomotion. Motility is connected with contractions and relaxations of the axial filament. The filaments of the spirochetes are structurally and chemically similar to the flagella of bacteria. The leptospires exhibit high velocity in vicious media. Under such conditions motility of the flagellated bacteria usually is markedly reduced. In vicious environments, such as body fluids, the spirochetes may thus have a selective advantage over the motile bacteria that are flagellated. The spirochetes are primarily found in aquatic environments and in warm-blooded animals. There exist free-living forms and a variety of pathogens causing disease in men and animals. The classification is largely based on cell size and structure of the axial filament. The number of fibrils in *Cristispira* may exceed 100, in *Borrelia* up to 18, in *Treponema* and *Leptospira* 4, and in *Spirochaeta* 2. Members of the genera

Spirochaeta and *Cristispira* attain cell lengths from 30–500 μm. These large spirochetes are obligately or facultatively anaerobic. The genera *Treponema* and *Borrelia* have lengths from 3–18 μm and live in anaerobic environments. The leptospires are 5–10 μm long and have an aerobic way of life. The members of the genus *Spirochaeta* are free-living organisms living in mud and water of ponds and swamps. Besides the freshwater forms halophilic organisms (*S. halophila*) also have been encountered. All members studied are saccharolytic, and together with many other microorganisms probably function in the breakdown of sugars. In natural anaerobic environments, the *Spirochaeta* are also involved in cellulose degradation since they utilize cellobiose. Although they are not cellulolytic, they exhibit a strong chemotactic response towards low concentrations of cellobiose. Since cellobiose at low concentrations may inhibit the activity of some cellulases (of cellulolytic organisms), the *Spirochaeta* may enhance the rate of cellulose breakdown in anaerobic environments by using cellobiose. *Spirochaeta plicatilis* is a large mud organism that lives in close association with *Beggiatoa*. It has been observed that lysis of *Beggiatoa* trichomes was accompanied by an increase in number of the large spirochetes.

The genus *Cristispira* comprises large spirochetes that live in the digestive tract of many molluscs, both marine and freshwater forms. Their occurrence in molluscs is not associated with pathogenicity. The individual cells have diameters of between 0.4 and 10 μm and attain lengths of up to 150 μm. *Cristispira* has not yet been studied in axenic culture. This explains the lack of physiological, biochemical, and genetic data. The facultatively anaerobic *Cristispira* has an optimum temperature of 15 °C. The symbiotic relationship between *Cristispira* and *Mollusca* is commensal. The bacteria live in the crystalline style within the digestive tract. Within a population of molluscs, not all individuals harbour *Cristispira*. The factors that select for the bacterium in certain hosts are not clearly understood. In the crystalline styles, only *Cristispira* is usually encountered. Occasionally they are accompanied by small spirochetes and eubacteria.

The genera *Treponema, Borrelia,* and *Leptospira* comprise a number of important pathogens in humans and animals. The cells are small in diameter, usually less than 0.5μm and attain cell lengths of 6–7 μm. The helically coiled *Treponema* occur in the oral cavity, the intestinal tract, and the genitalia of man. Treponemes have also been isolated from a great number of animals including insects, termites, and shrimps. Many of the treponemes from the flora of man and other animals have not yet been studied intensively. There are three important diseases in man caused by *Treponema* species. *Treponema pallidum* is the causal agent of syphilis, *T. pertenue* causes yaws, and *T. carateum* is the agent of pinta disease. These pathogens have not yet been cultivated in vitro, but only in laboratory animals. The members of the genus *Borrelia* have diameters of 0.2–0.5 μm and attain cell lengths between 3 and 20 μm. The anaerobic, Gram-negative, spiral-shaped bacteria have a specific nutritional requirement of long-chain fatty acids. *Borrelia recurrentis* causes relapsing fever in man. The pathogens are transmitted by the human body louse *Pediculus humanus* or by ticks. The infected lice remain infectious for their life span. Rodents are the reservoir of this pathogen.

The leptospires have a 'spinning' flexuous motility. They are obligately aerobic and have relatively simple nutritional requirements. Free-living leptospires are found in soil and water, while parasitic or pathogenic forms occur in vertebrates. Although leptospirosis is a zoonosis that primarily infects wild and domestic mammals, humans may occasionally be infected and become incidental hosts. *Leptospira icterohaemorrhagiae* is the causal agent of Weil's disease, an infectious jaundice. The major reservoirs of leptospira are rodents.

Some helical and curved bacteria
Members of the genus *Spirillum, Aquaspirillum,* and *Oceanospirillum* are vibrioid or helical, Gram-negative, chemoorganotrophic, and have a rotating motility by polar flagella (bipolar tufts). The rapidly moving organisms have the appearance of a corkscrew. The organisms are respiratory. Some are capable of using nitrate as the terminal electron-acceptor producing nitrite, others also denitrify.

The former genus *Spirillum* has presently been divided into the three genera *Spirillum, Aquaspirillum,* and *Oceanospirillum* on the basis of molecular data, in particular on the basis of DNA base composition. The spirilla are widely distributed in nature but do not predominate in any habitat. *Azospirillum lipoferum* is found in the rhizosphere of many plants and capable of N_2-fixation. *Spirillum minus* is a parasite of rats that may be transmitted to humans causing the so-called rat-bite fever. *Aquaspirillum* occurs in fresh-water sources, ponds, lakes, sewage, and soil. Members of the genus *Oceanospirillum* have been isolated from sea water, in particular from the intertidal zones along the coast. They do not occur in the open sea.

Bacteria of the genus *Campylobacter* are Gram-negative, vibrio-shaped rods that are motile with a single polar flagellum. Some representatives are pathogens of men and animals. *Campylobacter fetus* is the cause of infectious abortion in cattle, sheep, goats, and swine. The non-pathogenic *C. sputorum* occurs in the oral cavity of man. From sheep faeces nonpathogenic *C. fecalis* has been isolated.

Bacteria of the genus *Bdellovibrio* have the unique property of being parasites of other bacteria. The organism is highly motile by an unusually thick polar flagellum of 28 nm in diameter. A wild type *Bdellovibrio* cell attaches to the cell surface of a susceptible bacterial host, penetrates through the cell wall into the periplasmic space and finally causes lysis of the infested individual. In the periplasmic location, the invading *Bdellovibrio* cell grows into a large helical structure that generates a number of progeny swarmers by multiple fission. After the digestion of the host cell, the swarmers are released and may initiate a new life cycle, provided suitable bacterial host cells are present. Vibrioid to rod-shaped *Bdellovibrio* cells have a relatively small size (0.25–0.40 μm wide; 1–2 μm long). The bdellovibrios are widespread in nature and have been isolated from a variety of habitats. They probably occur in any aerobic environment that supports growth of suitable host bacteria and have been isolated from soil and sewage, polluted waters, fresh waters, and also from marine environments. The numbers of bdellovibrios in their natural habitats are relatively low compared to other bacteria. Titres have been reported of up to 10^5 cells/g of soil, 10^5 cells/ml of sewage, and 10–100 cells/ml of polluted river water. The bdellovibrios exclusively attack and lyse Gram-negative bacteria. They are incapable of attacking Gram-positive bacteria, cyanobacteria or eukaryotic organisms. As recently shown by oligonucleotide cataloguing, the bdellovibrios are probably phylogenetically related to the sulphate-reducing bacteria and the myxobacteria. During periplasmic growth, the *Bdellovibrio* cell utilizes nucleoside monophosphates derived from the host cell for the synthesis of nucleic acids. The phosphate-ester bonds existing in the nucleic acids of the host are conserved by the parasite. Also fatty acids from the host cells are directly taken up and incorporated into the fatty acids of *Bdellovibrio*. Thus the energy expenditure of the parasite during periplasmic growth is reduced. Y_{ATP} values (g dry weight per mole ATP) for periplasmic growth are up to 26. The unusually high energy efficiency approaches the theoretical maximum value and indicates that *Bdellovibrio* needs only little energy during periplasmic growth.

Bacteria of the genus *Microcyclus* have a ring-like morphology, are nonmotile and Gram-negative. They are widely distributed in fresh water ponds and have occasionally been isolated from soil.

Pelosigma (formerly *Spiromonas*) are bacteria living in bundle-shaped aggregates. The individual cells have a length of up to 20 μm. Attempts to cultivate the organism in axenic culture have failed. They have been found in aerobic environments where low temperatures prevail.

Brachyarcus is a rod-shaped organism that has the appearance of a pretzel. The bacteria possess gas vesicles which enable them to float in water. As with *Pelosigma*, attempts to culture *Brachyarcus* have failed. *B. thiophilus* is an anaerobic, chemoorganotrophic bacterium.

The pseudomonads and related bacteria
The family of the Pseudomonadaceae comprises a large group of Gram-negative bacteria, strictly aerobic, catalase-positive, and oxidase-positive. There are no members capable of fixing atmospheric nitrogen. The genera combined in this group are: *Pseudomonas, Xanthomonas, Gluconobacter,* and *Zoogloea*.

The pseudomonads are unicellular rods motile by polar flagella. They are respiratory chemoorganotrophs. Some are capable of using nitrate or other nitrogenous oxides as terminal electron acceptors. Others are facultative chemoorganotrophs with the ability to oxidize H_2. The pseudomonads are important organisms in the microbiology of soils and waters, in human and veterinary medicine, in plant pathology, and in industrial microbiology. They possess an extreme metabolic versatility and are well known for their ability to metabolize a vast array of synthetic organics including pesticides. Pseudomonads are widespread in nature and are encountered in soils, fresh waters, marine environments, and many other habitats. Some are 'opportunistic pathogens', only a few are true pathogens. In the soil, the pseudomonads often are the dominant group. The same is true for marine habitats. Some species are adapted to low temperature growth and are involved in spoilage of meat, poultry, eggs, and seafood. The pseudomonads play an important role in the mineralization of organic matter and in nitrogen cycling.

Among the pseudomonads are two true pathogens for humans and animals: *P. mallei* and *P. pseudomallei*. *P. mallei* causes glanders (respiratory disease, ulcers) in horses, mules, donkeys; *P. pseudomallei* melioidosis (a granulomatous disease) in men and animals. *P. aeruginosa* is an opportunistic pathogen that often is encountered in patients with low resistance against infections. Disease develops when local or general defense mechanisms are impaired. In a susceptible host, *P. aeruginosa* may invade wounds, the urinary tract, the respiratory tract, or may cause endocarditis, meningitis, pneumonia, otitis, vaginitis, or conjunctivitis.

Apart from *P. aeruginosa*, a number of other *Pseudomonas* species have occasionally been isolated from clinical specimens, in particular from compromised human patients.

A variety of plant diseases is caused by pseudomonads. They cause either necrotic lesions and spots on fruit, stem, or leaves, or hyperplasias (galls, scabs), tissue maceration (soft rots), cankers, blights, and wilts (vascular disease). The *P. syringae* group is associated with foliar diseases. Soil-borne pathogens are *P. marginalis*, *P. gladioli*, *P. caryophylli*, and several others. *P. solanacearum* causes some of the most serious infections in plants.

Bacteria of the genus *Xanthomonas* have exclusively been isolated from diseased plants. Some xanthomonads, e.g. *X. citri*, or *X. malvacearum* have a high host specificity. The yellow-pigmented xanthomonads possess a unique xanthomonadin pigment which does not occur in any other bacterial taxa. These pigments are mixtures of unusual, brominated aryl-polyene esters. Compared to the plant pathogenic pseudomonads, the xanthomonads grow rather slowly.

Zoogloea is ubiquitous in organically enriched oxygenated waters. *Z. ramigera* forms typical aggregates, and the cells are surrounded by a gelatinous matrix. The extracellular matrix polymer is a polysaccharide, which enables the zoogloeal masses to adhere to solid objects suspended in lakes and ponds.

Gluconobacter and *Acetobacter* occur in sugary solutions and also in flowers, fruits, beehives, and palm wine. *Gluconobacter oxydans* oxidizes ethanol to acetic acid while *Acetobacter aceti* performs the complete oxidation of ethanol to CO_2 and H_2O. *Gluconobacter* has also been isolated from soil and shown to be capable of degrading 1,1-diphenylethylene.

Some dinitrogen-fixing bacteria
The capability of dinitrogen fixation is limited to prokaryotes. It is represented in organisms of a variety of unrelated groups. Nitrogen fixation is found in free-living organisms and in symbiotic associations. Since nitrogenase is a O_2-labile enzyme, aerobic N_2-fixation usually requires lower pO_2. In *Azotobacter*, the O_2 concentration is reduced by excessive respiration (and partial uncoupling of phosphorylation). In cyanobacteria, a low pO_2 is maintained in heterocysts that have thick cell walls preventing O_2 diffusion. Certain bacteria that are capable of nitrogen fixation can express this capacity only at reduced pO_2, e.g. *Corynebacterium autotrophicum*, *Methylosinus trichosporium*, *Azospirillum lipoferum*. In anaerobic free-living bacteria possessing nitrogenase,

the problem of protection against O_2 does not exist. There are a great many bacteria that fix N_2 under anaerobic conditions, e.g. *Klebsiella, Enterobacter*, phototrophs, and clostridia. In leguminous symbiotic N_2-fixation by rhizobia, leghaemoglobin functions to protect nitrogenase from O_2 inactivation. The intimate association of N_2-fixing cyanobacteria and fungi in lichens allows growth in N_2-deficient habitats.

The family of the Azotobacteraceae includes the genera *Azotobacter, Azomonas, Beijerinckia*, and *Derxia*. These are free living aerobic chemo-organotrophs that are capable of fixing N_2 in a N_2-free or N_2-poor environment, in the presence of organic carbon as the energy source. The cells of these N_2-fixers are Gram-negative, usually motile, and some form cysts. Growth factors are not needed for growth, but Mo is required for dinitrogen fixation because it is a component of nitrogenase. *Azotobacter* occurs in soil, waters, and particularly in the rhizosphere. *A. paspali* is associated with the root surface (rhizoplane) of the grass *Paspalum notatum*. It has been claimed that the associative growth in the rhizo-sphere is beneficial for the plant growth. In alkaline soils, *A. vinelandii* is the prevailing *Azotobacter* species. *Azomonas agilis* and *A. insignis* are obligately aquatic organisms (in freshwater habitats). *Beijerinckia* is widely distributed in acidic soils of the tropics. In Africa, *Beijerinckia* species are widely distributed. *Derxia gummosa* is a nitrogen-fixing organism that is highly sensitive to O_2. Although the ecological distribu-tion of *Azotobacter* appears to depend to some degree on the availability of soil moisture, it has been shown that the organism is also present in dry and arid soils.

The rhizobia have the capacity to nodulate legume host plants and to fix nitrogen in this symbiotic association. Legumes nodulated by *Rhizobium* are found from subarctic to temperate and tropical regions. The occur-rence of rhizobia in soil is influenced by pH, moisture, temperature, and the nutritional conditions. The *Rhizobium* strains differ with respect to their host specificity and efficiency.

Agrobacteria and rhizobia are taxonomically related. *Agrobacterium tumefaciens* lives in association with plant roots and causes gall formation. Pathogenicity of *A. tumefaciens* depends on the presence of a large extrachromosomal DNA element, the T_i-plasmid (T_i = *tumour induc-ing*). More than 600 species from about 300 plant genera are susceptible hosts of *Agrobacterium*.

Physiologically defined assemblages of bacteria
A variety of bacteria from different taxonomic groups are capable of oxidizing molecular H_2. These chemolithotrophs or chemolitho-

autotrophs are members of the genera *Pseudomonas, Alcaligenes, Spirillum,* or belong to the Gram-negative cocci, coryneforms, bacilli, mycobacteria, rhizobia and nocardiae. H_2, which is preferentially used by many bacteria as an electron donor, is mainly produced during anaerobic fermentation. Some H_2 reaches the aerobic zones in water bodies, soils, and mud. These locations, therefore, are the major habitats of the aerobic H_2-oxidizers. H_2 is also produced by N_2-fixing organisms due to the hydrogenase activity of nitrogenase. It has been shown that H_2 evolved from root nodules is not lost from the soil plant ecosystem but is metabolized by H_2-oxidizing soil bacteria.

The methylotrophic bacteria are an assemblage of organisms capable of metabolizing C_1-compounds. They primarily utilize methane and methanol, but also methylamine, dimethylether, formaldehyde, and other C_1-compounds. The organisms differ with respect to their metabolic specialization. The obligate methanotrophs depend on methane which in the first step is oxidized by a monooxygenase. The methanolotrophs are unable to oxidize methane but only use methanol or other C_1-compounds as carbon and energy source. Facultative methylotrophs, by definition, metabolize, in addition to C_1-compounds, a variety of other substrates. Physiologically, the methylotrophs comprise two groups. One uses the ribulose monophosphate-cycle of formaldehyde fixation (RuMP pathway), the other assimilates the C_1-compound via the serine pathway. Compared to methane, methanol is used by a greater number of bacteria and can also be oxidized by some yeasts. The occurrence in nature of methane oxidizing bacteria is related to the presence of methane producing bacteria. These organisms, therefore, occur in greatest numbers in, or on, the surface of sediments and above organic muds.

The carboxydobacteria have the unique capability of using CO as the sole source of carbon and energy. Several bacteria have been encountered that belong to this metabolic type, e.g. *Pseudomonas carboxydovorans, P. gazotropha,* and *Seliberia carboxydohydrogena.* The organisms are found in the upper mud layers of polluted waters.

Hydrocarbon-oxidizing bacteria are widely distributed in all natural habitats. In non-contaminated soils, about 1–10% of the bacteria have been found to be capable of growing on hydrocarbons as their sole source of carbon and energy. The origin of the hydrocarbons is related to the synthesis of plant and microbial biomass. In sediments significant quantities of aliphatic and aromatic hydrocarbons are present.

Denitrifying bacteria are ubiquitous in terrestrial and aquatic habitats. A great number of bacteria are capable of using nitrate as the terminal electron acceptor (instead of oxygen) in anaerobic environments. Among those bacteria that play a major role in denitrification are the pseudomonads, *Bacillus* and *Alcaligenes*. In heavily fertilized agricultural soils, denitrifying bacteria are abundant. The rhizosphere has been regarded as an area of intensive denitrification. Here, the organisms are supplied with organic materials excreted by the roots.

The dissimilatory sulphate-reducing bacteria comprise a physiological–ecological group capable of using sulphate as the terminal electron-acceptor and reducing sulphate to sulphide. The sulphate-respiration is performed by a restricted number of bacteria belonging to the genera *Desulfovibrio, Desulfomonas, Desulfotomaculum*, and some recently discovered new genera. H-donors are low molecular weight compounds that are produced during anaerobic degradation of organic materials such as acetate, propionate, butyrate, ethanol, lactate, higher fatty acids, and also hydrogen. With respect to the oxidation of the organic acids, two groups exist. Some execute only partial oxidation of the organic H-donor and produce acetate as the end product (*Desulfovibrio, Desulfotomaculum*). Others have the capability of oxidizing acetate and higher fatty acids (*Desulfotomaculum acetoxidans*, and members of the new genera *Desulfobacter, Desulfococcus, Desulfosarcina*, and *Desulfonema*). Certain sulphate-reducing bacteria such as *Desulfovibrio salexigens*, and *Desulfovibrio desulfuricans* var. *aestuarii* depend on NaCl. All sulphate-reducing bacteria are strict anaerobes. Bacteria with a capacity of dissimilatory sulphate reduction are encountered in anaerobic aquatic and terrestrial environments. Their occurrence is associated with the blackening of waters and sediments, and the smell of H_2S. It has been estimated that sulphate-reducing bacteria are accountable for the anaerobic oxidation of more than 50% of the organic matter in sediments. In marine and saline habitats, the formation of methane is insignificant because the sulphate-reducing bacteria are more competitive than the methanogens, and because the reduction of sulphate to H_2S is thermodynamically more favourable than the reduction of CO_2 to methane. Anaerobic CH_4 oxidation at the expense of SO_4^{2-} reduction is thermodynamically feasible, but has not been shown to exist. Anaerobic organisms capable of using CH_4 as the sole carbon source are unknown. The desulphurizers obviously belong to the oldest forms of bacterial life. Their activities have been traced back more than three billion years by sulphur isotope fractionation in minerals and rocks. Most sulphur deposits are of biogenic origin.

A bacterium capable of dissimilatory sulphur reduction is *Desul-*

furomonas acetoxidans. This organism lives in syntrophic association with phototrophic green bacteria. *Desulfuromonas* reduces elemental sulphur to H_2S at the expense of acetate which is oxidized to CO_2. The green bacteria, on the other hand, oxidize the produced H_2S and excrete elemental sulphur. Thus sulphur serves as the electron transfer catalyst for the growth of both organisms. By the capacity of growing with acetate and sulphur, the organism occupies a highly specialized ecological niche.

Obligately chemolithotrophic bacteria

Several groups of bacteria living in soil and water have the capability of oxidizing reduced inorganic substances, using the energy and the reducing power for biosynthesis of cellular materials and maintenance of metabolism. The reduced compounds used by such organisms are ammonium, nitrite, sulphide, thiosulphate, sulphite, iron(II)-ions, elemental sulphur, and hydrogen. The mechanisms of electron-transport and energy-conservation are essentially the same as in chemoorganotrophs.

Most of the chemolithotrophs use CO_2 as the sole carbon source and thus are chemolithoautotrophs. The assimilation of CO_2 occurs via the ribulosebisphosphate-cycle (Fig. 2.6). Besides the obligate chemolithotrophs, there also exist facultative chemolithotrophs which are able to grow at the expense of organic compounds, as do the heterotrophs. These organisms are characterized as mixotrophic, i.e. they obtain their energy, and/or carbon, from both inorganic and organic sources. A third category are the chemolithotrophic heterotrophs that use inorganic energy substrates to effect the assimilation of organic compounds. CO_2-assimilation is the major source of carbon in many chemolithotrophs but is not strictly coupled with chemolithotrophy. While the majority of the chemolithotrophs use O_2 as the terminal electron-acceptor, a few specialists are capable of coupling the oxidation of the reduced compound with the reduction of nitrate, nitrite, or N_2O. They effect 'anaerobic respiration'. The following chemolithotrophic oxidation reactions are known: $H_2 + O_2, H_2 + NO_3^-, H_2 + CO_2, NH_4^+ + O_2, NH_4^+ + NO_2^-, NO_2^- + O_2,$ $H_2S + O_2, S^0 + O_2, HS^- + O_2, S_2O_3^{2-} + O_2, S_2O_3^{2-} + NO_3^-, Fe^{2+} + O_2.$ Before the appearance of O_2 in the atmosphere, bacterial photosynthesis and fermentation processes using H_2 and H_2S as reductants must have been characteristic for this period. It has been assumed that during this time the earliest chemolithotrophs evolved, first the methanogens that oxidize H_2 and reduce CO_2, second the sulphate reducers that oxidize H_2 (or other reductants) and reduce SO_4^{2-}. The chemolithotrophs that depend on oxygen- or nitrate-respiration, therefore, must be viewed as relatively recent organisms that evolved after the appearance of molecular oxygen in the biosphere.

The main chemolithotrophs are the nitrifying bacteria and the thiobacilli. The nitrifying bacteria comprise two groups of Gram-negative chemolithotrophic bacteria that fix CO_2 via the Calvin cycle. They derive their energy and reducing power from oxidation of ammonia or nitrite. The organisms are obligate chemolithotrophs that use CO_2 as the major source of carbon. A particular strain of *Nitrobacter winogradskyi* can also grow chemoheterotrophically. The nitrifying bacteria grow relatively slowly and have generation times of between 8 and 24 hours. Optimal growth is observed at substrate concentrations of less than 20 mM, and at temperatures between 25 and 30 °C. Growth does not occur at pH values below 5.

The nitrifying bacteria are widely distributed in nature and are encountered in almost all aerobic environments. They exist in soils (except acid forest soils), compost piles, fresh waters, and marine habitats. In soil, the highest concentration is observed in the upper 10 cm, in rivers, nitrification occurs at the sediment–water interface. In marine environments, nitrification has been shown in the upper 200 m of the water column. The most studied species are *Nitrosomonas europaea* and *Nitrobacter winogradskyi*. In addition, a variety of species belonging to different genera (*Nitrosococcus, Nitrosospira, Nitrosolobus, Nitrospina, Nitrococcus*) have been described. The nitrifiers either oxidize ammonium or nitrite. Nitrite oxidizers depend on ammonium oxidizers in a sequential metabolic association.

The oxidation of reduced inorganic S-compounds for energy production is restricted to the genus *Thiobacillus*, Gram-negative polarly flagellated bacteria, the genus *Thiomicrospira*, bipolarly flagellated spirilla, and the genus *Sulfolobus*, thermophilic bacteria that belong to the archaebacteria. Most of the thiobacilli are obligate chemolithoautotrophs and depend on CO_2-fixation. Others are facultative autotrophs and are capable of growing with organic compounds as the energy and carbon source. Some of the thiobacilli can also couple the oxidation of S-compounds to the reduction of nitrate or nitrite (*T. denitrificans*). Certain strains of the thiobacilli (*T. ferrooxidans*) can use iron(II) ions or other metal ions as an energy source. The facultative chemolithotrophic thiobacilli have a versatile physiology and can grow autotrophically, mixotrophically or heterotrophically. A variety of *Thiobacillus* species has been described (*T. denitrificans, T. neapolitanus, T. novellus, T.*

thioparus, T. intermedius, T. thiooxidans, T. ferrooxidans, T. acidophilus). The thiobacilli are capable of a number of oxidation reactions. The product of oxidation of sulphide, elemental sulphur, and thiosulphate is sulphate. The various species differ considerably with respect to the pH required or tolerated. They cover the range from pH 1 to pH 11. Some strains tolerate temperatures up to 60 °C. The thiobacilli are encountered in H_2S-containing sediments from rivers, estuaries, acid sulphate soils, and mine drainage effluents. They are ubiquitous in soil, fresh waters, and marine environments. As aerobic sulphur oxidizers, the thiobacilli are often found in zones where sulphide and oxygen (or nitrate) coexist. The simultaneous presence of H_2S and O_2 is characteristic of border areas between aerobic and anaerobic layers in surface waters. In this ecological niche H_2S is unstable due to the presence of O_2, and several sulphur compounds are produced by spontaneous oxidation of H_2S depending on pH, temperature, and other factors. The generated products such as elemental sulphur, polysulphides, thiosulphates, and sulphite, are all potential substrates for the chemolithotrophic organisms. By transformation of sulphur in soil and sediments, the thiobacilli play an important role in element cycling. In addition, there are also heterotrophic bacteria involved in the oxidation of reduced inorganic sulphur compounds. In the presence of organic materials these heterotrophic S-oxidizers compete for the oxidizable sulphur compounds.

Sulfolobus acidocaldarius inhabits hot acid springs. This organism is typically acidophilic; because it lacks the rigid cell-wall structure (murein) it is a member of the archaebacteria. This acidophilic organism grows at pH values of 2–3.

In an environment characterized by the simultaneous presence of H_2S and O_2, there are – in addition to *Thiobacillus, Thiomicrospira*, and *Sulfolobus* – several morphologically conspicuous sulphur-oxidizing bacteria involved in the cycling of S-compounds. Organisms of this type have been described as *Achromatium, Macromonas, Thiobacterium*, and *Thiospira*. Besides the listed genera, also filamentous sulphur bacteria such as *Beggiatoa, Thiothrix*, and *Thioploca* are encountered in habitats where H_2S is produced. These organisms are absent in habitats devoid of H_2S. Since many of these bacteria have not yet been obtained in pure culture, our knowledge of the physiological and biochemical properties is limited.

Microorganisms involved in the transformation of sulphur compounds have played and are still playing an important role in the biogeochemical cycle of sulphur. It is generally agreed that the sulphur deposits mined today are of biogenic origin. They are the result of sulphate reduction followed by an oxidation, a process in which colourless sulphur bacteria are involved. In certain habitats – the so-called sulphureta – sulphur is accumulating by chemical and photosynthetic sulphide oxidation. Biological sulphide oxidation is also involved in the generation of acid soils.

Aerobic, Gram-negative bacteria of medical importance
Members of the genus *Brucella* are small aerobic, Gram-negative coccobacilli that are pathogenic for men and animals. Brucellosis is caused by *Brucella abortus* (cattle), *B. melitensis* (goats and sheep), and *B. suis* (pigs). The organism causes infectious abortion and sterility in domesticated livestock, and produces undulant fever in humans (Malta fever). Brucellosis is one of the most widely distributed zoonotic diseases. The facultative intracellular parasites are localized in the reproductive tract of the animals and occur in the reticuloendothelial tissue. The bacteria are transferred venereally, by ingestion through the skin or by inhalation. High incidence of abortion up to 50% is not uncommon. The marked specificity for the reproductive tract is related to the presence of erythritol in the fetal tissue which stimulates growth of the bacteria. The reservoirs of infection are cattle, swine, sheep, and goats; many other animals are affected. The pathogens survive under certain environmental conditions outside their hosts. Survival in urine (49 days), in potable water (72 days), and in dry organic matter (9 months) has been reported. There is no geographic limitation as to the distribution. The pathogens have the ability to convert to L-forms. This behaviour favours the persistence *in vivo* and contributes to the chronicity of the disease. The transmission from cow to man usually occurs by contaminated milk. The pathogens inhabit the mucous membranes of the gastrointestinal tract, and, after invading the lymphatics and the blood stream, they selectively multiply in the spleen, the liver, and the kidneys. The symptoms associated with the disease are primarily caused by an endotoxin.

Bordetella pertussis and *B. parapertussis* are pathogens that occur only in human beings. They inhabit the ciliated epithelium of the respiratory tract and cause 'pertussis', the whooping cough of children. The disease is highly communicable by droplets from coughing or sneezing. The organisms apparently require the ciliated epithelium for growth *in vivo*, and symptoms are caused by the liberation of a toxic substance. *Bordetella* is recoverable from nasal passages, trachea, bronchi, lungs, and secretions. *Bordetella bronchiseptica* causes a respiratory disease mainly in lower mammalian species and only occasionally affects man.

Francisella tularensis is the causal agent of tularaemia, a disease occurring among wild rodents, especially squirrels and rabbits. Tularaemia is an acute pulmonary disease with high mortality. Small wild animals are the principal reservoirs in nature, and the pathogen is transmitted by blood-sucking insects. It may be transmitted by the bite of a variety of ectoparasites (flies, ticks, mites), by contaminated water, or by inhalation of dusts bearing the pathogen. The principal reservoir of the disease is the cottontail rabbit. Therefore, the disease in man is known as 'rabbit fever'. *Francisella tularensis* var. *tularensis* is found only in North America. It was first isolated from a 'plague-like disease' of squirrels in California. The pathogen does not grow on ordinary media but requires special substrates meeting the particular sulphhydryl requirements of the organism.

Legionella pneumophila is the causal agent of the legionnaires' disease (legionellosis). It is a newly recognized bacterial infection of man affecting the respiratory system. The flagellated Gram-negative rods represent a group of bacteria that are genetically unrelated to many organisms examined (enterobacteria, *Pasteurella, Francisella, Vibrio, Flavobacterium, Bordetella, Rickettsia, Flexibacter*). The first isolation of the aetiological agent was in 1977. Since then the disease has been found in several countries, and the causal agent probably is distributed throughout the world. The organism has been isolated from water, mud, wet sand, from cooling towers, condensers of air-conditioning systems, and natural soft water ponds. Also a natural association between legionellae and blue-green algae has been described. Although legionnaires' disease has been studied intensively, there is relatively little known about the natural habitats of the legionellae, the host–parasite relationships, the pathogenesis, and the epidemiology of the disease.

Enterobacteriaceae and Vibrionaceae
The enterobacteria comprise a rather homogeneous group of rod-shaped, Gram-negative, oxidase-negative, and asporogenous bacteria. They have peritrichous flagellation or are non-motile. As facultative aerobic organisms they possess cytochromes and catalase, and are capable of generating energy both by respiration (aerobic) and by fermentation (anaerobic). During fermentation they produce gas and acid. Although of minor quantity, the enterobacteria produce formic acid as a characteristic end product during fermentation. There are two groups of enterobacteria with respect to the end products of fermentation, (a) bacteria performing mixed-acid fermentation and (b) bacteria performing

butylene glycol fermentation. The latter produce large amounts of 2,3-butylene-glycol. Bacteria representing the type of formic acid fermentation have the capacity to inhabit the intestinal tract (enteron), and, therefore, have been combined in the Enterobacteriaceae. *Escherichia coli* is the most studied microorganism. This bacterium has become a primary tool in bacterial genetics, molecular biology, and microbial metabolism. The rapid generation time under suitable conditions and the ability to grow on defined and simple media has contributed to the importance that *E. coli* has gained in scientific research.

Some enterobacteria are parasites of men and animals. Members of the genus *Salmonella* cause a variety of illnesses. Enteric pathogens are also the cause of food- and waterborne diarrhoeal diseases. Pathogenicity of the enterobacteria is associated with the production of enterotoxins. A high percentage of nosocomial infections is caused by enterobacteria such as *Escherichia coli, Klebsiella, Enterobacter, Citrobacter, Proteus,* and *Serratia marcescens.* The susceptibility to nosocomial infections is particularly high in compromised hosts. Taxonomically the enterobacteria comprise a variety of genera. The subgroups are differentiated mainly on the basis of lactose utilization, indole formation, methyl-red reaction, acetyl-methyl carbinol production, utilization of citrate, formation of H_2S, urease activity, gas production from glucose, motility, and pigmentation. The genera have considerable homogeneity. Nevertheless, there is extensive subdivision in several groups. The genus *Salmonella* comprises more than 1500 different serotypes. Apart from immunological reactions, bacteriophage typing is used for identification of individual strains in epidemiological work.

Escherichia coli is a normal inhabitant of the human intestine and is regarded an opportunistic pathogen. There is evidence that only special strains have a pathogenic capacity. It is generally agreed that *E. coli* is not indigenous in soil and water but can survive for some time outside the intestine. Finding the organism in water, therefore, is regarded as an indication of faecal contamination. With respect to abundance *E. coli* represents only 1% of the bacterial flora present in the colon. The majority of colon bacteria belong to the genera *Bacteroides* and *Bifidobacterium.* Coliform bacteria produce a highly toxic lipopolysaccharide that normally is detoxified and does not enter the blood stream. Special serotypes prevail in diarrhoeal diseases of men and animals. Resistance to antibiotics is often observed. In many cases resistance has been shown to be determined by plasmid-carried determinants.

The genus *Enterobacter* comprises three species, *E. aerogenes* found in the intestine, milk and dairy products, *E. cloacae* present in the faeces of men and animals but also found in soil, sewage, and water, and *E. agglomerans* associated with many plants and animals. Strains of *Enterobacter* are considered to be opportunistic pathogens. They are a serious cause of nosocomial infections. As in other enterobacteria, its identification is mainly based on biochemical tests.

Members of the genus *Hafnia* are isolated from animals, and sometimes also from soil, sewage, and water. *Hafnia alvei* is the causative agent of an intestinal disorder.

Members of the genus *Klebsiella* are non-motile enterobacteria. *Klebsiella pneumoniae* is the cause of a small percentage of acute pneumonia in man. The organism is regarded an opportunistic pathogen that may become the causal agent of many kinds of infections, particularly in compromised patients. They are mainly involved in urinary tract infections and in bacteremia. The same is true for *K. aerogenes* (formerly *Aerobacter aerogenes*). Strains of *Klebsiella* are known to fix N_2. The *nif* genes are located on the chromosome.

Members of the genus *Salmonella* cause diseases in men and animals. *Salmonella typhi* is the causal agent of typhoid fever. This serious disease was first observed in 1880 by Ebert. Four years later Gaffky isolated and cultivated this organism. The many serotypes of *Salmonella* are mainly characterized on the basis of the O (somatic) and the H (flagella) antigens. The Vi antigen is primarily associated with the salmonellae causing typhoid fever. The different serotypes correspond to defined chemotypes based on the chemical nature of the complex polysaccharides of the outer membrane. A special trait of the polysaccharides is the presence of unusual kinds of sugars belonging to the dideoxyhexoses. The pathogenicity of the salmonellae is related to the action of an endotoxin. *Salmonella* serotypes cause diverse clinical symptoms. There is a correlation between serotype and degree of pathogenicity. Some serotypes are highly pathogenic while others are not. In general, immunosuppressed patients are more susceptible. The potential danger for transmission of the disease are chronic carriers that are without any symptoms. Salmonellae are transmitted through human or animal excretions in water and soil. *Salmonella typhimurium* often is the cause of food poisoning. The intoxication is related to the production of lipopolysaccharides that affect the mucosa. The symptoms usually appear 12 hours after ingestion and last for two to five days. Identification of the salmonellae is based on a set of characteristic features and on serotyping. The most important representatives are *S. typhi, S. paratyphi, S. enteritidis,* and *S. typhimurium.*

Shigellosis is a dysentery of global distribution. The causal agent is *Shigella dysenteriae*. The organism causes acute inflammation with ulceration of the rectum and large intestine of humans. In contrast to a high infecting dose with food-poisoning salmonellae, the infecting dose of *Shigella* is extremely small (10 to 100 cells).

Bacteria of the genera *Proteus, Providencia* and *Morganella* are involved in serious infections but are not primary disease producing pathogens. *Proteus vulgaris* and *P. mirabilis* are ubiquitous in nature and participate in the decomposition of organic matter. They have been isolated from rivers, manure, faeces and from nosocomial infections, e.g. from septic lesions, the respiratory tract, and infantile enteritis. *Proteus* is often the cause of urinary tract infection. Strains of *Providencia* and *Morganella* likewise occur in nosocomial infections.

Citrobacter, which is capable of utilizing citrate as the sole source of carbon, occurs in soil and water, sewage, food, and many other habitats. The organism causes diarrhoea in humans, and has frequently been isolated from clinical specimens.

Members of the genus *Edwardsiella* cause opportunistic infections in humans, including bloody diarrhoea. They have also been found in urinary tract infections and in endocarditis. The organisms are identified on the basis of a set of biochemical test results and their pattern of antibiotic susceptibility.

Serratia marcescens is a red-pigmented enterobacterium frequently involved in nosocomial infections. This applies especially to non-pigmented strains of the organism which are a threat to surgical and intensive care units because of their marked resistance to antibiotic treatment. In hospitalized patients they cause serious problems in respiratory tract and surgical wound infections. The organism is widely distributed in soil and water, on plants, vegetables, insects, vertebrates, and men. Their identification is based on biochemistry, serotyping, phage typing, and bacteriocin typing.

Yersinia pseudotuberculosis causes a disease in rodents and fowl in which visceral miliary 'pseudotubercles' are apparent. *Yersinia enterocolitica* has been isolated from the stool of patients suffering from enterocolitis. There are many open questions in the epidemiology of yersiniosis. The organism seems to be involved in terminal ileitis, in acute enteritis, septicaemia, and arthritis. *Yersinia pestis* is a Gram-negative rod or coccobacillus and is the aetiological agent of plague. The natural reservoir of this pathogen is in rodents, mainly in rats. The bacteria are transmitted to humans by the bite of an infected flea. In the

Middle Ages the 'Black Death' was a threat to mankind. In the four-teenth century a quarter of the European population was extinguished by the plague. Although the disease has been virtually eradicated by appropriate sanitary conditions, cases of plague have been reported now and then.

The genus *Erwinia* comprises phytopathogens causing soft-rot (*E. carotovora*) and fire blight (*E. amylovora*). *Erwinia herbicola* is recognized by the yellow pigmentation. Non-pigmented strains of *Erwinia* have been isolated from clinical sources and are regarded as opportunistic pathogens.

The most important *Vibrio* species is *V. cholerae*, the causative agent of cholera. An enterotoxin is involved in the disease which is accompanied by diarrhoea causing dehydration and electrolyte imbalance. The pathogen is primarily transmitted by contaminated water and food.

Plesiomonas has been isolated from humans and animals suffering from intestinal disorders. The organism is also an inhabitant of fresh waters.

Aeromonas is primarily an inhabitant of fresh waters but has also been isolated from human patients and is regarded an opportunistic pathogen. *A. salmonicida* causes furunculosis and bacteraemia in fishes.

Photobacterium and *Beneckea* are marine enterobacteria. *B. parahaemolytica* is the causative agent of a gastroenteritis contracted from contaminated sea food. Some species of the genera *Photobacterium* and *Beneckea* have the property of emitting light. These luminous bacteria occur free in sea water, on the surfaces of marine animals, in the gut tracts of marine animals, or as symbionts in the light organs of marine fishes and other animals.

Facultatively anaerobic, Gram-negative, rod-shaped bacteria
Zymomonas mobilis (formerly *Pseudomonas lindneri*) is a polarly flagel-lated, large, Gram-negative rod that is microaerophilic and thus adapted to growth in liquid media. This bacterium ferments sugars quantitatively to ethanol and CO_2. With respect to the end product it resembles yeasts, such as *Saccharomyces cerevisiae*. However, yeasts ferment sugar by the Embden–Meyerhof–Parnas pathway (FBP) while *Zymomonas* ferments via the Entner–Doudoroff pathway (KDPG). The organism metabolizes only glucose, fructose, and sucrose but not other sugars, and is resistant to alcohol. The bacteria occur in fermented beverages, such as palm wine of the tropics, Mexican agave sap (pulque), and Brazilian sugar.

Chromobacterium violaceum is conspicuous for its production of a blue-violet pigment, violacein. The pigment, an indole derivative, has been suggested to serve as a protectant against visible and ultraviolet radiation. It also confers some resistance against predation by protozoa. A similar organism, *C. libidum*, is psychrophilic and present in cooler habitats. The chromobacteria are ubiquitous in nature and found in soil and waters from polar regions to the tropics. *Chromobacterium* has also been encountered as an opportunistic pathogen involved in septicemia. The organism can easily be enriched and isolated from polished or precooked rice grains placed on wet soil. After 5 days at 23–25 °C, bluish spots develop almost regularly on the grains.

Members of the genus *Flavobacterium* are yellow-pigmented, non-fermentative, Gram-negative bacteria. They have been isolated from soil, fresh water, marine water, ocean sediments, foods, and also from clinical specimens. The pathogenicity, however, is doubtful, and the taxonomy of this group is still uncertain.

Organisms of the genus *Haemophilus* are rod-shaped, Gram-negative, aerobic, facultative anaerobic, and fastidious. They have a growth requirement for haemin or related porphyrins and/or NAD. The haemin requirement only exists under aerobic conditions. Temperature for optimum growth is 35–37 °C. The haemophili are strict parasites. *H. influenzae* is an important pathogen in men and animals. It causes bacterial meningitis, chronic bronchitis, and occasionally pneumonia. In pandemics of influenza, a respiratory disease caused by an RNA virus, *H. influenzae* often has set up severe infections in persons compromised by the virus attack. In the 1918 flu pandemic, this pathogen played a prominent role as the fatal secondary invader. *H. aphrophilus* and *H. segnis* are preferentially found on the surfaces of teeth and are involved in dental plaque formation. The factors determining the ability to colonize specific surfaces are not yet known.

Bacteria of the genus *Pasteurella* are small, Gram-negative rods, non-motile, facultatively anaerobic, fermentative, catalase-positive, and oxidase-positive. According to present taxonomic views *Pasteurella pestis*, *P. pseudotuberculosis*, and *P. enterocolitica* are now regarded as *Yersinia*, and *P. tularensis* and *P. novocid* are now placed in the genus *Francisella*. In the genus *Pasteurella* remain the species *P. multocida* and *P. haemolytica*. *P. multocida* is the primary cause of fowl cholera. The organism also causes sporadic infections as a secondary invader. The pasteurellae are commensals on mucous membranes in many healthy animals. Dogs and cats are the usual source of human infection due to *P. multocida*.

Actinobacillus comprises short bacillary or coccobacillary forms that are pleomorphic. The organisms live as commensals in the alimentary, respiratory or genital tracts of animals (cattle, horses, swine), and occasionally occur as pathogens of animals, especially in domesticated stock.

Cardiobacterium hominis is an indigenous commensal of the human respiratory flora. The organism originally isolated from a case of bacterial endocarditis (hence the name!) is of low virulence and does not possess pathogenicity for any laboratory animal.

Streptobacillus moniliformis is the causal agent of rat-bite fever in humans, an acute illness with significant mortality. Rat and mouse are the chief reservoirs. The organism is fastidious and requires blood or serum supplementation.

Calymmatobacterium granulomatis is a Gram-negative, non-motile pathogen that causes granulomatous lesions in the inguinal region (donovanosis). It is pathogenic only for man and prevails in warm and humid climates.

Anaerobic, Gram-negative, rod-shaped bacteria
The strictly anaerobic, Gram-negative cocci comprise the genera *Bacteroides, Fusobacterium, Leptotricha, Butyrivibrio, Succinivibrio, Succinomonas, Lachnospira,* and *Selenomonas.* The non-pathogenic *Bacteroides* are widespread in the oral cavity and common inhabitants of the alimentary tract of warm-blooded animals (cecum, colon, rumen). Compared to *E. coli, Bacteroides* are much more numerous in the human faeces (ratio up to 1000 : 1). *Bacteroides* possesses cyt b and is capable of generating ATP by oxidative phosphorylation in addition to ATP production by substrate level phosphorylation. The organism ferments sugars and amino acids. *B. succinogenes* (in the rumen reticulum) also has cellulolytic capacity. Members of the genus *Bacteroides* cause disease in man, chiefly in compromised patients that have undergone surgery or have been treated with gamma-ray irradiation or immunosuppressants. They are involved in various diseases and have been reported to occur in almost all organs.

The members of the genus *Fusobacterium* are obligately anaerobic, nonsporeforming, motile or nonmotile, Gram-negative rods. They inhabit the mucous membranes of men and animals. All species are parasitic, and *F. nucleatum* and *F. necroforum* are most frequently isolated from human sources. The pathogenic fusobacteria are involved in inflammatory processes accompanied by necrosis and ulceration. They also have been isolated from abscesses in brain and liver.

The Gram-negative, anaerobic *Leptotricha buccalis* is a filamentous organism. It only exists in the oral cavity of man and has no specific pathogenicity. The highly saccharolytic organism is found in dental plaques and participates in the development of tooth decay. Growth in an anaerobic environment is promoted by the presence of 5–10% CO_2.

The *Butyrivibrio* are anaerobic, motile rods with tapered ends. They are common inhabitants of the rumen of all ruminants and have also been isolated from faecal materials of other animals and humans. Because of a wide biochemical diversity, these bacteria are regarded as the anaerobic equivalents of the pseudomonads that are known to exhibit extreme metabolic diversity. *Lachnospira, Succinivibrio,* and *Succinomonas* all live in the bovine rumen. *Lachnospira* is the main pectin fermenter of the rumen. *Succinivibrio* is specialized in fermentation of dextrins and starch whereas *Selenomonas* ferments soluble carbohydrates and starch. Many selenomonads also ferment lactate which is not readily fermented by other organisms of the rumen.

Gram-negative cocci and related bacteria
The Gram-negative cocci and coccobacilli contain both common soil and water bacteria and organisms pathogenic to man. There are two important pathogens in the genus *Neisseria, N. meningitidis* and *N. gonorrhoeae. N. meningitidis* is a common inhabitant of the human nasopharynx. Up to 7% of healthy individuals have been shown to carry the organism in inter-epidemic periods. Since the organism is part of the normal flora, a relatively high natural immunity to meningococcal disease in men is observed. The carriers have no recognizable symptoms. Under certain conditions, the organism enters the bloodstream and initiates a general infection of the body. In some cases, the central nervous system is affected leading to meningitis. The clinical symptoms are associated with the production of an endotoxin. *N. gonorrhoeae* is the causal agent of gonorrhoea. The organism inhabits the surfaces of the genital tissues. Both pathogens are extremely fastidious and also require an increased concentration of CO_2 (2–10%). The former '*Neisseria catarrhalis*' has been removed from the true *Neisseria* on the basis of molecular data. Its taxonomic position is now in the genus *Acinetobacter*. While the genera *Moraxella* and *Branhamella* mainly contain pathogens in humans and animals, members of *Acinetobacter* usually are found in soil, water, and sewage. Members of the genus *Acinetobacter* are oxidase-negative aerobes and penicillin-resistant. They are capable of degrading aromatic compounds, such as 1,1-diphenylethylene. Their versatility is comparable to that of the pseudomonads.

Lampropedia hyalina has a distinctive appearance. The cells are arranged in rectangular or square tablets or sheets of one cell thickness (monolayered). The relatively large cells are aerobic and do not grow under anaerobic conditions. This organism lives in highly eutrophic waters.

Gram-positive cocci

The Gram-positive cocci are an assemblage of bacteria that have been grouped together primarily because of common morphological characteristics. Bacteria of the genus *Micrococcus* (micrococci) are obligate aerobes which are indigenous to soil, water, mud, plants, meat, and dairy products. The dominating organism is *Micrococcus luteus*. The mammalian skin is a natural habitat of the micrococci. In a pertinent study on men, 96% carried cutaneous populations of micrococci. *M. varians* plays a role in meat processing.

The genus *Staphylococcus* is physiologically and genetically different from *Micrococcus*. It is a facultative anaerobe which contains teichoic acids as a cell wall component, and has a lower mole % of G+C (30–38) than *Micrococcus* (66–73). The staphylococci are non-motile bacteria which form irregular clumps because cell division is unorganized along an axis or plane. Staphylococci are consistently found on mammalian skin, and almost everybody is a carrier of staphylococci. Some species are pathogens which are involved in a variety of infections, such as furuncles, carbuncles, pneumonia, acute endocarditis, myocarditis, pericarditis, cystitis, bacteriemia, and others. Serious staphylococcal infections occur in patients having limited resistance. *S. epidermidis* (formerly *S. albus*) is a non-pigmented and non-pathogenic form inhabiting the skin and mucous membranes. Coagulase production generally is associated with pathogenicity, but coagulase-negative strains have also been shown to cause disease. *S. aureus* often is associated with food poisoning. The heat-stable enterotoxin produced by the organism causes a severe diarrhoea. The symptoms may appear within 30 minutes following ingestion of the interotoxin, but may take as long as 8 hours.

Members of the genus *Planococcus* are arranged in pairs or tetrads and are motile by 1–3 flagella. They are obligate aerobes and possess both catalase and cytochrome oxidase. A typical representative of this group is *P. citreus*, which is indigenous to marine environments.

The genus *Streptococcus* according to present taxonomy comprises 21 species. The Gram-positive cells are arranged in chains. They do neither possess respiratory cytochromes nor catalase but grow by homofermentative lactate fermentation (i.e. they produce only lactate). The non-pathogenic lactic streptococci play an important role in industrial fermentations. They are particularly important in the dairy industry. The lactic streptococci are usually associated with plant and dairy materials; the soil is not a natural habitat. Before the era of antibiotics, the infection by pathogenic streptococci often caused death in men. The main representative is *S. pyogenes*. Certain types of streptococci are part of the normal flora in the human oral cavity and the upper respiratory tract. They are frequently the cause of sore or 'strep' throats of susceptible individuals. Streptococci are also the causative agent of rheumatic fever. These bacteria also occur in considerable numbers in the oral cavity, and are involved in dental diseases. *S. mutans* is the most cariogenic organism (causing dental caries). It metabolizes sucrose and produces extracellular polysaccharides of a sticky nature that are insoluble in water. The produced acids act upon the dental enamel and dentin, which eventually causes caries.

Bacteria of the genus *Leuconostoc* are present in the fermentation of wine, sauerkraut, starter cultures for cheese, and other materials. *L. mesenteroides* is a heterofermentative lactic acid bacterium and is characterized by excessive slime production (dextran) on saccharose. The mass production of the organism in the tube system of sugar factories can cause technical problems.

Bacteria of the genus *Pediococcus* perform a homofermentative lactic acid fermentation. These microaerophilic organisms are involved in spoilage of beer.

The anaerobic cocci comprise a number of genera: *Peptococcus, Peptostreptococcus, Veillonella, Acidaminococcus, Megasphaera,* and *Ruminococcus*. These bacteria are common members of the normal endogenous flora of men and animals, and some are opportunistic pathogens. The organisms inhabit the skin, the upper respiratory, gastro-intestinal, and urogenital tracts, and are also found in soil, sediments, and mud. *Peptococcus* utilizes amino acids and peptones and produces fatty acids. *Peptostreptococcus* is strictly anaerobic and catalase-negative. Some members take part in the decomposition of cellulose in the rumen. Certain anaerobic cocci are involved in different types of infection and have been isolated from cases of chronic otitis media, sinusitis, and brain abscesses. *Veillonella* is an oxidase-negative, anaerobic coccus present in the oral cavity. The organism does not ferment carbohydrates, but instead metabolizes lactate and succinate. *Acidaminococcus* is specialized to the fermentation of peptones and amino acids and, as *Veillonella*, does not ferment carbohydrates. *Megasphaera* is a rumen organism. It is involved in the fermentation of carbohydrates and produces fatty acids, CO_2, and H_2. Several species of *Ruminococcus* have been isolated from the large intestine of man and the intestinal tract or rumen of animals. Contrary to *Megasphaera*, *Ruminococcus* does not produce volatile acids with more than three carbons.

Gram-positive, asporogenous, rod-shaped bacteria
The genus *Lactobacillus* contains Gram-positive nonsporulating and non-motile rods that are anaerobic or facultatively anaerobic and have complex nutritional requirements (carbohydrates, amino acids, peptides, fatty acids, nucleic acid derivatives, and vitamins). The lactobacilli ferment in the presence of ambient O_2 and produce lactic acid by homofermentative (only lactate) or heterofermentative (lactate and acetate or ethanol) metabolism. They occur in the intestinal tract, predominantly in the stomach and small intestine, but are a minority of the anaerobic flora. The lactobacilli are primarily associated with milk and dairy products such as cheese and fermented milk. *L. bulgaricus* is involved in the manufacture of yoghurt. Other species occur in silage, fermented vegetables and fermented beverages. The lactobacilli grow at pH values of as low as 5, and thus cause protection of the organic substrate from other bacteria and preservation of the fermented product. *L. acidophilus*, *L. lactis*, *L. casei*, and *L. plantarum* are homofermentative, while *L. fermentum* and *L. brevis* are heterofermentative. Presently 27 species are differentiated within the genus *Lactobacillus*.

Bacteria of the genus *Listeria* have been isolated from healthy humans and animals, in particular from faeces and tonsils. Besides the non-pathogenic forms there also exist pathogens. *L. monocytogenes* is associated with diseases and has various clinical manifestations. Listeriosis mainly occurs in sheep and birds and is occasionally found in other warm-blooded animals. Members of the genus are aerobic or microaerophilic and possess catalase.

A catalase-negative, aerobic, Gram-positive, rod-shaped bacterium is *Erysipelothrix*. This organism is common in swine erysipelas and is also associated in the infections of other animals and may cause acute septicaemia. The usual symptoms are reddish spots in the skin. *E. rhusiopathiae* is the etiological agent of erysipeloid, a skin infection of humans. It is transmitted from infected animals or animal products. Systemic dissemination in the body is known and may become the cause of arthritis or endocarditis.

An obligately aerobic, gram-positive, peritrichously flagellated organism is *Caryophanon latum*. This organism produces trichomes 10–20 μm in length; it has been isolated from ruminant manure and sewage.

Endospore-forming bacteria

Endospores that confer resistance to heat exist in the genera *Bacillus* and *Clostridium, Sporolactobacillus, Desulfotomaculum* and in *Sarcina ureae*. The bacilli comprise aerobic, facultatively anaerobic, and anaerobic organisms. The endospores are the most heat-resistant biological structures known. They even resist boiling for long periods of time. Heat resistance is related to the extremely low water contents of the spores (15%) and to their high contents of dipicolinic acid. In dry soil, endospores can survive for decades. When dormancy is broken the spores germinate and develop into heat-sensitive vegetative cells. Because of the tremendous stability of the bacterial endospores, sterilization procedures in microbiology are directed towards destruction of the heat-resistant spores in addition to the vegetative cells, which necessitates application of temperatures above 100°C (moist heat sterilization in an autoclave or dry heat sterilization in a hot-air oven).

Members of the genera *Bacillus* and *Clostridium* are usually motile by means of peritrichous flagella. Bacilli are catalase-positive, whereas clostridia are negative in catalase and do not possess cytochromes. Both genera are extremely heterogeneous which is mirrored by the broad scale of G + C mole % values ranging from 32–62 in *Bacillus* and from 22–36 in *Clostridium*. The considerable genetic heterogeneity has also been shown in studies on nucleic acid homologies.

The ubiquitous bacilli grow well in simple media containing sugars or organic acids as the sole carbon source, ammonium as the sole nitrogen source, and minerals. Many bacilli metabolize polysaccharides, nucleic acids, and lipids by means of extracellular hydrolytic enzymes. Some produce antibiotics (e.g. polymyxin, gramicidin). Well-studied representatives are *B. subtilis, B. cereus, B. polymyxa,* and *B. megaterium*. Most bacilli are mesophilic but there exist also thermophilic members that do not grow below 40°C (e.g. *B. stearothermophilus*), and psychrophilic members (e.g. *B. psychrophilus*). Some representatives are involved in food spoilage. *B. pasteurii* hydrolyses urea constitutively and is adapted to alkaline conditions. The only pathogenic species causing disease in humans is *B. anthracis*. The discovery and conclusive demonstration of the anthrax bacillus as a causative disease agent by Robert Koch was a

milestone in the development of microbiology. *Bacillus anthracis* is a
rather large bacterium, attaining lengths between 4 and 8 μm. The
virulent cells produce a unique polypeptide capsule that inhibits obsoniza-
tion and phagocytosis. The capsule production is an important factor for
the invasiveness. The toxin causes severe symptoms including acute
kidney failure. Without treatment anthrax is often fatal.

Several bacilli are known to be insect 'pathogens'. They have attracted
much interest in phytopathology because of their potential use in the
biological control of plant infesting insects. *B. thuringiensis* and *B.
popilliae* form a crystalline protein during sporulation (parasporal body)
that is located outside the spore. After ingestion of sporulated cells the
crystals become solubilized in the gut of the larvae. The crystal toxin
affects the gut epithelium which then favours the invasion of the
haemocoel by the germinated bacilli causing a lethal septicaemia. *B.
thuringiensis* is active against larvae of lepidoptera but does not affect
other insects. *B. popilliae* acts against the Japanese beetle (*Popillia
japonica*) and is the cause of the 'milky disease'.

The strictly anaerobic clostridia do not start growth when the redox
potential (E_0') of the environment is above +115 mV. Because of their
oxygen sensitivity, the organisms are restricted to anaerobic habitats. The
clostridia are separated into two large groups, the saccharolytic (e.g. *C.
butylicum, C. acetobutylicum*) and the proteolytic clostridia (*C. perfringens, C. botulinum*). Some clostridia are true pathogens associated
with various types of infection. *C. perfringens* is the cause of gas gangrene.
C. septicum is associated with infections of the central nervous system
(e.g. brain abscesses) and causes also endocarditis, septic arthritis, and
other diseases. *C. botulinum* is the causal agent of the most serious food
poisoning (botulism). This is not an infection *sensu stricto* but a severe
intoxication by a neurotoxin. Botulinus toxin is the most poisonous
substance known. The fatality rate in man is extremely high approaching
100%. 1 mg of the toxin is enough to kill a million guinea pigs. The toxin
blocks neural transmission and leads to death by paralysis of the respiratory system. *C. tetani* causes tetanus in various domestic animals and in
man. The clostridia associated with human diseases exist in many environments. They have been isolated from soil, water, vegetables, milk, meat,
faeces, canned food, and smoked fish. Soil appears to be the major
habitat. A variety of clostridia are capable of N_2-fixation.

Sporolactobacillus inulinus is an endospore-forming homofermentative lactic acid bacterium that has been isolated from chicken feed.

Sporosarcina urea is an obligately aerobic and motile bacterium widely distributed in soil. It can easily be enriched from soil in a medium containing 5% urea and 1% yeast extract. Compared to spores of *Bacillus*, heat resistance of the spores of *Sporosarcina* is less.

The coryneform bacteria

The coryneform bacteria have the following characteristics: aerobic or anaerobic, Gram-positive to Gram-variable rods, non-acid-fast, non-branching, rod-shaped, non-motile, pleomorphic. These organisms are widespread in nature. Some occur as saprophytes in soil, others are the causal agents of plant diseases or diseases in men and higher animals.

Bacteria of the genus *Arthrobacter* are the predominating organisms of the autochthonous soil microflora. They have an uncommon morphogenesis. Physiologically young cells are pleomorphic long rods that fragment into coccoid forms when growing old. Although they do not produce spores they are remarkably resistant to desiccation, and, therefore, can easily be isolated from dry soil. Arthrobacters have a considerable nutritional versatility and are capable of degrading pesticides, nicotine, and other aromatic compounds.

Cellulomonas is a Gram-variable soil bacterium that degrades cellulose. *Curtobacterium* and *Brevibacterium* are taxonomically less well-defined genera. *Brevibacterium linens* is associated with the ripening of cheese. *Curtobacterium* is a group of coryneforms that differ from *Cellulomonas* by containing ornithine in the cell wall peptidoglycan.

Saprophytic corynebacteria have been isolated from butter, cheese, marine fish, and also from sea water. The taxonomic position of the phytopathogenic coryneforms is still a matter of debate. Some favour retention of the genus *Corynebacterium*, others plead for rearrangement. Pathogens of economic importance are *C. sepedonicum*, the causal agent of potato ring rot, *C. insidiosum*, the causal agent of alfalfa wilt, and *C. fascians*, the causal agent of fasciation in a variety of plants.

Taxonomically, *Corynebacterium, Mycobacterium,* and *Nocardia* belong to the actinomycetes. All are Gram-positive, non-motile, aerobic, and catalase-positive. An organism that has been intensively studied is *C. diphtheriae*, the causal agent of diphtheria.

The genus *Kurthia* comprises Gram-positive, obligate aerobic bacteria that form long chains of coccoid cells. The organisms are regularly isolated from meat, meat products, and from animal faeces. Very little is known about this organism.

The bacteria of the genus *Propionibacterium* are Gram-positive, rod-shaped, non-sporing, non-motile, and anaerobic. Despite their anaerobic mode of life, most propionibacteria possess catalase. The propionic-acid producing bacteria occur in dairy products, particularly in cheese, and are also present in soil and silage. A common representative is *P. freuden-reichii*. Among the cutaneous propionibacteria is *P. acnes*, an occasional pathogen. The relationship of this organism to the disease known as 'acne vulgaris' is obscure.

Bacteria of the genus *Eubacterium* are anaerobic, non-spore-forming, Gram-positive rods. They occur in the oral cavity, the rumen, and in large numbers in stool. Some species are involved in human infections, but only a few have been shown to be truly pathogenic.

The actinomycetes
The actinomycetes comprise a large variety of bacteria. They are Gram-negative and generally non-motile. There exists a morphological continuum from coccoid to rod-shaped to filamentous and branched forms of fungal appearance. The organisms grow on ordinary laboratory media but usually slower than other bacteria. With respect to oxygen they are obligate aerobes, microaerophilic, facultative anaerobes, or strict anaerobes. Their natural habitat primarily is the soil. The main subgroups of the actinomycetes are the genera *Actinomyces, Bifidobacterium, Mycobacterium, Frankia, Nocardia,* and *Streptomyces*.

Members of the genus *Actinomyces* comprise common bacteria of the oral cavity, animal parasites, and soil inhabitants. *A. bovis*, the causal agent of lumpy jaw of cattle, is not transmitted to humans. The soil actinomycetes produce a typical earthy odour caused by the production of geosmin. A thermophilic representative of this group, *Thermoactinomyces vulgaris,* produces conidia that contain dipicolinic acid in quantities comparable to the endospores of the bacilli.

Bacteria of the genus *Bifidobacterium* are common in the alimentary tract of new-born infants. The pleomorphic rods are strict anaerobes or facultative aerobes. *B. bifidum* predominates in the intestine of breast-fed infants.

Members of the genus *Mycobacterium* differ from actinomycetes by the property of acid-fast staining. This character is related to the possession of long chain mycolic acids (C79–C85) in the cell wall. The mycobacteria are Gram-positive, non-motile, non-sporulating, aerobic rods that produce branched cells but do not form mycelia. They are common in soil as free-living saprophytes, and many are capable of utilizing molecular hydrogen and hydrocarbons. Most important pathogens are *M. tuberculosis*, the causal agent of tuberculosis, and *M. leprae*, the causal agent of leprosy. The latter organism cannot be cultured on artificial media but grows in armadillos. *M. bovis* causes tuberculosis in cattle but is also virulent in humans.

Bacteria of the genus *Frankia* are N_2-fixing root-nodule symbionts of non-leguminous plants, such as *Alnus, Casuarina equisetifolia*, and *Hippophaë*. Isolation and continuous cultivation of the *Alnus glutinosa* endophyte has been reported.

Nocardia (Proactinomycetes) is an aerobic and branching actinomycete that does not produce conidia. Many are capable of growing with H_2. Members of this group are important in the degradation of branched-chain hydrocarbons and saturated cyclic hydrocarbons.

The members of the genus *Streptomyces* are typical soil inhabitants. *S. scabies* is the causal agent of potato scab. The taxonomy of the streptomycetes is mainly based on morphology, arrangement of filaments, and the types of spore-bearing structures. These strict aerobic bacteria are nutritionally versatile; many utilize cellulose, chitin, and other polymers. A great number of streptomycetes produce antibiotics (e.g. streptomycin, chloramphenicol, tetracyclines). Thermophilic and marine forms are known.

Some obligately symbiotic bacteria
The main groups of obligately endosymbiotic bacteria are the rickettsiae and the chlamydia which live as parasites in men and animals.

The rickettsiae are obligate intracellular parasites that cannot be cultured in common bacteriological media. Cultivation is possible in animals (e.g. guinea pigs, mice), chicken embryos, and tissue cultures. Because of changes in the permeability of their membranes they are incapable of controlling the influx and efflux of the metabolites. *Rickettsia prowazekii* is the causal agent of epidemic typhoid fever. The natural reservoir is man, and the human body louse is the vector. Other rickettsiae are transmitted by fleas, ticks, or mites. Rickettsiae also occur as pathogens in invertebrates, and *Rickettsia*-like bacteria have recently been described as plant pathogens.

The *Chlamydia* are intracellular parasites in humans. They only grow in living cells or in tissue culture. Because of the lack of an independent energy metabolism they depend on ATP supply from the host, and are regarded as 'energy parasites'. Their cell membranes are highly permeable to ATP. The intracellular parasites are thought to be the result of a regressive development. They have lost synthetic capacities and largely depend on the metabolism of the host. *C. trachomatis* is the agent of trachoma, the Egyptian eye disease. *C. psittaci* causes psittacosis which is transmitted by avian carriers.

Cell wall-deficient bacteria

Members of the *Mycoplasma* group are the smallest prokaryotes known (0.2–0.3 μm in diameter). They are devoid of a cell wall and, therefore, are osmotically labile and only grow in an isotonic environment. Most mycoplasmas require highly complex growth media supplemented with fresh serum or ascitic fluid containing unsaturated fatty acids and sterols. Members of *Mycoplasma* require sterols while members of *Acheloplasma* and *Thermoplasma* (thermophilic) do not. Mycoplasmas are widespread in nature and occur in warm-blooded animals, insects, plants, soil, sewage and other natural habitats. Because of their frequent occurrence in animals, they often contaminate tissue cultures. While most mycoplasmas are harmless saprophytes, some are pathogens. *M. mycoides* causes a contagious bovine pleuropneumonia. Members of the genus *Spiroplasma* cause disease in plants.

The archaebacteria

The archaebacteria comprise a group of prokaryotic organisms that differ fundamentally from the classic eubacteria and eukaryotes. The establishment of the kingdom of archaebacteria is based on a variety of common properties such as nucleotide sequences of the rRNAs and tRNAs, cell wall composition, nature of membrane lipids, and antibiotic sensitivity. Although known for some time, these bacteria have only recently been recognized as members of the 'Ur-kingdom' Archaebacteria, comprising the methanogenic bacteria, the halobacteria, *Sulfolobus*, *Thermoplasma*, and *Desulfurococcus*.

The methanogens are Gram-variable, strict anaerobic bacteria that produce CH_4 as the major product. Morphologically they comprise diverse groups of bacteria, long or short rods, cocci, spirilla, and aggregates. The genera of the presently known methanogens are *Methanobacterium*, *Methanococcus*, *Methanosarcina*, *Methanobrevibacter*, *Methanomicrobium*, *Methanogenium*, and *Methanospirillum*. Most methanogens are chemolithotrophs capable of using H_2 as an energy source and CO_2 as the terminal e-acceptor. They produce CH_4 according to $4 H_2 + CO_2 \rightarrow CH_4 + 2 H_2O$. Many are capable of forming CH_4 from formate, methanol, methylamine, or acetate. Most methanogens grow at pH 6.5 to 7.5, but not below 6.0 or above 8.0. Because of their strictly anaerobic life, the methanogens are found in habitats where E_0' values are -200 mV or less. The methanogens are metabolically associated with certain non-methanogens via interspecies hydrogen transfer. This inter-relationship was first detected in a culture of *Methanobacterium omelianskii* which for years was thought to be a pure culture. In fact, this culture was a mixture of two organisms. It consisted of a non-methanogen oxidizing ethanol to acetate and H_2, and a H_2-oxidizing methanogen not using ethanol (*Methanobacterium bryantii*). The physiological interaction with respect to H_2-transfer reactions has an important ecological function for the methanogenic bacteria. They execute the terminal steps in the anaerobic cycling of organic matter resulting in the production of the C_1-compounds CH_4 and CO_2. The methanogens thus use the hydrogen generated by other bacteria during anaerobic decomposition of organic materials.

The methanogens occur in freshwater and marine sediments. At high concentrations of sulphate, dissimilatory sulphate reduction predominates. Sulphate reducers and CH_4 producers appear to be mutually excluded in marine environments. Apart from anoxic environments where the organic matter undergoes decomposition under anaerobic conditions, e.g. sediments of ponds, marshes, lakes, and oceans, methanogens occur in the rumen of cattle and other herbivores, and even in the heart wood of living trees.

The halobacteria are adapted to life in concentrated or saturated salt solutions. The extreme halophiles grow best at salt concentrations between 20% (wt/vol) and saturation (*c*. 30%). The halobacteria *Halococcus* and *Halobacterium* are obligate aerobic chemoorganotrophs that utilize proteins and amino acids rather than carbohydrates. Some are capable of nitrate respiration. The organic matter decomposed by halobacteria is primarily supplied by algae, such as the 'brine algae' *Dunaliella salina* and *D. viridis*. Since these algae do not grow above 12% salt concentration the halobacteria and algae do not grow in close proximity but at different salt gradients. The bacteria feed on the products of excretion and use the autolysates of the algae. In addition to their chemoorganotrophic mode of life, the halobacteria have the unique property of generating energy by a pigment (bacteriorhodopsin) located in the cell membrane. The so-called 'purple membrane' allows photo-phosphorylation. Contrary to the true anoxic phototrophic bacteria, the halobacteria depend on aerobic conditions. Their phototrophic energy production is only an additional energy source. The halobacteria are found in hypersaline ecosystems such as the Great Salt Lake or the Dead Sea and are also present in the alkaline and extremely saline lakes of the Wadi Natrun in Egypt.

Sulfolobus acidocaldarius is a sulphur-oxidizing bacterium that grows at low pH and high temperature (pH 2.0; up to 85 °C). The facultative autotroph also oxidizes a variety of organic compounds such as glutamate or peptone. The organism attaches to sulphur crystals, and pili are suspected to be involved in the attachment to the sulphur particles.

Thermoplasma acidophilum is a free-living thermophilic and acidophilic bacterium that grows at pH values of 1 to 2, and at temperatures around 60 °C.

The genus *Desulfurococcus* comprises thermophilic archaebacteria isolated from acidic hot springs in Iceland. These bacteria have a temperature optimum of more than 80 °C. They oxidize various carbon sources via sulphur respiration producing H_2S and CO_2, or derive their energy from fermentation.

Eukaryotic microorganisms
Fungi

The fungi are chemoorganotrophic eukaryotes. They have an aerobic metabolism and generate energy from oxidation of organic compounds. Compared to the eukaryotic plants, the morphological differentiation of the fungi is rather limited. Some fungi form hyphae, some form yeast cells, and others develop both cell types depending on the growth conditions. The diameter of the hyphae is usually around 5 μm. The hyphae are either without septae or have a cellular morphology by septate hyphae. The mass of hyphae represents the mycelium. The fungi possess rigid cell walls (usually chitin). They have a chemoorganotrophic metabolism and live as saprophytes on dead organic matter or as parasites on animals, plants (including microscopic algae), protozoa, or even other fungi. The classification is largely based on the pattern of spore formation and the type of sexual reproduction. There are three main groups of fungi, (1) Phycomycetes, (2) Ascomycetes, and (3) Basidiomycetes. Because of the production of macroscopic mycelial structures (e.g. fruiting bodies) many ascomycetes and basidiomycetes are not microorganisms *sensu stricto*. Those fungi that do not exhibit sexual reproduction have beeen combined in the Fungi imperfecti.

The Phycomycetes (lower fungi) have branched hyphae without septa and are multinuclear. Spores are usually produced within sporangiae. Certain types adapted to life in water produce motile spores and gametes. In terrestrial phycomycetes motile stages are rare. Many of them contain cellulose, rather than chitin, as the primary cell wall constituent.

Chytridiomycetes are aquatic fungi living on detritus; the zoospores have one flagellum. Some species are parasitic, e.g. *Rhizophydium planktonicum*, causing collapse of blooms of the freshwater diatom *Asterionella*. Economically important is *Synchytrium endobioticum*, the causal agent of wart disease of potato.

Oomycetes are aquatic and terrestrial forms. Their zoospores have two flagella. Some important examples are *Saprolegnia* spp., *Phytophthora infestans* (causing late blight of potato), and *Plasmopara viticola* (causing downy mildew of vine).

Zygomycetes have a coenocytic mycelium, i.e. a mycelium without regular crosswalls. Sexual reproduction occurs by gametangial fusion and production of a zygospore which is a thick-walled resting structure. Representatives are *Mucor mucedo* (saprophyte on soil and dung), and *Rhizopus nigricans* (common on moulding bread).

The Ascomycetes have septate hyphae and produce asci containing ascospores. The production of ascospores is the result of sexual reproduction. Asexual reproduction is connected with the production of conidia.

A number of technologically important microorganisms, such as *Saccharomyces cerevisiae*, *Aspergillus niger*, and *Penicillium notatum* belong to the Ascomycetes.

The Basidiomycetes (mushrooms and toadstools) are the most-developed fungi. They produce basidia containing four basidiospores. The mycelium consists of septate hyphae. Members of the basidiomycetes are the phytopathologically important uredinales or rusts, and ustilaginales or smuts.

The slime moulds (myxomycota) represent a heterogeneous group of eukaryotic microorganisms, some of which have been classified both in mycological and in protozoological taxonomic systems. This group includes the cellular slime moulds (Acrasiomycetes), the acellular slime moulds (Myxomycetes), the net slime moulds (Labyrinthulales), and the endoparasitic slime moulds (Plasmodiophorales). The latter are obligate intracellular parasites in a variety of higher plants. For example, *Plasmodiophora brassicae* is the causal agent of clubroot of cabbage.

The microalgae

The algae are eukaryotic organisms capable of oxic photosynthesis. They are mainly aquatic living in habitats exposed to daylight. Some algae can live heterotrophically (chemoorganotrophically), e.g. diatoms in the darkness of the deep seas. Others occur as phototrophic symbionts in invertebrates (e.g. dinoflagellates as intracellular symbionts of corals). Many algae have close phylogenetic relationship to organisms classified as flagellated protozoa. By treatment with streptomycin,

Euglena gracilis loses its chloroplasts and is thus changed into a 'protozoan' resembling *Astasia longa*. In some groups of algae, both multicellular macroorganisms and unicellular microorganisms occur during their development cycle.

The classification of algae is traditionally based on pigmentation, life cycle, type of flagellation, and cell-wall composition. Algae resemble higher plants with respect to the presence of chlorophyll a in the algal photosynthetic pigments. During photosynthesis, O_2 is evolved. The aquatic algae occur in fresh, brackish, and marine waters. As primary producers they are of major ecological importance. The terrestrial algae are found on damp soils, on rocks, tree-trunks, on ice and snow, and as symbionts of lichens. In microbial ecology, planktonic and single-celled algae are of particular interest. The main algal groups can be characterized as follows:

Rhodophyceae (red algae) are predominantly marine and mostly multicellular forms. Unicellular red algae occur in sand or encrusting rock pools. The life cycles are often complex. Certain red algae are used as sources of agar and carrageenan.

Chlorophyceae (green algae) occur in fresh water as well as marine and terrestrial environments. Among the terrestrial species some are the symbionts (phycobionts) of lichens; others occur as endosymbionts (zoochlorellae) in protozoans. Sexual processes occur in most species, some exhibiting an alternation of generations.

Euglenophyceae are freshwater, brackish and marine algae, some also found in soil. All species are unicellular and motile by biflagellation.

Bacillariophyceae (diatoms) are freshwater, marine and terrestrial forms. They are typically unicellular and exhibit gliding motility. The cell wall is a silicaceous structure which consists of two parts that fit together like a box and the overlapping lid.

Dinophyceae (dinoflagellates) are typically found as microplankton in seas and lakes. Most are free-living, some occur as endosymbionts in radiolarians and corals. 'Red tides' caused by *Gonyaulax tamarensis* result in fish mortality due to the production of a toxin. *Gonyaulax polyedra* is a luminescent dinoflagellate causing the nocturnal phosphorescence of warm seas.

Chrysophyceae (golden algae) are predominantly freshwater algae. Most are unicellular and motile by one or two apical flagella. Non-flagellated, amoeboid species occur. Some marine species possess silicaceous scales.

Haptophyceae are predominantly marine algae. They are typically biflagellate planktonic algae, and many of them are found in the nano-plankton. Haptophyceae blooms give the sea a milky appearance.

Xanthophyceae (yellow-green algae) are predominantly freshwater organisms. Some are marine, others terrestrial. They are chiefly multi-cellular; unicellular forms occur in plankton or soil.

The protozoa

The protozoa are eukaryotic, typically unicellular micro-organisms. They are usually classified within the animal kingdom although certain forms (e.g. the slime moulds) have been included in botanical classificatory schemes.

Many protozoa are predators on bacteria, fungi, algae, and other protozoa, and some are parasitic in animals. Because of the phylogenetic affinities with certain unicellular algal forms, there is no universally accepted classification. For ecological considerations, it is appropriate to separate the photosynthetic organisms as algae and their colourless counterparts as protozoa. The evolutionary relationships between proto-zoans and the multicellular animals (metazoa) are not yet fully elucidated.

The free-living protozoa typically inhabit aquatic environments (fresh-water ponds, rivers and lakes, estuaries, seas and oceans). In fresh water, ciliates and flagellates predominate while in marine habitats, foraminife-rans and radiolarians are common. In addition, many species are found in muds and moist soils. When available water is minimal, some protozoa can survive in encysted form. Parasitic and pathogenic species generally occur in the blood or alimentary or reproductive tracts of their hosts. Some protozoa are also involved in symbiotic relationships with bacteria, insects, or other organisms. Fossil protozoans have been found at the bottom of seas and oceans, and in sedimentary rocks.

Apart from the phytoflagellates, which are typically photolithotrophic, the protozoans are chemoorganotrophs. Feeding is saprozoically, by pinocytosis (e.g. in *Trypanosoma*), or holozoically (e.g. in amoebae and ciliates). The protozoa comprise 'herbivorous', 'carnivorous', and 'omni-vorous' species. Some protozoa exhibit growth requirements including amino acids and/or vitamins.

Most protozoans are aerobic. Some free-living and parasitic species can grow microaerophilically or anaerobically (e.g. the rumen ciliates).

The Sarcomastigophora are flagellated and amoeboid protozoa; free-living forms are common as predators in soil. The foraminiferans and radiolarians have internal or external skeletal structures. Some are pathogens (e.g. *Entamoeba histolytica*) in the mammalian gut; others are symbionts in the termite gut.

The Ciliphora (ciliates) comprise more than 6000 species of freshwater or marine forms. They cover a wide morphological array, with cell sizes ranging from *c*. 10 μm to several mm. They are ciliated during at least some stages of their life cycle. Freshwater types (e.g. *Vorticella*) are important in sewage treatment where they feed on bacteria and on detritus. Pathogenic species include *Balantidium coli*, the causal agent of an enteric disease in man, and *Ichthyophthirius multiphiliis*, an ectoparasite of freshwater fish. Other well-known representatives are *Paramecium* and *Stentor*.

The Sporozoa and Cnidospora are parasitic in animals and men. *Plasmodium* spp. cause malaria, and *Babesia* spp. a tick-borne disease of cattle, the so-called red-water fever.

Further reading

Books
General characterization of microorganisms
Doetsch, R. N. & Cook, T. M. (1973). *Introduction to Bacteria and Their Ecobiology*. Baltimore: University Park Press.
Esser, K. (1976). *Kryptogamen, Praktikum und Lehrbuch*. Berlin: Springer–Verlag.
Esser, K. (1982). *Cryptograms. Cyanobacteria, Algae, Fungi, Lichens*. London: Cambridge University Press.
Leadbetter, E. R. & Poindexter, J. S. (eds) (1985). *Bacteria in Nature*. Vol. I. Bacterial activities in perspective. New York: Plenum Press.
Starr, M. P., Stolp, H., Trüper, H. G., Balows, A. & Schlegel, H. G. (eds) (1981). *The Prokaryotes – A Handbook on Habitats, Isolation, and Identification of Bacteria*, published in two volumes, 2284 pages, 169 chapters. New York: Springer–Verlag.

Cyanobacteria
Carr, N. G. & Whitton, B. A. (eds) (1973). *The Biology of Blue-Green Algae*. Oxford: Blackwell Scientific Publications.

Phototrophic bacteria
Clayton, R. K. & Sistrom, W. R. (eds) (1978). *The Photosynthetic Bacteria*. New York: Plenum Press.

Chemolithotrophic and chemoorganotrophic bacteria
Postgate, J. R. (1979). *The Sulphate-Reducing Bacteria*. New York: Cambridge University Press.

Archaebacteria

Gunsalus, I. C., Sokatch, J. R. & Ornston, L. N. (eds) (1985). *The Bacteria. A Treatise on Structure and Function*. Vol. VIII, *Archaebacteria* (Woese, C. R. & Wolfe, R. S. eds.). New York: Academic Press.

Fungi

Alexopoulos, C. J. & Mims, C. W. (1979). *Introductory Mycology*, 3rd ed. New York: John Wiley.
Burnett, J. H. (1976). *Fundamentals of Mycology*, 2nd ed. London: Edward Arnold.
Deacon, J. W. (1980). *Introduction to Modern Mycology*. New York: John Wiley & Sons, Inc.
Domsch, K. H. & Gams, W. (eds) (1972). *Fungi in Agricultural Soils*. London: Longman.
Griffin, D. M. (1972). *Ecology of Soil Fungi*. London: Chapman and Hall.
Hudson, H. J. (1986). *Fungal Biology*. London: Edward Arnold.
Loomis, W. F. (ed.) (1982). *The Development of Dictyostelium discoideum*. New York: Academic Press.
Ross, I. K. (1979). *Biology of the Fungi*. New York: McGraw–Hill Book Co.
Webster, J. (1980). *Introduction to Fungi*. London: Cambridge University Press.

Algae

Bold, H. C. & Wynne, M. J. (1978). *Introduction to the Algae: Structure and Reproduction*. Englewood Cliffs, N.J.: Prentice–Hall.
Round, F. E. (1976). *The Biology of the Algae*. London: Edward Arnold.
Round, F. E. (1981). *The Ecology of the Algae*. Cambridge: Cambridge University Press.
Trainor, F. R. (1978). *Introductory Phycology*. New York: John Wiley and Sons.
Van den Hoek, Ch. (1978). *Algen*. Stuttgart: Thieme.

Protozoa

Corliss, J. O. (1979). *The Ciliated Protozoa*. New York: Pergamon Press.
Farmer, J. N. (1980). *The Protozoa*. St. Louis: The C.V. Mosby Co.
Levandowsky, M. & Hutner, S. H. (eds) (1980). *Biochemistry and Physiology of Protozoa*. New York: Academic Press.
Sleigh, M. (1973). *The Biology of Protozoa*. London: Edward Arnold.

Articles

General characterization of microorganisms

Burchard, R. P. (1981). Gliding motility of prokaryotes: ultrastructure, physiology, and genetics. *Annual Review of Microbiology*, **35**, 497–529.
Fox, G. E., Stackebrand, E., Hespell, R. B., Gibson, J., Maniloff, J., Dyer, T. A., Wolfe, R. S., Balch, W. E., Tanner, R. S., Magium, L. H., Zablen, L. B., Blakemore, R., Gupta, R., Bonen, L., Lewis, B. J., Stahl, D. A., Luehrsen, K. R., Chen, K. N. & Woese, C. R. (1980). The phylogeny of prokaryotes. *Science*, **209**, 457–63.
Woese, C. R. & Fox, G. E. (1977). Phylogenetic structure of the prokaryotic domain: the primary kingdoms. *Proceedings of the National Academy of Science U.S.A.*, **74**, 5088–90.

Cyanobacteria

Stanier, R. Y. & Cohen-Bazire, G. (1977). Phototrophic prokaryotes: the cyanobacteria. *Annual Review of Microbiology*, **31**, 225–74.

Phototrophic bacteria

Pfennig, N. (1978). General physiology and ecology of photosynthetic bacteria. In *The Photosynthetic Bacteria*, eds. R. C. Clayton & W. R. Sistrom, pp. 3–18. New York & London: Plenum Publishing.

Chemolithotrophic and chemoorganotrophic bacteria

Balch, E., Fox, G. E., Magrum, L., Woese, C. R. & Wolfe, R. S. (1979). Methanogens. Re-evaluation of a unique biological group. *Microbiological Reviews*, **43**, 260–96.

Ferguson, T. J. & Mah, R. A. (1983). Isolation and characterization of an H_2-oxidizing thermophilic methanogen. *Applied and Environmental Microbiology*, **45**, 265–74.

Hanson, R. S. (1980). Ecology and diversity of methylotrophic organisms. *Advances in Applied Microbiology*, **26**, 3–39.

Harrison, A. P. jr. (1984). The acidophilic thiobacilli and other acidophilic bacteria that share their habitat. *Annual Review of Microbiology*, **38**, 265–92.

Harwood, C. S. & Canale-Parola, E. (1984). Ecology of spirochetes. *Annual Review of Microbiology*, **38**, 161–92.

Hespell, R. B., Paster, B. J., Macke, T. J. & Woese, C. R. (1984). The origin and phylogeny of the bdellovibrios. *Systematic and Applied Microbiology*, **5**, 196–203.

Higgins, I. J., Best, D. J., Hammond, R. C. & Scott, D. (1981). Methane-oxidizing microorganisms. *Microbiological Reviews*, **45**, 556–90.

Holt, S. C. (1978). Anatomy and chemistry of spirochetes. *Microbiological Reviews*, **42**, 114–60.

Marbach, A., Varon, M. & Shilo, M. (1976). Properties of marine bdellovibrios. *Microbial Ecology*, **2**, 284–95.

Moore, R. L. (1981). The biology of *Hyphomicrobium* and other prosthecate, budding bacteria. *Annual Review of Microbiology*, **35**, 567–94.

Poindexter, J. S. (1981). The caulobacters: ubiquitous unusual bacteria. *Microbiological Reviews*, **45**, 123–79.

Razin, S. (1978). The mycoplasmas. *Microbiological Reviews*, **42**, 414–70.

Reichenbach, H. (1981). Taxonomy of the gliding bacteria. *Annual Review of Microbiology*, **35**, 339–64.

Starr, M. P. & Seidler, R. J. (1971). The bdellovibrios. *Annual Review of Microbiology*, **25**, 649–75.

Stolp, H. & Starr, M. P. (1963). *Bdellovibrio bacteriovorus* gen. et sp. n., a predatory ectoparasitic and bacteriolytic microorganism. *Antonie van Leeuwenhoek*, **29**, 217–48.

Whitcomb, R. F. (1981). The biology of spiroplasmas. *Annual Review of Entomology*, **26**, 397–425.

Zeikus, J. G. (1983). Metabolism of one-carbon compounds by chemotrophic anaerobes. *Advances in Microbial Physiology*, **24**, 215–89.

Archaebacteria

Stoeckenius, W. & Bogomolni, R. A. (1982). Bacteriorhodopsin and related pigments of halobacteria. *Annual Review of Biochemistry*, **51**, 587–616.

Van Valen, L. M. & Maiorana, V. C. (1980). The archaebacteria and eukaryotic origins. *Nature*, **287**, 248–50.
Woese, C. R. (1981). Archaebacteria. *Scientific American*, **244**, 98–122.
Woese, C. R., Magrum, L. J. & Fox, G. C. (1978). Archaebacteria. *Journal of Molecular Evolution*, **11**, 245–52.

4

The natural environments of microorganisms

The continents and the oceans of this planet are inhabited by a multitude of organisms. Microorganisms are found in virtually all locations where life can exist. They are even encountered in extreme environments with abiotic conditions unfavourable for most forms of life. There are many ecosystems on earth, both natural and man-made, that are exclusively inhabited by prokaryotic organisms. The higher forms of eukaryotic life are excluded from the strictly anaerobic regions such as the bottom of freshwater lakes and the marine estuary sediments. Also in environments that are extreme with respect to temperature, acidity, salt and other factors, eukaryotes do not find appropriate living conditions.

Bacteria are ubiquitous in nature mainly for four reasons. (1) Their small size allows easy dispersal. (2) The energy conversion is not restricted to aerobic conditions, but also allows growth and multiplication in anaerobic environments; in addition to the chemoorganotrophic (heterotrophic) and phototrophic higher animals and plants, chemolithotrophic bacteria exist that are capable of generating energy by the oxidation of reduced inorganic compounds. (3) Bacteria have an extreme metabolic versatility and have a much broader range of utilizable nutrients than eukaryotes; some prokaryotes also dispose of a unique capability, the fixation of molecular nitrogen from the air. (4) Many bacteria have the ability to tolerate unfavourable environmental conditions.

In a particular habitat, according to the given abiotic and biotic conditions, certain species predominate while others are only present in low numbers or are absent. In most soils and in sea water, the microorganisms usually are present in low numbers but in many different species. Such habitats are rather indistinct with respect to physicochemical and nutritional conditions. In ecosystems of distinct environmental conditions, on the other hand, a few species and relatively high numbers of individuals occur. The metabolic versatility of the prokaryotes allows microbial life in many parts of the biosphere.

The basic unit of an ecosystem is the community (biocoenosis), comprising the biotic components. The community, as the entirety of organisms living together, is not an independent matter but is under constant influence of the physical and chemical conditions governing the ecosystem. The abiotic and biotic components of the ecosystem characterize the environment. The term environment is used here as synonymous with the term habitat. Defined ecosystems may have huge differences with respect to their spatial extension. The system can be as large as an ocean or as small as a grain of sand. A variety of ecosystems such as arable field, human skin, the phyllosphere, or the rhizosphere are governed by moderate ('normal') environmental conditions. Others, like hot springs, or acid mine waters are characterized by very distinct environmental factors which pose a strict selective pressure upon any potential invader.

The same type of bacteria is often found in more than one habitat. Rhizobia, for example, live as symbionts in root nodules or as free-living organisms in the soil; *Pseudomonas aeruginosa* is found both in aquatic and in soil habitats; it may also occur as opportunistic pathogen in animal hosts. The same applies to *Clostridium tetani, Erwinia amylovora* (the fireblight organism) and several other pathogens. Symbiotic luminescent bacteria may live as free organisms or in association with animals in light emission organs. Organisms of a specific physiological group may also be found in different habitats. The methanogens, for instance, occur in sediments, in the rumen, and in man-made habitats such as sewage fermenters.

The ecology of bacteria is characterized by a multiplicity of microbial environments. These comprise natural, terrestrial and aquatic environments, but also man-made environments such as cooling systems of power plants and dumping sites of organic compounds such as pesticides or solvents. The best-studied environments of microorganisms are those which do not allow life of higher plants and animals but which permit development of a limited number of microbial species. Such extreme environments include virgin volcanic soils, desert soils, hot springs, and other uninviting localities.

Microorganisms in their natural environments can be divided into two categories. (1) The autochthonous (indigenous) flora, and (2) the allochthonous (nonindigenous, zymogenous) flora. The autochthonous microflora is native to a distinctive soil (or water), and by definition is a permanent component of the specific environment. Humic soil, plant surfaces, lake waters, intestinal tracts, rumen, skin, and many other habitats have their characteristic autochthonous flora. The allochthonous flora, on the other hand, depends on the transmittance to this locality from the outside. The allochthonous organisms are aliens or transients in their new environment. In the absence of a suitable substrate they die off or survive in a dormant stage. The allochthonous (non-autochthonous) organisms are incidentally introduced into a habitat by air currents, dust dispersal, rain, animal vectors, or other means of transportation (e.g. aeroplanes, boats).

In some distinct habitats, highly specialized organisms exist and are restricted to that habitat. Since they have become typically adapted to that particular habitat, they are members of the indigenous flora. This applies to obligately parasitic bacteria living in tissues of plants and animals and also to specialists inhabiting hot springs or other extreme environments. In contrast to the native bacterial flora of distinct habitats, ubiquitous bacteria are found in a variety of habitats. The concept of the 'ecological niche' describes the function of a particular species in a community. It originally also referred to a location characterized by properties that allow life of the particular species. Each organism has its characteristic structures and features, has its specific nutritional requirements, disposes of distinct biochemical abilities, and has a defined tolerance to the environmental conditions. All these properties together decide on the functions the organism can fulfil in a given ecosystem. Many cellulose-decomposing bacteria, for instance, are found in a variety of habitats and occupy a rather broad niche. However, in some habitats, as in insect symbiosis, they occupy a very narrow niche. In a particular ecosystem, a given microorganism can only function if it is adapted to the physical and chemical environment, and also tolerates the biotic influences of that community. The concept of the microbial niche as defined in terms of function has 'relativized' (modified) the sharp separation of aquatic and terrestrial microbiology, which is defined in terms of locations.

The terrestrial environment
Composition and structure of the soil
The overall composition of the lithosphere by mass is as follows: O (46%), Si (28%), Al (8.1%), Fe (5.1%), Mg (2.1%), Ca (3.6%), Na (2.8%), K (2.6%). Some elements that are of major importance for the growth of organisms occur in lower concentrations, P (0.12%), C (0.09%), S (0.06%), N (0.0046%). The soil is a complex mixture of inorganic and organic components. In agricultural soils, the mineral

constituents amount to 50% by volume, while the organic matter is 10–15%. The rest, by volume, is air and water distributed in a pore system. The organic contents of different soils may vary considerably. Peat contains up to 30%, tundra and desert soils only 0.1% of organic matter by mass. There are two main groups of soils, (a) mineral soils that originate from initial weathering of rocks, and (b) organic soils laid down in bogs and marshes. Physical, chemical, and biological processes are involved in the weathering of rocks. The parent rock is mainly altered by temperature changes, water, and effects produced by biological activities.

Microorganisms play a central role in weathering. Lichens, algae, fungi, and bacteria participate in this process. They mediate weathering by production of organic acids. Rock-associated fungi accelerate decomposition of natural silicates by the production of citric or oxalic acid. By the process of weathering, the surface layer of the raw soil is physically and chemically altered and thus differs from the underlying materials. Associated with weathering is the occurrence of clays consisting of aluminosilicate particles. These represent in the mineral fraction the smallest size class of particles measuring less than 0.002 mm. Because of their negative charge the clay particles adsorb cations to the surface including those cations that are plant nutrient. Soils with a high concentration of clay, therefore, are particularly fertile.

The primary minerals in soil occur as gravel, coarse or fine sand, and silt. Four main types of clay are differentiated (illite, montmorillonite, kaolinite, and amorphous clay). While clay soils are poorly drained and have a high nutrient content, the sandy soils are well drained but low in nutrients. Loam soils made up of clay + sand + silt are the best agricultural soils as far as drainage and nutrient supply are concerned. The structure of the soil is characterized by soil aggregates containing both inorganic and organic components. They are composed of primary mineral particles associated with clay platelets, organic materials, and various organisms. The aggregates contain pores, some of which are too small to allow access of microorganisms.

After the formation of raw soil, pioneer plants start to develop. By the introduction of biomass to the system they physically and biologically affect the soil structure. Organic root exudates promote microbial growth in the rhizosphere of the plants, as does the decay of any plant material. To some extent, the generation of soil is counteracted by erosion. Above the unweathered parental material the soil is not uniform throughout all depths. By movement of materials downward, several distinct layers (horizons) are formed. A typical soil profile comprises the surface litter

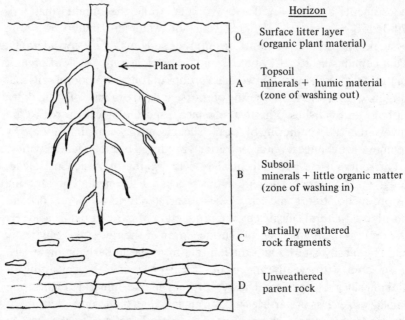

	Horizon
0	Surface litter layer (organic plant material)
A	Topsoil minerals + humic material (zone of washing out)
B	Subsoil minerals + little organic matter (zone of washing in)
C	Partially weathered rock fragments
D	Unweathered parent rock

Fig. 4.1 Vertical soil profile

layer, and the A-, B-, and C-horizon (Fig. 4.1). The A-horizon is the layer which contains a mixture of minerals and organic matter. In the B-horizon the material leached from the upper layers may accumulate. The C-horizon consists of unweathered parent material and is not directly affected by biological processes. The layers differ with respect to mineral content, organic matter, colour, texture, and other properties. Because of the vast diversity of soils, there exist numerous different types of soil profiles, for instance, oxisols (leached soils in tropical rain forests), aridisols (desert soils), or histisols (bog soils with high contents of organic material).

A major part of the organic material in soil is the humic substances. They represent a fraction of brown and insoluble residues derived mainly from lignin and partly from microbial products. Certain bacteria, actinomycetes, and fungi also produce such dark polymers in laboratory culture. The humus fraction in soil is relatively persistent because of its resistance to microbial attack. The turnover of humus compounds is a long-time process related to the recalcitrance of lignin. The residence time of humic substances may last up to 2000 years in cold areas of Siberia or Canada, or only 20 years as in Southern California.

Physicochemical conditions affecting microorganisms

As will be explained in Chapter 5, the water content in soil *per se* does not indicate the amount of water which is available to plants and soil microorganisms. The availability is a complex function of adsorptive and solution factors. In order to take up water, the organism must overcome the forces that retain it. The water potential (ψ) describes the amount of work that has to be done by an organism to obtain water from its environment. In soil microbiology, the water potential is usually used in order to describe the water regime of a soil. The total water potential in soil is mainly influenced by the matric potential (ψ_m) which is an indicator of the surface tension forces acting in the capillary pores. The relationship between matric potential and pore diameter is as follows:

$$\psi_m \, (\text{N} \cdot \text{cm}^{-2}) = 2\gamma \cdot r^{-1}$$

r = effective radius of the pore
γ = surface tension of water (N $\times$ cm^{-1}).
N = Newton (1 N = 1 kg m/s^2)

Water potentials are usually measured in MPa (or bar). Most plants are unable to generate a sufficient suction to overcome ψ_m values of -15 bar. This water potential value is known to be the 'permanent wilting point' for the majority of crop plants.

Many microorganisms in soil exist in a sorbed state. They colonize only a small part of the available surface area of the soil (Fig. 4.2). The clay fraction is particularly important with respect to the sorptive effects on microorganisms. The sorption of microorganisms to surfaces in soil has

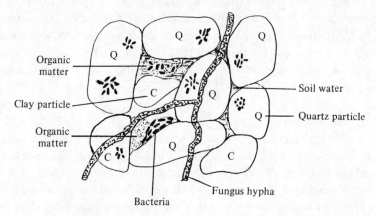

Fig. 4.2 Diagrammatic representation of microbial colonization on soil particles

implications upon the techniques used for enumeration. The liquid phase of a soil suspension contains only a fraction of the bacteria because many do not get released, even after vigorous shaking of the soil aggregates. For this reason, the number of bacteria determined by plating of suitable solutions usually is underestimated. The adhesion of the bacteria to particle surfaces is mediated by the production of sticky substances such as polysaccharides, and is supported by appendages such as holdfasts, fimbriae, or pili.

The pores in soil aggregates are filled either with water or air. Since the gas exchange between the soil atmosphere and the overlying air is rather slow, the composition of air in the soil differs from that in the air. O_2 tends to become depleted, and CO_2 is increased. The pCO_2 in the soil atmosphere usually is between 0.002 and 0.02 atm (in the air it is normally 0.0003 atm).

Substrates for microbial growth

The substrates available in soil for microbial growth mainly originate from the primary production of higher plants. Degradation of the plant litter by herbivorous animals is restricted to those components the animals are able to metabolize. The major components of plants, i.e. cellulose and lignin, are metabolized by microorganisms. Animals can utilize cellulose and lignin only in symbiotic association with the appropriate microbial symbionts. On a global basis, the deposition of plant residues amounts to 1.5×10^{12} tons/year. It has been estimated that 40–60% of the cellulose and the proteins will be mineralized in the first year, while 20% remain in the soil up to five years. A variety of biogenic compounds such as polyaromatics derived from lignin, tannin, or melanin are recalcitrant and require longer periods for decomposition, which may be several thousands of years as estimated by radiocarbon dating. 'Recalcitrance' does not mean absolute resistance to degradation but refers to a retarded decay.

Energy flow

Virtually all energy on earth originates from the sun and is lost as heat. The total energy reaching the earth's atmosphere has been estimated to be 54.4×10^{20} kJ/year. This equals $c.$ 10^7 kJ/m^2 × year. About 50% of this amount of energy reaches the earth's surface. Not more than 1% of the radiation energy entering the biosphere is conserved in the gross primary production. Some of the energy contained in the organic matter that is produced by the photosynthetic organisms is dissipated by

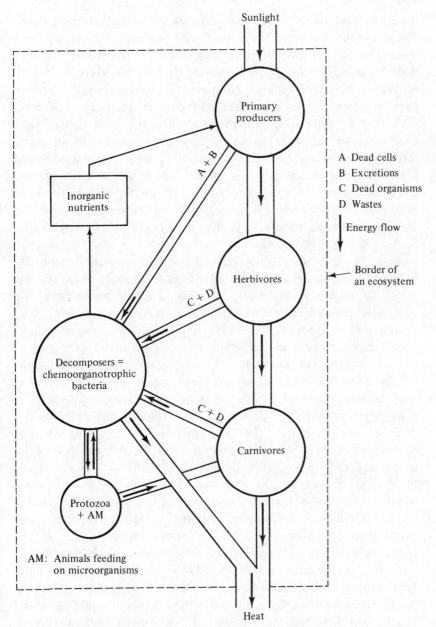

Fig. 4.3 Food chain and energy flow through an ecosystem (simplified representation)

the primary producers themselves, as a consequence of their respiration. The rest of the chemically bound energy is taken over by herbivores and by microorganisms involved in the degradation of the primary production. Again, a part of the energy entering the herbivores is dissipated by respiration, and the biomass is consumed by carnivores which, on their part, are eaten by other carnivores, and so on. At each step of the food chain, a part of the energy is dissipated as heat (Fig. 4.3). Chemical energy (organic substance) is passed from one organism to another, going through different trophic levels. The fate of the primary production is not a linear sequence but rather a complicated food web. Besides the grazing food chain, there is also a detritus food chain, i.e. the decomposition of dead plants and animals that have died by natural causes, injuries, or diseases. The dead bodies are finally decomposed by microorganisms. Since each stage of the food chain is connected with a loss of energy, the biologically useful energy conserved in the primary production eventually is dissipated. Thus, energy continuously flows through an ecosystem. While all chemical energy finally is dissipated as heat and lost from the ecosystem, the bioelements do not get lost but are recycled. The role of microorganisms in the energy flow is mainly related to the decomposition of dead organic matter and excretion products (detritus food chain).

The steady input of biomass into the soil does not occur continuously at the same rate, but rather in pulses. According to the supply varying in time, microbial activities also change periodically. The overall activity is equalized by successions of populations. When large temporal and spatial dimensions are considered (i.e. over years and hectares), the activities can be considered to be more or less constant. The energy supply of the microbial flora in terrestrial environments primarily originates from leaf litter, crop residues, root exudates, and root materials. Plant biomass returned to the soil is chemically complex, e.g. cellulose, hemicelluloses, and lignin. Fungi are the primary decomposers of such compounds. The important role of fungi in the decomposition of plant materials is reflected by the relatively large amounts of fungal biomass in soil. On a dry matter basis, the bacteria have been estimated to represent 10%, and the fungi 90% of the total biomass amounting to 500 kg per ha. Compared to these components, the biomass of protozoa estimated to be around 1 kg/ha and of earthworms estimated to be in the order of 12 kg/ha are relatively low. Since on a global base CO_2-release by decomposition and CO_2-fixation by the photosynthetic organisms are balanced, the carbon level remains constant in most ecosystems. In some anaerobic and closed environments, the organic matter levels may increase with time, because decomposition is retarded while primary production continues. This situation exists for instance in bogs and marshes.

Abundance, distribution, and survival of microorganisms

Soil is a suitable habitat and a giant reservoir for all types of microorganisms comprising bacteria, fungi, protozoa, and algae. Data on the abundance, distribution, and composition of the soil microflora are plentiful. The occurrence of microorganisms has been studied in relation to the type of soil, seasonal variation, depth, temperature, water regime, and other environmental factors. The estimation of microbial numbers by cultural methods is difficult and limited because a substantial fraction of the microbial population escapes isolation. This is particularly true for the bacteria. There is not a general substrate available that allows growth and multiplication of all types of bacteria, and even use of different media does not assure isolation of all existing types. A further difficulty for estimation of the total number is related to the fact that many types of organisms develop as microcolonies on the surface of soil particles and do not become quantitatively detached and suspended in the solution used for isolation. Despite the limitations due to inadequate techniques, our present knowledge on numbers and types of microorganisms primarily has been derived from isolation studies.

It has generally been observed that microbial numbers vary considerably in samples taken from sites that are not far apart, and the same variation is also observed between replica counts. Although the variation must partly be attributed to imperfection of methodology, there are, without doubt, also real differences because of heterogeneity. The abundance of microorganisms at a given site primarily depends on the availability of suitable carbon and energy sources, and the presence of other essential nutrients. It has generally been observed that, with respect to bacteria in non-rhizosphere soil, the Gram-positives predominate. Coryneform bacteria, *Arthrobacter*, bacilli, and micrococci often amount to 70% of the total population. Among the Gram-negatives the pseudomonads, flavobacteria, and *Alcaligenes*, among the anaerobes, the clostridia prevail. *Acinetobacter, Agrobacterium, Brevibacterium, Cellulomonas, Corynebacterium, Nocardia*, and *Streptomyces* are also indigenous in many soils. The numbers of microorganisms can be related to a variety of factors, in particular to the amount of organic matter, to moisture content, temperature, and pH. Bacilli are usually more prevalent in soils under temperature and water stress because of their production of resistant endospores. Increased numbers of bacteria are encountered on the root surface (rhizoplane) and in the immediate vicinity around the plant roots (rhizosphere). Large numbers are also found in the humus-rich A-horizon of a soil profile. Anaerobic bacteria in soil are not only found in the deeper layers but also encountered in the upper layers. Obviously, anoxic microenvironments exist at any depth.

Compared to the total population, specific physiological groups such as nitrifying bacteria, N_2-fixing organisms, sulphur oxidizers or sulphate-reducing bacteria usually constitute but a small fraction. Cyanobacteria are often the primary colonizers, particularly under alkaline conditions. In relation to the total biomass, algae and protozoa are insignificant components, each representing only about 1% of the total biomass. Protozoa in soil are often encysted if the water supply is insufficient. Pores of 10 μm in diameter already drain at $\psi_m = -0.1$ bar, thus limiting growth of the protozoa. The Fungi imperfecti are a major group of fungi in soil. Because of their production of conidiospores, isolation of imperfect fungi such as *Penicillium, Aspergillus, Cephalosporium*, and *Cladosporium* is common. It has to be considered that the soil also contains mycorrhizal fungi, including the vesicular-arbuscular type that are up to the present time non-cultivable and thus escape isolation. Because of the large numbers of bacteria in plate counts compared to fungi, the occurrence of fungi often is underestimated. Although the fungus biomass usually exceeds the biomass of bacteria by the factor 10, the metabolic activities of bacteria because of their small volume and their relatively large surface area exceed that of the fungi.

It is a general feature of the microbial flora that their abundance in soil is subject to seasonal variation. Increase in temperature and input of organic matter (litter) is accompanied by an increase in microbial numbers. A major factor in the distribution of microorganisms over long distances is the dispersal by clouds of dust particles carrying microorganisms from the soil into the atmosphere. The air, however, is not a genuine habitat of microorganisms; air-borne microbes originate from the terrestrial environment. Therefore, the flora in the atmosphere over terrestrial areas in some way reflects the flora of the adjacent soil. The bacteria prevailing in the atmosphere are Gram-positives. The numbers of bacteria found above the soil usually are between 10^3 and 10^6 cells/m^3. At an altitude of 1000 m the concentration is reduced to 10^2 to 10^3/m^3. Above the ocean in 5000 m there are even less, 1 to 10 bacteria/m^3.

Microorganisms have developed a variety of survival mechanisms and are able to persist in soil during periods of unfavourable growth conditions. A few bacteria, in particular the aerobic bacilli, anaerobic clostridia, fungi, and actinomycetes, are capable of producing spores resistant to environmental stress. It is an established fact that not only such spore-producing organisms but also nonsporeformers can be isolated from environments which at the moment of sampling are unsuitable for growth. Such organisms must persist as vegetative cells. The nature of their apparent resistance to the adverse conditions is not yet fully understood. Factors causing stress conditions are mainly lack of nutrients for growth, unavailability of water or oxygen, development of acidic conditions, temperature changes, and radiation at the soil surface. As the soil is a highly structured habitat, environmental conditions may vary between adjacent sites. In apparently well-aerated soils even anaerobic microzones exist. The same is true for the occurrence of neutral conditions in acid soils and for other factors influencing growth. In view of this situation, survival of microorganisms in natural environments is difficult to define. Survival is favoured by the production of resistant structures, such as spores, or vegetative cells that have the ability to overcome periods of suppressed growth.

The survival of animal and plant pathogens in soil has attracted much interest. Most pathogens usually disappear rapidly. Survival periods for shigellae in soil were found to be 6 to 39 days, and for salmonellae 6 weeks. Strains of *Proteus* and *Providencia* were shown to have a decimal reduction time in soil of 6 days at 18 to 20 °C. Contrary to these enterobacteria, survival of *Chlamydia* spp. and *Coxiella burnetii* was found to last for weeks, months, or years. Survival was especially favoured in dried status and under conditions of protection by organic matter coating the cell. The survival time of various plant pathogens differs considerably. A potato strain of *Pseudomonas solanacearum* has been reported to survive in soil for up to two years. Possibly, the organisms do not survive that long in plain soil but in infested pieces of host debris. Following separation from the host tissue and inoculation into soil, *Xanthomonas campestris* was no longer recoverable after two weeks. When protected by cabbage stem tissue, the pathogen, however, survived in large numbers and could be recovered from plant debris for up to three-quarters of a year. The symbiotic rhizobia have rather high survival rates in soil. With *Rhizobium japonicum* introduced into soil, the bacteria could be recovered after five years, even without any soybean crop during this period. Experiments on the survival in soil of the opportunistic human pathogen *Pseudomonas aeruginosa* point to the existence of a dormant form which in some ways resembles a cyst. Clay minerals in soil appear to have a profound effect on the survival of microorganisms. The nature of the effects has still to be elucidated in detail.

Macro- and microhabitats

If we regard soil and water as macrohabitats, we have to recognize that the effective habitat of a microorganism is its microhabitat. This is the locality where the cells live in close vicinity and where metabolic actions occur and interactions are possible. The term 'microhabitat' is often used synonymously with 'microenvironment', or sometimes with 'microecosystem'. In microbial ecology the term 'habitat' is often used with the meaning of 'ecosystem', comprising the entirety of the biotic and abiotic factors a particular organism is exposed to. Synonymous use of habitat and ecosystem is admissible because the operational area of the bacteria is usually small. The concept of microenvironments has greatly eliminated the former sharp division between terrestrial and aquatic habitats. The soil represents a highly complex ecosystem composed of a great many microenvironments inhabited by many different microorganisms. The same is true for the sediments of waters. In more homogeneous environments such as the ocean water bodies, the microbial community, as a rule, is less diverse than in soil. The homogeneity is most pronounced in extreme environments which usually only harbour representatives of a few microbial species. Soil and water are characterized as macrohabitats by varying proportions of two phases, the solid surface and the water. With respect to the phase proportions, there exists a continuum of habitats ranging from arid deserts with no or little bound pore water to offshore sea water that has only traces of particulate matter, and thus lacks any solid surfaces. Some factors in macro- and microenvironments may be the same, e.g. temperature and pressure. Certain factors, however, may differ within a microenvironment from the surrounding macroenvironment. Thus, a soil may, and usually will, contain several microenvironments differing with respect to moisture content, nutrients, pH, and some other factors. There are presently no means to determine the chemical situation in microhabitats because the small space does not allow measuring local concentrations of environmental components at the site of microcolonies. The O_2-tension, for instance, in the vicinity of a microcolony adsorbed to a surface may be zero in an environment of overall aerobic conditions.

Compared to laboratory cultures, bacteria in nature live in a heterogeneous environment which is exposed to chemical and physical gradients influencing uptake of nutrients and metabolic activities. In natural habitats the adsorption to surfaces is of great importance because insoluble matter preponderates both in aquatic and terrestrial environments. Localized environmental changes in a microhabitat may markedly alter the microbial balance in this particular habitat without affecting adjacent environments. It has been found that local changes, e.g. in redox potential and pH, may be different over short distances. The effects are drastic with respect to O_2 conditions. While larger pores may contain air space and thus may allow aerobic processes, smaller pores in the vicinity may be drained by water and easily become anoxic due to microbial activity and poor oxygen transfer. The diffusion coefficient of O_2 in water is known to be 10 000 times smaller than in air. Pores of 10 μm in diameter and smaller are filled with water at $\psi_m = -0.1$ bar. This explains the occurrence of denitrification and other anaerobic processes in relatively well-drained soils. The numerous microhabitats distributed at random allow oxic and anoxic processes to occur simultaneously and side by side.

The study of the organisms located in a microenvironment, with respect to spatial relation to one another and to their metabolic activities, is virtually impossible because of the complex situation and the very many factors involved. While there is some access to the spatial situation by direct electron microscopy of natural materials, other factors of ecological interest such as metabolism, response to environmental factors, nutritional situation, and so on, cannot be determined because of methodological limitations.

Surfaces and gradients as habitats

Growth on surfaces is of minor interest in laboratory cultures although it is occasionally observed, e.g. at the rim of a culture vessel. In nature, however, growth on surfaces is most common and a very important ecological determinant. There are three kinds of interfaces between solid and liquid matter. (1) The solid–liquid interface is represented by detritus particles, food particles, by the inner surface of body holes (mouth, intestine), and many other locations. (2) The liquid–gas interface is represented by water surfaces of rivers, lakes, and oceans, flooded soil, gas bubbles in agitated waters, and similar situations. (3) The liquid–liquid interface occurs in an aqueous solution containing oil droplets.

The various particles existing in soil can be classified according to their size into gravel, sand, silt, and clay. There is a reciprocal relationship between the diameter of particles and the surface per unit of weight. 1 g of fine gravel (particles measuring 2000 μm in diameter) has a surface of *c*. 11 cm^2. The surface per g of clay (particles measuring 2 μm in diameter), however, is 11 000 cm^2. The surface area of clay, thus, is 1000 times that of fine gravel of the same weight. Clay in soil or sediments, therefore, causes an extension of the surface area which strongly influences the adsorptive properties of the soil, and also has a bearing on the colonization by microorganisms. Because of the great surface area, clay minerals are significant in sorption processes. Montmorillonite, which is a very important clay mineral, can adsorb large amounts of organic substances. Enzymes can also be adsorbed to clay minerals. Proteases, phosphatases, urease, and other enzymes of microbial origin are able to function in the state of being adsorbed to the soil particles. The sorptive properties of a soil are also influenced by quartz sand. The adsorption of organic matter to a glass surface is a well-known phenomenon and can readily be demonstrated in an aquarium. Part of the organic matter in soil exists in the form of complex materials called humus. It consists of organic polymers containing sugars, amino acids, phosphates, and other components. Humus substances form complex aggregates with clay minerals, and there is evidence that most microorganisms in soil are associated with these colloidal complex aggregates. It is difficult to describe exactly the physical and chemical conditions at the surface of a given particle to which microorganisms are attached. While liquid solutions are rather homogeneous with respect to physical and chemical properties, the conditions on the surface of particles tend to more variation.

The distribution of nutrients in nature, contrary to laboratory conditions, is not even. In many habitats a vertical gradient of nutrient concentration exists. This is particularly observed in standing waters. If nutrients from the sediment diffuse into the upper layers above, a concentration gradient is formed, provided currents or convections are absent. Such gradients are built up on a macroscale in lakes and oceans, but they also exist on a microscale in sediments and soil. The gradients formed refer to nutrients as well as physical and chemical environmental factors such as oxygen, temperature, radiation intensity, or reduction–oxidation potential. For the distribution of microorganisms in nature, gradients of organic acids, of hydrogen sulphide, O_2, and CO_2 have major importance. Despite the heterogeneous conditions in soil, gradients in microhabitats are a determinant for distribution. Solid organic matter on, or near, the soil surface is decomposed mainly aerobically. Part of the materials is transported downwards by soil animals and is further degraded aerobically or anaerobically depending on aeration and moisture conditions. From the local introduction of nutrients, gradients develop which influence the distribution of the microorganisms. Because of the heterogeneous conditions in soil, diffusion processes and gradients of nutrients and other factors cannot as easily be recognized as in aquatic environments.

The aquatic environment

Seventy-one per cent of the earth's surface is covered by oceans. Waters, therefore, are the dominant environment of this planet. The border line between terrestrial and aquatic environments is not as clear-cut as it seems to be, but is rather diffused. Aquatic environments comprise springs, ponds, rivers, lakes, oceans, but also ground waters, acid mine waters, sewage lagoons, and other aquatic habitats. Compared to terrestrial environments, the aquatic ecosystems show a more pronounced constancy of the environmental conditions. The temperature in the surface layers of waters fluctuates less than in soil. The oceanic waters have a rather low temperature; many of the oceanic water bodies never have more than $4\,^{\circ}C$. The constancy is also expressed by the more even distribution of nutrients. These are available in dissolved and ionic form and are continuously dispersed by diffusion, convection, and currents. The productivity in aquatic environments is essentially limited to the euphotic surface layers. In total, it is in the order of magnitude of the terrestrial primary (photosynthetic) production.

Physicochemical conditions affecting microorganisms

With respect to the ionic composition, the aquatic environments exhibit a broad range of variation. Compared to river and lake waters, sea water is distinguished by a high concentration of sodium, chloride, sulphate, and magnesium ions. In mg/l, the figures are as follows (first the concentration in lake waters, second the concentration in sea waters): Na^+ (7.5; 11 000), Cl^- (7.4; 20 000), SO_4^{2-} (15; 2700), Mg^{2+} (4.9; 1300). The concentration of dissolved CO_2 in sea water is about twice that of lake water. As to the concentration of organic matter, fresh waters contain twice as much as sea water. With respect to C, N, and P, the natural waters generally have lower contents than soils. All elements in waters to some degree show spatial discontinuities. This is most obvious for the organic carbon.

Carbon dioxide in gas form is in equilibrium with dissolved CO_2. It reacts with water according to the equation

$$CO_2 + H_2O \rightleftharpoons H_2CO_3 \rightleftharpoons H^+ + HCO_3^- \rightleftharpoons 2H^+ + CO_3^{2-}$$

Carbonic acid which is only present at very low concentration (0.1% of the total) dissociates into H^+ and HCO_3^- ions. CO_2 in water is three times as soluble as O_2; therefore, CO_2 deficits in waters are rare. The solubility of CO_2 is strongly influenced by the pH value. At low acidity (pH 4), the concentration of dissolved CO_2 is prominent. Under alkaline conditions (pH 9) CO_3^{2-} predominates. In the biological range, under more or less neutral conditions, HCO_3^- prevails, and CO_2 is also high in concentration. The average pH values in fresh waters are between 6 and 9, those of sea water between 8.0 and 8.3. With respect to the dissolved salts sea water has a concentration of 35 mg/ml. The prevailing ions Na^+ and Cl^- amount to about 11 g/kg and 19 g/kg sea water, respectively. The solubility of oxygen in water is low, pure water at $0\,°C$ containing 14.6 mg O_2/l. The oxygen solubility is lowered by solutes, by increase in temperature, and by increase in pressure.

The diffusion of oxygen from the atmosphere into water bodies and finally into the sediments is extremely slow. The consequences are anoxic conditions in sediments, where mixing of water is restricted. In the anoxic marine environments, sulphate is the most important anion. In the presence of organic materials it serves as the terminal electron-acceptor for a variety of organisms capable of dissimilatory sulphate reduction. The consequence is the emanation of H_2S which in turn serves as the H-donor for the anaerobic phototrophs, e.g. the green and purple bacteria.

Marine habitats are the largest anaerobic ecosystems in the biosphere. The Black Sea, for instance, is devoid of O_2 from 150 m to 2000 m depth. Almost the entire sulphide present originates from the reduction of sulphate (SO_4^{2-}). The oxidation of H_2S by phototrophic microorganisms occurs at the anoxic/oxic interface and is connected with the fixation of large amounts of CO_2. In anoxic marine waters, the concentration of methane (CH_4) is low compared to that of anoxic freshwater environments. In sediments with high sulphate concentrations (more than 10 mM), the degradation of organic materials is mainly mediated by the sulphate-reducing bacteria. Under conditions of low sulphate concentrations, however, methanogenesis is the major process in the degradation of carbon compounds. High concentrations of sulphate generally prevent methanogenesis in marine habitats (in particular sublittoral and estuarine sediments) due to competition between sulphate and CO_2 (and acetate) reduction.

An important ecological determinant in aquatic environments is light. Light absorption regulates the distribution of phototrophs as the primary producers. These, on their part, influence the distribution of the chemoorganotrophs. For each metre of depth, light intensity decreases by about 50%. Another factor that influences life of aquatic organisms is the hydrostatic pressure. It rises by 1 atm for every 10 m in depth.

Substrates for microbial growth

Growth of the aerobic photosynthetic organisms (phytoplankton) mainly depends on the presence of the mineral salts required for growth. The nutritional basis for the chemoorganotrophs is the organic carbon that occurs both in dissolved and in particulate form. The total organic carbon in sea water usually is around 1 mg/l, and the particulate matter is $\frac{1}{10}$ to $\frac{1}{5}$ of the dissolved carbon. Part of the particulate carbon, because of its chemical nature, is resistant to microbial decomposition.

Energy flow

The energy flow in aquatic environments starts with the primary production by photosynthetic organisms. The base of the zone of primary production (euphotic zone) is determined by the so-called compensation point, which occurs where the gain by photosynthesis is balanced by the respiratory losses. In clear lakes, the euphotic zone reaches down to depths of 200 m, in open oceans it is restricted to the upper 100 m, and in turbid estuaries it comprises the upper 2 m. The productivity in waters largely depends on the nutritional conditions. The rate of primary production (defined as g dry organic matter/m^2 × d) in polluted streams may be as high as 75, in coral reefs 18, in lakes during the summer 9, in lakes during the winter 1, and in the open ocean not more than 0.2. The limiting factors for production are mainly the inorganic nutrients nitrogen and phosphorus and for diatoms, silicon. In marine environments, carbon (as bicarbonate) and sulphur (as sulphate) are never limiting. The N-concentration in ocean waters, however, is four or more orders of magnitude less than in fertile land. In certain areas, where upwelling occurs, more nutrients are added to the euphotic zone.

The phytoplankton are chiefly consumed by zooplankton, in particular by small crustaceans. By excretion of the phytoplankton, the water is also supplied with soluble organic matter. The various forms of organic matter in sea water consist both of soluble and particulate organic matter. Much of the organic matter in fresh waters is allochthonous that has been introduced from the surrounding land in the form of dead leaves and other detrital components. These materials are degraded by microorganisms and thus partly converted into microbial protein. The bacteria have an important function as decomposers and mineralizers of the organic matter mediating the cycling of the bioelements. The microbial cells, on their part, finally die, and, by lysis, release nutrients that are used by other organisms.

Abundance, distribution, and survival of microorganisms

The aquatic environment can be divided into neustonic, planktonic, benthic, and epibiotic habitats. The neustonic habitat is confined to the air–water interface. The community belonging to this habitat is termed neuston. The planktonic environment comprises the water column which is inhabited by free-floating organisms, and the community of this habitat is called plankton. The organisms of the benthic habitat, the benthos community, live in, and on, sediments. Epibiotic habitats are characterized by the community of attached organisms, the periphyton. They exist as epiphyton on plants, as epizoon on animals, and as epilithic flora on rocks and stones. In most aquatic habitats the bacterial numbers are lower than in soil. They range from around 10^3/ml in oligotrophic waters to around 10^7/ml in eutrophic waters. In neustonic habitats the concentration of organic matter is high, the number of bacteria often exceeding 10^8/ml. At liquid–solid interfaces, nutrients accumulate by sorption and thus favour growth of microorganisms. The bacteria most common in aquatic habitats are Gram-negative rods. The majority of the isolates belong to the genera *Pseudomonas, Vibrio,* and *Flavobacterium.* In sediments, a higher proportion of Gram-positive bacteria (bacilli) is encountered.

The question whether truly 'marine' microorganisms exist has been a matter of debate for a long time. Bacteria isolated from the ocean do not necessarily have to be of marine origin because many organisms are washed in by the rivers. It is, therefore, necessary to differentiate between the organisms occurring in the open ocean and those isolated near the coast. The existence of genuine marine microorganisms as autochthonous inhabitants is now generally accepted. They have a requirement for NaCl and are psychrophilic with respect to temperature. The various groups of sheathed and/or appendaged bacteria are strictly aquatic, preferably in the benthic habitat. The bacterial primary producers (phototrophs) are also truly aquatic organisms which live in the planktonic habitat. Prosthecate bacteria are common in water bodies of low nutrient content. Many planktonic organisms have the ability to float in the water column. Buoyancy is related to the small size, to motility, and to the presence of gas vesicles which are known in phototrophs, cyanobac-

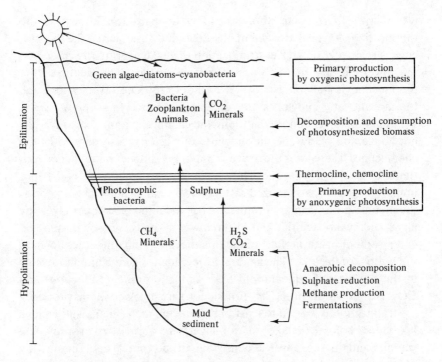

Fig. 4.4 Vertical profile of a stratified lake

teria, and others. Similar structures also occur in the halobacteria which keep them at the surface of brine pools.

The fungi are more prevalent in fresh waters as opposed to the sea. They are primarily involved in the decay of plant residues. Lower fungi, such as the chytrids, are parasitic on planktonic algae. Oomycetes are widespread in rivers, ponds, and lakes but are rare in the sea. The Thraustochytridiales are truly marine fungi. Ascomycetes and Fungi imperfecti are also found in rivers and lakes, where they are associated with the decay of leaves and other plant residues. Yeasts have been found in oceans down to 3000 m depth. Common representatives in coastal waters are *Rhodotorula* and *Torulopsis*.

The inland waters comprise both flowing and still environments. The flowing streams and rivers have more or less uniform conditions throughout all depths by continuous mixing of the water body. In a still lake, however, distinct water layers develop which differ in temperature, density, chemical composition, and biological conditions. The development of distinct layers is known as stratification (Fig. 4.4). As a result of surface heating, the upper layer is warmed up. At the lower base of the warm layer there is an abrupt drop in temperature, known as the thermocline. Vertical movement of solutes and gases across the thermocline is relatively slow. The stratification of a lake is primarily caused by the lower density of the warmer surface waters. The depth of the thermocline is generally between 8 and 15 m. The layers above the thermocline are known as the epilimnion, the layers below as the hypolimnion. Since redox conditions and chemical parameters are different above and below the thermocline, this layer is also defined as the chemocline. It separates the oxygen containing (upper) water layers from the anoxic (deeper) layers. The layer between epilimnion and hypolimnion which is characterized by temperature and chemical gradients is the metalimnion. Primary production occurs in the oxic upper layers by algae and cyanobacteria, and in the lower anoxic layers by purple and green sulphur bacteria. Part of the organic matter finally settles down to the bottom of the lake. The anaerobic degradation of the biomass occurs in the sediment. Fermentation, SO_4^{2-}-reduction (H_2S-production) and CO_2 (acetate)-reduction (CH_4-production) are involved in this process.

Stratification is known to exist in holomictic, meromictic, and amictic lakes. In a holomictic lake, the top layers are warmed up in spring and summer and thus become less dense than the bottom layers. The stability of stratification during the summer leads to an oxic epilimnion and an anoxic hypolimnion. When, during fall and winter, the temperature of the epilimnion cools down below that of the hypolimnion the two layers become turned over and mixed. The deeper layers thus get to the top and are oxygenated. By this circulation the nutrient-rich bottom waters are evenly distributed and cause blooms of greeen algae and cyanobacteria as the lake warms up in the spring. This effect is more pronounced in eutrophic lakes, which contain more nutrients and have shallower depths than in oligotrophic lakes, where these processes are less distinctive. In meromictic and amictic lakes stratification is more or less permanent and independent of the season. Permanent stratification is common in tropical regions where the surface water of lakes does not get colder than that of the hypolimnion and, therefore, does not sink to the bottom. In temperate climate zones, both holomictic and meromictic lakes occur.

Phytoplankton development in the top layers of a holomictic lake leads to the production of organic material that finally sinks to the bottom. It is first aerobically, and, after exhaustion of oxygen, anaerobically decomposed. The anaerobic processes are accompanied by the production of H_2, H_2S, CH_4, and CO_2. Because of lack of convection, these products slowly diffuse upwards. Part of the methane, rising to the surface in form of bubbles, is dissolved and aerobically oxidized by the methylotrophs. In the anaerobic environment, organic fermentation products are oxidized by means of nitrate and sulphate respiration. The H_2S produced is oxidized anaerobically just below the chemocline by purple sulphur and green phototrophic bacteria. Many bacteria living in this zone have gas vacuoles and are capable of buoyancy. The primary production by anoxic photosynthesis is considerable, as noted by the development of secondary producers (consumers) in the adjacent upper zone. Here, protozoa and copepods are especially abundant. The sulphate produced by H_2S-oxidizing anoxic phototrophs is in turn used by sulphate-reducing bacteria. In the hypolimnion, at depths usually between 10 and 20 m, the conditions are anoxic, and the temperature is constant. Anoxic photosynthesis is restricted to a layer adjacent to the thermocline while oxic photosynthesis mainly occurs close to the surface (down to 5 m). The most striking feature of a stratified lake is the presence of two layers of photosynthetic primary production. Sulphate respiration likewise has two zones, one near the bottom layers of the hypolimnion, i.e. in the sediment, and the second just below the chemocline.

Natural rivers that are little contaminated are clear in appearance and have a low concentration of microorganisms. Small amounts of organic matter are easily decomposed (self-purification). In highly contaminated waters, however, there is a drastic alteration of the microflora and fauna. The occurrence of *Sphaerotilus natans* is indicative of contamination (eutrophicated waters).

Marine habitats usually contain high concentrations of sulphate. Under anoxic conditions, the production of H_2S by sulphate-reducing bacteria is abundant provided that organic matter is available. The presence of H_2S exerts a selective pressure on the microbial flora and the food chain. In the deep sea which is characterized by the absence of light, by temperatures between 2° and 3 °C, and by high hydrostatic pressure, the concentration of organic energy sources is low, which is mirrored by the scantiness of life. Nevertheless, microorganisms including barophiles have been detected in the sediments of the deep sea.

The numbers of bacteria in aquatic habitats depend on a variety of factors. The active primary producers are the starting point of the food chain. They are followed by the chemoorganotrophs. In oligotrophic waters, the bacterial concentration per ml is 10^3 to 10^4 while in eutrophic waters the concentration is 10^7 to 10^8. In the detritus on the sediment surface of lakes, concentrations of as high as 10^9 cells/g of sediment have been estimated. In oceans where less detritus reaches the ocean floor, the concentration of bacteria is 10^4 to 10^5/g. Since the supply of nutrients needed by microorganisms for growth is usually low in aquatic habitats, the doubling time is relatively long. In oligotrophic lakes doubling times for bacteria between 60 h and 180 h have been estimated. In nutrient-rich and warm waters rapid microbial growth has been observed in the vicinity of the phytoplankton, with 4 h generation time reported for bacteria.

Luminescent bacteria are largely restricted to the marine environment. Two genera prevail: *Beneckea* and *Photobacterium*. Both occur as free-living organisms, photobacteria also as symbionts in marine fishes and invertebrates. The survival of pathogenic bacteria in rivers, lakes, and the sea shore has attracted much attention. The results suggest that the persistence of potentially pathogenic bacteria generally is restricted.

Growth at interfaces and gradients

In aquatic environments, a variety of interfaces provide specific and selective conditions for growth. The interface between the water surface and the air is occupied by the neuston. An aqueous–solid interface is common to sediments and to many kinds of submerged particle surfaces. A specific interface is that between the oxygenated and the anoxic water. In stagnant waters, growth of microorganisms is strongly influenced by gradients of light, temperature, and other factors. In surface films formed during calm weather on lakes and ponds, the diversity of bacteria is high, and is comprised of *Pseudomonas, Caulobacter, Hyphomicrobium, Flavobacterium, Alcaligenes, Micrococcus,* and many others. The attraction of microorganisms to liquid surfaces is mediated by the surface tension. The surface tension of water is higher than that of many other liquids, and it is decreased by addition of solutes or other liquids. Insoluble substances such as hydrocarbons spread on the surface and form films. The formation of surface films has attracted much attention because of oil pollution accidents. Common surface films on water contain fatty acids, lipids, polysaccharides, and proteins. The liquid–gas interface has characteristic features such as high intensities of light, exposure to air, and accumulation of hydrophilic substances. The concentration of organisms in the surface film usually is much higher than in the water body.

Gradients at the macroscale are characteristic for the stratified lake (Fig. 4.4). From the anaerobic decomposition of organic matter, a chemical gradient (chemocline) develops. In particular, H_2S, CH_4, H_2, and CO_2 diffuse upwards, and thus form concentration gradients. Gradients at a microscale are produced in the sediments. The degradative and biosynthetic processes in sediments are similar to those occurring in stratified lakes. In coastal marine sediments, the organic material necessary for life is mainly allochthonous (leaves, other plant residues, and detritus). Because of an excess of sulphate in most marine ecosystems, the anaerobic food chain yields H_2S and induces activities of bacteria of the S-cycle. In the presence of molecular oxygen, H_2S is unstable. Therefore, a habitat containing both components will have a limited size. Vertical gradients also occur with respect to light, temperature, oxygen, and hydrostatic pressure. Horizontal gradients occur around hot springs (temperature gradient) or sulphur springs (H_2S gradient), and are also common in running waters.

Extreme environments

When discussing 'normal' or 'extreme' conditions, one has to take into consideration that the greatest portion of the biosphere is in the realm of environmental extremes. The oceans cover the greatest part of the earth's surface, and many marine habitats are continuously cold and under pressure. While higher forms of life, both animals and plants, require moderate environmental conditions, the prokaryotes have developed structural and chemical mechanisms that allow growth of a number of representatives also in extreme environments. It is a general experience that the number of species that can be isolated from a natural habitat decreases with increase of the environmental adversity. The abundance of physiological types is restricted, but the few species adapted to the extreme conditions may be present in high numbers of individuals. Organisms possessing the ability to grow under extreme conditions have usually lost the ability to develop in other environments. Low numbers of species with high specialization are characteristic for any extreme conditions such as high or low temperature, high salt concentration, high or low pH, low moisture content, low nutrient concentration, etc. Under less rigid conditions, a greater number of microbial species is present. These may obligately be bound to the special environment or live in it facultatively. From an ecological point of view, 'normal' conditions exist where the greatest species diversity is allowed. Organisms living under highly extreme conditions, also known as 'extremophiles', not only tolerate the specific conditions but usually depend on them.

Pressurized deeps of the oceans, strongly acid and alkaline areas, the cold polar regions, and the hot geothermal regions are unsuitable habitats for most forms of life. Wherever environmental conditions become demanding, higher organisms are excluded, and microorganisms predominate.

The range of environmental extremes tolerated by microorganisms is much broader than that of other forms of life. The limits for growth and reproduction with respect to temperature range from $-12\,°$ to more than $+100\,°C$ ($118\,°C$ under pressure). There exist organisms that grow at pH 0 (*Thiobacillus thiooxidans*) or at pH 13 (*Plectonema nostocorum*). Deep sea bacteria can endure hydrostatic pressures up to 1400 atm. Some highly specialized and adapted bacteria and algae live in saturated brines (*Halobacterium, Halococcus, Dunaliella*). In addition to natural extreme environments, man has also created habitats with extreme conditions, e.g. coolhouses and acid mine waters. Life in extreme environments has been intensively studied with respect to the molecular and regulatory mechanisms that are involved. Proteins of extreme thermophiles are also of great interest to biotechnology because higher temperature would give faster rates of substrate conversion. In addition, this field of research has also attracted attention because of its impact on the question of possible existence of life on other planets.

Microbes at low water potential

Common laboratory growth media have water potentials around -1.5 bar. In soil, the water potential easily becomes decreased, at least in microhabitats, due to drainage. A drastic decrease of metabolic activity is generally observed below -3 bar, and, at lower water potentials, many microorganisms are inhibited. Bacteria as a whole are more sensitive to water stress than fungi.

Low water potentials are mainly encountered in certain aquatic environments of high salinity. In sea water containing 3.5% NaCl, the water potential is -28 bar ($0.980\ a_w$). Most freshwater and terrestrial bacteria do not tolerate this potential, and consequently are only transients which do not survive in the marine environment. Organisms that are adapted to, and grow best at, high concentrations of NaCl are called halophiles. Slight halophiles prefer NaCl concentrations between 2 and 5%, moderate halophiles are adapted to 5–20% NaCl, and extreme halophiles grow best at concentrations between 20 and 30% NaCl. Most bacteria living in the ocean and in marine mud are slightly halophilic. Extreme halophiles are inhabitants of salt lakes at saturated concentration. They prefer water potentials between -274 and -422 bar (a_w 0.83–0.75). Only few microorganisms are capable of growing at saturated salt conditions. Members of the characteristic flora are the alga *Dunaliella viridis* and the halophilic bacteria, e.g. *Halobacterium cutirubrum, Halobacterium salinarium,* and *Halococcus morrhuae*. With respect to salt-induced low water potential, halophilic and halotolerant organisms can be distinguished. While the halophiles have a specific requirement for salt, the halotolerant organisms grow also in the absence of salt. This category includes a variety of bacteria, yeasts, filamentous fungi, cyanobacteria, and algae. At conditions of salt saturation (5.2 M NaCl, −422 bar, 0.75 a_w), which exists in solar evaporation ponds, only a few types of microorganisms can grow. The halobacteria exclude Na^+ from the interior and concentrate K^+. It has been shown that the halobacteria have a specific requirement for high levels of KCl necessary for stability and maximum activity of their enzymes. The stability of the cell envelope requires 1 to 2 M NaCl; at lower concentrations the cells lyse. The halobacteria are physiologically interesting microorganisms not only because of their ability to grow at low water potentials but also because of their ability to exert a non-chlorophyll-mediated photophosphorylation. This special ability confers a selective advantage to the bacteria in a habitat of high light intensity. Photosynthesis of the halobacteria occurs under microaerophilic conditions and is mediated by a 'purple membrane'. This structure contains bacteriorhodopsin, a light-sensitive pigment similar to vertebrate rhodopsin. Induced by illumination, protons are released producing a proton flux that creates an electrochemical gradient across the membrane and allows ATP production. The halobacteria possess C_{50} carotenoids and ether-linked lipids in the cell membrane. The latter property reflects the nature of these organisms as members of the archaebacteria.

Other organisms capable of growing at low water potentials compensate the external solutes by producing osmotically active pools of 'compatible solutes'. Polyols such as glycerol, arabitol, mannitol, proline, and betain are known to be produced by microorganisms for osmoregulation.

Environments with low water potential due to non-ionic solutes are rare in nature. Certain yeasts and filamentous fungi can grow on dry foods. These are xerotolerant or osmotolerant and live at water potentials of as low as −700 bar. The most xerotolerant fungus, *Xeromyces bisporus*, is known to tolerate −726 bar (a_w 0.61). With *Saccharomyces rouxii* the limit of salt-induced growth is at −200 bar, while in the presence of sugars the organism can grow even at −700 bar. The response of bacteria to ionic and non-ionic solutes (same water potential) is different.

Microbes at extreme temperatures

Based on the adaptation of microorganisms to specific temperature ranges, mesophilic, thermophilic, and psychrophilic organisms are distinguished. The optimum temperature is usually higher than that present in the natural environments of soils and waters. In a temperate climate the average soil temperature is around 12 °C, but the optimum growth temperature of most mesophilic organisms found in these environments is considerably higher. The mesophiles, however, have the ability to tolerate a rather broad range of temperature which covers the seasonal fluctuations that may reach 30 °C. Since the behaviour of microorganisms with respect to temperature is different, obligate and facultative thermophiles are differentiated. By definition, the obligate thermophilic organisms are incapable of growth in the mesophilic range. Facultative thermophiles, on the other hand, are capable of growth at high temperatures, but also grow in the mesophilic range. Thermophiles are classified as extreme when the temperature optima are above 65 °C. Obligate psychrophilic bacteria are unable to grow above 20 °C, but do grow at low temperatures down to and below 0 °C. Facultative psychrophiles, on the other hand, are capable of growing at low temperature but also grow above 20 °C.

Extreme temperatures are only tolerated by prokaryotes. The temperature maximum known for eukaryotic organisms is between 50 and 60 °C. This group is chiefly represented by fungi, e.g. members of *Rhizopus, Penicillium, Humicola*, and *Mucor*. Among the protozoa, only a few can grow and survive at temperatures between 50 and 55 °C. Temperatures above 60 °C are exclusively tolerated by prokaryotic organisms. Self-heating of organic material (e.g. hay) is a process related to microbial successions. Thermotrophic fungi such as *Aspergillus fumigatus* and *Geotrichum candidum* are involved in the degradation up to temperatures of 50–60 °C. Then, thermophiles such as *Mucor pusillus* and *Humicola lanuginosa* come into action, and further heating beyond 65 °C is related to the activity of bacteria and actinomycetes. It is a striking experience that thermophiles can also be isolated from temperate soils. However, obligate thermophiles have only been isolated from hot habitats. The higher the temperature, the smaller the number of species present in the extreme environment. *Thermus aquaticus* grows continuously at temperatures around 70 °C, and its maximum temperature is 79 °C. The organism is common in hot springs but has also been isolated from domestic hot-water systems. Another extreme thermophile is *Sulfolobus acidocaldarius*. This organism has been isolated from hot and acid aqueous and soil habitats. It grows at pH between 1 and 6 and has a growth maximum temperature of 85 °C, with optimum growth between 70 and 75 °C. Thermophilic thiobacilli are common in Icelandic thermal areas and have growth optima between 60 and 75 °C. Some thermophilic iron and sulphur-oxidizing bacteria are involved in metal leaching. A thermophile similar to *Sulfolobus acidocaldarius* is *Caldariella acidophila* occurring in volcanic hot springs. This bacterium is also capable of oxidizing ferrous iron. From alkaline hot springs, the cyanobacterium *Synechococcus lividus* and the phototroph *Chloroflexus aurantiacus* have been isolated. Thermophilic bacteria growing between 50 and 75 °C are common in many soils and waters. The ability to grow at temperatures above 50 °C is not restricted to a few specialists but is found in several genera of bacteria such as *Bacillus, Thermoactinomyces, Methanobacterium,* and *Methylococcus*. Until not long ago, the upper temperature reported for microbial activity was 92 °C. Recently, new extreme thermophilic archaebacteria, *Pyrococcus furiosus* and *Pyrodictium occultum*, have been described growing at optimum temperatures of 100 °C and 105 °C, respectively (cp. Fig. 5.3). An astonishing fact is the occurrence of thermophilic bacteria even in cold lake sediments.

Many organisms, isolated from soils and waters, which are capable of growing at temperatures between 0 ° and 5 °C are not truly psychrophilic but psychrotrophic, i.e. these organisms tolerate low but prefer higher temperatures. Genuine psychrophiles are sensitive to temperatures above 20 °C. Exposure to higher temperature causes death, which has to be considered in isolation and enumeration procedures. From permanently cold habitats of polar regions, the psychrophilic alga *Raphidonema nivale* and the fungus *Sclerotina borealis* have been isolated. Among the terrestrial psychrophiles are members of the genera *Pseudomonas, Cytophaga,* and *Flavobacterium*. Psychrophiles also occur in other genera, e.g. *Arthrobacter glacialis, Micrococcus cryophilus,* and *Bacillus psychrophilus*. The marine psychrophiles comprise representatives of the genera *Pseudomonas, Vibrio,* and *Spirillum*. *Vibrio marinus* is a common organism found below the thermocline in the oceans. Some bacteria from arctic waters have growth optima of around 10 °C, but do not tolerate 20 °C. The isolates from the deep sea have to live with two types of stress, low temperature and high pressure. In the dry valleys of the Antarctic, bacteria have been found that are adapted to temperatures below 0 °C and to extremely low humidity. The main primary producer is a small psychrophilic cyanobacterium of the genus *Gloeocapsa*. There obviously exists an entire psychrophilic community comprising yeasts (*Cryptococ-*

cus vishniacii, Leucosporidium antarcticum), filamentous fungi, and bacteria.

Bacteria isolated from preserved food and growing around the freezing point are usually facultative psychrophiles that have their maximum growth temperatures above 20 °C.

Growth at extremely high or low temperatures requires that the structural integrity of the cell and the stability and function of the membrane is maintained under these conditions. It has been shown that thermophiles contain a larger proportion of high melting temperature membrane lipids. As demonstrated in *Thermus aquaticus*, the thermophiles are capable of modulating the synthesis of lipids, and thus can adapt to changing growth temperatures. Increase in temperature causes a higher proportion of the higher melting point C_{16} straight-chain fatty acids. Decreasing temperature induces the synthesis of C_{17} branched fatty acids. In psychrophiles, large amounts of unsaturated low-melting point fatty acids have been found. Thermophily and psychrophily are thus correlated with the fatty acid pattern of the cell. Extreme thermophiles produce proteins and nucleic acids that are stable at high temperatures. It is not yet known, however, why the thermophiles do not grow at lower temperatures. The biochemical and genetical basis of growth at extremely high and extremely low temperatures is still obscure.

Microbes at extreme pH values

Growth of microorganisms is strongly affected by hydrogen and hydroxyl ions. The influence is either direct or indirect via the ionic state and the availability of inorganic ions. Most bacteria prefer neutral or slightly alkaline conditions and do not grow below pH 3 and above pH 10. A few are known to tolerate and grow at pH 0 or pH 11 and above. Under moderately acidic conditions (pH 3 to 5.5) as existing in many lakes, bogs, and forests, the microbial activity is reduced, and degradation of plant materials is slow, especially in anaerobic zones. In acid bogs, specific bacteria are common that are rarely encountered in other habitats. These include *Planctomyces, Bactoderma, Caulobacter, Microcyclus,* and other stalked and prosthecate bacteria. In acidic soils, nitrification by autotrophic nitrifyers and heterotrophs is rather slow. In acidic waters, most allochthonous chemoorganotrophic bacteria die, and yeasts and moulds predominate. The acidic rain and its influence on the ecological conditions in fresh waters and lakes is presently a most serious problem in many parts of the world. Acidic rain, mainly originating from industrial emissions, has not only caused worldwide damage to forests but is also regarded as being responsible for the biological collapse of ponds and lakes. It was ascertained that a great number of the Canadian lakes are biologically dead by the effects of acidic rains due to industrial emissions.

Extreme acid conditions are found in volcanic lakes, geothermal springs, mine effluents, and leach pile effluents. These habitats are dominated by chemolithotrophic sulphur-oxidizing bacteria, the thiobacilli. Many of these iron- and sulphur-oxidizing bacteria have pH optima between 2 and 4, and do not grow at neutrality. In certain instances the pH is decreased to 1.0 or less. *Thiobacillus ferrooxidans* occurring in metal-leaching processes tolerates pH values of 1.0. Acidophilic thermophiles are found in acid hot springs. Representative inhabitants of such environments are *Sulfolobus acidocaldarius, Cyanidium caldarius,* and *Bacillus acidocaldarius.* Other thermophilic acidophiles are *Thiobacillus thermophilica* and *Thermoplasma acidophilum.*

Growth in alkaline environments is restricted to a few fungi, diatoms, cyanobacteria, and members of the genera *Flavobacterium, Agrobacterium, Bacillus,* and *Ectothiorhodospira.* While cyanobacteria are excluded from strictly acidic habitats, they are quite common under alkaline conditions. True alkalophiles do not grow at pH 7 but have their optimum at or above pH 9. There are some alkaline man-made environments such as cement factory effluents with pH values of pH 12. The microflora of such habitats, however, has not yet been intensively studied. Strictly alkaline conditions exist in the soda lakes and the soda deserts. Lakes of the Wadi el Natrun (Egypt) have pH values between 9 and 11. The prevailing microorganisms are cyanobacteria (*Anabaenopsis arnoldii, Spirulina platensis*) and phototrophs (*Ecothiorhodospira* spp.). In soda lakes with high concentrations of sodium, chloride, sulphate, and carbonate/bicarbonate (17%), alkalophilic halobacteria prevail. There is still a lack of information about the organisms inhabiting such extreme alkaline environments.

Since, at low pH, metal ions are more soluble, acidophilic organisms must tolerate higher concentrations of metals, such as Cu and Mo, that are toxic to most organisms in the concentrations present. At high pH, the divalent ions Mg^{2+} and Ca^{2+}, by being precipitated as carbonate, become limited. Therefore, alkaline organisms must concentrate the ions required for growth. The main inhibitory effect under alkaline conditions is the occurrence of free NH_3 accumulating by conversion of NH_4^+. Many microorganisms do not tolerate the presence of free ammonia. The internal pH of microbial cells is near neutrality. This is true for both acidophiles and alkalophiles. Their pH values deviate only for maximally two units. The stability of the internal pH is essential, because many enzymes do not function at pH values where acidophilic or alkalophilic organisms grow. The differences in pH outside and inside the cell are compensated by extrusion of OH^- or H^+. In alkalophilic organisms, the normal pH gradient across the membrane must be reversed. This situation causes problems in the generation of energy according to the chemiosmotic theory. The mechanism of H^+ exclusion in strongly acidophilic bacteria is not yet completely understood; the same is true for the exclusion of OH^- in alkalophilic bacteria. Tolerance of extreme acidic conditions seems to be related to structural features of the cell envelope. It has been shown that *Thermoplasma acidophilum* requires high concentrations of H^+ in order to maintain the structural integrity of the outer cell envelope. This property is not shared by other thermophiles but is specific in this thermophilic and acidophilic organism.

Microbes at low nutrient concentration

Lack of certain mineral nutrients, and particularly of the organic compounds essential for growth of chemoorganotrophs, may occur transiently in many habitats. There are, on the other hand, a variety of habitats that are permanently low in nutrients. Such conditions exist in desert soils, oligotrophic lakes, and oceans. On an average, the concentration of organic C in sea water is extremely low (around 1 mg C/l). Compared to laboratory media, the concentration in sea water is about 1/1000. In various parts of the oceans, the concentration of nutrients may be considerably higher. The local differences are usually related to the decay of plankton organisms or to the high primary productivity in upwell areas.

The ability of an organism to grow at low nutrient concentration is known as oligotrophy. The organisms have to face and to live permanently under starvation conditions. For survival under such conditions, the organisms have developed two strategies. (a) They make most efficient use of the poor nutrient supply; (b) they bridge over a period of insufficient nutrition by the production of dormant stages, and start growing as soon as nutrients become available. Studies of the mechanisms of adaptation to low nutrient conditions have revealed that high-affinity mechanisms work in the assimilation of nutrients. The adapted organisms possess a high substrate affinity expressed by a low substrate saturation constant (K_s). At low concentration, for example, ammonium is assimilated into glutamate via ATP-dependent glutamine synthetase, and glutamate synthase, while at high ammonium levels direct amination of 2-oxo-glutarate (to glutamate) occurs by means of glutamate dehydrogenase. The assimilation of glycerol is at low concentrations mediated by glycerol kinase; at sufficient glycerol supply, assimilation occurs via the glycerol dehydrogenase route. Oligotrophic organisms have been enriched in chemostats under low nutrient conditions, combined with slow dilution rates.

In habitats of low nutrient concentration, solid surfaces play an important role and have a strong effect on colonization resulting in microbial films and layers. The stalked caulobacters are typical low-nutrient organisms. They have developed both an efficient metabolic and structural response to low nutrient conditions. The structural response is connected with the production of holdfast material which allows sessile life at an interface, providing improved nutritional conditions. The production in cyanobacteria of heterocysts is another example of adaptation to specific oligotrophic environments. Cell differentiation thus allows N_2-fixation in a N-depleted habitat under conditions of oxygenic photosynthesis.

Microbes at extreme hydrostatic pressure

Organisms living at the ocean floor and in the deep sediments have to withstand high hydrostatic pressures amounting to several hundred atmospheres. They are known as barophiles. Any microorganism exposed to pressures of more than 300 atm has a reduced metabolic activity. The average hydrostatic pressure on the ocean floor, however, is almost 400 atm. For a long time it has been a matter of debate whether truly barophilic bacteria exist. By definition, such barophilic organisms should require high pressure for growth. Barotolerant organisms, on the other hand, are characterized by their ability to tolerate high pressures, although preferring growth at normal pressure. Studies with special pressure chambers have revealed that there are no true barophiles among the planktonic bacteria. There is much evidence, however, that true barophilic bacteria exist in the guts of deep sea animals. Because of the methodological difficulties in studies on deep-sea microorganisms, our present knowledge is still limited.

146   *The natural environments of microorganisms*

Further reading

Books
General environmental microbiology

Aaronson, S. (1970). *Experimental Microbial Ecology*. London: Academic Press.
Alexander, M. (1971). *Microbial Ecology*. New York: John Wiley & Sons.
Atlas, R. M. & Bartha, R. (1981). *Microbial Ecology: Fundamentals and Applications*. Massachusetts: Addison–Wesley.
Brock, T. D. (1966). *Principles of Microbial Ecology*. Englewood Cliffs, N.J.: Prentice–Hall.
Burns, R. G. & Slater, J. H. (eds) (1982). *Experimental Microbial Ecology*. Oxford, London, Edinburgh, Boston, Melbourne: Blackwell Scientific Publications.
Campbell, R. (1983). *Microbial Ecology*, 2nd edn Oxford, London, Edinburgh, Boston, Melbourne: Blackwell Scientific Publications.
Edmonds, P. (1978). *Microbiology – An Environmental Perspective*. New York: Macmillan.
Ellwood, D. C., Hedger, J. N., Latham, M. J., Lynch, J. M. & Slater, J. H. (eds) (1980). *Contemporary Microbial Ecology*. London: Academic Press.
Grant, W. D. & Long, P. E. (1981). *Environmental Microbiology*. Glasgow, London: Blackie.
Klug, M. J. & Reddy, C. A. (eds) (1984). *Current Perspectives in Microbial Ecology*. Washington, D.C.: American Society for Microbiology.
Laskin, A. I. & Lechevalier, H. (eds) (1974). *Microbial Ecology*. Boca Raton, Florida: CRC Press Inc.
Loutit, M. & Miles, J. A. R. (eds) (1978). *Microbial Ecology*. Berlin: Springer–Verlag.
Lynch, J. M. & Poole, N. J. (eds) (1979). *Microbial Ecology: A Conceptual Approach*. Oxford, London, Edinburgh, Melbourne: Blackwell Scientific Publications.
Marshall, K. C. (1976). *Interfaces in Microbial Ecology*. Cambridge, Mass: Harvard University Press.
Mitchell, R. (1974). *Introduction to Environmental Microbiology*. Englewood Cliffs, N.J.: Prentice–Hall.
Odum, E. P. (1971). *Fundamentals of Ecology*, 3rd edn Philadelphia, London: Saunders.
Russel, A. D. & Fuller, R. (1979). *Cold Tolerant Microbes in Spoilage and the Environment*. London: Academic Press.

Terrestrial environments

Alexander, M. (1977). *Introduction to Soil Microbiology*, 2nd edn New York: John Wiley & Sons.
Swift, M. J., Heal, O. W. & Anderson, J. M. (1979). *Decomposition in Terrestrial Ecosystems*, Studies in Ecology, 5. Oxford: Blackwell.

Aquatic environments

Cairns, J. (ed.) (1977). *Aquatic Microbial Communities*. New York, London: Garland Publications.
Holm-Hansen, O., Bolis, L. & Gilles, R. (eds) (1984). *Marine Phytoplankton and Productivity*. Berlin: Springer–Verlag.
Levinton, J. S. (1982). *Marine Ecology*. Englewood Cliffs, N.J.: Prentice–Hall.
Morris, I. (1980). *The Physiological Ecology of Phytoplankton*. Oxford: Blackwell Scientific Publications.
Moss, B. (1980). *Ecology of Fresh Waters*. Oxford: Blackwell Scientific Publications.

Raymont, J. E. G. (1980). *Plankton and Productivity in the Oceans*. 2nd edn Oxford: Pergamon Press.

Rheinheimer, G. (ed.) (1977). *Microbial Ecology of a Brackish Water Environment*. Berlin: Springer–Verlag.

Rheinheimer, G. (1980). *Aquatic Microbiology*, 2nd edn Chichester, London: John Wiley & Sons.

Sieburth, J. McN. (1979). *Sea Microbes*. New York: Oxford University Press.

Skinner, F. A. & Shewan, J. M. (eds) (1977). *Aquatic Microbiology*, Society for Applied Bacteriology Symposium Series, 6. London: Academic Press.

Extreme environments

Brock, T. D. (1978). *Thermophilic Microorganisms and Life at High Temperatures*. New York: Springer–Verlag.

Gould, G. W. & Corry, J. E. L. (eds) (1980). *Microbial Growth and Survival in Extremes of Environment*, Society for Applied Bacteriology Technical Series, 15. London: Academic Press.

Heinrich, M. R. (ed.) (1976). *Extreme Environments: Mechanisms of Microbial Adaptation*. New York: Academic Press.

Kushner, D. J. (ed.) (1978). *Microbial Life in Extreme Environments*. London: Academic Press.

Shilo, M. (ed.) (1979). *Strategies of Microbial Life in Extreme Environments*, Dahlem Conference Report. Weinheim, New York: Verlag Chemie.

Articles
General environmental microbiology

Brown, A. D. (1976). Microbial water stress. *Bacteriological Reviews*, **40**, 803–46.

Griffin, D. M. & Luard, G. J. (1979). Water stress and microbial ecology. In *Strategies of Microbial Life in Extreme Environments*, ed. M. Shilo, Dahlem Conference Report, **13**, pp. 49–64. Weinheim, New York: Verlag Chemie.

Kjelleberg, S., Humphrey, B. A. & Marshall, K. C. (1983). Initial phases of starvation and activity of bacteria at surfaces. *Applied and Environmental Microbiology*, **46**, 978–84.

Kuznetsov, S. I., Dubinina, G. A. & Lapteva, N. A. (1979). Biology of oligotrophic bacteria. *Annual Review of Microbiology*, **33**, 377–88.

Last, F. T. & Warren, R. C. (1972). Non-parasitic microbes colonizing green leaves: their form and functions. *Endeavour*, **31**, 143–50.

Marshall, K. C. (1980). Reactions of microorganisms, ions and macromolecules at interfaces. In *Contemporary Microbial Ecology*, eds. D. C. Ellwood, J. N. Heger, M. J. Latham, J. M. Lynch & J. H. Slater, pp. 93–106. London: Academic Press.

Pfaender, F. K. & Swatek, F. E. (1970). Interenvironmental transfer of microorganisms on the exterior surfaces of jet aircraft. *Applied Microbiology*, **20**, 227–32.

Poindexter, J. S. (1981). Oligotrophy: feast and famine existence. *Advances in Microbial Ecology*, **5**, 63–89.

Schlegel, H. G. & Jannasch, H. W. (1981). Prokaryotes and their habitats. In *The Prokaryotes, a Handbook of Habitats, Isolation, and Identification of Bacteria*, eds M. P. Starr, H. Stolp, H. G. Trüper, A. Balows & H. G. Schlegel, pp. 43–82. New York: Springer–Verlag.

Von Sprockhoff, H. (1980). Zur Tenazität von Chlamydien und *Coxiella burnetii*. Survival capacity of chlamydiae and *Coxiella burnetii* under environmental conditions. *Deutsche Tierärztliche Wochenschrift*, **87**, 273–5.

148   The natural environments of microorganisms

Terrestrial environments

Bewley, R. J. F. & Stotzky, G. (1983). Simulated acid rain (H_2SO_4) and microbial activity in soil. *Soil Biology and Biochemistry*, 15, 425–9.

Crozat, Y., Cleyet-Marel, J. C., Giraud, J. J. & Obaton, M. (1982). Survival rates of *Rhizobium japonicum* populations introduced into different soils. *Soil Biology and Biochemistry*, 14, 401–5.

Fuller, W. H. & Hanks, K. (1982). Distribution of *Azotobacter* in arid soils. *Plant and Soil*, 64, 355–61.

Heal, O. W. & Ineson, P. (1984). Carbon and energy flow in terrestrial ecosystems: relevance to microflora. In *Current Perspectives in Microbial Ecology*, eds M. J. Klug & C.A. Reddy, pp. 394–404. Washington, D.C.: American Society for Microbiology.

Kanazawa, S. & Filip, Z. (1986). Distribution of microorganisms, total biomass, and enzyme activities in different particles of brown soil. *Microbial Ecology*, 12, 205–15.

Leonardopoulos, J., Papakonstantinou, A., Kourti, H. & Papavassiliou, J. (1980). Survival of shigellae in soil. *Zentralblatt für Bakteriologie, Mikrobiologie und Hygiene, I Abt. B*, 171, 459–65.

Lynch, J. M. (1979). The terrestrial environment. In *Microbial Ecology: A Conceptual Approach*, eds J. M. Lynch & N. J. Poole, pp. 67–91. Oxford, London, Edinburgh, Melbourne: Blackwell Scientific Publications.

O'Brien, B. J. (1984). Soil organic carbon fluxes and turnover rates estimated from radiocarbon enrichments. *Soil Biology and Biochemistry*, 16, 115–20.

Papaconstantinou, A. T., Leonardopoulos, J. G. & Papavassiliou, J. T. (1981). Survival of *Proteus* and *Providencia* strains in soil. *Zentralblatt für Bakteriologie, Mikrobiologie und Hygiene, I Abt. C.*, 2, 362–4.

Paul, E. A. & Voroney, R. P. (1980). Nutrient and energy flows through soil microbial biomass. In *Contemporary Microbial Ecology*, eds D. C. Ellwood, J. N. Hedger, M. J. Latham, J. M. Lynch & J. H. Slater, pp. 215–38. London: Academic Press.

Platz, S. (1981). Modellversuche zur Persistenz von Salmonellen auf landwirtschaftlichen Nutzflächen. (Studies on Survival of Salmonellae on agricultural areas). *Zentralblatt für Bakteriologie, Mikrobiologie und Hygiene, I Abt. B*, 173, 452–6.

Rodriguez-Kabana, R., Godoy, G., Morgan-Jones, G. & Shelby, R. A. (1983). The determination of soil chitinase activity: conditions for assay and ecological studies. *Plant and Soil*, 75, 95–106.

Schaad, N. W. & White, W. C. (1974). Survival of *Xanthomonas campestris* in soil. *Phytopathology*, 64, 1518–20.

Skujins, J. (1984). Microbial ecology of desert soils. *Advances in Microbial Ecology*, 7, 49–92.

Tinker, P. B. (1984). The role of microorganisms in mediating and facilitating the uptake of plant nutrients from soil. *Plant and Soil*, 76, 77–91.

Aquatic environments

Caldwell, D. E. (1977). The planktonic microflora of lakes. *Critical Reviews in Microbiology*, 5, 305–70.

Conrad, R., Aragno, M. & Seiler, W. (1983). Production and consumption of hydrogen in a eutrophic lake. *Applied and Environmental Microbiology*, 45, 502–10.

Federle, T. W., Hullar, M. A., Livingston, R. J., Meeter, D. A. & White, D. C. (1983). Spatial distribution of biochemical parameters indicating biomass and community composition of microbial assemblies in estuarine mud flat sediments. *Applied and Environmental Microbiology*, 45, 58–63.

Fenchel, T. M. & Jørgensen, B. B. (1977). Detritus food chains of aquatic ecosystems; the role of bacteria. *Advances in Microbial Ecology*, 1, 1–58.

Fletcher, M. (1979). The aquatic environment. In *Microbial Ecology: A Conceptual Approach*, eds J. M. Lynch & N. J. Poole, pp. 92–114. Oxford, London, Edinburgh, Melbourne: Blackwell Scientific Publications.

Imhoff, J. F., Sahl, H. G., Soliman, G. S. H. & Trüper, H. G. (1978). The Wadi-Natrum: chemical composition and microbial mass developments in alkaline brines of eutrophic desert lakes. *Geomicrobiology Journal*, 1, 219–34.

Jannasch, H. W. (1978). Microorganisms and their aquatic habitat. In *Environmental Biogeochemistry and Geomicrobiology*, vol. 1, ed. W. E. Krumbein, pp. 7–24. Ann Arbor, Michigan: Ann Arbor Scientific Publications.

Jannasch, H. W. (1984). Microbial processes at deep sea hydrothermal vents. In *Hydrothermal Processes at Seafloor Spreading Centers*, eds P. A. Ronn, K. Bostrom, L. Laubier & K. L. Smith jr pp. 677–709. New York: Plenum Publishing Corporation.

Jannasch, H. W. (1985). The chemosynthetic support of life and the microbial diversity at deep-sea hydrothermal vents. *Proceedings of the Royal Society of London B*, 225, 277–97.

Jannasch, H. W. & Taylor, C. D. (1984). Deep-sea microbiology. *Annual Review of Microbiology*, 38, 487–514.

Jannasch, H. W. & Wirsen, C. O. (1977). Microbial life in the deep sea. *Scientific American*, 236, 42–52.

Karl, D. M., Jannasch, H. W. & Wirsen, C. O. (1977). Deep-sea primary production at the Galapagos hydrothermal vents. *Science*, 207, 1345–7.

McLeod, R. A. (1965). The question of the existence of specific marine bacteria. *Bacteriological Reviews*, 29, 9–23.

Miyamoto, S. (1981). Physiological and ecological studies on marine bdellovibrios. *Journal of the Osaka Medical Center*, 28, 501–20.

Morris, I. (1982). Primary production of the oceans. In *Experimental Microbial Ecology*, eds R. G. Burns & J. H. Slater, pp. 239–52. Oxford, London, Edinburgh, Boston, Melbourne: Blackwell Scientific Publications.

Mountfort, D. O. & Asher, R. A. (1981). Role of sulphate reduction versus methanogenesis in terminal carbon flow in polluted intertidal sediment of Waimea Inlet, Nelson, New Zealand. *Applied and Environmental Microbiology*, 42, 252–8.

Novitsky, J. A. (1983). Heterotrophic activity throughout a vertical profile of seawater and sediment in Halifax Harbor, Canada. *Applied and Environmental Microbiology*, 45, 1753–60.

Novitsky, J. A. (1983). Microbial activity at the sediment-water interface in Halifax Harbor, Canada. *Applied and Environmental Microbiology*, 45, 1761–6.

Phelps, T. J. & Zeikus, J. G. (1985). Effect of fall turnover on terminal carbon metabolism in lake Mendota sediments. *Applied and Environmental Microbiology*, 50, 1285–91.

Pomeroy, L. R. (1984). Significance of microorganisms in carbon and energy flow in marine ecosystems. In *Current Perspectives in Microbial Ecology*, eds M. J. Klug & C. A. Reddy, pp. 405–11. Washington, D.C.: American Society for Microbiology.

Williams, H. N. & Falkler, W. A. jr (1984). Distribution of bdellovibrios in the water column of an estuary. *Canadian Journal of Microbiology*, 30, 971–4.

Williams, H. N., Falkler, W. A. jr & Shay, D. E. (1982). Seasonal distribution of bdellovibrios at the mouth of the Patuxent River in the Chesapeake Bay. *Canadian Journal of Microbiology*, 28, 111–16.

Extreme environments

Baross, J. A. & Morita, R. Y. (1978). Microbial life at low temperatures. In *Microbial Life in Extreme Environments*, ed. D. J. Kushner, pp. 9–71. London: Academic Press.

Baross, J. A., Deming, J. W. & Becker, R. R. (1984). Evidence for microbial growth in high-pressure, high-temperature environments. In *Current Perspectives in Microbial Ecology*, eds. M. J. Klug & C. A. Reddy, pp. 186–95. Washington, D.C.: American Society for Microbiology.

Belkin, S., Wirsen, C. O. & Jannasch, H. W. (1986). A new sulphur-reducing, extremely thermophilic eubacterium from a submarine thermal vent. *Applied and Environmental Microbiology*, **51**, 1180–5.

Cometta, S., Sonnleitner, B., Sidler, W. & Fiechter, A. (1982). Population distribution of aerobic extremely thermophilic microorganisms in an Icelandic natural hot spring. *European Journal of Applied Microbiology and Biotechnology*, **16**, 151–6.

Deming, J. W. & Baross, J. A. (1986). Solid medium for culturing black smoker bacteria at temperatures to 120 °C. *Applied and Environmental Microbiology*, **51**, 238–43.

Fiala, G. & Stetter, K. O. (1986). *Pyrococcus furiosus* sp. nov. represents a novel genus of marine heterotrophic archaebacteria growing optimally at 100 °C. *Archives of Microbiology*, **145**, 56–61.

Friedmann, E. I. & Ocampo-Friedmann, R. (1984). Endolithic microorganisms in extreme dry environments: analysis of a lithobiontic microbial habitat. In *Current Perspectives in Microbial Ecology*, eds. M. J. Klug & C. A. Reddy, pp. 177–85. Washington, D.C.: American Society for Microbiology.

Innis, W. E. & Ingraham, J. L. (1978). Microbial life at low temperatures: mechanisms and molecular aspects. In *Microbial Life in Extreme Environments*, ed. D. J. Kushner, pp. 73–104. London: Academic Press.

Jones, W. J., Leigh, J. A., Mayer, F., Woese, C. R. & Wolfe, R. S. (1983). *Methanococcus jannaschii* sp. nov., an extremely thermophilic methanogen from a submarine hydrothermal vent. *Archives of Microbiology*, **136**, 254–61.

Kristjansson, J. K., Ingason, A. & Alfredsson, G. A. (1985). Isolation of thermophilic obligately autotrophic hydrogen-oxidizing bacteria, similar to *Hydrogenobacter*, from Icelandic hot springs. *Archives of Microbiology*, **140**, 321–5.

Lynch, J. M. & Fletcher, M. (1979). Extreme environments. In *Microbial Ecology: A Conceptual Approach*, eds J. M. Lynch & N. J. Poole, pp. 138–9. Oxford, London, Edinburgh, Melbourne: Blackwell Scientific Publications.

Marquis, R. E. & Matsumara, P. (1978). Microbial life under pressure. In *Microbial Life in Extreme Environments*, ed. D. J. Kushner, pp. 105–58. London: Academic Press.

Marshall, K. C. (1975). Clay mineralogy in relation to survival of soil bacteria. *Annual Review of Phytopathology*, **13**, 357–73.

Morita, R. Y. (1975). Psychrophilic bacteria. *Bacteriological Reviews*, **39**, 144–67.

Rodriguez-Valera, F., Juez, G. & Kushner, D. J. (1983). *Halobacterium mediterranei* spec. nov., a new carbohydrate-utilizing extreme halophile. *Systematic and Applied Microbiology*, **4**, 369–81.

Sandbeck, K. A. & Ward, D. M. (1982). Temperature adaptations in the terminal processes of anaerobic decomposition of Yellowstone National Park and Icelandic hot spring microbial mats. *Applied and Environmental Microbiology*, **44**, 844–51.

Smith, D. W. (1982). Extreme natural environments. In *Experimental Microbial Ecology*, eds R. G. Burns & J. H. Slater, pp. 555–74. Oxford, London, Edinburgh, Boston, Melbourne: Blackwell Scientific Publications.

Stetter, K. O. (1982). Ultrathin mycelia-forming organisms from submarine volcanic areas having an optimum growth temperature of 105 °C. *Nature*, **300**, 258–60.

Stetter, K. O. (1985). Extrem thermophile Bakterien. *Naturwissenschaften*, **72**, 291–301.

Stetter, K. O., König, H. & Stackebrandt, E. (1983). *Pyrodictium* gen. nov., a new genus of submarine disc-shaped sulphur reducing archaebacteria growing optimally at 105 °C. *Systematic and Applied Microbiology*, **4**, 535–51.

Further reading   151

Sullivan, C. W. & Palmisano, A. C. (1984). Sea ice microbial communities: distribution, abundance, and diversity of ice bacteria in McMurdo Sound, Antarctica, in 1980. *Applied and Environmental Microbiology*, **47**, 788–95.

Yayanos, A. A., Dietz, A. S. & Van Boxtel, R. (1979). Isolation of a deep-sea barophilic bacterium and some of its growth characteristics. *Science*, **205**, 808–10.

Zillig, W., Stetter, K. O., Schäfer, W., Janekovic, D., Wunderl, S., Holz, I. & Palm, P. (1981). Thermoproteales: a novel type of extremely thermoacidophilic anaerobic archaebacteria isolated from Icelandic solfataras. *Zentralblatt für Bakteriologie und Hygiene, I Abt. C.* **2**, 205–27.

5

Structure, behaviour and growth of microorganisms as related to the environment

Cell structure and environment
Size and shape

The size of microorganisms varies over a broad range. Their morphology and structure greatly influences their interactions with the environment. The surface-to-volume ratio increases with the decrease in size. The smaller the cells, the better their stability under suspended conditions. Very small cells do not settle in the gravitational field. Settling is influenced by the density of the cell and also by the viscosity of the medium. A counterforce to gravitation is Brownian movement. It is significant only with respect to small bacteria. These settle to the bottom when the gravitational field is increased in the common laboratory centrifuge. Bacteria almost never occur singly. They form chains (*Streptococcus, Lactobacillus*), pairs (*Neisseria*), clusters (*Staphylococcus*), tetrads (*Aerococcus*), packets (*Sarcina*), or sheets (*Lampropedia*). Others produce coryneform structures (*Corynebacterium*), form a network of cells (*Pelodictyon*), stellate aggregates (*Agrobacterium*), or fruiting bodies (myxobacteria). Some bacteria produce filaments. In *Leucothrix mucor*, growth occurs throughout the filament. The basal region is attached to a surface by holdfast material, and the apex forms cells which separate and start colonization on new surfaces. Stalked bacteria, such as *Caulobacter*, go through a development cycle and produce cells differing in shape and function (cp. Fig. 3.3).

Growth and extension of fungal hyphae allows exploitation of the surroundings. In running waters, filamentous algae grow attached to rocks and thus are prevented from drifting away. Bacteria, such as *Thiothrix* and *Sphaerotilus*, produce dense mats which are attached to rocks in running waters.

Rigidity, flexibility

Most prokaryotes have rigid cells and maintain a definite shape. When living in a hypotonic environment, the cell walls counteract the tendency to osmotic shock. They also withstand hypertonicity which occurs in environments with concentrated soluble materials. The halophiles which live in concentrated salt solutions are in an osmotic equilibrium by accumulation of high concentrations of K^+-ions. Some bacteria are elastically flexible (cp. Fig. 3.4). They can bend and flex, and return to their original form. Despite the presence of a rigid murein layer, the spirochetes are flexible. Cell-wall deficient bacteria such as *Mycoplasma* are deformable in shape and form bizarre cellular structures. The chemical nature of cell walls determining cellular rigidity is different with different groups of organisms. The cell wall of bacteria contains murein (peptidoglycan), diatoms and radiolaria form cell walls of silica, foraminiferae and some algae possess walls of $CaCO_3$, while green algae produce walls of cellulose. The cell walls of fungi are composed of glucan, chitin, or cellulose, and those of yeasts contain glucan, mannan, or protein.

Spores, cysts, storage materials

Resting structures such as spores (in eubacteria) and heterocysts (in cyanobacteria) have ecological impact. Such structures resist drying, survive under nutrient deficiencies, and withstand adverse conditions concerning temperature, ultraviolet light, and toxic effects. Only a few groups of bacteria form resting cells that are more resistant to deleterious effects than vegetative cells. The production of such resting stages often occurs when the nutrients are depleted. Typical resting cells are the endospores of bacteria (in *Bacillus, Clostridium, Sporosarcina, Thermoactinomyces, Desulfotomaculum*). The endospores of the bacilli and clostridia are extremely resistant to heat, desiccation, radiation, and chemicals. Bacterial spores are known to survive for hundreds of years. Spore germination is controlled by external factors such as temperature and humidity. Production of exospores in bacteria is rare. It is only known in *Methylosinus trichosporium*, a methylotrophic bacterium. The exospore formed by a process similar to budding lacks dipicolinic acid and, therefore, is not endowed with heat resistance.

Some bacteria form cysts, i.e. thick-walled structures which confer resistance to desiccation and ultraviolet radiation, but not to heat. This type of resting structure is known in *Azotobacter* and in myxobacteria. The cysts of myxobacteria are called myxospores. Coccoid cells of *Arthrobacter* also possess a modest resistance to desiccation.

The survival of bacteria is influenced by the presence of resting stages but also depends on many other factors such as growth conditions and presence of storage materials. Storage products represent a potential of energy allowing survival under conditions of nutrient depletion. The presence of storage products often characterizes the physiological status of a cell in its natural environment. Poorly fed bacteria usually do not produce internal reserves. The nature of the storage material varies with the organism. Starch is produced by algae, oil droplets occur in algae, bacteria, and fungi, PHB (polyhydroxybutyric acid) is exclusively found in bacteria, polyphosphates are formed by bacteria and fungi, and sulphur is deposited in purple sulphur and colourless sulphur bacteria. The storage of polymers does not cause osmotic complications, which would otherwise occur with monomers.

Cell behaviour and environment
Motility

Most aquatic and many terrestrial microorganisms are capable of locomotion. Motility occurs by flagella (bacteria), by contractile fibres of an axial filament (spirochetes), or by gliding. The mechanism of locomotion by gliding, as known in myxobacteria and in *Beggiatoa*, is still obscure. Motile organisms react to light or chemical stimuli. Phototactic and chemotactic reactions indicate that motility has an adaptive value. By phototaxis or chemotaxis, bacteria respond to changes in their environment. Amoeboid motion only occurs in contact with a solid surface; free motility is associated with flagella or cilia. While the molecular basis of motility has been intensively studied, the ecological role of motility has attracted much less attention.

All motile phototrophic bacteria react phototactically. They are capable of responding to differences in light intensity and thus attain a favourable position for photosynthesis. When a phototrophic cell enters an area of insufficient light intensity, the cell reacts with reversal of the flagellar movement and re-enters the area of more intense illumination. Phototactic reactions may have significance for the vertical distribution of phototrophs in lakes. Tactic behaviour may also be related to natural rhythms. It has been found that algae become negatively phototactic at high tide. This causes burying in the mud and thus prevents the cells from being washed out to sea at high tide.

Chemotaxis is a widespread phenomenon. It has ecological importance in so far as the organisms move towards favourable growth conditions and leave areas of adverse conditions. A bacterial cell capable of chemotactic response in an isotropic medium swims straight ahead in one direction, then stops and tumbles, and at random continues to swim in another direction. Movement occurs in almost equal intervals. If a concentration gradient of an attractant is effective, the frequency of tumbling is reduced as long as the cell moves towards the optimum concentration. In negative chemotaxis, the swimming periods are short, and tumbling occurs frequently. By this behaviour, the organism escapes unfavourable situations. Chemotaxis is mediated by the possession of chemoreceptors. A special case of chemotaxis is homotaxis. It describes the locomotion of individual cells which move towards each other and form aggregates. This type of taxis operates in slime moulds. The myxamoebae are known to produce acrasin, an intrinsic factor of the cell which is responsible for the attraction of other amoebae. Homotaxis, which also occurs in myxobacteria, is a phenomenon of population dynamics.

A special type of chemotaxis is aerotaxis. Aerotactically active organisms dispose of a mechanism to find the most favourable O_2 concentration. The aerotactic response can easily be demonstrated in a slide preparation of suspended bacteria. The motile aerophiles accumulate at the rim of the cover glass and in the vicinity of enclosed air bubbles. Anaerobic bacteria, on the other hand, tend to accumulate in the central part under the cover glass.

The isolation of bacteria capable of orientation in a magnetic field has been discovered during the past decade. The cells move towards the south pole of a magnet. It has been shown that these bacteria contain magnetite crystals (ferromagnetic iron oxide $FeOFe_2O_3$) which are located in granula close to the insertion point of the flagella. The cells have an unusually high iron content which amounts to 0.4% of the dry mass. The ecological significance of the magnetotactic response is still obscure.

Buoyancy

An alternative to active movement by flagella is passive movement by buoyancy. This type of locomotion occurs exclusively in aquatic bacteria. The organisms regulate buoyancy through the control of gas vacuoles and thus are able to attain particular depths, where they find favourable conditions for growth. Control of position in water by retaining or releasing gas is known in cyanobacteria, phototrophic bacteria, extreme halophiles, and both aerobic and anaerobic chemoorganotrophs. More than 80 species of gas-vacuolated bacteria have been described. They are most abundant in the anaerobic hypolimnia formed in lakes that are stratified during the summer. In halobacteria, the ability to produce gas vacuoles has been found to be plasmid-coded. Buoyancy is also influenced by the viscosity of the medium, is decreased by rising temperatures, and increased by the production of slimes and oozes.

In *Metallogenium*, an organism present in oligotrophic lakes containing manganese, movement is correlated to the concentration of manganese and O_2. After precipitation of manganese oxide at the cell surface, the cell sinks to the sediment. In this anaerobic environment manganese is reduced and thus made soluble. The reduction is accompanied by an increase in buoyancy causing the cells to go again upward to the aerobic layers. In *Acetobacter xylinum*, the excretion of cellulosic microfibrils allows floating of the organism near the oxygen-rich surface of its habitat.

Attachment to surfaces

Adsorption of cells to surfaces is a well-known phenomenon in biology. Not only microorganisms but also animal and plant cells can attach to glass surfaces or other materials. Bacteria stick to solid surfaces by a variety of mechanisms, (1) attachment by the outer layers of the cell envelope, (2) attachment by a sheath, (3) attachment by a holdfast, and (4) attachment by filamentous appendages (fimbriae, pili). The holdfast usually is a gum-like substance consisting of polymers. The attachment by polymers is widely distributed. Charge interactions between cells and surfaces also cause binding of cells to materials such as clay minerals. Adhesion occurs not only to abiotic surfaces but also to other living cells (host cells or prey cells). The attachment is related to the fine structure of the extracellular polysaccharide material that forms a fibre network. This network is called 'glycocalyx'. For establishing infectious disease, glycocalyx formation is an important structure. It plays a decisive role in the attachment of bacteria to the epithelium of the mucosa. The pathogenesis of a specific disease is often directly related to the ability of the pathogen to adhere to specific host tissues. Thus, *Neisseria gonorrhoeae* adheres to the epithelial cells of the urogenital tract, *Streptococcus mutans* attaches to the teeth causing dental plaques, *Streptococcus pyogenes* has an affinity to the epithelium of the human throat, *Streptococcus salivarius* to the tongue, and *Vibrio cholerae* to the epithelium of the small intestine.

Since nutrients adsorb to surfaces, an increase in microbial cells is observed in stored waters due to the adsorption of organic matter to surfaces. For growth and multiplication of bacteria, a minimum concentration of nutrients is required. This is demonstrated by the observation that sea water containing but a few hundred cells per ml, after transfer into a bottle, causes intense multiplication and high increase in bacteria due to the adsorption of nutrients to the bottle glass. A suspension of bacterial cells (*E. coli* and many others) as a rule does not grow at concentrations of 0.5 to 1 mg of organic compounds per litre. Growth, however, occurs after addition of glass beads. Without glass beads, good growth is only observed at higher nutrient concentrations. This observation proves that solid surfaces by adsorption of organic nutrients may favour microbial growth in environments of low organic matter content. Adhesion to surfaces consequently is an important determinant in natural environments. In rushing rivers, the organisms sticking to solid surfaces have better nutritional conditions. Attachment to solid surfaces may cause mass development as observed with *Sphaerotilus natans, Leptothrix ochracea* and *Crenothrix polyspora. Leucothrix mucor*, which lives in marine habitats, is the counterpart of *Sphaerotilus natans* living in fresh water. This sessile organism has a filamentous mode of life and grows as an epiphyte on seaweed. *Thiothrix nivea* has been found to grow in tufts attached to paddles in the runoff of a sulphur spring. It is a general experience that, in sea water, better microbial growth occurs on floating particles (silt, clay, detritus) due to the nutrients adsorbed to their surfaces. Attachment thus is a means to escape the adverse conditions of a low-nutrient environment. Bacteria that attach to rocks are termed epilithic. They have been shown to be particularly abundant and active in shallow water systems such as streams. The rate and extent of microbial colonization depends on the type of substrate and other environmental factors.

Caulobacters live as epiphytes on solid surfaces. Since the usual laboratory culture media have a high concentration of organic nutrients, adsorption is irrelevant under such conditions. In corrosion of metals, the attachment of organisms to the metal surface plays an important role. The same is true for the weathering of rock surfaces caused by attached bacteria. The epiphytic flora ('Aufwuchsflora') on filamentous algae is favoured both by the adsorption of nutrients to the surface and by cellular excretions. Exudation by plant roots is involved in establishing an epiphytic microflora in the plant rhizosphere. Attachment of microorganisms to the upper parts of terrestrial plants may likewise be favoured by plant excretions. A special form of microbial attachment is the close contact between cytophaga cells and cellulose fibres, which is necessary for expressing cellulolytic activity. The thin cells align according to the orientation of the microfibrils. Rumen bacteria tend to attach to particles from plant materials. Sulphur oxidizers adhere to sulfide minerals. Infection of root hairs by rhizobia requires specific binding of the bacteria to the plant specific lectins (phytohaemagglutinins). This type of attachment depends on the recognition of the corresponding plant. Some bacteria attach to solid surfaces or to other organisms by means of fimbriae, which are filamentous appendages (not flagellae) that are widely distributed among enterobacteria and pseudomonads. Specific attachment of *Pseudomonas tolaasii* to the surface of fungal hyphae of *Agaricus bisporus* has recently been reported. For organisms that attach to abiotic surfaces, to other microbes or host tissues by means of secreted holdfasts, fimbriae, or other surface components, the attachment undoubtedly is an advantage for nutrition and survival. Specific attachment of bacteria to solid surfaces can also be used as a selective factor for isolation (e.g. caulobacters).

Microbial growth as affected by environmental factors
Growth of microorganisms is affected by a variety of environmental factors. From a mixed population, the organisms that are best adapted to the given situation are selectively favoured.

Water regime
Water is an essential prerequisite of life and needed by macro- and microorganisms. Availability of water is the decisive factor. The amount available does not only depend on the water content of a substrate (e.g. soil), but is rather a complex function of adsorptive and solution factors. The adsorptive factors represent a matric effect, the solute factors an osmotic effect. In order to incorporate water, the organism must overcome the forces tending to retain it. There are several ways in which availability of water, as influenced by adsorption and solution factors, can be expressed. Water activity (a_w) and water potential (ψ) are commonly used to characterize the availability of water. Water activity as well as water potential is a measure of the amount of free water in a system. When solutes are dissolved in water, these become more or less hydrated, and the available free water is decreased. The a_w-value is the ratio of the vapour pressure of a given solution (substrate) to the vapour pressure of pure water at the same temperature. It is estimated by measuring the equilibrium relative humidity (RH) of the vapour phase. In meteorological usage, RH is expressed as a percentage, whereas a_w is given as a fraction, $a_w = \text{RH}/100$. A relative humidity of 80% thus equals $a_w = 0.80$. Since temperature affects the amount of water that air can hold, temperature must be specified when measuring a_w-values. In soil microbiology the term 'water potential' (WP; ψ) is preferentially used for characterizing the water regime. Water potential likewise expresses the availability of water; it is, however, defined as the difference in free energy between the substrate (e.g. soil) and a pool of pure water at the same temperature. The water potential can be expressed in units of Pascal

or bar. Similar to suction pressure, values of water potentials are always negative.

The total soil water potential (ψ) is defined as

$$\psi = \psi_p + \psi_s + \psi_m$$

ψ_p: hydrostatic pressure potential; is negligible in terrestrial situations.
ψ_s: solute potential; the potential of water as reduced by the presence of solutes.
ψ_m: matric potential; the potential of water as reduced by the interactions of water/solid and water/gas interfaces. As an energy term, ψ is defined as work per unit of mass (or volume, respectively) and has the dimension joule·kg^{-1}. Since

(1) $1\ J = 1\ N \cdot m$ (J = joule; N = newton), and
(2) $1\ Pa = 1\ N \cdot m^{-2}$ (Pa = pascal)
(3) $1\ J \cdot kg^{-1} = 1\ N \cdot m \cdot kg^{-1} = 1\ Pa \cdot m^3 \cdot kg^{-1} = 10^3\ Pa$
   $= 1\ kPa$ $(1\ kg = 10^{-3}\ m^3)$

It follows that $1\ MPa = 1\ kJ \cdot kg^{-1}$. By definition, $1\ bar = 10^5\ N \cdot m^{-2} = 10^5\ Pa$; then

(4) $1\ MPa = 10\ bar$

There is a direct relationship between ψ and a_w according to

(5) $\psi_{(MPa)} = R \cdot T_K \cdot \ln a_w \cdot V_w^{-1}$
   $R = 8.314\ J \cdot mol^{-1} \cdot K^{-1}$ (molar gas constant)
   a_w = rel. humidity $\cdot 10^{-2}$ (water activity)
   $V_w = 0.018\ l \cdot mol^{-1}$ (partial molal volume of water)
   T_K = temperature (Kelvin)

According to (1) and (2)

$$1\ J = 1\ Pa \cdot m^2 \cdot m = 1\ Pa \cdot 10^3\ l = 1\ MPa \cdot 10^3\ l \cdot 10^{-6}$$
$$= 1\ MPa \cdot l \cdot 10^{-3}\ (1\ m^3 = 10^3\ l)$$

Then, $R = 8.314 \cdot (MPa) \cdot l \cdot 10^{-3} \cdot mol^{-1} \cdot K^{-1}$, and

(6) $\psi_{(MPa)} = \dfrac{8.314 \cdot l \cdot T_K \cdot \ln a_w \cdot mol}{10^3 \cdot mol \cdot K \cdot 0.018 \cdot l}$

$\psi_{(MPa)} = \dfrac{8.314 \cdot T_K \cdot \ln a_w}{18}$

$\psi_{(MPa)} = 0.462 \cdot T_K \cdot \ln a_w$

$$(7) \quad \ln a_w = \frac{\psi_{(MPa)}}{0.462 \cdot T_K}$$

$$a_w = \exp \frac{\psi_{(MPa)}}{0.462 \cdot T_K}$$

Since $0 < a_w < 1.0$, ψ-values are negative. At 25 °C: $T_K = 298.15$ K

$$\psi_{(MPa)} = 0.462 \cdot 298.15 \cdot \ln a_w$$
$$(8) \quad \psi_{(MPa)} = 137.75 \cdot \ln a_w, \text{ and}$$

$$(9) \quad a_w = \exp \frac{\psi_{(MPa)}}{137.75}$$

Example: $a_w = 0.75$ (minimum for growth of halobacteria)
$$t = 25 \,°C$$
$$\psi_{(MPa)} = 137.75 \cdot \ln 0.75 = -39.628 \text{ (MPa)}$$

$$a_w = \exp \frac{-39.628 \text{ (MPa)}}{137.75} = 0.75 \ (a_w)$$

The most important criterion with respect to the water relations of a particular organism is the minimal water potential (WP) permitting growth and multiplication. The majority of bacteria have maximum growth rates at water potentials above -28 bar ($0.980 \ a_w$). Nutrient broth, a widely used growth medium for many chemoorganotrophic bacteria, has a WP of -1.5 bar (a_w 0.999). The various microorganisms vary considerably in their tolerance to decreasing WP. In general, Gram-negative rods are more sensitive to reduced WP than are bacilli, Gram-positive cocci, halophiles, and fungi (Fig. 5.1). The minimal WP found in non-halophilic bacteria is as low as -257 bar (a_w 0.83) tolerated by some Gram-positive cocci. Extreme halophiles living in salt lakes and concentrated brines grow even at WP of -396 bar (a_w 0.75). Minimal water potentials for growth of bacteria and substrates of corresponding values are given in Fig. 5.2. The lowest WP tolerated by a xerophytic fungus is -681 bar (a_w 0.61). Growth of bacteria and fungi under conditions of extreme water stress has been discussed in Chapter 4. Compared to microorganisms, higher plants are much more sensitive to water stress; the permanent wilting point of most plants is around -15 bar.

Since a bacterium growing at low WP due to the addition of a solute must do more work to extract water from the solution it usually grows

a_w	Bar	MPa (25 °C)	Organism
0.96-0.94	−56 to −85	−5.6 to −8.5	Gram-negative rods
0.93-0.90	−100 to −145	−10.0 to −14.5	Bacilli
0.95-0.83	−71 to −257	−7.1 to −25.7	Gram-positive cocci
0.83-0.75	−257 to −396	−25.7 to −39.6	Halophiles
0.80-0.60	−307 to −703	−30.7 to −70.3	Xerophytic fungi
0.71	−472	−47.2	*Aspergillus glaucus*
0.61	−681	−68.1	*Xeromyces bisporus*

Fig. 5.1 Minimum water potential for growth of bacteria and fungi

a_w (25 °C)	Bar	Bacterium	Substrates of responding values
0.999	−1.38	*Spirillum* spp.	Nutrient broth
0.99	−14	*Bac. cereus* var. mycoides	
0.97	−42	*Pseudomonas fluorescens*	
0.95	−71	*Bac. megaterium* *Escherichia coli* most *Salmonellae*	Bread
0.94	−85	*Aerobacter aerogenes* *Lactobacillus viridescens*	
0.93	−100	*Clostridium botulinum* *Bac. stearothermophilus* *Micrococcus lysodeicticus*	
0.92	−115	*Salmonella typhimurium*	
0.90	−145	*Bac. subtilis*	Ham
0.88	−176	*Staphylococcus albus*	
0.86	−208	*St. aureus* *Vibrio costilocus*	
0.85	−224	*Staphylococci*	Salami
0.75	−396	*Halobacterium* *Halococcus*	Salt lake
0.40	−1262		Egg powder
0.30	−1659		Biscuits
0.20	−2217		Milk powder, Cornflakes

Fig. 5.2 Minimum water potential for growth of selected bacteria

more slowly. In many instances, there will be a comparable result with any solute that lowers the WP. However, certain solutes may also have a specific (toxic) effect on the cells. Therefore, two media of the same WP may affect growth to different degrees. For instance, growth of bacteria is less affected by glycerol than by sucrose or NaCl used to adjust the growth medium to the same WP. Microorganisms often respond to excessive water stress by dormant survival. In particular, bacterial spores and cysts are highly resistant to desiccation. Although vegetative cells are much more sensitive, part of a population survives under conditions of low WP in soils. The degree of survival not only depends on the intensity of the water stress but also on the type of soil and on the velocity of the drying process.

In soil, the bacteria mainly develop in water films on the surface of soil particles. Consequently, they are primarily affected by the matric water potential. In small pores, ψ_m is considerably reduced compared to larger pores. At a pore diameter of 100 μm, ψ_m is -0.03 bar; at 10 μm it is -0.3 bar, and at 1 μm it is -3 bar. A drop of ψ_m to values below -0.30 bar (a_w 0.9978) already causes a drastic decrease in the overall respiratory activity. In general, at low WP in soil, the activity of fungi is less affected than that of bacteria. Water stress also restricts movement of the bacteria, and thus impairs metabolism through nutrient deficiencies. When comparing data obtained in pure culture studies and in field investigations, it becomes obvious that laboratory investigations in growth media are of only limited value in understanding the effects of water stress on microorganisms in their natural environments. The metabolic activities of different physiological groups of bacteria are limited at distinct water potentials. Fluctuations in soil water potential is one of the most important factors influencing microbial activity under field conditions. A linear relationship exists between microbial biomass and soil moisture. When studying the influence of relative humidity on the survival of phytopathogenic bacteria, large differences were observed. Survival was better at 34% relative humidity than at 0% or 75%. Coliform bacteria such as *E. coli* and *S. typhimurium*, stored for 14 days in dry soil, were shown to grow again when the soil was moistened.

In fungi, the response to WP is as manifold as in bacteria. Saprophytic growth of *Fusarium roseum* was stimulated by osmotic WP between -10 and -20 bar. After three days of incubation at 25 °C growth was negligible at -140 to -150 bar. It was found that growth decreased linearly with the decrease of the matric water potential from zero to -77 bar. Formation of sporangia by *Phytophthora* occurs within a limited range of

WP. Large numbers of sporangia were formed between −0.3 and −4 bar, whereas few or no sporangia were formed at zero WP or values below −4 bar. *Phytophthora drechsleri* remained viable in soil at WP values down to −40 bar. For *Verticillium dahliae*, the minimum osmotic potential which allowed conidial germination, mycelial growth, and sporulation was between −100 and −120 bar. Colonization by microorganisms of ergot honeydew was largely controlled by the WP. Conidia of *Fusarium heterosporum* did not germinate at less than −110 to −120 bar on sucrose-amended agar, and mycelial growth ceased at −150 to −160 bar. The low water potential of honeydew outside the glumes is a major factor preventing colonization by *Fusarium* and other microorganisms.

In addition to the water potential, the physico-chemical properties of water also affect microbial growth. Since water has a high viscosity it influences the rate of settling of particles and organisms. The higher absorption of water for red than for blue light influences the organismic life in deep-water bodies. The density of water, which is greatest at 4 °C, is related to the stratification of lakes.

Range of temperature
Temperature is one of the most important factors affecting microbial growth. According to their temperature requirements organisms are divided into psychrophiles, mesophiles, and thermophiles. The psychrophilic organisms prefer temperatures below 20 °C. The mesophiles, comprising most bacteria living in soils and waters, grow best at temperatures between 25 and 40 °C. Thermophiles are adapted to higher temperature and prefer temperatures above 55 °C. The temperature requirements of an organism are characterized by defined cardinal temperatures referring to minimum, optimum, and maximum growth temperatures (Fig. 5.3). The temperature range which allows growth at different growth rates spans about 30 to 40 °C for the majority of bacteria. Some have a narrow range of acceptable growth temperature, which may be less than 10 °C (*Neisseria gonorrhoeae, Fusobacterium polymorphum*). Others dispose of a broad range of 40 °C or more (*Bacillus coagulans, B. stearothermophilus*). Optimum and maximum temperatures are usually close together, and often differ only between 3 and 5 °C. When at increasing temperature the maximum is surpassed, the growth rate quickly drops to zero. This is caused by thermal denaturation of the proteins and other vital structures of the cell. The response to temperature and the cardinal temperature values are characteristic features in bacterial taxonomy. At high temperatures, bacteria may require growth

164   *Cell structure, behaviour and growth*

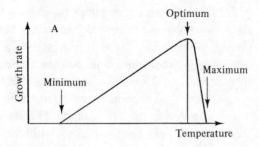

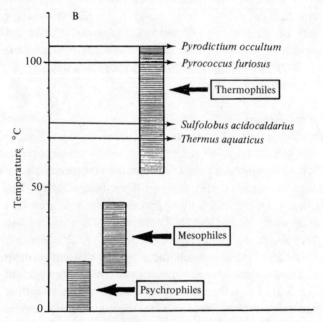

Fig. 5.3 A Cardinal growth temperatures
B Ranges of growth temperature and optimum growth temperatures of some thermophilic bacteria

factors that they do not need at low temperatures. In general, intensity of growth due to increased temperature and metabolic activity are coupled. Coupling, however, may deviate with respect to particular activities.
The relationship between temperature and growth has been subject to intensive investigation. At any temperature at which liquid water exists, i.e. also under subcooled conditions below 0 °C, microbial growth is

possible. In terrestrial environments, the temperature fluctuation with time is broader than in aquatic habitats. In midsummer the upper surface of soils may measure temperatures of up to 40 °C while during winter the same site will be subject to freezing temperatures. Microorganisms have to adapt to the temperature of their environments as they do not have specific means of regulating their body temperature. Bacteria that are used to living below 10 °C have temperature optima considerably higher, usually around 20 to 25 °C. It has been shown that both psychrophilic and thermophilic bacteria, after having been shifted away from the temperatures to which they were adapted, exhibited an increased metabolic activity. This increase indicates that the thermophilic and psychrophilic populations are permanently under thermal stress. Microorganisms associated with warm-blooded animals are adapted to temperatures of between 35 and 40 °C. Thermophilic bacteria involved in composting and silage fermentation are also common in mesophilic environments. Life at extreme temperatures has been discussed in Chapter 4.

Range of pH

Each bacterium can be characterized by the pH range it tolerates and by the optimum pH which allows maximum growth. According to their pH requirements the bacteria are divided into acidophilic, neutrophilic, and alkalophilic organisms. The majority of microorganisms prefer neutrality. Life under extreme pH conditions has been discussed in Chapter 4.

Osmotic conditions

The concentration of solutes outside a microbial cell, i.e. in media or in natural substrates, in general, is lower than the concentration of osmotically active solutes inside the cell. Passive and active processes are involved in the transport of molecules into the cell. Diffusion (small molecules and ions) is a passive process. Facilitated diffusion is mediated by substrate-specific permeases. This type of transport does not depend on metabolic energy, but is controlled by the substrate concentration of the medium. Active transport and group translocation, on the other hand, require energy-dependent substrate-specific permeases which allow entrance of molecules into the cell against a concentration gradient. The permeases are membrane proteins with the properties of enzymes. In many cases they are inducible by the substrate and possess substrate-specific activity. The transport systems ensure constant osmotic conditions inside the cell, irrespective of the osmotic conditions outside.

In natural environments, high osmolarity is often related to high concentrations of NaCl. The osmotic tolerance to NaCl is different and allows division of the organisms into four major groups: non-halophiles, marine organisms, moderate halophiles, and extreme halophiles. Whereas non-halophiles do not require Na^+-ions, the marine bacteria have a specific requirement for NaCl. Extreme halophiles are capable of growing at NaCl-concentrations of up to 36% (wt/vol). Some require NaCl-concentrations of at least 12% for growth. In these organisms, NaCl is needed for the stability and activity of certain enzymes. The requirement for NaCl is reduced in marine and in halophilic bacteria by Mg^{2+} and Ca^{2+} ions. Most bacteria have a rather broad osmotic tolerance, but those organisms that lack the rigid murein structure, such as mycoplasmas and other cell-wall defective bacteria, exhibit an extreme osmotic fragility. The marine microorganisms are adapted to NaCl-concentrations of around 3.5%; they usually grow poorly below and above this concentration. The response of fungi to salinity is comparable to that of bacteria. Tolerance to salinities and ecological distribution of aquatic fungi are directly related: while terrestrial ascomycetes have limited tolerance to high salinity, the marine ascomycetes show a high tolerance to low-salinity conditions. The sporulation of a variety of Fungi imperfecti was shown to have a broad tolerance to high- and low-salinity conditions irrespective of their ecological origin.

Atmospheric conditions

The atmosphere is composed of nitrogen (76%), oxygen (23%), and carbon dioxide (0.03%). In spite of the high concentration of atmospheric oxygen, this biologically important gas often becomes limited in soils and waters. This is due to the low solubility of oxygen and its poor diffusion rate in water. Molecular diffusion into a water body is extremely small if the surface is undisturbed. Since diffusion is proportional to the surface area, the O_2 supply is increased by agitation. Good growth of aerobic organisms in nutrient solutions, therefore, requires agitation and aeration. While strictly aerobic bacteria depend on O_2 supply, facultative anaerobes and strictly anaerobic bacteria grow in the absence of molecular oxygen. In soils, aerobic and anaerobic bacteria grow side by side. Obligate anaerobes are not restricted to O_2-depleted habitats such as mud or the intestinal tract, but also occur in seemingly aerobic locations. This fact can be explained by the existence of microenvironments and the close association of anaerobes with oxygen-consuming bacteria. The occurrence of O_2 in nature at concentrations higher than in air or in air-saturated water is rare. In blooms of cyanobacteria and algal mats near the water surface, bubbles of O_2 may occur. Under such conditions, epiphytic bacteria may become exposed to concentrations of oxygen higher than in equilibrium with the air. Such bacteria tolerate oxygen concentrations up to 40%. At 100% oxygen, growth is usually suppressed. If atmospheric oxygen gets access to formerly anaerobic environments, the obligate anaerobic bacteria are inhibited due to the lack of defence mechanisms that protect against the deleterious effects of oxygen. The sensitivity is primarily due to the absence of catalase and superoxide dismutase.

CO_2, which is rather limited in the atmosphere (0.03%), in contrast to molecular oxygen, is highly soluble in water. Provision of CO_2 is necessary for photolithotrophs and chemolithotrophs that assimilate CO_2 via the Calvin cycle. Some chemoorganotrophs such as *Brucella* and *Neisseria* require higher concentrations of CO_2 (up to 10% v/v) for cultivation. They incorporate CO_2 by means of anaplerotic reactions, e.g. the production of oxaloacetate from phosphoenolpyruvate and CO_2.

Oxidation–reduction potential

The oxidation–reduction potential (ORP) is a quantitative measure of the tendency of chemical compounds or elements to donate or accept electrons. It refers to the normal hydrogen electrode (pH = 1.0; partial pressure of H_2 = 1 bar) which is defined to have zero potential. ORP is strongly influenced by the H^+ concentration. The respiratory chain is composed of a sequence of redox systems that oscillate between the oxidized and the reduced state. In biological systems the redox potential is mainly controlled by the oxygen concentration. A system that is in equilibrium with the partial O_2 pressure of 1 bar, has a redox potential at pH 7 and 25 °C of about +0.8 volt. While surface waters measure potentials around +0.5 volt, the redox potential of reducing sediments is about zero. Growth of strict anaerobes is only possible at low oxidation–reduction potentials.

Light and radiation

Light and radiation of the sun is the primary energy source of the living world. The pigments involved in photosynthesis absorb radiation at specific wavelengths. Microbial pigments of ecological interest are the chlorophylls, phycobilins, and carotenoids. In strict anaerobes, carotenoids are uncommon. Carotenoid pigments act as photoprotective agents. It has been shown that carotenoidless mutants of pigmented bacteria are quickly killed on exposure to sunlight. This effect is not observed when irradiation occurs in the absence of air. Killing is known to be caused by photooxidation which requires both light and O_2. During exposure to light, bacterial cells become affected by oxygen if pigments are present which function as photosensitizers. The product of this reaction is singlet-state oxygen, a powerful oxidant. By the action of certain pigments (e.g. carotenoids), singlet-state oxygen is quenched, and the organism is protected from photodynamic death. In phototrophic bacteria, bacteriochlorophyll acts as a photosensitizer. The effects of photooxidation, however, are prevented by the action of carotenoids and other pigments. Also in non-phototrophic bacteria, carotenoids protect the cell from the effects of photosensitizing components. For bacteria which in their natural environments are exposed to high light intensities, the protective action of carotenoids against singlet oxygen has ecological significance. Whether common pigments such as pyocyanin, violacein, and prodigiosin, are involved in compensating photooxidation, is still unknown.

The spectral absorption of green algae, cyanobacteria, purple bacteria and green bacteria is different and characteristic for each group. The absorption peaks of the green and purple bacteria correspond to wavelengths at which algae do not absorb. This demonstrates that different photosynthetic organisms use different wavelengths for photosynthesis. In deep waters and at the surface of muds bacterial photosynthesis is possible because of the complementarity of pigment absorption in the algae living in the upper regions and the phototrophic bacteria. The phototrophs use the light which the algae allow to pass (far-red and infra-red).

Further reading

Books

Berkeley, R. C. W., Lynch, J. M., Melling, J., Rutter, P. R. & Vincent, B. (eds) (1980). *Microbial Adhesion to Surfaces.* Chichester: Ellis Horwood.

Bitton, G. & Marshall, K. C. (eds) (1980). *Adsorption of microorganisms to surface.* New York: Wiley–Interscience.

Boedeker, E. C. (ed.) (1984). *Attachment of Organisms to the Gut Mucosa,* vol. I and II. Boca Raton, Florida: CRC Press. Inc.

Goldman, R. (ed.) (1976). *Cell motility.* Cold Spring Harbor, N.Y.: Cold Spring Harbor Laboratory.

Hazelbauer, G. L. (ed.) (1978). *Taxis and behavior.* New York: Chapman & Hall.

Horikoshi, K. & Akiba, T. (1982). *Alkalophilic microorganisms.* New York: Springer–Verlag.

Marshall, K. C. (ed.) (1985). *Microbial Adhesion and Aggregation*, Dahlem Workshop Reports, vol. 31. New York, Heidelberg: Springer–Verlag.
Savage, D. C. & Fletcher, M. (eds) (1985). *Bacterial Adhesion. Mechanisms and Physiological Significance*. New York: Plenum Press.

Articles

Cell structure and environment
Doetsch, R. N. & Sjoblad, R. D. (1980). Flagellar structure and function in eubacteria. *Annual Review of Microbiology*, **34**, 69–108.
Gray, T. R. G. (1976). Survival of vegetative microbes in soil. In *The Survival of Vegetative Microbes*, eds T. R. G. Gray & J. R. Postgate, pp. 327–64. London: Cambridge University Press.
Petras, S. F. & Casida, L. E. jr (1985). Survival of *Bacillus thuringiensis* spores in soil. *Applied and Environmental Microbiology*, **50**, 1496–501.
Poindexter, J. S. (1984). Role of prostheca development in oligotrophic aquatic bacteria. In *Current Perspectives in Microbial Ecology*, eds M. J. Klug & C. A. Reddy, pp. 33–40. Washington, D.C.: American Society for Microbiology.

Cell behaviour and environment

Absolom, D. R., Lamberti, F. V., Policova, Z., Zingg, W., Van Oss, C. J. & Neumann, A. W. (1983). Surface thermodynamics of bacterial adhesion. *Applied and Environmental Microbiology*, **46**, 90–7.
Armstrong, R. E., Hayes, P. K. & Walsby, A. E. (1983). Gas vacuole formation in hormogonia of *Nostoc muscorum*. *Journal of General Microbiology*, **128**, 263–70.
Bayer, E. A., Kenig, R. & Lamed, R. (1983). Adherence of *Clostridium thermocellum* to cellulose. *Journal of Bacteriology*, **156**, 818–27.
Blakemore, R. P. (1975). Magnetotactic bacteria. *Science*, **190**, 377–9.
Blakemore, R. P. (1982). Magnetotactic bacteria. *Annual Review of Microbiology*, **36**, 217–38.
Blakemore, R. P., Frankel, R. B. & Kalmijn, A. J. (1980). South seeking magnetotactic bacteria in the southern hemisphere. *Nature*, **286**, 384–5.
Brooker, B. E. & Fuller, R. (1975). Adhesion of lactobacilli to the chicken crop epithelium. *Journal of Ultrastructure Research*, **52**, 21–31.
Burchard, R. P. (1981). Gliding motility of prokaryotes: ultrastructure, physiology, and genetics. *Annual Review of Microbiology*, **35**, 497–529.
Burns, R. G. (1979). Interactions of micro-organisms, their substrates and their products with soil surfaces. In *Adhesion of Micro-organisms to Surfaces*, eds D. C. Ellwood, J. N. Hedger, M. J. Latham, J. M. Lynch & J. H. Slater, pp. 109–38. London: Academic Press.
Burns, R. G. (1980). Microbial adhesion to soil surfaces: consequences for growth and enzyme activities. In *Microbial Adhesion to Surfaces*, eds R. C. W. Berkeley, J. M. Lynch, J. Melling, P. R. Rutter & B. Vincent, pp. 249–62. Chichester: Ellis Horwood.
Busscher, H. J., Weerkamp, A. H., Van der Mei, H. C., Van Pelt, A. W. J., De Jong, H. P. & Arends, J. (1984). Measurement of the surface free energy of bacterial cell surfaces and its relevance for adhesion. *Applied and Environmental Microbiology*, **48**, 980–3.
Caldwell, D. E. & Lawrence, J. R. (1986). Growth kinetics of *Pseudomonas fluorescens* microcolonies within the hydrodynamic boundary layers of surface microenvironments. *Microbial Ecology*, **12**, 299–312.
Chet, I. & Mitchell, R. (1976). Ecological aspects of microbial chemotactic behavior. *Annual Review of Microbiology*, **31**, 221–39.

Dazzo, F. B. (1984). Attachment of nitrogen-fixing bacteria to plant roots. In *Current Perspectives in Microbial Ecology*, eds M. J. Klug & C. A. Reddy, pp. 130–5. Washington, D.C.: American Society for Microbiology.

Fletcher, M. & McEldowney, S. (1984). Microbial attachment to nonbiological surfaces. In *Current Perspectives in Microbial Ecology*, eds M. J. Klug & C. A. Reddy, pp. 124–9. Washington, D.C.: American Society for Microbiology.

Gibbons, R. J. & Van Houte, J. (1975). Bacterial adherence in oral microbial ecology. *Annual Review of Microbiology*, **29**, 19–44.

Hastings, J. W. & Nealson, K. H. (1977). Bacterial bioluminescence. *Annual Review of Microbiology*, **31**, 549–95.

Jones, G. W. (1984). Mechanisms of the attachment of bacteria to animal cells. In *Current Perspectives in Microbial Ecology*, eds M. J. Klug & C. A. Reddy, pp. 136–43. Washington, D.C.: American Society for Microbiology.

Kennedy, M. J. & Lawless, J. G. (1985). Role of chemotaxis in the ecology of denitrifiers. *Applied and Environmental Microbiology*, **49**, 109–14.

Konopka, A. (1984). Effect of light-nutrient interactions on buoyancy regulation by planktonic cyanobacteria. In *Current Perspectives in Microbial Ecology*, eds M. J. Klug & C. A. Reddy, pp. 41–8. Washington, D.C.: American Society for Microbiology.

Koshland, D. E. jr (1979). Bacterial chemotaxis. In *The Bacteria*, vol. 7, eds. J. R. Sokatch & L. N. Ornston, pp. 111–68. New York: Academic Press.

Macnab, R. M. & Aizawa, S.-I. (1984). Bacterial motility and the bacterial flagellar motor. *Annual Review of Biophysics and Bioengineering*, **13**, 51–83.

Mett, H., Kloetzlen, L. & Vosbeck, K. (1983). Properties of pili from *Escherichia coli* SS142 that mediate mannose-resistant adhesion to mammalian cells. *Journal of Bacteriology*, **153**, 1038–44.

Mills, A. L. & Maubrey, R. (1981). Effect of mineral composition on bacterial attachment to submerged rock surfaces. *Microbial Ecology*, **7**, 315–22.

Nealson, K. H. & Hastings, J. W. (1979). Bacterial bioluminescence: its control and ecological significance. *Microbiological Reviews*, **43**, 496–518.

Preece, T. F. & Wong, W. C. (1982). Quantitative and scanning electron microscope observations on the attachment of *Pseudomonas tolaasii* and other bacteria to the surface of *Agaricus bisporus*. *Physiological Plant Pathology*, **21**, 251–7.

Pringle, J. H. & Fletcher, M. (1986). Adsorption of bacterial surface polymers to attachment substrate. *Journal of General Microbiology*, **132**, 743–9.

Salas, S. D. & Geesey, G. G. (1983). Surface attachment of a sediment isolate of *Enterobacter cloacae*. *Microbial Ecology*, **9**, 307–15.

Simon, M. (1985). Specific uptake rates of amino acids by attached and free-living bacteria in a mesotrophic lake. *Applied and Environmental Microbiology*, **49**, 1254–9.

Thomas, R. H. & Walsby, A. E. (1985). Buoyancy regulation in a strain of *Microcystis*. *Journal of General Microbiology*, **131**, 799–809.

Vesper, S. J. & Bauer, W. D. (1986). Role of pili (fimbriae) in attachment of *Bradyrhizobium japonicum* to soybean roots. *Applied and Environmental Microbiology*, **52**, 134–41.

Walsby, A. E. (1977). The gas vacuoles of blue-green algae. *Scientific American*, **237**, 90–7.

Environmental factors affecting growth

Bayley, S. T. & Morton, R. A. (1978). Recent developments in the molecular biology of extremely halophilic bacteria. *CRC Critical Reviews in Microbiology*, **6**, 151–205.

Brock, T. D. (1971). Microbial growth rates in nature. *Bacteriological Reviews*, **35**, 39–58.

Brown, A. D. (1976). Microbial water stress. *Bacteriological Reviews*, **40**, 803–46.

Griffin, D. M. (1982). Water and microbial stress. *Advances in Microbial Ecology*, **5**, 91–136.

Hellebust, J. A. (1985). Mechanisms of response to salinity in halotolerant microalgae. *Plant and Soil*, **89**, 69–81.

Imhoff, J. F. & Rodriguez-Valera, F. (1984). Betaine is the main compatible solute of halophilic eubacteria. *Journal of Bacteriology*, **160**, 478–9.

Jannasch, H. W. (1969). Estimations of bacterial growth rates in natural waters. *Journal of Bacteriology*, **99**, 156–60.

Jannasch, H. W. & Wirsen, C. O. (1977). Microbial life in the deep sea. *Scientific American*, **236**, 42–52.

Jannasch, H. W. & Wirsen, C. O. (1977). Retrieval of concentrated and undecompressed microbial populations from the deep sea. *Applied and Environmental Microbiology*, **33**, 642–6.

Krinsky, N. I. (1976). Cellular damage initiated by visible light. In *The Survival of Vegetative Microbes*, eds T. R. G. Gray & J. R. Postgate, pp. 209–39. New York: Cambridge University Press.

Kröckel, L. & Stolp, H. (1984). Influence of soil water potential on respiration and nitrogen fixation of *Azotobacter vinelandii*. *Plant and Soil*, **79**, 37–49.

Kröckel, L. & Stolp, H. (1985). Influence of oxygen on denitrification and aerobic respiration in soil. *Biology and Fertility of Soils*, **1**, 189–93.

Kröckel, L. & Stolp, H. (1986). Influence of the water regime on denitrification and aerobic respiration in soil. *Biology and Fertility of Soils*, **2**, 15–21.

Lodhi, M. A. K. (1982). Effects of H ion on ecological systems: effects on herbaceous biomass, mineralization, nitrifiers and nitrification in a forest community. *American Journal of Botany*, **69**, 474–8.

Lund, V. & Goksoyr, J. (1980). Effect of water fluctuations on microbial mass and activity in soil. *Microbial Ecology*, **6**, 115–23.

Mahler, R. L. & Wollum, A. G. (1980). Influence of water potential on the survival of rhizobia in a Goldsboro loamy sand. *Journal of the Soil Science Society of America*, **44**, 988–92.

Moreno, J., Gonzales-Lopes, J. & Vela, G. R. (1986). Survival of *Azotobacter* spp. in dry soils. *Applied and Environmental Biology*, **51**, 123–5.

Morita, R. Y. (1975). Psychrophylic bacteria. *Bacteriological Reviews*, **39**, 144–67.

Padan, E. (1984). Adaptation of bacteria to external pH. In *Current Perspectives in Microbial Ecology*, eds M. J. Klug & C. A. Reddy, pp. 49–55. Washington, D.C.: American Society for Microbiology.

Polonenko, D. R., Mayfield, C. I. & Dumbroff, E. B. (1986). Microbial responses to salt-induced osmotic stress. V. Effects of salinity on growth and displacement of soil bacteria. *Plant and Soil*, **92**, 417–25.

Schnürer, J., Clarholm, M., Boström, S. & Rosswall, T. (1986). Effects of moisture on soil microorganisms and nematodes: A field experiment. *Microbial Ecology*, **12**, 217–30.

Tison, D. L. & Pope, D. H. (1980). Effect of temperature on mineralization by heterotrophic bacteria. *Applied and Environmental Microbiology*, **39**, 584–7.

Wilson, J. M. & Griffin, D. M. (1975). Water potential and the respiration of microorganisms in the soil. *Soil Biology and Biochemistry*, **7**, 199–204.

Yayanos, A. A., Dietz, A. S. & Van Boxtel, R. (1981). Obligately barophilic bacterium from the Mariana trench. *Proceedings of the National Academy of Science, U.S.A.*, **78**, 5212–15.

6

Dispersal of microorganisms and development of microbial populations

In their natural environment many organisms of different systematic categories, representing populations of different 'species', form a natural community. The habitat which is defined by distinct physical and chemical conditions is also known as biotope. The community and the habitat together represent an ecosystem. There are numerous habitats in nature where microorganisms live. Ecosystems can have small or large dimensions. A pond or a lake represents a clearly bordered ecosystem which, within its boundaries, harbours a characteristic community. Because of the multitude of existing species and the multitude of habitats, the ecology of microorganisms is intricate and complex. The ecologist, therefore, looks for general principles that govern the manifold relationships. While autecology tends towards the study of interrelations between one particular species and its environment, synecology is directed towards the study of interrelations among the various species and between the organisms and their environment. Synecology thus is more comprehensive and aims at an understanding of the complex ecosystem in its entirety. An ecosystem can be viewed at the level of individuals, populations, or the community.

In general the environment is heterogeneous, yet within the loosely defined boundaries there are established communities. The composition of such communities in a larger habitat (e.g. soil, lake, skin, etc.) is defined by the physical and chemical characteristics which select for those organisms best adapted and able to exploit the environment. Based on the complex relations to the abiotic and biotic environmental factors, each organism has its specific position in the structure of an ecosystem that determines the existence of the population. This specific position represents the 'ecological niche'. The term niche, in this context, has not a spatial but a functional meaning.

The organisms present in a natural environment are either autochthonous or allochthonous. The autochthonous species are indigenous, permanent, and functional members of the community. Allochthonous forms represent aliens, have been introduced from outside, and are transient members of the community. The allochthonous organisms, on their part, are autochthonous in other habitats. Although most microorganisms are ubiquitous in nature, they are not randomly distributed but exist in defined patterns of distribution. This is obvious in particular with pathogenic bacteria and protozoa affecting men, animals and plants.

Microorganisms are found in all regions of the biosphere. Soils and waters are the primary habitats. It has been estimated that in fertile soils the upper 10 cm contain per ha about 4 tons of bacteria and fungi, i.e. 400 g/m^2. The numbers of microorganisms inhabiting 1 g of fertile soil, roughly estimated, are 10^8 bacteria, 10^4 fungi (spores and pieces of hyphae), 10^3 protozoa and 10^2 algae. These figures relate to cultural counts. By direct counting (fluorescence microscopy), the figures are 10 to 100 times higher. There are several reasons for this discrepancy, (a) microscopy also includes dead and nonproliferating cells, (b) a number of colonies may arise from cell conglomerates instead of single cells, (c) not all types of microbes start growing on the substrates used for enumeration.

In soil, the total number of microorganisms decreases with depth. This decrease is mainly related to the lack of organic matter; it is accompanied by a relative increase of anaerobes. The concentration of bacteria at a depth of 1 m usually is around 10^4 to 10^5 cells per g of soil.

As in soil, the concentration of microorganisms in waters varies with the nature of the habitat. Ground water is poor in microorganisms, surface waters of rivers, lakes, and oceans have higher concentrations, and the highest numbers are found in waste waters. In a clear lake, the concentration of microorganisms in the upper layer is about 10^2 microorganisms per ml, whereas the sediment contains 10^4 to 10^5 cells per ml.

The air is not a primary habitat. In 1 m^3 of clean air, usually not more than a few hundred bacteria are encountered. They are associated with dust particles and are brought into the atmosphere by air currents.

The spatial extension of a microbial population, i.e. the colonization of a new habitat, often is a stringent requirement for securing the existence of a species. A great number of individuals is necessary for successful dispersal, and discontinuities in space and time have to be overcome in order to secure continuity. This requirement is accomplished by mechanisms that obviate unfavourable periods, e.g. by the production of resting stages.

Dispersal

Microorganisms are spread in nature by active and passive dispersal. Active dispersal is known in fungi by growth of hyphae, which is limited to short distances. Active dispersal is also possible by motility. This applies to flagellated bacteria, to zoospores of fungi, to flagellated and ciliated protozoa, and to gliding microorganisms. A few organisms have a development cycle in which a motile and a nonmotile phase alternate. *Caulobacter*, for instance, has a sessile and a motile stage (cp. Fig. 3.3). The distances that can be covered by active motility are relatively short. The bdellovibrios, measuring about 1 μm in length, are extremely fast bacteria; they move $\frac{1}{10}$ of a millimetre per second.

Passive dispersal occurs through air, water, and by means of vectors. Microorganisms moved by wind and turbulences can bridge large distances. In dusty air, bacteria, yeasts, spores of fungi, cysts of protozoa, and algae are transported long distances, even at great heights. It has been shown that spores of *Puccinia graminis* or spores of *Peronospora tabacina* are transported over hundreds of kilometres. The air microflora has its origin mainly in terrestrial environments. Dispersal of microorganisms through the air is particularly important for plant and animal pathogens. Air dispersal of bacteria is favoured by the low mass and by structures resistant to drying. Some fungi have developed mechanisms that favour dispersal through the wind (anemochoric dispersal). A special type of active dispersal by ejecting sporangia is known in *Pilobolus* and other zygomycetes.

Passive dispersal through water (hydrochoric dispersal) mainly occurs in rivers. Freshwater lakes and oceans may thus receive inocula from terrestrial environments. The ground water contains much less microorganisms than the surface waters. By vertical movement of water through the soil most microorganisms are retained due to adsorption to soil particles. This process is important for the hygienic condition of ground water used as drinking water supply. Microorganisms that are transported from land into the ocean do not become established because they are not adapted to the special marine environment, and eventually disappear.

Microbial dispersal by animals (zoochoric dispersal) is particularly important in the transmission of disease-causing microorganisms. A variety of pathogens are transmitted by fleas, *Rickettsia* by lice, *Trypanosoma gambiense* (sleeping sickness) by the tsetse fly, *Plasmodium* (malaria) by *Anopheles*, the yellow-fever virus by *Aedes*, a species of mosquito. By conquering the vectors it is possible to reduce or eliminate the disease.

Man has been involved in the transmission of pathogens from one continent to another. Among the phytopathogenic fungi, introduced to Europe from America, were *Phytophthora infestans* (first appearance in Europe 1830), *Plasmopara viticola* (1878), and *Sphaerotheca morsuvae* (1901). *Pseudomonas tabaci*, the causal agent of wild fire in tobacco, first appeared in Europe in 1924. *Erwinia amylovora*, the pathogen causing fire blight in pears and apples, was originally restricted to the USA, appeared in New Zealand in 1919, and was introduced to England in 1958. Since then it has spread to The Netherlands, Denmark (1969), and Germany (1970).

Human dispersal plays an important role in the dissemination of pathogens. Some can survive outside their host for several months (e.g. *Salmonella* and *Vibrio cholerae* in water), while others are extremely susceptible outside their natural habitat (e.g. *Treponema pallidum*, the causal agent of syphilis).

Although most microorganisms are ubiquitous in nature, there are certain organisms that have a geographic preference. Some marine algae are known to occur periodically in defined areas. Many pathogens are bound to the habitats of their hosts, and thus have a fixed geographical distribution (e.g. plant pathogens in coffee trees, or citrus). On the other hand, the area of distribution of a specific pathogen may be smaller than the area of the potential host. This situation applies to leprosy caused by *Mycobacterium leprae*, the sleeping sickness caused by *Trypanosoma gambiense*, and to a variety of other tropical diseases. The nature of the geographic boundaries usually is unknown; in some cases, it is related to the distribution of the appropriate vector.

Development of microbial populations
Colonization and successions
The colonization by microorganisms of a complex organic substrate leads to a sequence of successions which are connected with alterations of the community. The first organisms to attack fresh organic residues are pioneer species which are only transient. In the decay of organic plant materials, phycomycetes often act as pioneers in the decomposition of the more labile carbohydrate polymers and sugars. They decline in numbers as these substrates become depleted, whereupon the succession of another community, often Fungi imperfecti, arises and begins to utilize the more resistant cellulosic fraction. Finally, the climax community of Basidiomycetes arises in response to the remaining lignin portion of the plant residue. At the different stages, also various bacteria and other microorganisms are involved in the process of decomposition.

The nature of colonization depends on the physical and chemical conditions of the habitat. The intestinal flora of a suckling represents a *quasi*-pure culture of *Bifidobacterium bifidum*. The favoured development of this bacterium is related to the presence of N-acetylglucosamin in mother's milk. This compound is essential for synthesis of murein and is required as a growth factor by the bifidobacteria. In the colonization of habitats containing no available organic carbon, e.g. lava fields, cyanobacteria and lichens play a dominating role.

Although many microorganisms have a global distribution, not every species is found in every habitat. New invaders are often excluded from establishing and multiplying because they do not find an ecological niche. The barriers for colonization may be mechanical, as in the case of an egg shell, or chemical as in the examples of long-chain fatty acids on the skin, or lysozyme in tears and in the mucosa. Colonization of a natural habitat and multiplication of a given microorganism are strongly influenced both by biotic and abiotic factors. Among the abiotic factors, temperature, humidity, pH, light intensity, osmotic conditions, redox potential, toxins and other deleterious metabolites produced by other organisms, play a major role. Even in the case of optimal nutritional conditions, the propagation of an organism may be inhibited. The 'ecological amplitude' defines the range and the limits of a selection factor. If the limits of tolerance of the population are surpassed, the organism is unable to establish and grow.

Changes of the microbial community in a given habitat may be caused by two different types of succession, autogenic or allogenic. Autogenic successions are caused by biotic factors, such that the sequence of populations is related to changes caused by the activities of the present populations. A classic example is the production of nitrite from ammonia by *Nitrosomonas*, which allows for the subsequent development of *Nitrobacter* oxidizing nitrite to nitrate. Allogenic successions are caused by abiotic factors. This type of succession often has a cyclic nature and is caused by seasonal changes of temperature, light intensity, nutrients, or other factors.

Population growth

While a single cell increases in mass at an arithmetic rate, a microbial population increases in mass at an exponential rate. A growing population can be regarded as an autocatalytically reproducing system. Growth kinetics has been discussed in Chapter 2.3.

There are differences in growth of unicellular and filamentous microorganisms. Growth of fungus hyphae occurs at the tips of the filaments and is an arithmetic function.

Growth rates or doublings per unit of time differ considerably with the types of organism. As a general rule, the growth rates increase with decrease in cell size. Maximal growth rates (as doublings per day) in pure culture are as follows: green algae 4, protozoa 10, phototrophic bateria 10, cyanobacteria 11, fungi 12, chemoorganotrophic bacteria up to 85. The last figure relates to *Escherichia coli* and equals a doubling time of 17 min. Some treponema have doubling times of more than 30 h. Under natural conditions, the most rapidly growing organism must not necessarily be the most successful. Actually all organisms in a community are successful, otherwise they would not be present. Which organism prevails, in the mixture of different populations, is influenced by a variety of factors in addition to the growth rate. While the limitation of a population in axenic culture is mainly related to the exhaustion of nutrients and the production of toxic metabolites, the population density in open systems such as natural environments is also influenced by other factors, e.g. predation and sedimentation.

A bacterial population cannot be regarded as homogeneous in the narrow sense. It is genetically heterogeneous because of the presence of mutants and variants, and it is also heterogeneous with respect to the physiological status of the individual cells. Even during exponential growth cell divisions do not occur synchronously. Because of the nature of the development of a population, the age of a cell is different from the age of the population.

It has occasionally been observed that single cells do not grow in liquid media although they start growth and form colonies on agar media of the same composition. This phenomenon is probably related to a cooperative action of individual cells. On the solid medium, the progeny of a dividing cell remains together and thus secures conditions necessary for multiplication, while the cells in a liquid medium separate and thus are prevented from cooperation. The growth conditions on a soil particle may be analogous to the growth on a solid agar surface. Another cooperative phenomenon is known from the freezing of bacteria. High population densities can better withstand freezing than low population densities. Possibly, microcolonies on solid surfaces in nature might also survive freezing temperatures better than individual cells in the liquid phase.

Natural selection

Natural selection is an essential element of ecology. Under the specific conditions prevailing in the natural environments over a given period of time, certain representatives are favoured and selected. Not only the members of different species, but also variants and mutants of one and the same species, are exposed to selection pressure. The best adapted organisms finally succeed and dominate. By alteration of a distinctive factor, an organism that was formerly in a minimum position may become the dominating component. The nature of dominance is rather complex, and many biotic and abiotic factors may be involved. In order to explain the dominance of a species and the factors conferring the selective advantage, nutrition and growth kinetics of mixed cultures have been studied. Dominance in nature is often related to competition. In the H_2S-containing zone of lakes, large chromatiae (*Chromatium okenii, C. weissei*) and small chromatiae (*C. vinosum*) are found side by side. Both types coexist, or the large phototrophs dominate. It has been shown that organisms dominating in nature may become suppressed under laboratory chemostat conditions. As the small phototroph has a higher substrate affinity (lower K_s) for H_2S, it has a higher maximum growth rate. In continuous light, most H_2S is consumed by *Chromatium vinosum* leading to overgrowth of that organism. The observed dominance of the large chromatiae in nature is related to the diurnal rhythm of illumination. This example demonstrates that kinetic growth properties are important factors in competition. For the understanding of the ecological behaviour of organisms living together, laboratory studies both with pure cultures and mixed cultures are indispensable.

In certain habitats, the factors, conferring selective advantage are obvious. This applies to temperature resistance of organisms in hot springs, to salt tolerance in salt lakes, or to spore formation in dry localities. Usually, the nature of the selective advantage in a given habitat is less obvious and unknown. The critical property related to selection can be one specific enzyme that allows degradation of a substrate not attacked by the other members of the community. Under other conditions, it may be the concurrence of several physiological properties that allows faster growth and occupation of an ecological niche by a particular organism.

Natural selection from a mixture of organisms operates in enrichment cultures, where it is amenable for study. If the particular properties and requirements of a given microorganism are known, it is possible to construct conditions for its specific enrichment. Enrichment and subsequent isolation of *Azotobacter*, for instance, is possible in a medium containing a suitable carbon source but devoid of combined nitrogen. Under aerobic conditions, N_2-fixing bacteria of the *Azotobacter* type will then develop. Other examples are the enrichment of nitrifying bacteria in a mineral medium containing ammonium, or the enrichment of *Thiobacillus denitrificans* under anaerobic conditions with sulphur or thiosulphate

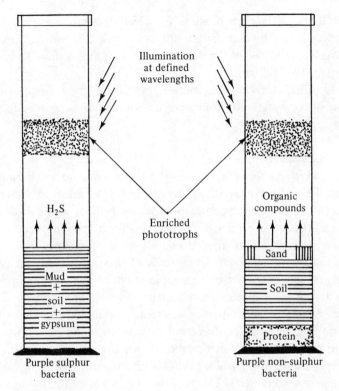

Fig. 6.1 Winogradsky Column for enrichment of phototrophic bacteria

as H-donor and nitrate as the terminal electron acceptor. Successful enrichment, of course, requires the presence of the organism to be enriched in the material used for inoculation. The selection of mutants from a parental population is based on the same principle. Actually, any physiological property can be used in selection.

Interspecific selection refers to the selection of a particular species from a mixture of different species, whereas intraspecific selection refers to the selection of mutants (variants) from a population of one species. Specific abiotic factors of selective value are, in particular, light (quality and intensity), nutrients, growth factors, acidity, pO_2, CO_2-concentration, and osmotic conditions. The control of selection by different wavelengths of light can easily be demonstrated in a Winogradsky column (Fig. 6.1). In the presence of H_2S, enrichment of the green Chlorobiaceae occurs at 720–770 nm, and for the purple Chromatiaceae at 800–900 nm. Under anaerobic conditions with an organic substrate serving as H-donor, rhodospirillae (e.g. *Rhodospirillum rubrum*) are enriched between 800 and 1100 nm. It is even possible to select distinctive species of the Rhodospirillaceae by using different wave lengths: *Rhodospirillum rubrum* is selected at 800–900 nm, whereas *Rhodopseudomonas viridis* is selected at 900–1100 nm.

Intraspecific selection is of practical importance in infectious diseases because of the outgrowth from a population of strains possessing resistance against antibiotics.

Adaptation

Microorganisms have the ability to adapt to environmental changes. This adaptive capacity is the reason for the observed physiological flexibility. In phenotypic adaptation, all cells of a population are involved. This type of change is not genetically conditioned. It is a modification that under altered conditions is reversible. Phenotypic adaptation often is related to the presence of enzymes that are induced by a particular substrate. Another example of phenotypic adaptation is the production of compatible solutes under conditions of low water potentials. In genotypic adaptation, the altered population originates from mutation or gene transfer. Most mutants occurring during growth in a population do not survive because the cells are already optimally adapted. Genotypic adaptation usually becomes effective after a change of the environmental conditions. The presence of an antibiotic, for instance, causes selective development of resistant mutants, and thus leads to a population change. The mutational step to resistance is known to occur independently of the antibiotic.

Further reading

Books

Bazin, M. J. (ed.) (1982). *Microbial Population Dynamics*. Boca Raton, Florida: CRC Press, Inc.

Articles

Atlas, R. M. (1984). Diversity of microbial communities. *Advances in Microbial Ecology*, **7**, 1–48.

Belser, L. W. (1979). Population ecology of nitrifying bacteria. *Annual Review of Microbiology*, **33**, 309–34.

Caldwell, D. E., Malone, J. A. & Kieft, T. L. (1983). Derivation of a growth rate equation describing microbial surface colonization. *Microbial Ecology*, **9**, 1–6.

Federle, T. W. & Vestal, J. R. (1982). Evidence of microbial succession on decaying leaf litter in an Arctic lake. *Canadian Journal of Microbiology*, **28**, 686–95.

Kieft, T. L. & Caldwell, D. E. (1983). A computer simulation of surface microcolony formation during microbial colonization. *Microbial Ecology*, **9**, 7–13.

Slater, J. H. (1979). Microbial population and community dynamics. In *Microbial Ecology: A Conceptual Approach,* eds. J. M. Lynch & N. J. Poole, pp.45–66. Oxford, London, Edinburgh, Melbourne: Blackwell Scientific Publications.
Slater, J. H. (1984). Genetic interactions in microbial communities. In *Current Perspectives in Microbial Ecology*, eds. M. J. Klug & C. A. Reddy, pp. 87–93. Washington, D.C.: American Society for Microbiology.
Swift, M. J. (1982). Microbial succession during the decomposition of organic matter. In *Experimental Microbial Ecology*, eds R. G. Burns & J. H. Slater, pp. 164–77. Oxford, London, Edinburgh, Boston, Melbourne: Blackwell Scientific Publications.

7

Interactions

Types of interactions

Contrary to life in the laboratory, where they are usually kept as pure cultures, microorganisms in nature are associated with other microbes and with macroorganisms. The existence in nature of pure cultures of microorganisms is extremely rare and actually does not exist if related to a larger area. A spatially separated microcolony developing in a microhabitat may be regarded as a 'pure culture'.

The interactions among microbial populations and between populations of microorganisms and macroorganisms are extremely diverse. If 'living together' in its broadest meaning is defined as symbiosis, the variety of interactions can be classified as mutual symbioses or as parasitic symbioses. The mutualistic symbioses comprise both ectosymbioses and endosymbioses. Since all types of mutualistic symbioses possess also certain traits of parasitism, symbiosis can be regarded as a dynamic process of mutual exploitation. Therefore, the terms 'mutualistic symbiosis' and 'mutualistic parasitism' occasionally are used as synonyms.

Microbial interactions with other microorganisms, plants, or animals may be absent, weak or strong. Organisms that live together, but have dissimilar requirements for nutrients or other factors and do not interact, are considered as neutral.

In the range of mutualistic relationships, ectosymbioses are widespread in nature. The symbiont occurs on the external surface of the host or on the external lining of body cavities. This type of association includes the microflora of the rhizosphere and the phyllosphere. It also refers to the symbionts living in the intestine or the rumen. True endosymbioses (in the cytoplasm of a cell) are only known in eukaryotic organisms. Endosymbiotic fungi usually are not completely inside the cell, but act into the interior by means of haustoria from the outside. Ecto- and endosymbiotic relationships have evolved in a vast array of microorganisms, plants, and animals. There is now much evidence that such symbioses have originated from loose associations between different partners. Lichens are the product of the association of algae or cyanobacteria and fungi; mycorrhiza has developed from the association of fungi and plant roots. True endosymbionts usually resist cultivation as pure cultures outside the host. In a number of symbioses the nutritional advantages of the partners are obvious, as exemplified in lichens by the close association of the nonphototrophic fungi and the phototrophic algae.

According to a currently favoured hypothesis, mitochondria and chloroplasts of eukaryotic cells originate from endosymbionts. The mitochondria have descended from aerobic bacteria, while the chloroplasts are thought to originate from cyanobacteria. Since the electron transport chain of mitochondria is very similar to that of *Paracoccus denitrificans*, it has been speculated that this organism may be a present-day descendant of a protomitochondrion. The alga *Prochloron* living in symbiosis with didemnids, on the other hand, has been regarded as a present-day descendant of a protochloroplast of the green algae and higher plants. The endosymbiont hypothesis is supported by the fact that the RNAs of the organelles (mitochondria, chloroplasts) resemble the RNAs of present-day prokaryotes, while the cytoplasmic rRNA of eukaryotic cells is largely unrelated to any prokaryotic rRNA. The rRNA is considered to be highly conserved because of the vital importance that RNA has for the maintenance of the cellular life. For this reason, differences in nucleotide sequences or base modifications in rRNA are regarded as indicating ancient evolutionary divergencies. rRNA comparison at the molecular level thus has become a very effective tool for the elucidation of evolutionary relationships. Another fact supporting the endosymbiont hypothesis is the existence in mitochondria and chloroplasts of DNA and ribosomes of the 70S type.

Parasitic symbiosis is as manifold and versatile as is mutualistic symbiosis. The antagonistic relationships range from competition for nutrients to parasitism and predation. As among microorganisms themselves, the relationships between micro- and macroorganisms may be neutral, beneficial, or antagonistic. Symbionts and parasites may be obligate or facultative. This separation is not stringent but depends on the possibility of its cultivation separate from the host. A formerly obligate parasite becomes facultative if someone succeeds in cultivating the organism on artificial media. From the cultivation of parasites in the laboratory it is not possible to make predictions on the saprophytic growth in nature, where the organism has to compete with other saprophytic organisms. *Salmonella typhi*, the causal agent of typhoid fever, can be cultivated in laboratory but seems to be an obligate parasite in nature.

The organism does not survive in soil and water for longer periods, but dies out. The situation is different with the causal agent of botulism, *Clostridium botulinum*, which is a successful saprophyte in soil. An example of facultative symbionts are the rhizobia that live in association with the host plant but are also successful saprophytes in nature and can be grown in the laboratory.

Microbe–microbe interactions
Metabolic associations

Mutualistic symbioses comprise ectosymbiotic and endosymbiotic associations. Primary forms of ectosymbioses are represented by metabolic or syntrophic associations. Such metabolic interdependencies have sometimes been discovered in cultures presumed to be axenic. A classical example is the original culture of *Methanobacterium omelianskii* which was regarded to be a pure culture of a methanogen, but later was found to be a mixture of two organisms. One (S-organism) produced hydrogen from ethanol, the other (MOH-strain) oxidized hydrogen and produced methane from CO_2 as the terminal e-acceptor. In this system, the phenomenon of interspecies hydrogen transfer was discovered. It represents a metabolic symbiosis with unidirectional substrate supply. But both organisms profit from the syntrophic association. As a pure culture growing on ethanol, the S-organism is inhibited by its own production and accumulation of hydrogen, according to

$$2 \ C_2H_5OH + 2 \ H_2O \rightarrow 2 \ CH_3COOH + 4 \ H_2$$

The methanogen (MOH-strain), by oxidizing H_2, reduces the partial pressure of hydrogen. Thus, both organisms benefit from the syntrophic association. This type of interaction exists in a variety of H_2-evolving and H_2-consuming bacteria. Another example of unidirectional transfer of metabolites is the production of nitrite by ammonia-oxidizing chemolithotrophs. The end product nitrite is the substrate of the associated organism that oxidizes nitrite to nitrate. This type of metabolic mutualistic association is also known as metabiosis. Syntrophic associations occur in many examples. During the decomposition of milk, for instance, bacteria and yeasts cooperate in a syntrophic way. The bacteria produce glucose and galactose from lactose. Subsequently, glucose is fermented with the production of ethanol and CO_2. Since yeasts do not possess β-galactosidase they depend on the preceding action of the bacteria. Another interesting example of metabolic syntrophy is the combined growth of *Mucor ramanianus* and *Rhodotorula rubra* in a growth medium devoid of vitamin B_1 (thiamine), although both organisms depend on that growth factor. By production of the pyrimidine portion of the molecule by one partner and production of the thiazol portion by the other organism, both partners are capable of synthesizing vitamin B_1 when living together. In this type of mutualistic interaction, one organism excretes a precursor used by the other for synthesis of the final product.

A close syntrophic association based on bidirectional transfer of small molecules is operating in a mixed culture of sulphate reducing and hydrogen sulphide oxidizing bacteria. In the presence of sulphate and organic acids in anaerobic environments, sulphate is converted into hydrogen sulphide by dissimilatory sulphate reduction (sulphate respiration). The hydrogen sulphide is used as e-donor in anoxic photosynthesis of phototrophic bacteria, which on their part produce sulphate by oxidation of the hydrogen sulphide. Such type of metabolic association, for instance, exists between *Desulfovibrio* and *Chromatium*. A similar association is known between sulphur reducing and hydrogen sulphide-oxidizing bacteria. During oxidation of ethanol *Desulfuromonas acetoxidans* reduces elemental sulphur to hydrogen sulphide. This in turn is oxidized by the green phototroph *Chlorobium*, resulting in the production of elemental sulphur. By direct coupling of the e-donor and the e-acceptor, both organisms grow in that interdependent syntrophic association.

The fact that certain bacteria cannot be grown or grow poorly in axenic culture may be related to their natural growth in syntrophic association. For a better understanding of the function of microorganisms in their natural habitats, it is, therefore, indispensable to do experimental studies with mixed cultures. It is a well-established fact that mixed populations have a greater potential in the decomposition of organic materials. Cellulose, for instance, is digested more effectively by mixed cultures than by pure cultures. The nature of such combined action is usually unknown. It may be related to syntrophy, to an alteration of the physicochemical environment, or to other factors. The destruction of toxic products may also be involved.

Ectosymbiotic relationships among microorganisms are characterized by close physical contact. The association of cyanobacteria with flagellates and with spirillae, and the occurrence of spirochetes on protozoa are two well-known examples. True microbial endosymbionts are only found in the eukaryotes. They occur intracellularly in the cytoplasm or the nucleus. Endosymbiotic fungi usually do not enter the cell completely but act via haustoria. Bacteria are known to occur as endosymbionts of amoebae, flagellates, ciliates, and sporozoa. These symbionts usually have resisted cultivation outside the host. For this reason, they have not been studied to a great extent. Green algae are common in freshwater protozoa, and dinoflagellates occur in seawater protozoa. In the flagellate *Cyanophora*, cyanobacteria occur as endosymbionts. Cell division of these so-called cyanellae is regulated by the host. A cell of *Cyanophora* contains two cells of cyanobacteria which divide synchronously within the protozoa.

The classical example of symbiosis among microorganisms is the association of algae and fungi in lichens. More than 15 000 species of lichens have been described. In the majority of lichens, ascomycetes are the mycobionts, although Fungi imperfecti and basidiomycetes – albeit . very rarely – do occur. Many mycobionts have been successfully cultured in the laboratory, but they do not grow in nature without their algal partners. Reconstitution of the partners in the laboratory has proved to be extremely difficult. The majority of phycobionts belong to the green algae, and about 10% are cyanobacteria (formerly known as blue-green algae). Many can live without the fungus. The lichen symbiosis reveals traits of parasitism on the side of the fungus (mycobiont). This becomes obvious by the formation of haustoria which penetrate into the algal cells. In typical lichens, highly ordered structures (thalli) are produced. Their growth rate in nature is extremely slow, and radial expansion is often less than 1 mm per year. The lichens are typical inhabitants of wetting and drying rock surfaces and barks, but also occur in vegetated soils. Lichens are highly resistant to desiccation, heat, cold, and sunlight. The role of the phycobionts in this association is the supply of the chemoorganotrophic fungus with organic carbon. The benefits to the phycobiont (alga; cyanobacteria) is the greater availability of minerals due to the metabolic activities of the fungal hyphae. Some pigments produced by lichens have been found to possess antibacterial properties and possibly protect the association from bacterial attack. Resistance to drying and existence in the presence of low water potentials are related to the algal production of polyols, which function as compatible solutes.

For the description of mutualistic (symbiotic) relationships, the term 'commensalism' is occasionally used. It has several meanings. (1) Two species of organisms live in close physical association; one derives benefit and the other is neither benefited nor harmed. (2) Two species of organisms live in close physical association, and each derives some benefit from the association. This type of commensalism is synonymous with mutual symbiosis. (3) Two species of organisms live in close physical association, both being neither benefited nor harmed as a result of their association.

Commensalism in terms of metabolic association, where one organism is benefited by the action of another, is widespread in nature. A few examples may be given. By growth of osmophilic yeasts in concentrated sugar solutions, the osmolarity is reduced and then allows secondary growth of less osmotolerant organisms. By changing the physiological conditions of the environment, e.g. by alteration of pH or consumption of O_2, one organism may favour the development of others specifically adapted to the new conditions. Growth of obligate anaerobes in apparently aerobic environments in soils is conditioned by the depletion of O_2 in microhabitats due to the respiration of the aerobes. In the degradation of organic materials, intermediates are produced that are essential nutrients for other organisms. The excretion of organic matter from plant roots or from algae is another form of commensalism in which microorganisms benefit from the activities of higher organisms. In a broader sense, all transformations of bioelements such as carbon, nitrogen, and sulphur, are accompanied by population changes in which one type of organism paves the way for other succeeding organisms. For instance, deamination (ammonification) precedes and effects nitrification, CH_4-production is followed by CH_4-oxidation, production of H_2S by dissimilatory sulphate reduction is a prerequisite for growth of organisms depending on the presence of H_2S. In this sense, there are numerous metabolic interconnections among microorganisms and between microorganisms and macroorganisms.

Antagonisms

Antagonistic (parasitic) relationships between two organisms are characterized by an advantage to one partner and a disadvantage to the other partner. Within the range of antagonistic relationships, various forms of interactions can be differentiated.

In competition, organisms compete for a compound which is present only in limited amounts. The essential compound can be an energy and carbon source, a mineral component, or a growth factor. Success in competition largely depends on the relative growth rates of the competing organisms. The organism that grows fastest has a selective advantage and will replace the other. In order to understand population shifts due to competition and dominance of a species in its natural habitat, it is indispensable to study the nutritional requirements and growth kinetics of the organisms in pure culture, and to extend the study on the situation in mixed culture. When studying a microorganism in pure culture, the interactions with other members of a community cannot be revealed in this condition. The pure culture studies give an idea of the ecological potential with respect to certain environmental factors under control, but do not allow predictions on the behaviour in natural habitats. An organism showing good growth under laboratory conditions may be overgrown in nature by competing organisms. Competition has been studied both in closed systems and in open continuous culture systems. Also mathematical models for competition have been developed. The dependency of the specific growth rate (μ) on the limiting (minimal) nutrient concentration (S) is described by the equation

$$\mu = \mu_{max} \frac{S}{K_s + S}$$

μ_{max} = the maximum growth rate possible with the given substrate,

K_s = the substrate concentration that allows growth at half
the maximum growth rate.

Under high nutrient concentrations organisms with a high maximum growth rate (μ_{max}) have a considerable selective advantage. Under extremely low nutrient concentrations, however, organisms with a low maximum growth rate are selectively favoured provided they have a greater affinity for the substrate (low K_s). Organisms with the greatest affinity for the substrate, therefore, have a chance to survive in oligo-trophic environments. Because of their low μ_{max}, they are outgrown in culture media containing higher substrate concentrations.

The term amensalism has been used to describe the antagonistic situa-tion in which metabolic products (e.g. toxins) of one organism cause deleterious effects to another. Competition and amensalism to some extent overlap. A special case of amensalism is antibiosis, referring to dam-age of a partner by the production of an antibiotic. In laboratory tests, the production and action of antibiotics can easily be demonstrated, but the ecological implications of antibiotics are not yet fully understood. Produc-ers of highly potent antibiotics obviously have no selective advantage in their natural environments. On the contrary, they are relatively rare.

Antagonistic effects may also be induced by metabolites, for example by methanol, ethanol, or organic acids. Such metabolic end products may limit or inhibit growth of other organisms. Organic acids produced by lactobacilli play an important role in the conservation of sauerkraut and in pickle fermentation. An antagonistic effect may also result from the production of O_2 by photosynthetic organisms influencing or inhibiting the growth of anaerobes.

Although parasitic relationships are most striking between microor-

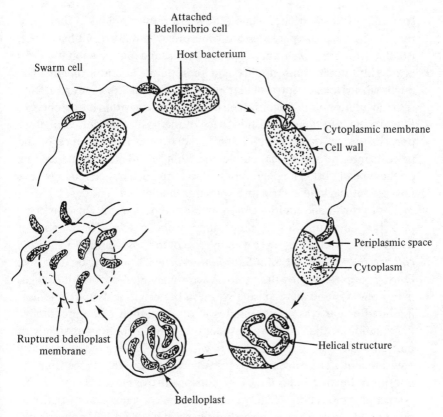

Fig. 7.1 Development cycle of *Bdellovibrio*

ganisms and higher plants, animals, and men, such interactions also do occur among microorganisms. Protozoa are known to be affected by ecto- and endoparasitic bacteria and fungi. Fungi, on their part, can be attacked by other fungi. Members of the phycomycetes, in particular *Rhizophydium* and *Phytridium*, parasitize algae.

The bdellovibrios are bacteria with the unique property of being parasites of other bacteria. A wild-type *Bdellovibrio* cell attacks and attaches to a viable host cell, penetrates the cell wall, and multiplies within the periplasm, which is the space between cytoplasmic membrane and cell wall. In this location, the entered parasite grows into a helical structure that generates progeny swarm cells by multiple fission. These are finally released from the digested host cell and start a new lifecycle if a suitable host bacterium is present. The life cycle of *Bdellovibrio* sp. is presented in Fig. 7.1. The bdellovibrios have been shown to possess lytic activity only against Gram-negative bacteria. Some strains have a broad spectrum of host activity, while others are rather limited in their host range. The bacterial parasites are widespread in nature and have been isolated from soil, fresh waters, waste waters, and marine habitats. They are highly motile, and motility is a prerequisite for attachment. The bdellovibrios are not 'intracellular' parasites *sensu stricto*. They penetrate into the interior of the bacterial cell but do not grow within the cytoplasm. Penetration into the periplasmic space of the host cell requires an entry pore in the cell-wall layers of the invaded cell. The entrance of the parasite into the host cell is completed within 5 to 20 minutes, depending on the type of host. The penetration is accompanied by conversion of the host cell into a globular structure known as bdelloplast. The development cycle of growth and multiplication within the periplasmic space is completed within 1 to 3 hours, depending on the system. The number of daughter cells released varies with the size of the host cell. In *Escherichia coli* are released about 6, in *Spirillum serpens* 20 to 30, daughter cells. During periplasmic growth, the host bacterium undergoes drastic changes in morphology and metabolism. Synthesis of nucleic acids and proteins is inhibited as early as a few minutes after attachment. The progressive degradation of the cellular constituents secures a continuous supply of nutrients into the periplasmic space, which has been looked at as a 'cosy environment'. The cell envelope prevents considerable leakage from the interior of the infested cell into the outside environment. Therefore, the system of exploitation is highly effective and economic. During periplasmic growth, *Bdellovibrio* directly utilizes nucleoside monophosphates derived from the host cell for the synthesis of nucleic acids. Since the phosphate ester bonds preexisting in the nucleic acids of the host bacterium are taken over and conserved by *Bdellovibrio*, the energy requirements for periplasmic growth are considerably reduced. Also the direct uptake of fatty acids from the host cell and its incorporation into *Bdellovibrio* fatty acids contributes to the minimal energy expenditure required during growth. Due to these abilities, *Bdellovibrio* spends very little energy during periplasmic growth, which is indicated by unusually high values of Y_{ATP} (up to 26). Lysis of bacteria by *Bdellovibrio* is not comparable to lysis caused by bacterial viruses (bacteriophages). Viruses are biological entities devoid of essential properties that characterize organismic life. Their multiplication depends on the metabolic activities of the living host cell.

Whereas in parasitism the consumer as a rule is smaller than the consumee, predatation usually involves ingestion of a smaller organism by a larger one. The dynamics of predator-prey relationships has been intensively studied, especially in protozoan predation on bacteria.

Interactions between microorganisms and plants
The phyllosphere
Leaf surfaces representing the phyllosphere are generally inhabited by a specific microflora. Inoculation occurs by deposition of airborne microorganisms or by splash-dispersion during rain and wind. Most species are saprophytes growing on plant materials of different kinds. Bacteria are most abundant on leaf surfaces, and the first to colonize newly emerged leaves. The highest numbers are encountered close to the meristematic leaf basis. The composition of the microbial flora is distinct and differs from that of the soil. The nutritional conditions on the leaf surface exert a selective pressure on the development of specifically adapted organisms. Among the bacteria, pigmented forms predominate. Most common are the yellow pigmented *Erwinia herbicola*, as well as flavobacteria and pseudomonads. In certain plants, e.g. *Ardisia crispa*, leaf nodules occur that contain bacterial symbionts transmitted through the seed. The presence of plant pathogenic bacteria and fungi in the phyllosphere is of particular interest to phytopathology.

The rhizosphere
The zone in soil adjacent to plant roots is defined as the rhizosphere. The extension is but a few millimetres around the roots. Because of the presence of organic materials, the rhizosphere is a site of increased microbial activity. Compared to the root-free soil, the numbers of microorganisms in the vicinity of or on, the roots are considerably higher, generally by two or more orders of magnitude. The R/S-ratio is defined as the ratio of numbers of organisms in the rhizosphere versus numbers in the adjacent soil. It varies according to type of soil and plant. The organic compounds present in the rhizosphere comprise root exudates, polysaccharide mucigel production by root cap and epidermal cells, dead root hairs, sloughed-off root cap cells, and dead epidermal and cortical tissue. Because of methodological difficulties, it is a practical impossibility to identify root exudates with respect to the chemical composition and the quantity in the soil. At the moment of exudation and thereafter, the organic materials are subject to microbial attack, and thus cannot be enriched and separated from the roots in their natural environments. Data on the nature and quantity of root exudates have been obtained from sterile hydrocultures; the results, however, cannot be extrapolated to the plant in its natural environment.
Root exudation has been quantified by measuring the production of labelled CO_2 in rhizosphere of ^{14}C-labelled plants, and it has been estimated that about 20% of the photosynthate is released into the

rhizosphere. Since microbial respiration is directly related to the amount of organic matter, the rate of exudation in the rhizosphere can be calculated from the rate of CO_2 production. The data obtained with this method, however, give only an approximation of the actual root exudation because both microbial respiration and root respiration are measured. Determination of microbial respiration alone and exclusion of the root respiration has been achieved by measuring dissimilatory nitrate reduction in the rhizosphere, kept under anaerobic conditions. Thus, organic matter excreted by the roots is exclusively respired by the denitrifying bacteria, added in excess to the root system. By addition of acetylene (10% v/v), denitrification, due to inhibition of N_2O reductase, leads to the production of N_2O which is measured by gas chromatography. Production of N_2O occurs according to the equation

$$C_6H_{12}O_6 + 6HNO_3 \xrightarrow{C_2H_2} 6CO_2 + 3N_2O + 9H_2O$$

Root exudation estimated by this indirect method amounted to 10 to 15% of the net photosynthate produced by four-week-old corn plants.

By their intense activity in the rhizosphere, the microorganisms affect pH, O_2 tension, CO_2 concentration, and possibly also influence plant growth. Microbial products such as phytotoxins, released in the rhizosphere, may affect plant growth directly. The significance of growth regulators produced by certain bacteria *in situ* is still a matter of debate. Other microbial products such as polysaccharides may influence plants in an indirect way by modifying the soil structure. The main influence on plant growth by the rhizosphere flora is probably related to promotion or inhibition of ion uptake. In recent years, the association between plant roots and N_2-fixing azospirilla has been the subject of intensive studies. It has been speculated that nitrogen supply of cultivated plants may be improved by establishing in the rhizosphere azospirilla or other N_2-fixing bacteria. The results obtained in field trials are contradictory. The bacterial flora of the rhizosphere are composed mainly of Gram-negatives, with pseudomonads as the prevailing group. The fungi are chiefly represented by saprophytic members like *Penicillium nigricans* and *Trichoderma koeningii*, but phytopathogenic fungi like *Fusarium solani* and *Phytophthora cinnamoni* are also common.

Mycorrhiza

A great many terrestrial plants live in close association with fungi. The features of this association, which is known as mycorrhiza, are those of a mutualistic symbiosis. Both partners benefit from the interac-

Ectomycorrhiza

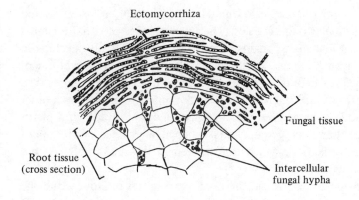

Root tissue
(cross section)

Fungal tissue

Intercellular
fungal hypha

Endomycorrhiza

Vesicles

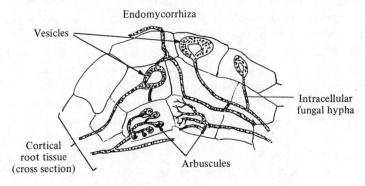

Intracellular
fungal hypha

Cortical
root tissue
(cross section)

Arbuscules

Fig. 7.2 Mycorrhizae

tion; the fungus is supplied with an energy source by the plant, and the plant is supplied with minerals and water by the fungus. There are two types of mycorrhizae (Fig. 7.2). In ectomycorrhiza, a fungal sheath develops around the root, and part of the mycelium also invades the intercellular space of the peripheral cortical root tissue. In endomycorrhiza, the fungus penetrates the root tissue and lives in an intercellular and intracellular position. The ectotrophic mycorrhiza is mainly found with forest trees. The root-inhabiting fungi obtain their organic nutrients for growth from the roots. The fungi participating in the ectotrophic association, include (a) agaric basidiomycetes (*Amanita, Boletus, Tricholoma*), (b) gasteromycetes, (c) ascomycetes, and (d) Fungi imperfecti. Some of the fungi are obligate symbionts, while others also have the capacity to live as decomposers. Species specificity in the interactions is usually low. Up to 40 species of fungi have been found to be associated with one particular plant species. The mycorrhiza is essential for most gymnosperms and many angiosperms. The fungal sheath develops in response to root exudates. The fungus profits from the photosynthate of the tree, and growth of the tree is enhanced by the associated fungus. The beneficial effect to the plant is related to the supply of phosphorus, other minerals, and water. It has been demonstrated that mycorrhizal plants grow better than uninfected plants, when living under nutrient-poor conditions. N_2-fixation, which is restricted to the prokaryotes, is not involved in mycorrhiza.

In endotrophic mycorrhiza, the fungus penetrates the root tissue and does not spread into the surrounding soil. The most widespread of all forms of mycorrhiza is the vesicular-arbuscular type. It is characterized by specific structures within or between the root cortical cells. This type of endomycorrhiza exists in bryophytes, vascular plants, ferns, trees, grasses, and a variety of crop plants. The symbiotic partners of the endotrophic mycorrhizas are zygomycetes of the family Endogonaceae (*Endogone*). Some fungi, e.g. *Glomus mosseae*, have a broad host range and infect both monocotyledons and dicotyledons. Because of their nature as obligate symbionts, the present knowledge of this group of fungi is still restricted, despite the important role the mycorrhizal fungi play in nature.

Root nodule systems

Among the various nitrogen-fixing symbioses, the symbiotic relationship between rhizobia and leguminous plants has attracted much interest. This endosymbiotic association is the most differentiated symbiotic relationship known. The bacteria causing root nodule formation in leguminous plants are included in the genus *Rhizobium*. These are free-living, Gram-negative rods that are strictly aerobic and require organic compounds as carbon and energy source. Because of the agronomic and ecological importance, the root nodule symbiosis of leguminous plants has been intensively studied by both microbiologists and agronomists. Two main groups of rhizobia are separated, the fast-growing represented by *R. leguminosarum*, and the slow-growing, represented by *R. japonicum, R. lupini*, and many of the 'cowpea' rhizobia. The infection of the host plant is exclusively initiated at young root hairs (Fig. 7.3). The bacteria invade a root hair close to the tip and grow into the root tissue forming an infection thread that is surrounded by a cellulose membrane. From the basis of the infected root hair, the bacteria penetrate into the epidermal and root-cortex cells. When they invade a

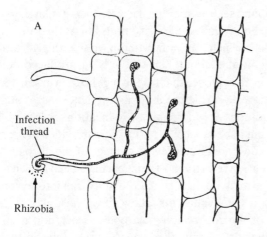

Fig. 7.3 The legume–*Rhizobium* symbiosis
A Primary steps of infection (longitudinal section)
B Root nodule cell filled with bacteroids

tetraploid cell of the cortex tissue, proliferation of the root cells is initiated. The result is the production of a nodule. Within the nodule cells, the rhizobia multiply rapidly and turn into bacteroids which have up to ten times the volume of free-living rhizobia. The nodule tissue containing the bacteroids is red, pigmented by leghaemoglobin. This pigment protects the nitrogenase from deleterious effects of oxygen. Fixation of molecular nitrogen occurs only in nodules containing leghaemoglobin. Presence of the pigment and initiation of N_2-fixation coincide. The pigment is located between the bacteroids and the surrounding membrane. Both the bacteroids and the plant participate in the production of leghaemoglobin. The prosthetic group (protohaem) is synthesized by the bacteroids, the protein part by the plant. Leghaemoglobin possesses a high affinity to oxygen. It has been suggested that the diffusion of molecular oxygen to the surface of the bacteroids is facilitated by leghaemoglobin. The function of this compound secures that the bacteroids do not lack oxygen for the energy production required in N_2-fixation, but at the same time prevent high pO_2 values which are known to interfere with N_2-fixation. The nodule bacteria consume about 30% of the NH_4^+ produced during N_2-fixation. There is much evidence that free-living rhizobia in soil do not participate in N_2-fixation. According to general experience, pure cultures under laboratory conditions are incapable of N_2-fixation. Basically, the rhizobia, however, seem to be capable of N_2-fixation, provided the partial pressure of oxygen is low enough to prevent damage of the nitrogenase. During the past few years, a few strains of rhizobia have been shown to fix nitrogen even during growth on agar media. Possibly, the interior of the bacterial colonies secures pO_2 values that allow nitrogenase activity. The nature of specificity of the *Rhizobium*–host plant association is still a matter of debate. Specific proteins known as lectins (glycoproteins) appear to be involved in the primary attachment of rhizobia to the root hairs. It has been suggested that interactions between lectins at the surface of a root hair and the polysaccharides at the surface of the rhizobia decide on the success of the infection. In soils with high nitrogen content, nodule formation is suppressed.

In addition to the *Rhizobium*–legume relationship, there exist a number of non-legumes possessing root nodules with the ability to fix nitrogen. In many of these symbioses, actinomycetes of the genus *Frankia* are the endosymbionts. They occur in woody and herbaceous plants and have a world-wide distribution. Compared to the N_2 fixation of legumes, which amounts to a gain of 100 to 300 kg N/ha per year, the efficiency of the *Frankia* symbiosis is nearly of the same order of magnitude; in some plants it amounts to 150 to 300 kg N/ha per year. N_2 fixation is known to be most effective in *Casuarina equisetifolia*, in *Alnus*, *Hippophaë*, and *Ceanothus*. Considerable amounts are also fixed by *Myrica*, *Dryas*, and *Elaeagnus*. Trees such as the alder are characteristic pioneers in nitrogen-poor habitats. They colonize bare soils, and this capacity obviously is related to their ability to enter into a symbiotic relationship allowing N_2 fixation. Members of the genus *Frankia* are slow-growing microaerophilic filamentous organisms that induce adventitious lateral root formation. A pigment comparable to leghaemoglobin is not produced, and it is not yet known how nitrogenase is protected in these associations. The root nodules of the woody plants may have considerable size. They consist of branched and coralloid structures representing roots that have ceased growing.

Apart from symbiotic associations characterized by root nodules containing N$_2$-fixing microorganisms, there are several other forms of symbiosis known in higher plants lacking the formation of nodules. The water fern *Azolla*, for instance, harbours within its leaves N$_2$-fixing cyanobacteria. The symbiont *Anabaena azollae* produces a great number of heterocysts involved in nitrogen fixation. In rice paddies, nitrogen fixation by *Anabaena* in *Azolla* amounts to 300 kg N/ha per year, and thus meets the total nitrogen requirement.

Plant pathogens

A wide variety of bacteria and fungi cause disease in plants. Also *Mycoplasma* and *Rickettsia* occur as plant pathogens. Because of the non-organismic nature of viruses, diseases caused by virus agents are beyond the scope of this treatise.

Plant diseases are caused by bacteria of the following genera, *Pseudomonas, Xanthomonas, Erwinia, Corynebacterium, Agrobacterium* and *Streptomyces*. The symptoms caused by bacterial attack include necroses, wet rots, vascular diseases, tumour production and scab-like surface lesions. *Agrobacterium tumefaciens* causing crown gall, a tumourlike disease of roots in many plant species, has attracted much interest during the past few years, not only by phytopathologists but particularly by molecular biologists. It has been discovered that the tumour-inducing principle is related to the presence of a plasmid in the bacterium. On the basis of physiological and molecular data, *Agrobacterium* and *Rhizobium* are taxonomically related. Another *Agrobacterium, A. rhizogenes,* causes hairy-root disease of apple trees and other plants. True phytopathogenic bacteria have rarely been found in habitats other than the diseased plant, or the adjacent soil. Some potentially phytopathogenic bacteria, in particular members of the genera *Pseudomonas* and *Erwinia*, also occur as opportunistic pathogens causing nosocomial infections in man.

Fungi are the economically most important plant pathogens. Plant pathogenic fungi are found in all major taxonomic groups, ascomycetes, basidiomycetes, and also in lower fungi such as the Peronosporales (Oomycetes) and the Chytridiomycetes. Although pathogenic fungi may affect all kinds of plants, their study has understandably been focussed on diseases of crop plants. Serious diseases in economically important plants are caused by the rusts and smuts. *Puccinia graminis,* the causal agent of wheat rust, has a complex two-host life cycle, one in wheat, the other in the wild barberry (*Berberis vulgaris*). The parasitic symbiosis is obligate, and it has not yet been possible to cultivate this pathogen in laboratory culture. Rye, barley, and oats are also attacked by rust fungi. The smut fungi cause economically important diseases in certain crops. These organisms typically produce masses of dark-coloured teliospores on, or within, the tissues of the infected hosts.

Although all parts of a plant are susceptible to attack, the fungi (as other pathogens) have developed a marked specificity for distinct organs such as roots, leaves, flowers, or fruits. The nature of damage to a plant may be related to the production of a toxin, to the blocking of vessels involved in water and nutrient transport, or to other factors.

In response to fungus attack, higher plants may produce fungistatic substances known as phytoalexins. The production of such compounds appears to be a local effect; translocation has not yet been proven unequivocally. By the ability to produce phytoalexin, the plant may resist infection. As an example, the infection of soybean by *Phytophthora megasperma* f. sp. *glycinea* may be mentioned. Resistance to a particular race of *Phytophthora*, possessing potential pathogenicity for other susceptible plant varieties, is related to the production of glyceollin. In some cases, production of phytoalexins appears to be associated with a hypersensitivity reaction. Hypersensitivity involves the rapid death of plant cells at the site of infection, resulting in the formation of small necrotic lesions to which the infection is confined.

Interactions between microorganisms and animals

There exist in nature innumerable interactions between microorganisms and animals that can be classified as mutualistic or parasitic symbioses. The non-parasitic relationships range from loose associations to obligate symbioses. External and internal surfaces of animals are inhabited by a variety of microorganisms representing an indigenous microflora. The interaction between microorganism and host is neutralistic, when the prokaryote feeds on waste products, mutualistic, when both organisms benefit, or parasitic, when the host's health is impaired. The normal microbiota found in higher organisms on surfaces, in body cavities, and in the intestinal tract include bacteria, yeasts, other fungi, and protozoa. Studies with gnotobiotic animals have revealed that the presence of microorganisms in, or on, the host more probably is related to maintaining the health of the host, rather than undermining it. The indigenous flora protects the host against potentially harmful microorganisms. One major effect of the normal microflora is the maintenance of the normal immunoglobulin concentration in the host. Under normal conditions, the presence of microorganisms is restricted to certain parts of the host. For a variety of reasons, indigenous microorganisms can temporarily inhabit other areas and function as opportunistic pathogens. The skin of man harbours a characteristic microflora including corynebacteria, mycobacteria, micrococci, streptococci, propionibacteria, and yeasts. The skin is a homogeneous habitat with respect to temperature, but varies considerably with respect to moisture. In locations of relative high humidity such as the axilla, the bacterial populations are especially dense. The organisms of the skin derive their nutrients from sweat. Also sweat glands and hair follicles are inhabited and secure the repopulation of the skin after cleaning. The normal microflora of the skin is not of any known disadvantage to the health of man. On the contrary, it seems to have a useful function. By internal application of antibiotics, massive development of potentially pathogenic yeasts and other fungi has been elicited. Production of fatty acids by the skin organisms is known to be involved in the exclusion of pathogens. The normal microflora of the mouth have been intensively studied because of the interactions between oral streptococci and the enamel surfaces, involved in dental caries and tooth decay. The interactions are partially related to the production of extracellular polysaccharides.

Among the inner surfaces of animals and men, the intestinal tract is the ecosystem with the highest population density. The situation is well characterized by the fact that a human being is comprised of about 10^{13} body cells, yet is inhabited by more than 10^{14} microorganisms, living mainly in the intestines. The various sections of the entire human intestinal tract, from the mouth to the large intestine, all possess a particular bacterial flora. The microorganisms live on epithelial surfaces, free in the lumen, or hidden in crypts. Mouth, throat, and nasopharynx harbour both aerobic and anaerobic bacteria. Among these, *Streptococcus salivarius, S. mutans, Veillonella alcalescens, Treponema dentium, Fusobacterium, Actinomyces,* lactobacilli, corynebacteria, and cocci are the most important. Because of a continuous introduction of allochthonous organisms with the food, not all bacteria isolated from the contents of the intestinal tract must be regarded as autochthonous. In order to be a member of this latter category, the organism must be required to be capable of anaerobic growth, to be present in healthy individuals, to colonize particular areas of the intestinal tract, to maintain stable population levels, and to associate with the mucosal epithelium of the colonized area. Because of the acid conditions in the human stomach, this organ is not populated by a genuine autochthonous flora. The faeces produced in the intestinal tract harbour especially high numbers of microorganisms.

The concentration of bacteria amounts to 10^{11} cells/g of faeces. *Escherichia coli* which is used as an indicator of faecal contaminations, amounts to only 1% of the total population; the predominant organism is *Bacteroides*. In addition, other strictly anaerobic Gram-negative bacteria of the genera *Fusobacterium, Eubacterium,* and *Peptostreptococcus* as well as streptococci, lactobacilli, and bifidobacteria are present. The actual composition of the flora is largely related to the composition of the food. The beneficial function of the normal intestinal flora becomes apparent when the bacteria are excluded by the application of antibiotics or other chemotherapeutic agents. Under such conditions, disturbance of the intestinal flora may impair the health of the host. It is known from experiments with gnotobiotic animals that such sterile grown animals are much more susceptible to infectious diseases than are normal unsterile grown animals. The intestinal microflora obviously confers resistance to intruding opportunistic or pathogenic microorganisms.

During evolution, loose and, more or less, close associations have developed between animals and microorganisms. Certain higher organisms have succeeded in exploiting two unique abilities of prokaryotic organisms. (a) The fixation of molecular nitrogen. Symbiotic relationships with nitrogen-fixing microorganisms have not only developed in plants, but also in animals. (b) The decomposition of cellulose. Higher animals lack the ability to hydrolyse cellulose, but some have established symbiotic relationships with cellulolytic bacteria.

Microbes as symbionts

Mutualistic symbioses between microorganisms and animals occur with ectosymbionts living outside of cells and tissues of the host, and endosymbionts inhabiting the interior of cells and tissues. The ectosymbiosis between microorganisms and ruminants has been intensively studied; the rumen represents the best-known anaerobic ecosystem (Fig. 7.4). Since ruminants live mainly on grasses and leafy plants but lack the enzymes for digestion of cellulose, the function of the microbial symbionts is obvious. By their cellulolytic activity, the rumen organisms make available to animals otherwise nondigestible materials. Among the ruminants, cattle, sheep, and goats are the most important domestic animals. Also deer, moose, elk, and antelope possess a rumen. The main carbohydrates subjected to anaerobic fermentation stem from hay, straw, and grass. Chemically, cellulose, fructosanes, and xylanes prevail. The symbiosis has developed special anatomical features, and the bovine stomach consists of the rumen and the reticulum. The rumen is compar-

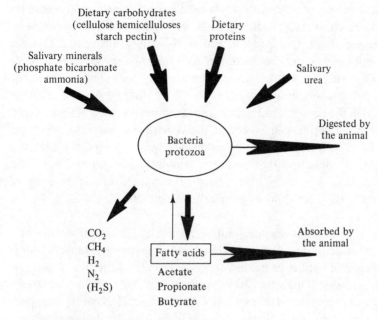

Fig. 7.4 The ruminant symbiosis

able to a digestive vessel (a fermenter) containing 100 to 250 l. The fermentation conditions maintained by the animal are as follows: temperature 37–39 °C, and pH 5.8–7.3. The phosphate concentration is between 10 and 50 mM, the concentration of bicarbonate 100 to 140 mM. The animal supports the digestive process by secreting 100 to 200 l of saliva per day, and by mechanically agitating the rumen through contractions.

In terms of growth physiology, the rumen represents a semicontinuous culture of anaerobic microorganisms. Their numbers per ml of the rumen contents are around 10^{10}–10^{11} bacteria, and 10^5–10^6 protozoa. The oxidation–reduction potential (E_0') is –350 mV. The main cellulose digestors include *Ruminococcus albus*, *R. flavefaciens*, *Bacteroides succinogenes*, *Butyrivibrio fibrisolvens*, *Eubacterium cellulosolvens*, and *Clostridium lochheadii*. The rumen, however, also contains a great number of other bacteria that do not ferment cellulose but which depend on carbohydrates or the products thereof. Among these may be mentioned *Bacteroides amylophilus*, *B. ruminicola*, *Succinimonas amylolytica*, *Selenomonas ruminantium*, *Streptococcus bovis*, *Veillonella alcalescens*, *Lachnospira multiparus*, *Peptostreptococcus elsdenii*, and *Desulfotomaculum ruminis*. In addition, the rumen harbours a variety of other organisms that have not yet been grown and studied in pure culture.

Cellulose is degraded to glucose via cellobiose. Fermentation occurs by bacteria that also utilize pectins, starch, fructosanes, proteins, and lipids. The products of the fermentation process are mainly fatty acids, CO_2, and H_2. Methanogens, such as *Methanobacterium ruminantium*, convert H_2 and CO_2 or acetate into methane. The methanogens play an important role in the interspecies hydrogen transfer. More than 80% of the cellulose digested in the rumen terminates in fermentation products. These mainly consist of fatty acids such as acetate, propionate, and butyrate, which are assimilated as nutrients by the animal. About 10% of the digested cellulose is converted into microbial biomass, and about 5% of the cellulose is dissipated as heat. Hence, the rumen represents a highly effective system for utilization of cellulose-containing materials by the animal.

Many herbivorous animals, and, in particular, insects, make use of a hindgut fermentation. It is not as efficient as the rumen symbiosis, but is widespread in nature. Many insects depend on the activities of their gut microorganisms. Often they have evolved a diversity of intestinal structures containing the symbiotic microorganisms. The symbionts apparently serve two main functions: (a) degradation of cellulose which the host cannot digest, (b) supply of growth factors, such as vitamins and amino acids, which are lacking in the diet. Termites live in symbiosis with flagellates. These, on their part, contain bacterial symbionts that are capable of producing cellulase. In this type of symbiosis, the flagellate protozoa live as ectosymbionts within sacciform dilatations of the hindgut, and the protozoa depend on the production of cellulases by endosymbiotic bacteria. Leaf-cutting ants live in a nutritional symbiosis with fungi domesticated by the insect. The ants arrange leaves in heaps on which the fungus *Hypomyces hippomoeae* grows. The ants actually cultivate the fungus. They feed the fungus with leaf fragments and construct chambers within which the fungi grow. The developing mycelium is finally grazed by the insects. Termites are also known to cultivate fungi for the nutrition of their offspring. A wood-boring insect, known as the 'ambrosia' beetle, has developed an ectosymbiotic association with fungi which they cultivate in tunnels within the trees. They possess a special organ in which they store spores of the fungus. The spores they inoculate into the tunnels, and the fungus grows at the expense of nutrients which seep into the tunnel from the wood sap. The developing mycelium is finally ingested by the beetle and used as the primary source of food. The insect–fungus relationship is highly specific, each species of insect being associated with only one or a few fungal species. The insects only ingest a part of the fungus population, and thus assure continuity of the association. By such type of symbiosis, the insects obviate their otherwise unbalanced diet and make use of the wood-degrading fungi as a source of protein and vitamins.

Another highly developed and intensively studied ectosymbiosis is that of luminous bacteria and fish, bacteria and cephalopods, bacteria and tunicates. The specific luminous organs are located at different sites of the body and have a variety of shapes. The organs are usually formed by an invagination of the body or gut surface and often exhibit special morphological structures acting as lenses or reflectors. Although the majority of the relationships are ectoparasitic by definition, there also exist examples (in the tunicates) for endosymbiotic association with luminous bacteria inside of mesodermal cells. Some fish possess bean-shaped organs with luminous bacteria located close to their eyes and have the ability of flashing the light periodically. Such light organs are known in deep-sea and coastal fish. The light is produced through the luciferase-mediated oxidation of reduced flavin mononucleotide ($FMNH_2$), which is coupled to the oxidation of a long-chain aliphatic aldehyde (tetrade-canal). The system biochemically differs from that of the fire fly. The luminous bacteria of the genus *Photobacterium* exist in light organ symbioses and also as free-living forms. The advantage on the side of the bacteria, contained in light organs, obviously is related to their provision with nutrients by the host. The advantage of luminescence for the host is not yet understood. Possibly, the light source has some survival value in the darkness of the deep sea; and it may aid in recognition and attraction of potential prey. This function is supported by the observation that O_2 supply to the luminous bacteria is under control of the host, thus controlling the intensity of bioluminescence.

Apart from the endosymbiotic relationships among microorganisms and between microbes and plants already discussed, there also exist a variety of endosymbiotic relationships between microorganisms and animals. In many aquatic invertebrates, such as *Paramecium, Hydra,* and *Spongilla,* endosymbiotic chlorophytes (known as zoochlorellae) function as O_2 producers. In marine invertebrates such as the foraminiferae, radiolarians, coelenterates, sea anemones, corals, and clams, the endosymbionts usually belong to dinoflagellates such as *Ceratium, Noc-ticula, Peridinium* or *Amphidinium.* Zoochlorellae are also found in marine platyhelminths, and didemnid ascidians. In some molluscs, symbionts have been found in the form of isolated chloroplasts. The algal (plant) cell in this system is reduced to an organelle which is integrated into the animal cell.

Endosymbiotic relationships are common in insects. They have possibly evolved from ectosymbiotic associations. It is generally observed that insects supplied with a high quality diet do not harbour symbionts. Insects living on leaf sap, wood, and other materials of low nutritional value, however, have, as a rule, evolved symbiotic relationships. Malnutrition and in particular the need of growth factors are compensated by the metabolic activities of the symbiont. The endosymbionts of insects are usually bacteria or yeasts. Among the bacteria, Gram-negative rods, *Norcardia*, and corynebacteria prevail. The advantage of the endosymbiosis is the continuous presence of the symbiont in specialized cells. For transmittance of the symbionts to the progeny, a variety of mechanisms have evolved that secure a cyclic symbiosis. This is accomplished, for instance, by feeding on the faeces of imagines that contain the symbionts, or by inoculation of the eggs during ovoposition. In *Coctosoma scutellatum*, the females deposit eggs together with cocoons containing the symbionts. The hatching larvae suck out the cocoons, and thus incorporate the symbionts. In this particular case, the symbiosis is coupled to a genetically determined behaviour. Symbioses also exist that are based on an intracellular infection of the eggs. In this case the symbionts enter the egg cytoplasm during egg formation in the ovaria. The nutritional significance of an endosymbiotic association has been proved by removing the symbionts from the host and studying the two partners separately. Removal of the symbionts has been possible by heat treatment or by application of antibiotics and lysozyme. It has also been achieved by sterilization of infected eggs or, in case of fungi, by mechanical removal of the mycetomes. The symbiont-free insects are characterized by a retardation of growth and a change in morphogenesis. Absence of the symbionts could be compensated by a diet rich in vitamins. By entering into an association with symbionts, the insects can escape and compensate the one-sided nutrition which is typical in their natural habitats. With the aid of the symbionts, they have the capacity of occupying ecological niches that otherwise would not be occupied by insects. The study of insect symbioses is still fragmentary because most endosymbiotic microorganisms cannot be propagated in axenic culture.

Microbes as pathogens

Microbiology as a science is closely related to the discovery of microorganisms pathogenic to men and animals, to the attempts of understanding the nature of the harmful effects, and to the need to control the diseases. The ability to cause disease is one of the most significant properties of microorganisms in relation to higher organisms. It has largely influenced the development not only in areas of medical interest but also in other fields of basic and applied microbiology. A parasite lives on, or in, another organism and causes damage or even death to the host. The interaction between a parasite (parasitic symbiont) and its host are dynamic, and each partner has a mutual influence on the activities and functions of the other. The outcome of a disease does not exclusively depend on the pathogen but also on the susceptibility (or resistance) of the host. The specificity of the parasite may be distinctive and restricted to one or a few hosts, or may be broad. Several diseases such as pneumonia may be caused by a variety of pathogens, in which the symptoms are identical, or similar. Other diseases originate from infection by only one specific organism, e.g. tuberculosis by *Mycobacterium tuberculosis*, or syphilis by *Treponema pallidum*.

Parasitic symbiosis can be caused by ectoparasites living on surfaces of the host, or by endoparasites living in the interior of cells and tissues. True endoparasites only occur in eukaryotic cells and tissues. With respect to the degree of adaptation to the host, facultative and obligate parasites can be differentiated. There exist in nature legions of parasite–host interactions between microorganisms and animals. Only a few will be considered in this chapter. If a parasite causes death of its host and lives on the constituents, it is called necrotrophic. If the relationship is based on nutrient exchange between the living host and the parasite during contact, the relationship is called biotrophic. In essence, all predators that devour and metabolize the prey must be classified as necrotrophs. Predation on bacteria by protozoa is a characteristic example. While parasitic relationships among microorganisms are relatively rare, there are numerous cases of parasitic relationships between microorganisms and eukaryotic macroorganisms. Since many parasites are capable of growth on simple artificial media or on dead tissue, the nutritional advantage of the parasitic mode of life of such organisms is usually obscure. A fascinating example of parasitism (and predation) are the interactions between fungi and nematodes. Some nematode-trapping soil fungi have developed special capture organs: *Nematoctonus*, a basidiomycete, has knobs, and *Arthrobotrys*, a hyphomycete, has constricting rings. Most nematode trappers belong to the hyphomycetes. If a nematode passes through the hyphal ring, a quick closure of the ring is induced, and the nematode is trapped. Then, hyphae originating from the trap invade the prey. The production of immobilizing toxins and possibly also of attractants is involved in the capture process. Predatory fungi are known to occur among the oomycetes, hyphomycetes, and basidiomycetes. They have evolved parasitic interactions also with amoebae and rotifers.

There exist a great many bacteria that are significant as human or animal pathogens. The relationship is characterized by a continuum in parasite–host interactions. Most diseases of man caused by pathogenic bacteria are well known and have been intensively studied. Nevertheless, now and then, a new disease is discovered that previously has not been encountered. An example is the occurrence of the legionnaires' disease caused by *Legionella pneumophila*. It has also been reported that already known bacteria which had been thought to be non-pathogens may be related to a 'new' disease.

Pathogenic bacteria are found in almost all taxonomic groups. Just a few genera including pathogens may be listed: *Micrococcus, Staphylococcus, Streptococcus, Neisseria, Listeria, Salmonella, Shigella, Yersinia, Pseudomonas, Vibrio, Brucella, Bordetella, Haemophilus, Pasteurella, Bacillus, Clostridium, Corynebacterium, Mycobacterium, Actinomyces, Spirochaeta, Treponema, Borrelia, Leptospira, Mycoplasma, Rickettsia, Coxiella, Bartonella,* and *Chlamydia.* Viruses also play an important role, but remain unconsidered in this treatise because of their non-organismic nature.

The majority of pathogenic bacteria and fungi can be cultured on artificial media and, therefore, have to be classified as facultative parasites. Only a few obligately intracellular bacteria are known. Their mode of life is usually related to a degeneration of their metabolism. The *Rickettsia* and *Chlamydia* are obligate pathogens causing disease in men and animals. The natural hosts of the *Rickettsia* are arthropods (ticks, mites, fleas, and lice). In these hosts, they usually live as compatible parasites or symbionts. After transmittance to man, or other susceptible hosts, severe symptoms of disease are provoked. *Rickettsia prowazekii* is the causal agent of typhoid fevers and has its main reservoir in man. The pathogens grow within the cell's cytoplasm and reproduce by transverse binary fission typical of bacteria. They are transmitted by lice. The *Chlamydia* likewise are obligate intracellular parasites in a variety of vertebrates, including man and other mammals. *Chlamydia trachomatis* is the causal agent of trachoma that starts as inclusion conjunctivitis and ends in blindness. *Chlamydia psittaci*, the causal agent of psittacosis, causes severe pneumonia. The chlamydia can only be propagated in living cells or in tissue culture. They are devoid of an ATP-generating system, and therefore have been regarded as 'energy parasites'. Obviously, the intracellular bacteria are the result of a regressive development. The adaptation to the host cell is related to the loss of a variety of metabolic properties.

Pathogens of any kind (bacteria, fungi, protozoa) enter the organism by penetrating the skin, mucosa, epithelial surfaces, wounds, or other portals of entry. Penetration into the skin often causes a focal infection with local propagation of the pathogen. This process is usually accompanied by pussy inflammation. When the pathogen enters the blood system, the infection results in a generalized sepsis (bacteriaemia). This type of spreading is relatively rare. As a rule, localization of the pathogen is restricted to a specific organ. *Brucella abortus*, the causal agent of brucellosis, has a predilection for the foetus and the placenta in cows. This specific organotrophy has been found to be related to the presence of erythritol, a substance which promotes the development of the pathogen; it is not present in other tissues of the host.

Bacterial infection often requires adhesion and penetration. The pathogen must have the ability to infiltrate the mucous surfaces or to penetrate epithelial surfaces in order to gain access to deeper tissue layers. For attachment and colonization, some bacteria have a preference for specific areas (defined anatomic sites). Thus, *Streptococcus salivarius* has a preference to the dorsal surface of the tongue. For microbial adhesion, the bacteria produce specific substances (adhesives) or specific structures. In many pathogens, adhesion is mediated by fimbriae (pili). The 'glycocalyx' consisting of exopolysaccharide fibres that surround the cells is involved in adhesion of many bacteria.

Invasion of the host requires overcoming of the natural barriers of defence. There are three ways to escape the defence barriers: (a) by the production of capsules; (b) by the production of leukocidins; (c) by the production of specific enzymes that allow spreading in the tissue. Encapsulated cells of pathogens such as *Bacillus anthracis*, *Diplococcus pneumoniae*, and *Pasteurella pestis* are not as easily phagocytized as are nonencapsulated cells. Leukocidins are produced by staphylococci and streptococci. They have the ability to destroy the white blood cells, and in addition, exhibit toxic or lytic activity also towards erythrocytes. Leukocidin is composed of several constituents which are essential for the leukocidal action. The consequence of leukocidin action is the formation of pus. A typical representative is *Streptococcus pyogenes*. The production of specific enzymes that favour spreading is known in staphylococci, streptococci, and clostridia. They produce hyaluronidase, an enzyme which depolymerizes hyaluronic acid. Because of the increase of invasiveness it was formerly known as the 'spreading factor'. Hyaluronic acid is the basal substance of connective tissue. Production of collagenase causes destruction of collagen, the main protein of connective tissue. This protein is generally resistant to enzymic degradation, but certain bacteria such as *Clostridium perfringens* and *Clostridium histolyticum* degrade collagen by specific collagenases, and thus enhance invasiveness of the tissue. Streptokinase is produced by certain streptococci. The enzyme assists the invasiveness of streptococci by lysing the fibrin barriers which may enclose streptococcal lesions. Coagulases exist as a variety of serologically distinguishable bacterial enzymes capable of plasma coagulation. In staphylococci, they have the function of so-called aggressines. In addition to the extracellular enzymes mentioned above, deoxyribonuclease and phospholipase are involved in the process of invasiveness.

In order to survive in a susceptible host, the bacteria must gain access to the required nutrients. Obviously, pathogenicity has nothing to do with the nutritional requirements of pathogenic strains as compared to non-pathogenic bacteria. Specific differences have not been documented. Among the factors determining pathogenicity, toxins play an important role. Many pathogens have the ability to produce exotoxins or endotoxins. Exotoxins are primarily produced by Gram-positive bacteria. *Clostridium botulinum* produces a highly toxic substance which causes paralysis in man. Another powerful neurotoxin is formed by *Clostridium tetani*, the causal agent of tetanus (lock jaw). A very potent toxin is produced by *Corynebacterium diphtheriae* causing diphtheria. The toxin may produce serious systemic effects with neurological and cardiac involvement. Toxigenic strains are lysogenic, and toxigenicity has been transferred to avirulent strains by temperate bacteriophages (lysogenic conversion). Endotoxins occurring in Gram-negative bacteria are only released during cell lysis. In enterobacteria, the toxic effect is caused by lipopolysaccharides and is believed to be related to the lipid portion, lipid A.

The virulence of a pathogenic microorganism describes the capacity to cause disease in terms of severity of symptoms in the host. There exist several degrees of virulence. A highly virulent strain may cause severe symptoms in a susceptible host, while a less virulent strain would cause less severe symptoms in the same individual. The virulence depends on the ability of the organism to invade tissue and on the capability of producing toxins. Both properties are often combined, but not necessarily. Thus, *Clostridium tetani* is little invasive but highly toxic. On the other hand, *Streptococcus pneumoniae* is highly invasive but does not produce toxins. Loss of virulence sometimes can be achieved by serial passages of a pathogen on artificial media. This phenomenon, known as attenuation, is related to a population shift due to the appearance of avirulent mutants.

Resistance to pathogens is related to constitutive or inductive defence mechanisms. The body's main defence system against invaders are the leukocytes (granulocytes, lymphocytes, monocytes–macrophages). Phagocytosis is the process in which particulate matter (e.g. bacteria) is ingested by a cell. It is carried out by special cells such as granulocytes and monocytes. Granulocytes (polymorphonuclear leukocytes) contain several enzymes such as lysozyme, proteases, phosphatases, nucleases, and lipases. During the process of phagocytosis, the metabolism of the granulocytes shifts from respiration to glycolysis. By the production of lactic acid, the pH of the cell is decreased causing an increase in enzyme activity. Thus, phagocytosis becomes more efficient. Another important mechanism of resistance to bacterial infection is inflammation. An inflammatory response is non-specific, and is also induced by other stimuli such as heat, mechanical affection, or chemical poisons. Such effects cause a local extension of blood vessels and an increase in capillary permeability. The consequence is an increased blood supply of the tissue which in turn brings more phagocytes into the inflamed area.

Induced specific defence mechanisms causing immunity to pathogens do not occur in animals below the vertebrates.

Only higher animals have the ability to produce specific antibodies. An antibody molecule is produced in direct response to the introduction and presence of an antigen. Antibodies have the properties of immunoglobulins and are capable of specific, non-covalent combination with the antigen which elicited its formation. *In vivo*, the antigen–antibody combination may confer benefits on the host organism, when the antigenic stimulus has derived from an invading pathogen. When the host is sensitized, re-exposure to the antigen will result in an allergic reaction.

Not all infections by pathogens induce clinically overt disease in individuals that are potentially susceptible. The outcome of success or failure of an invading microorganism largely depends on the status of the host. In compromised patients, the susceptibility to pathogens is increased and leads to the establishment of nosocomial infections. Although opportunistic pathogens are not truly pathogenic and lack the aggressiveness of typical transmissible pathogens, they may be the causal agent of severe disease.

Further reading

Books

General aspects of interactions

Cooke, R. (1977). *Biology of Symbiotic Fungi.* New York: John Wiley and Sons.
Margulis, L. (1981). *Symbiosis in Cell Evolution.* San Francisco: W. H. Freeman.

Microbe–microbe interactions

Brown, D. H., Hawksworth, D. L. & Bailey, R. H. (eds) (1976). *Lichenology: Progress and Problems.* New York: Academic Press.
Seaward, M. R. D. (ed.) (1977). *Lichen Ecology.* London: Academic Press.

Microorganisms and plants

Blakeman, J. P. (1981). *Microbial Ecology of the Phylloplane.* London: Academic Press.
Dommergues, Y. R. & Krupa, S. V. (eds) (1978). *Interactions between non-pathogenic soil microorganisms and plants.* Amsterdam: Elsevier Publishing Co.
Harley, J. L. & Scott, R. R. (eds) (1979). *The Soil–Root Interface.* London: Academic Press.
Jackson, R. M. & Mason, P. A. (1984). *Mycorrhiza.* The Institute of Biology's Studies in Biology no. 159. London: Edward Arnold.
Klingmüller, W. (ed.) (1982). *Azospirillum: Genetics, Physiology, Ecology.* Basel, Boston, Stuttgart: Birkhäuser Verlag.
Klingmüller, W. (ed.) (1983). *Azospirillum II: Genetics, Physiology, Ecology.* Basel, Boston, Stuttgart: Birkhäuser Verlag.
Klingmüller, W. (ed.) (1985). *Azospirillum III: Genetics, Physiology, Ecology.* Berlin, Heidelberg, New York, Tokyo: Springer–Verlag.
Vincent, J. M. (ed.) (1982). *Nitrogen Fixation in Legumes.* Sydney: Academic Press Inc.

Microorganisms as plant pathogens

Daly, J. M. & Uritani, I. (1979). *Recognition and Specificity in Plant Host–Parasite Interactions.* Tokyo: Japan Scientific Societies Press. Baltimore: University Park Press.
Fany, P. C. & Persley, G. J. (eds) (1983). *Plant Bacterial Diseases.* A Diagnostic guide. Sydney: Academic Press Australia.
Schippers, B. & Gams, W. (eds) (1979). *Soil-borne Plant Pathogens.* London: Academic Press.
Vanderplank, J. E. (1982). *Host–Pathogen Interactions in Plant Disease.* New York: Academic Press.

Microorganisms and animals

Barron, G. L. (1977). *The Nematode-Destroying Fungi.* Guelph: Canadian Biological Publications.
Batra, L. R. (ed.) (1979). *Insect-fungus Symbiosis.* Montclair: Allanheld & Osmun.
Clarke, R. T. J. & Bauchop, T. (eds) (1977). *Microbial Ecology of the Gut.* London: Academic Press.
Hobson, P. N. (1976). *Microflora of the Rumen.* Patterns of Progress. Durham: Meadowfield Press.
Krieg, A. (1986). *Bacillus thuringiensis, ein mikrobielles Insektizid.* Grundlagen und Anwendung. Berlin: Parey-Verlag.

Microorganisms as human and animal pathogens

Braude, A. I. (ed.) (1981). *Medical Microbiology and Infectious Disease*. Philadelphia: W. B. Saunders Co.

Lenette, E. H., Balows, A., Hausler, W. J. jr & Truant, J. P. (1980). *Manual of Clinical Microbiology*, 3rd edn Washington D.C.: American Society for Microbiology.

Mandell, G. L. (ed.) (1979). *Principles and Practice of Infectious Disease*. New York: John Wiley & Sons.

Rippon, J. W. (1982). *Medical Mycology*, 2nd edn Philadelphia: W. B. Saunders Co.

Wehrle, P. F. & Top, F. H. sr. (1981). *Communicable and Infectious Diseases*, 9th edn St. Louis: The C. V. Mosby Co.

Articles

General aspects of interactions

Alexander, M. (1981). Why microbial predators and parasites do not eliminate their prey and hosts. *Annual Review of Microbiology*, **35**, 113–33.

Gray, M. W. & Doolittle, W. F. (1982). Has the endosymbiont hypothesis been proven? *Microbiological Reviews*, **46**, 1–42.

Kuenen, J. G. & Harder, W. (1982). Microbial competition in continuous culture. In *Experimental Microbial Ecology*, eds R. G. Burns & J. H. Slater, pp. 342–67. Oxford, London, Edinburgh, Boston, Melbourne: Blackwell Scientific Publications.

Lynch, J. M., Fletcher, M. & Latham, M. J. (1979). Biological interactions. In *Microbial Ecology: A Conceptual Approach*, eds. J. M. Lynch & N. J. Poole, pp. 171–90. Oxford, London, Edinburgh, Melbourne: Blackwell Scientific Publications.

Schwartz, R. M. & Dayhoff, M. O. (1978). Origins of prokaryotes, eukaryotes, mitochondria and chloroplasts. *Science*, **199**, 395–403.

Veldkamp, H. (1985). Microbial interactions in nature and in the laboratory. *Antonie van Leeuwenhoek*, **51**, 457–72.

Microbe–microbe interactions

Chaturvedi, A. P. & Dwivedi, R. S. (1985). Mycoparasitic behaviour of *Fusarium oxysporum* Schlechtendahl towards *Aspergillus luchuensis* Inui. *Plant and Soil*, **84**, 419–22.

Curds, C. R. (1977). Microbial interactions involving protozoa. In *Aquatic Microbiology*, eds F. A. Skinner & J. M. Shewan, pp. 69–105. London: Academic Press.

Ferry, B. W. (1982). Lichens. In *Experimental Microbial Ecology*, eds R. G. Burns & J. H. Slater, pp. 291–319. Oxford, London, Edinburgh, Boston, Melbourne: Blackwell Scientific Publications.

Rittenberg, S. C. (1982). Bdellovibrios–intraperiplasmic growth. In *Experimental Microbial Ecology*, eds R. G. Burns & J. H. Slater, pp. 379–91. Oxford, London, Edinburgh, Boston, Melbourne: Blackwell Scientific Publications.

Rittenberg, S. C. & Thomashow, M. F. (1979). Intraperiplasmic growth – life in a cozy environment. In *Microbiology 1979*, ed. D. Schlessinger, pp. 80–6. Washington, D.C.: American Society for Microbiology.

Shilo, M. (1984). *Bdellovibrio* as a predator. In *Current Perspectives in Microbial Ecology*, eds M. J. Klug & C. A. Reddy, pp. 334–9. Washington, D.C.: American Society for Microbiology.

Starr, M. P. & Stolp, H. (1976). *Bdellovibrio* methodology. In *Methods in Microbiology*, vol. 9, ed. J. R. Norris, pp. 217–44. London, New York, San Francisco: Academic Press.

212   *Interactions*

Stolp, H. (1973). The bdellovibrios: bacterial parasites of bacteria. *Annual Review of Phytopathology*, **11**, 53–76.

Stolp, H. & Petzold, H. (1962). Untersuchungen über einen obligat parasitischen Mikroorganismus mit lytischer Aktivität für *Pseudomonas*-Bakterien. *Phytopathologische Zeitschrift*, **45**, 364–90.

Stolp, H. & Starr, M. P. (1965). Bacteriolysis. *Annual Review of Microbiology*, **19**, 79–104.

Varon, M. & Shilo, M. (1979). Ecology of aquatic bdellovibrios. *Recent Advances in Aquatic Microbiology*, **2**, 1–48.

Varon, M., Fine, M. & Stein, A. (1984). The maintenance of *Bdellovibrio* at low prey density. *Microbial Ecology*, **10**, 95–8.

Veldkamp, H., Van Gemerden, H., Harder, W. & Laanbroek, H. J. (1984). Competition among bacteria: an overview. In *Current Perspectives in Microbial Ecology*, eds M. J. Klug & C. A. Reddy, pp. 279–90. Washington, D.C.: American Society for Microbiology.

Williams, S. T. & Vickers, J. C. (1986). The ecology of antibiotic production. *Microbial Ecology*, **12**, 43–52.

Wolfe, R. S. & Pfennig, N. (1977). Reduction of sulfur by *Spirillum* 5175 and syntrophism with *Chlorobium*. *Applied and Environmental Microbiology*, **33**, 427–33.

Microorganisms and plants

Balandreau, J. & Knowles, R. (1978). The rhizosphere. In *Interactions Between Non-Pathogenic Soil Microorganisms and Plants*, eds Y. R. Dommergues & S. V. Krupa, pp. 243–68. Amsterdam: Elsevier.

Beck, S. M. & Gilmour, C. M. (1983). Role of wheat root exudates in associative nitrogen fixation. *Soil Biology and Biochemistry*, **15**, 33–8.

Bolan, N. S., Robson, A. D., Barrow, N. J. & Aylmore L. A. G. (1984). Specific activity of phosphorus in mycorrhizal and non-mycorrhizal plants in relation to the availability of phosphorus to plants. *Soil Biology and Biochemistry*, **16**, 299–304.

Bowen, G. D. (1980). Misconceptions, concepts and approaches in rhizosphere biology. In *Contemporary Microbial Ecology*, eds D. C. Ellwood, J. N. Hedger, M. J. Latham, J. M. Lynch & J. H. Slater, pp. 283–304. London: Academic Press.

Bowen, G. D. (1984). Development of vesicular-arbuscular mycorrhizae. In *Current Perspectives in Microbial Ecology*, eds M. J. Klug & C. A. Reddy, pp. 201–7. Washington, D.C.: American Society for Microbiology.

Brown, M. E. (1982). Nitrogen fixation by free-living bacteria associated with plants – fact or fiction? In *Bacteria and Plants*, eds M. E. Rhodes-Roberts & F. A. Skinner, pp. 25–41. London: Academic Press.

Dazzo, F. B. (1982). Leguminous root nodules. In *Experimental Microbial Ecology*, eds R. G. Burns & J. H. Slater, pp. 431–46. Oxford, London, Edinburgh, Boston, Melbourne: Blackwell Scientific Publications.

Halverson, L. J. & Stacey, G. (1986). Signal exchange in plant–microbe interactions. *Microbiological Reviews*, **50**, 193–225.

Hardarson, G., Zapata, F. & Danso, S. K. A. (1984). Field evaluation of symbiotic nitrogen fixation by rhizobial strains using ^{15}N methodology. *Plant and Soil*, **82**, 369–75.

Hayman, D. S. (1978). Endomycorrhizae. In *Interactions Between Non-pathogenic Soil Microorganisms and Plants*, eds Y. R. Dommergues & S. V. Krupa, pp. 401–42. Amsterdam: Elsevier Pub. Co.

James, D. W. jr, Suslow, T. V. & Steinback, K. E. (1985). Relationship between rapid, firm adhesion and long-term colonization of roots by bacteria. *Applied and Environmental Microbiology*, **50**, 392–7.

Lynch, J. M. (1982). Interactions between bacteria and plants in the root environment. In *Bacteria and Plants*, eds M. E. Rhodes-Roberts & F. A. Skinner, pp. 1–23. London: Academic Press.

Lynch, J. M. (1982). The rhizosphere. In *Experimental Microbial Ecology*, eds R. G. Burns & J. H. Slater, pp. 395–411. Oxford, London, Edinburgh, Boston, Melbourne: Blackwell Scientific Publications.

Mallik, M. A. B. & Tesfai, K. (1985). Pesticidal effect on soybean–rhizobia symbiosis. *Plant and Soil*, **85**, 33–41.

Marx, D. H. & Krupa, S. V. (1978). Ectomycorrhizae. In *Interactions Between Non-pathogenic Soil Microorganisms and Plants*, eds Y. R. Dommergues & S. V. Krupa, pp. 373–400. Amsterdam: Elsevier Pub. Co.

Mazzucchi, U. (1983). Recognition of bacteria by plants. In *Biochemical Plant Pathology*, ed. J. A. Callow, pp. 299–324. New York: John Wiley & Sons.

Mertens, T. & Hess, D. (1984). Yield increases in spring wheat (*Triticum aestivum* L.) inoculated with *Azospirillum lipoferum* under greenhouse and field conditions of a temperate region. *Plant and Soil*, **82**, 87–99.

Millet, E., Avivi, Y. & Feldman, M. (1985). Effects of rhizospheric bacteria on wheat yield under field conditions. *Plant and Soil*, **86**, 347–55.

Ocampo, J. A. & Barea, J. M. (1985). Effect of carbamate herbicides on VA mycorrhizal infection and plant growth. *Plant and Soil*, **85**, 375–83.

Powell, C. L. (1982). Mycorrhizae. In *Experimental Microbial Ecology*, eds R. G. Burns & J. H. Slater, pp. 447–71. Oxford, London, Edinburgh, Boston, Melbourne: Blackwell Scientific Publications.

Schmidt, E. L. (1979). Initiation of plant root–microbe interactions. *Annual Review of Microbiology*, **33**, 355–78.

Silsbury, J. H. (1977). Energy requirement for symbiotic nitrogen fixation. *Nature*, **267**, 149–50.

Smith, S. E. (1980). Mycorrhizas of autotrophic higher plants. *Biological Reviews*, **55**, 475–510.

Solheim, B. (1984). Infection process in the *Rhizobium*-legume symbiosis. In *Current Perspectives in Microbial Ecology*, eds M. J. Klug & C. A. Reddy, pp. 217–21. Washington, D.C.: American Society for Microbiology.

VanBerkum, P. & Bohlool, B. B. (1980). Evaluation of nitrogen fixation by bacteria in association with roots of tropical grasses. *Microbiological Reviews*, **44**, 491–517.

Whipps, J. M. & Lynch, J. M. (1986). The influence of the rhizosphere on crop productivity. *Advances in Microbial Ecology*, **9**, 187–244.

Yahalom, E., Kapulnik, Y. & Okon, Y. (1984). Response of *Setaria italica* to inoculation with *Azospirillum brasilense* as compared to *Azotobacter chroococcum*. *Plant and Soil*, **82**, 77–85.

Zambre, M. A., Konde, B. K. & Sonar, K. R. (1984). Effect of *Azotobacter chroococcum* and *Azospirillum brasilense* inoculation under graded levels of nitrogen on growth and yield of wheat. *Plant and Soil*, **79**, 61–7.

Microorganisms and animals

Aronson, A. I., Beckman, W. & Dunn, P. (1986). *Bacillus thuringiensis* and related insect pathogens. *Microbiological Reviews*, **50**, 1–24.

Barron, G. L. (1982). Nematode-destroying fungi. In *Experimental Microbial Ecology*, eds R. G. Burns & J. H. Slater, pp. 533–52. Oxford, London, Edinburgh, Boston, Melbourne: Blackwell Scientific Publications.

Bonar, D. B., Weiner, R. M. & Colwell, R. R. (1986). Microbial–invertebrate interactions and potential for biotechnology. *Microbial Ecology*, **12**, 101–10.

Bowden, G. H. W., Ellwood, D. C. & Hamilton, I. R. (1979). Microbial ecology of the oral cavity. In *Advances in Microbial Ecology*, vol. 3, ed. M. Alexander, pp. 135–217. New York: Plenum Press.

214   *Interactions*

Haanstad, J. O. & Norris, D. M. (1985). Microbial symbiotes of the ambrosia beetle *Xyloterinus politus*. *Microbial Ecology*, **11**, 267–76.

Hungate, R. E. (1978). Gut microbiology. In *Microbial Ecology*, eds M. W. Loutit & J. A. R. Miles, pp. 258–64. Berlin: Springer–Verlag.

Latham, M. J. (1979). The animal as an environment. In *Microbial Ecology: A Conceptual Approach*, eds J. M. Lynch & N. J. Poole, pp. 115–37. Oxford, London, Edinburgh, Melbourne: Blackwell Scientific Publications.

Lee, A. (1985). Neglected niches. The microbial ecology of the gastrointestinal tract. *Advances in Microbial Ecology*, **8**, 115–62.

Nealson, K. H. & Hastings, J. W. (1979). Bacterial bioluminescence: its control and ecological significance. *Microbiological Reviews*, **43**, 496–518.

Noble, W. C. & Pitcher, D. G. (1978). Microbial ecology of the human skin. *Advances in Microbial Ecology*, **2**, 245–89.

Nordbring-Hertz, B. & Jansson, H.-B. (1984). Fungal development, predacy, and recognition of prey in nematode-destroying fungi. In *Current Perspectives in Microbial Ecology*, eds M. J. Klug & C. A. Reddy, pp. 327–33. Washington, D.C.: American Society for Microbiology.

Orpin, C. G. (1982). Microbe–animal interactions in the rumen. In *Experimental Microbial Ecology*, eds R. G. Burns & J. H. Slater, pp. 501–18. Oxford, London, Edinburgh, Boston, Melbourne: Blackwell Scientific Publications.

Smith, D. C. (1978). Photosynthetic endosymbionts of invertebrates. In *Companion to Microbiology*, eds A. T. Bull & P. M. Meadow, pp. 387–414. London: Longman.

Trench, R. K. (1979). The cell biology of plant–animal symbioses. *Annual Review of Plant Physiology*, **30**, 485–531.

Walker, G. E. (1984). Ecology of the mycophagous nematode *Aphelenchus avenae* in wheat-field and pine-forest soils. *Plant and Soil*, **78**, 417–28.

Weis, D. S. (1982). Protozoal symbionts. In *Experimental Microbial Ecology*, eds R. G. Burns & J. H. Slater, pp. 320–41. Oxford, London, Edinburgh, Boston, Melbourne: Blackwell Scientific Publications.

Wolin, M. J. (1979). The rumen fermentation: a model for interactions in anaerobic ecosystems. *Advances in Microbial Ecology*, **3**, 49–78.

Microorganisms as human and animal pathogens

Fraser, D. W. & McDade, J. E. (1979). Legionellosis. *Scientific American*, **241**, 82–99.

Lysenko, O. (1985). Non-sporeforming bacteria pathogenic to insects: incidence and mechanisms. *Annual Review of Microbiology*, **39**, 673–95.

8

Microbial activities of ecological significance

The role of microorganisms in the cycling of bioelements

Life on earth is characterized by continuous interrelationships between production and consumption of organic matter. The green plants are the main producers of organic compounds, making use of sun energy and reduction of CO_2 in the process of photosynthesis. A minor part of the primary production results from CO_2 fixation by phototrophic and chemolithoautotrophic bacteria. All organic matter (live and dead plants, animals and microorganisms) is finally decomposed by chemoorganotrophic microorganisms. This process, known as mineralization, leads to the conversion of organic materials into inorganic components. Fixation of bioelements is counteracted by decomposition of the organic biomass, thus maintaining a continuous cycling of the bioelements within the biosphere. The energy conserved in the organic matter flows through the system and is finally dissipated as heat. On a large scale and over a sufficient length of time, the rate of production of organic matter and the rate of its consumption are in a steady state. The role of microorganisms in the biogeochemical cycles is not easy to assess because of the interference of nonbiological processes, such as photochemical reactions and spontaneous oxidations.

In most ecosystems, the largest part of the primary production is not consumed by animals, but becomes part of the pool of detritus originating from dead organisms. For a balance of the bioelements, this pool is required to remain in a steady state.

Microorganisms have an essential function in the cycling of carbon. By aerobic and anaerobic oxidation (mineralization) of the organic materials they produce CO_2, which is the basal compound in photosynthesis. In order to keep the relatively low concentration of CO_2 in the atmosphere constant (0.03%; 12 μM), a steady balance between CO_2 consumption and CO_2 production is essential. Without continuous generation, the CO_2 reserves in the atmosphere would already be exhausted due to photosynthesis of the green plants after some ten years. Including the enormous reserves of CO_2 in the oceans, photosynthesis would go on for about 2000 years. These figures illustrate the interdependence of all living creatures involved in the cycling of carbon. In anaerobic environments, part of the mineralized carbon enters the atmosphere as methane. This gaseous compound is oxidized either chemically, leading to CO_2 via CO, or biologically by the action of methylotrophic bacteria. Since sugars, polysaccharides, and related substances are the main products of the green plants, these compounds are the common nutrients for many organisms, which depend on organic materials.

Cycling of oxygen and hydrogen is intimately connected with the cycling of carbon. During photosynthesis, radiation energy from the sun is transformed into biochemical energy by splitting of water molecules, resulting in the production of oxygen (O_2) and hydrogen (electrons), used in photosynthesis for the production of carbohydrates. During aerobic respiration, the hydrogen from organic carbon compounds is oxidized and furnishes biochemical energy (ATP) with the production of water. The difference in redox potential between hydrogen and oxygen is the source of energy for all aerobically respiring chemoorganotrophs. The hydrogen bound in organic carbon compounds is also the source of energy for the anaerobic organisms, with the difference that hydrogen is not completely oxidized to water but incorporated into reduced fermentation products. Since each oxidation step in aerobic and anaerobic oxidation is connected with a loss of energy, all chemical energy eventually is dissipated as heat.

A variety of microbial processes are involved in cycling of nitrogen. By degradation of organic material, the nitrogen contained in proteins and other nitrogenous organic matter is released as ammonium. This process, known as ammonification, is counteracted by ammonium assimilation. In addition, there are a series of reactions in which nitrogen compounds are interconverted by microorganisms. The main processes are nitrification, assimilatory and dissimilatory nitrate reduction, and nitrogen fixation.

The sulphur cycle is characterized by a series of processes in which sulphur bound in sulphide, sulphate, and organic compounds, as well as elemental sulphur are interconverted.

Phosphorus in biomass is mainly present in the form of phosphate-esters. In soils and waters, the concentration of free ions of orthophosphate (PO_4^{3-}) often is low because of the production of P-complexes of low solubility. For this reason, P (and N) usually are the limiting bioelements in biomass production in both aquatic and terrestrial ecosystems.

The interdependence of macro- and microorganisms is obvious with respect to the essential cycling of the bioelements. Since the effects caused by microbial activities in their natural habitats are not easily detected, and usually remain as hidden as the organisms themselves, it has become an established practice to isolate the microbes, cultivate them in axenic culture, and examine their properties in laboratory experiments. By this classical approach to the study of microbial life, a vast body of information on the physiology and metabolic activities of the various groups of microorganisms has been gathered. Such information has often been interpreted under the tacit assumption that the properties and activities in axenic laboratory culture are comparable with those expressed in the natural environment. Although the laboratory approach has its limitations, it is presently the only way to get information on the properties and behaviour of individual microorganisms. For methodological reasons, it is extremely difficult to assess in situ activities of individual members of a microbial community, as will be discussed in Chapter 9 (Methods).

The carbon cycle
General aspects of carbon cycling
For many millions of years, the green plants have synthesized organic compounds on earth. Nevertheless, considerable amounts have not accumulated. Only a relatively small part of the carbon involved in photosynthesis has been preserved in the form of reduced carbon compounds such as natural gas, oil, and coal. It has been estimated that the CO_2 content of the atmosphere amounts to 2600×10^9 t. By photosynthesis of the green plants on land 129×10^9 t CO_2 are fixed per year. This amount is balanced by the yearly production of 37×10^9 t CO_2 due to respiration of plants and animals and 92×10^9 t CO_2 during microbial mineralization. The interdependence of all organisms on earth becomes particularly obvious in the C cycle (Fig. 8.1). The concentration of CO_2 in the atmosphere on earth (0.03%) has probably been constant for a long time. A local increase (up to 0.05%) has been observed in upwell areas, where CO_2 from beneath the chemocline is released into the atmosphere. In recent years, a small but steady increase of CO_2 in the atmosphere has been monitored. This increase is related to burning of considerable amounts of fossil fuels (oil, coal), which is of the order of 10^9 to 10^{10} t/year. The impact of an atmospheric CO_2 increase on global climate conditions has become a matter of controversial discussion.

Not only biological, but also geochemical processes are involved in the global carbon cycle. Most carbon of the biosphere exists in an oxidized

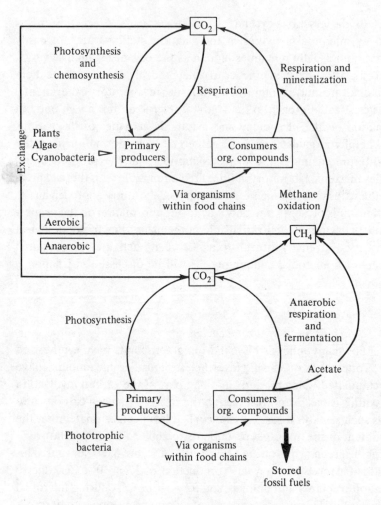

Fig. 8.1 The carbon cycle (biological reactions)

state. Carbonates occur in limestone and other rocks, while bicarbonates occur in the oceans. In the living cells, and also in the fossil fuels derived thereof, organic carbon occurs in the reduced state orginating from CO_2 fixation of algae, cyanobacteria, and vascular plants. The reduced carbon is transformed back to CO_2 by oxidation of organic compounds. Decomposition of biological matter is linked to the carbon and energy metabolism of the participating organisms. It leads to the loss of structure and organization of dead organic matter and is accompanied by the release of inorganic minerals. During decomposition, the carbon of organic matter partially is incorporated into the biomass of the degrading microorganisms and partially is respired with the production of CO_2. All compounds of natural origin are degradable. Depending on the type of organism and the nature of environmental conditions, the organic matter is either completely or partially degraded. Partial degradation results in the production of end products which, for their part, are totally, or again partially, degraded by other organisms. The fate of all natural organic molecules, regardless of their complexity, is the final degradation by microorganisms. In this sense, microorganisms are omnipotent and substantiate the principle of microbial infallibility. The situation has changed since man has synthesized low molecular weight compounds, such as detergents or pesticides, and high molecular weight synthetic polymers that resist microbial degradation, at least for the time under investigation.

Among the organic materials of natural origin, there exist great differences with respect to degradability. Many compounds are easily decomposed, while others are more resistant to microbial attack. The latter include lignins, humins, polyphenols, carotenoids, and waxes. Resistance of organic compounds to microbial attack is most expressed under anaerobic conditions. In the complex natural environments, it is difficult to associate the degradation of a distinct compound with the metabolic activity of a distinct organism. Information on the nature and speed of the degradation of organic molecules stems both from field studies and from laboratory experiments, in particular from enrichment cultures. Such studies have led to the isolation of a variety of microorganisms endowed with definite abilities. The enrichment technique, as usually applied, does not necessarily uncover all types of organisms possessing the ability to be tested. In basal mineral media, supplied with a particular substrate as the carbon and energy source and inoculated with a mixture of organisms present in soil or water, growth will be restricted to the non-fastidious organisms. Moreover, the organisms with the highest growth rate will dominate. Therefore, other more fastidious and slow-growing microorganisms with the same metabolic ability may remain uncovered.

The fate of organic matter from terrestrial plants, animals, and microbes is extremely complex because a great many organisms and a great many compounds are involved. For this reason, our present knowledge of the activities and interactions of microorganisms that participate in the decomposition of organic matter in the natural environment is only rudimentary. The organisms involved in the mineralization of organic matter represent, on their part, a pool of microbial biomass that itself is submitted to turnover and mineralization. Biomass in agricultural soils contains up to 5% of the total soil C, and up to 15% of the total soil N. The average quantities of N, P, K, and Ca, immobilized in the microflora of the soils, are about 100, 80, 70, and 10 kg/ha, respectively. In forest soils, less than 1% of the total C and around 0.2% of the total N are part of the microbial biomass. In conclusion, the microorganisms store considerable amounts of carbon and mineral elements in their own biomass and act both as a sink and a possible source for mineral nutrients.

The rates of carbon transformations have intensively been studied with ^{14}C-labelled compounds. In biogeochemistry and palaeomicrobiology, measurement of the relative contents of ^{12}C and ^{13}C in the various carbon components present in natural environments is a most informative technique. The principle is based on the fact that living organisms discriminate in their metabolic reactions against ^{13}C. Carbon compounds of biological origin, therefore, are lower in ^{13}C, when compared to the C-source used.

Degradation of organic matter

The organic matter underlying degradation originates from primary production. Gross primary production relates to the total carbon incorporated by photosynthesis, while net primary production is the organic matter that remains after loss of carbon (CO_2) by respiration of the primary producers. Estimations on the global net primary production range from 8.5×10^{10} to 1.8×10^{11} t/year. The biomass of plants produced on land mainly consists of wood. Approximately 5% of the terrestrial net primary production is consumed by herbivores, while most of the organic matter (95%) becomes litter (detritus), which is finally decomposed. The net primary production of the oceans is about the same as that on land. Main producers are the algae, particularly diatoms and dinoflagellates, in the upper euphotic zone.

The terrestrial detritus is composed of a broad spectrum of substrates. Most abundant are structural polymers of the plant cell walls. These include cellulose, hemicelluloses, pectins, and lignin. Cellulose is the main component of plant materials, and its production surmounts that of all other natural compounds. Plant residues that are decomposed in the soil consist of 50% or more of cellulose. Microbial degradation of cellulose, therefore, is an essential step in the mineralization process and in carbon cycling. Cellulose is a β-1,4-linked glucan (Fig. 8.2), and the chains of the β-D-glucose have a degree of polymerization of about 12 000. Decomposition of cellulose and of other plant cell wall polymers is mainly due to bacteria and fungi.

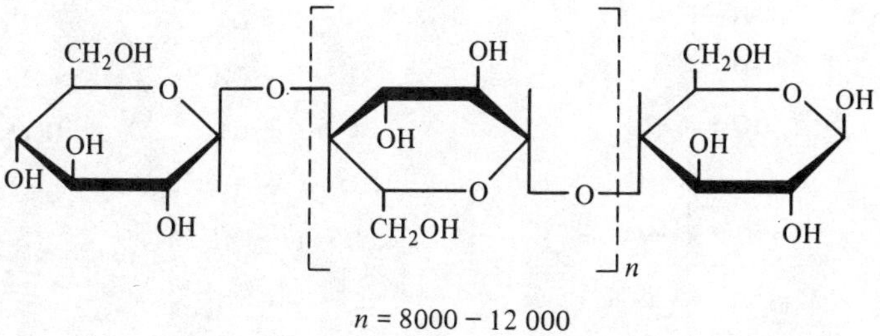

$n = 8000 - 12\ 000$

Fig. 8.2 The structure of cellulose (β-1,4-linked glucan)

After depolymerization the dissimilation of sugars follows the common pathways. Organisms involved in the degradation of the plant polymers must primarily dispose of extracellular enzymes capable of hydrolysing the glycosidic links. The cellulase-system in fungi consists of at least three enzymes: (1) Endo-β-1,4-glucanases, which act on polymers but not on dimers or trimers; (2) Exo-β-1,4-glucanases, which split off the disaccharide cellobiose, starting from the end of the cellulose chain; (3) β-glucosidases, which finally hydrolyse cellobiose resulting in the formation of glucose. In laboratory cultures, the cellulolytic microorganisms only produce these enzymes if cellulose is the only carbon and energy source available. Enzyme production is abated by the presence of other substrates, e.g. glucose.

Decomposition of cellulose is due to eubacteria, myxobacteria, and fungi. Under anaerobic conditions, breakdown of cellulose is performed mainly by mesophilic and thermophilic clostridia. Under aerobic conditions in soil, fungi play a major role. They dominate in particular under acid soil conditions and account for the breakdown of cellulose in wood. Involved are large numbers of Fungi imperfecti and a variety of basidiomycetes. Partly degraded cellulose is hydrolysed by members of the genera *Fusarium, Trichoderma, Cephalosporium, Truncatella, Gliocladium, Chaetomium, Rhizoctonia, Humicola, Penicillium*, and *Verticillium*. Among the bacteria, members of the general *Cytophaga, Sporocytophaga, Cellulomonas*, and some actinomycetes are involved in cellulose degradation.

The nutrition of the ruminants is mainly based on grass, hay, and straw containing about 50% of the dry mass as cellulose. The symbiotic interactions between microorganisms and ruminants have already been discussed (Chapter 7). The bacteria of the rumen degrade the polymeric carbohydrates and produce low molecular weight compounds such as fatty acids and alcohols. Rumen bacteria involved in the degradation of

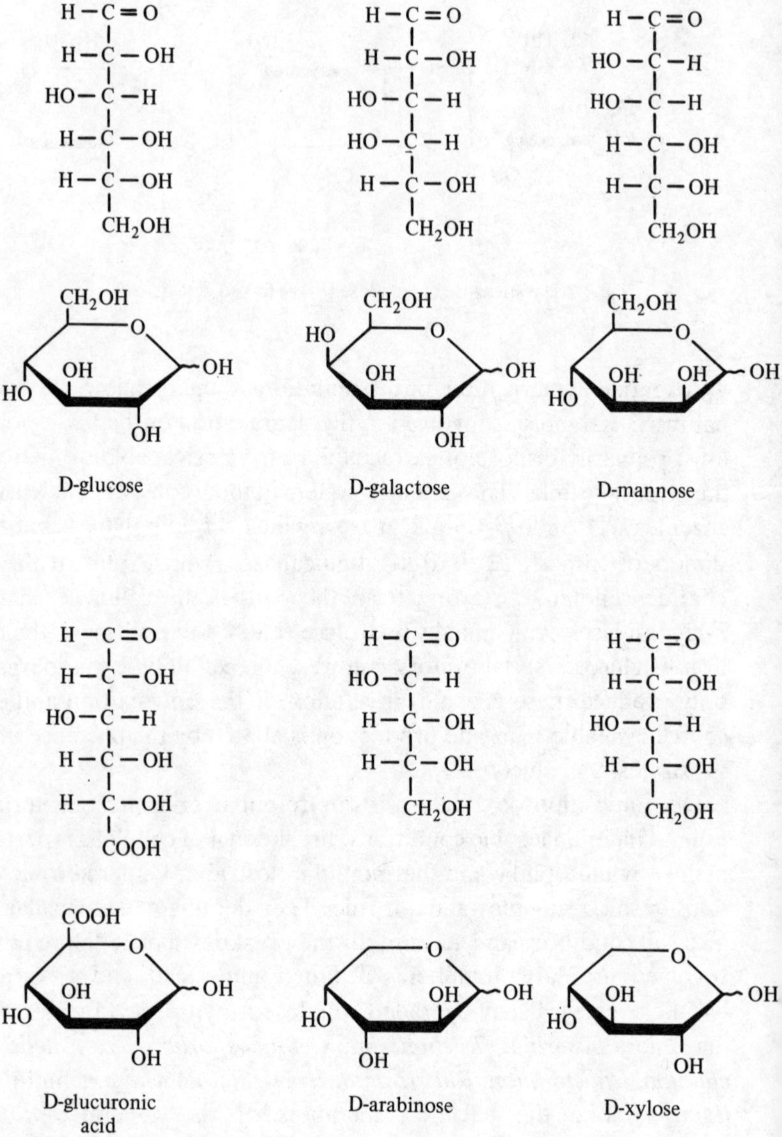

H — C = O
H — C — OH
HO — C — H
H — C — OH
H — C — OH
CH₂OH

H — C = O
H — C — OH
HO — C — H
HO — C — H
H — C — OH
CH₂OH

H — C = O
HO — C — H
HO — C — H
H — C — OH
H — C — OH
CH₂OH

D-glucose

D-galactose

D-mannose

H — C = O
H — C — OH
HO — C — H
H — C — OH
H — C — OH
COOH

H — C = O
HO — C — H
H — C — OH
H — C — OH
CH₂OH

H — C = O
H — C — OH
HO — C — H
H — C — OH
CH₂OH

D-glucuronic
acid

D-arabinose

D-xylose

Fig. 8.3 Components of xylans (hemicelluloses)

cellulose are *Ruminococcus albus, R. flavefaciens, Bacteroides suc-cinogenes, Butyrivibrio fibrisolvens,* and *Clostridium cellobioparum.*

Besides cellulose, xylan, also known as hemicellulose, is most abundant in nature. Xylans are composed of pentoses, hexoses, and uronic acids (Fig. 8.3). The basal xylan chain consists of β-D-xylose molecules that are

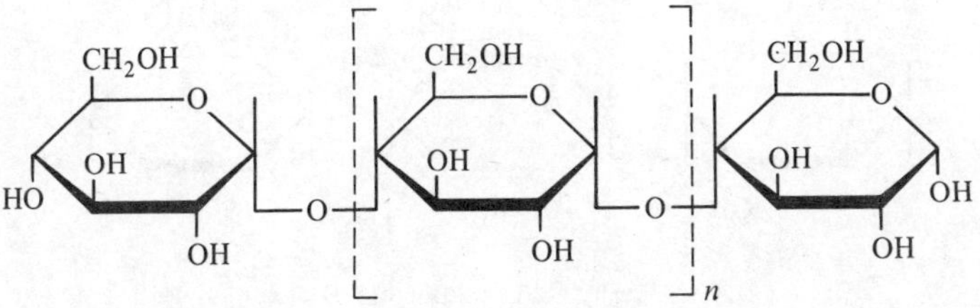

$$n = 200 - 5000$$

Fig. 8.4 Structure of amylose (α-1,4-linked glucan)

linked by β-1,4-glycosidic bonds. Xylan is more readily attacked by microorganisms than cellulose, and many cellulolytic microorganisms also produce xylanase. The majority of fungi is capable of utilizing xylan. Among the bacteria, bacilli, *Sporocytophaga*, and a variety of other bacteria are involved in xylan decomposition.

Starch as the dominating reserve material of many plants consists of amylose and amylopectin and is readily decomposed by microorganisms. Amylose is a polymer of D-glucose with α-glycosidic links in 1,4-position (Fig. 8.4). Amylopectin likewise is poly-α-1,4-D-glucose. The molecule, however, is branched in the 1,6-position. A great many fungi and bacteria produce α-amylases and are capable of degrading starch. A potent producer of amylase among fungi is *Aspergillus oryzae*, and among bacteria is *Bacillus macerans*. Under anaerobic conditions, starch is mainly decomposed by saccharolytic clostridia. Glucans, other than starch, are common products in microorganisms and function as reserve materials. Many plants, in particular grasses, have a relatively high content (12 to 15%) of fructans (laevans). Fructanases have been isolated from both fungi and bacteria and seem to be common in nature. Laevan production is also known in microorganisms, particularly in the presence of saccharose.

Pectins are a group of complex polysaccharides which basically consist of α-1,4-linked D-galacturonic acid residues (Fig. 8.5). The pectins are derived from protopectins that occur in plants in the middle lamellae or in the primary cell wall, in association with hemicelluloses. Many fruits have a high pectin content, and pectins also occur in the cell walls of certain algae. A wide range of fungi and bacteria are capable of degrading pectins. In some phytopathogenic fungi such as *Botrytis cinerea*, and bacteria such as *Erwinia carotovora*, pectinolytic activity is associated with pathogenicity. Pectinolytic organisms occur in the rumen and are also involved in the retting process in which stems of flax and similar

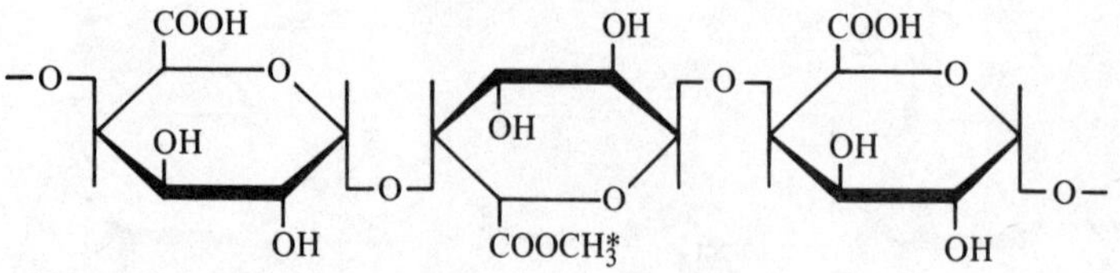

*Methylated building block

Fig. 8.5 Structure of pectin (poly α-1,4-galacturonic acid)

plants are attacked by microorganisms, causing release of fibres of cellulose. Some spore-forming bacteria such as *Bacillus macerans* and *Bacillus polymyxa* are very active in pectin degradation. Two types of enzymes are mainly involved in the breakdown of pectins: (a) pectin methyl esterases which split the ester bonds and remove the methyl groups, and (b) polygalacturonases which break down the D-galacturonan chain. Specificity and mode of action of these enzymes appears to vary considerably.

Lignins occur in the woody material of vascular plants, and are found in the plant cell walls in close association with cellulose and hemicelluloses. The woody plant tissues contain 18 to 30% by weight of lignin. Lignins are encrusted in the secondary lamellae of the cell wall. Among the plant materials produced in large quantity, the lignins are degraded most slowly. They are extremely resistant to microbial attack and represent the main source of the slowly decaying organic matter in soil. Lignins are attacked almost exclusively by fungi, especially by the 'white-rot' basidiomycetes. Some members of the ascomycetes (e.g. *Xylaria*) are also capable of attacking lignins. The fungi release enzymes that split the polymer into its constituent subunits, which are then susceptible to further degradation by a variety of microorganisms, both fungi and bacteria. The role of bacteria in the degradation of lignin is not yet clear. Studies with ^{14}C-labelled synthetic lignin polymers indicate that bacteria may be more important in lignin metabolism than hitherto assumed.

Chemically, the lignins represent a class of complex polymers that are composed of phenyl-propanoid subunits (Fig. 8.6). A common constituent is coniferyl alcohol (3-methoxy-4-hydroxyphenyl-prop-1-ene-3-ol). The complexity is based on the great number of different linkages of the subunits. Like coniferyl alcohol, coumaryl and sinapyl alcohols are derived from phenylpropane. The irregular structure of lignin is caused by the random non-enzymic polymerization of the free aromatic radicals which are produced enzymatically. The proportions of the monomers

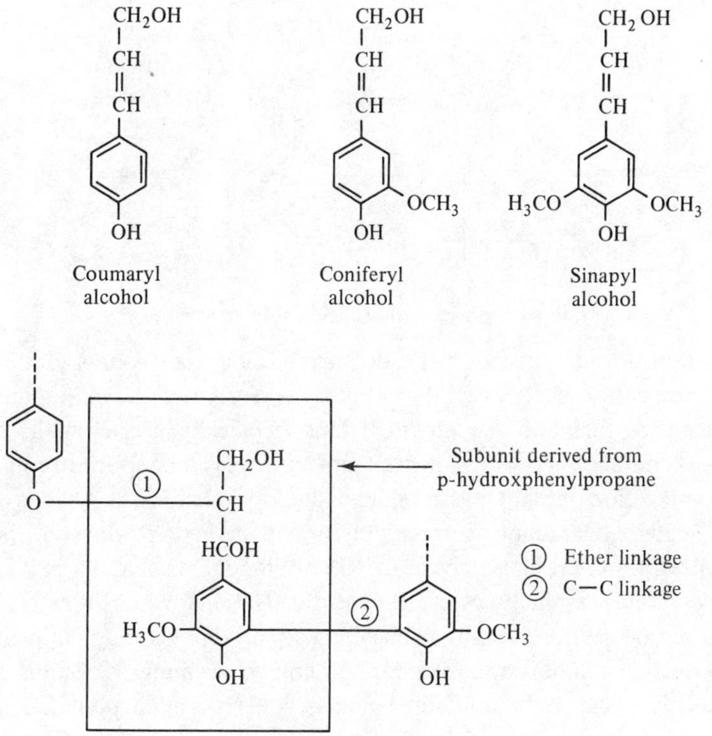

Fig. 8.6 Some components of lignin

vary in different groups of plants. The lignin of firs mainly consists of coniferyl alcohol, while deciduous trees contain coniferyl and sinapyl alcohol; grasses, in addition, contain coumaryl alcohol. The building blocks of lignin form a net containing ether and C-C linkages that are irregularly arranged (Fig. 8.6). These linkages are extremely resistant against enzymatic attack. Compared to cellulose and hemicelluloses, the lignins are only slowly degraded by wood-decaying fungi and bacteria. In the breakdown of lignins mono-oxygenases, di-oxygenases, and phenol-oxidases are involved. Basidiomycetes cause various forms of decay of wood, known as rots. The fungi causing 'brown rots' degrade the cellulose and hemicelluloses (xylans) of the wood and leave the lignin component intact. In 'white rots', all components of the wood are destroyed turning it soft and fibrous. The complete decay is performed by fungi that primarily attack lignin, and others that degrade both lignin and cellulose.

Lignin as the second most abundant naturally occurring organic polymer is a significant component of the carbon cycle. The microbiological and biochemical aspects of lignin biodegradation have attracted

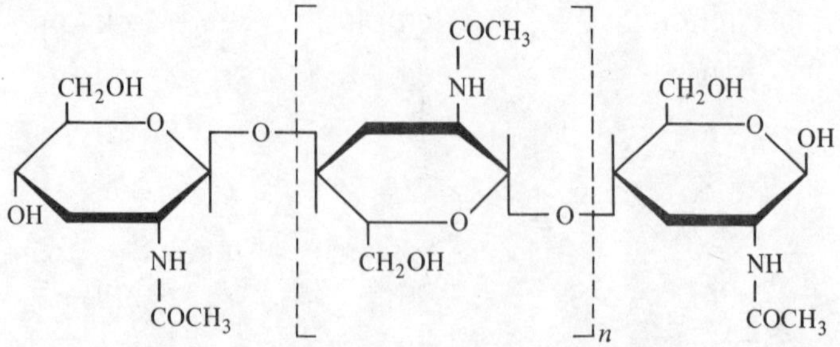

Fig. 8.7 Structure of chitin (β-1,4-linked N-acetylglucosamine)

much interest, but are not yet fully understood. In biodegradation studies, utilization of lignocelluloses extracted from radiolabelled plant materials and utilization of synthetic lignins specifically labelled with ^{14}C in distinct components of the complex molecule, play an important role.

Decomposition of plant and animal residues in soil occurs in a series of steps. Readily degradable components are immediately attacked and mineralized by microbial activities. Other components that are not as easily degraded remain intact and are preserved in soil for some time. The portion of material originating from biomass and representing an insoluble brown and amorphous residue, is known as humus. Humus is derived from decay of the soil fungal biomass and from lignin polymerization.

There is much evidence that bacteria and fungi, protozoa and worms are involved in humus production. Certain bacteria, actinomycetes, and fungi produce dark polymers that resemble humus. Humification of plant materials is accompanied by an increase in nitrogen. While the C:N-ratio of plant residues is around 40:1, it is 10:1 in humus. The persistence of humus in soils has been estimated to range from 5 to 2000 years depending on the type of soil. Humus production is under steady-state conditions in soil with constant humus concentration. In tropical soils, humus is usually scarce because of the rapid decay of all organic materials due to the higher temperatures. Long and cold winters and dry summers, on the other hand, favour the accumulation of humus as noted in most northern latitudes. The nature of plant materials, together with climatic and edaphic conditions, decide on the production of soil humus. It is generally observed that soils rich in humus, compared to mineral soils, have a more complex microflora.

In animal residues, chitin and keratin are the most important substrates. Chitin is composed of β-1,4-linked N-acetyl-D-glucosamine residues (Fig. 8.7). It occurs both in animals and plants and is the main component of exoskeletons of arthropods and of cell walls in fungi. A great number of soil and marine bacteria are capable of degrading chitin. Microorganisms with chitinolytic activity are known in the genera *Flavobacterium, Bacillus, Pseudomonas, Cytophaga,* and in many actinomycetes. There is a high portion of chitin-degrading microorganisms in soil, indicating that this substrate is ubiquitous and abundant. Some actinomycetes (*Streptomyces* spp.) are particularly favoured in the presence of chitin. Chitinase and chitobiase are involved in the degradation of chitin. Keratin, which is a highly insoluble protein, occurs mainly in hair, wool, horn, and skin. Relatively few organisms produce keratinases. Among the specialists attacking keratin are *Keratinomyces* spp., *Trichophyton* spp., and also the dermatophyte *Candida albicans*.

Apart from the macromolecular compounds discussed above, a broad spectrum of other organic substrates is likewise involved in carbon cycling. These include aliphatic and aromatic hydrocarbons as well as proteins and nucleic acids occurring in the plant and animal biomass. Hydrocarbons are not only fossil relics of primary production of early eras of the earth, but are secondary metabolites continuously produced by many microorganisms and plants. Among the hydrocarbons, methane is the most important compound. It is produced under anaerobic conditions by methanogens and is oxidized under aerobic conditions by methylotrophic bacteria such as *Methylomonas, Methylococcus, Methylosinus,* and *Methanomonas*. A wide variety of microorganisms are capable of utilizing aliphatic hydrocarbons as carbon and energy source. Straight-chain alkanes appear to be the most widely used, but branched-chain alkyl-alkanes and unsaturated hydrocarbons (alkenes) are also metabolized by some organisms. In general, long-chain hydrocarbons are more readily used than are short-chain hydrocarbons. A variety of bacteria (*Mycobacterium, Corynebacterium, Nocardia, Actinomyces, Pseudomonas*) and yeasts (*Candida, Hansenula, Torulopsis*) and filamentous fungi (*Aspergillus, Botrytis, Fusarium, Cladosporium*) are capable of degrading hydrocarbons. In this strictly aerobic process, a mono-oxygenase is involved that leads to the formation of a primary alcohol. The alcohol is then oxidized to the corresponding fatty acid which finally is degraded by β-oxidation. Plant and animal materials contain a range of organic compounds with aromatic rings. Splitting of the ring and further degradation is accomplished by many bacteria and fungi. Since breakdown of the aromatic ring is mediated by oxygenases, the process depends on the presence of molecular oxygen.

Degradation of organic matter in aquatic environments underlies the same principle as in terrestrial environments. There are, however, specific aspects related to the type of the aquatic habitat and to the nature of the organic materials present. In rivers of developed and industrialized areas, the carbonaceous materials mainly come from domestic, agricultural, and industrial sources. Depending on the amounts of degradable substances, drastic alterations of the O_2 balance occur. Because of the low O_2 solubility in water (1 litre of water, in equilibrium with air at atmospheric pressure and 20 °C, contains 6.2 ml of O_2), intense microbiological activity depletes the dissolved oxygen and induces oxygen-poor or anaerobic conditions, which influence life of the higher organisms. With extreme amounts of organic discharge into rivers and ponds, foul-smelling waters may develop that no longer allow existence of any higher forms of life. The O_2 demand in relation to the carbon content can be characterized by the COD (chemical oxygen demand) and the BOD (biological oxygen demand). Since COD estimates all the oxidizable materials including non-biodegradable substances, the influence of the carbon content on biological effects is more appropriately comprehended by BOD-values. A common test for evaluation of the biodegradable organic materials in water samples is BOD_5, which is based on the measurement of dissolved oxygen at the start and after five days of incubation at 20 °C in the dark. While in a 'clean' water course the bacterial numbers are around 10^2 to 10^3/ml, pollution by organic materials usually causes an increase in bacterial numbers of up to 10^6 to 10^7/ml, or even more. As a consequence of oxygen depletion, anoxic conditions arise that are accompanied by successions of organisms which by their metabolic activities lower the redox potential of the environment. In well-aerated waters, the ROP (reduction–oxidation potential) is between +200 and +600 mV. Between 0 and +200 mV, microaerophilic bacteria prevail, while at ROPs below 0 mV anaerobic phototrophs and chemoorganotrophs such as clostridia, H_2S producers, and methanogens are favoured. The strict anaerobes only develop at potentials below −150 mV. Habitats with such a low ROP generally are devoid of eukaryotes.

Organic matter in lakes, seas, and oceans predominantly originates from photosynthetic microorganisms. In shallow marshes and inshore waters, also plant materials and organic nutrients from land drainage are involved. The rate of primary production in offshore waters is limited by the lack of N and P. Because of the presence of large amounts of bicarbonate and sulphate, C and S are never limited in the open sea. Due to the extremely low concentration of nitrogen (0.000 05%), the rate of primary production is very low in oligotrophic lakes and the infertile open sea. In polluted streams and ponds as well as in estuaries, the rate of production is considerably higher. The phytoplankton is consumed mainly by the zooplankton, and the algae directly enter the animal food chain. The organic matter available for microbial mineralization originates from exudation of organic substances by phytoplankton and macroalgae, from excretion of animals, and from decay of dead organisms. In springs, oligotrophic lakes, and in the open sea, the concentration of organic matter is extremely low (less than 2 mg/l). The exudation products include amino acids, fatty acids, glycerol, carbohydrates, polysaccharides, and other soluble organics. The organic matter which is not consumed or mineralized in the surface layers, sinks to the bottom and becomes part of the sediments. In the anaerobic sediment and mud, acidic fermentation products accumulate and lower the pH, so that most bacteria are inhibited in their function. Under such conditions, many sea compounds escape decomposition and are preserved in the sediments. As long as anaerobic decomposition of organic matter is possible, it is accompanied by the production of CO_2, H_2, H_2S, and CH_4. The methanogens and the sulphate respiring bacteria (performing dissimilatory sulphate reduction) are the last groups in the anaerobic food chain. In the presence of high concentrations of sulphate, as common in sea water, a greater part of the organic matter is decomposed via sulphate reduction. The desulphurizing bacteria are particularly adapted to the utilization of fatty acids, alcohols, and H_2 that accumulate in the mud and impair the development of other anaerobic organisms. Their concentration in the mud amounts to 10^7 bacteria/ml.

Methane oxidation has long been regarded as an aerobic process that essentially depends on the presence of molecular oxygen. Although the mechanism is not yet understood, there is some evidence that methane oxidation to CO_2 in lake waters also occurs in the absence of oxygen. Enrichment cultures with acetate and methane, as the sole sources of carbon and energy, and with sulphate as the electron acceptor, resulted in the growth of bacteria capable of methane oxidation. Acetate was not oxidized to CO_2 but assimilated by the cells, while methane was not assimilated but oxidized to CO_2 in the absence of oxygen.

Degradation of fossil fuels
The fossil fuels, coal and oil, originate from partial decomposition of organic materials. The process characterized by incomplete decomposition of organic matter results in the removal of carbon from the biological carbon cycle. The generation of peats, which develop in waterlogging of

litter, can be regarded as the progenitors of coal deposits. The most significant factor in the incomplete decay of plant residues is the absence of oxygen, causing anaerobic degradation with the production of metabolites that inhibit microbial activities. In peats, therefore, lignin, humic acids, and phenolics, accumulate and are preserved from further decomposition. An impressive proof and demonstration of the accumulation of some preservative chemicals is the known preservation of animal and human corpses in bogs. The conversion of peats or peat-like substrates into coal has involved burial by inorganic sediments and changes in temperature and pressure during geological periods. By such alterations the relative carbon content, which is about 55% in peats, has increased to 73% in lignites, 83% in bituminous coal, and 94% in anthracite. Coal, as presently found in collieries, is regarded as the product of the great freshwater forest swamps existing in carboniferous times.

Also crude oil is of biological origin. It is the predominant fossil fuel in marine environments and has been derived from anaerobic alteration of masses of marine algae. Crude oil contains alkanes, pristanes, isoprenoids, and porphyrins which have accumulated in marine sediments in the ancient seas. The phytoplankton that escaped degradation later were buried by inorganic sediments and subjected to high temperatures and pressure. By polymerization and condensation, the materials were transformed into an isoluble complex which, after additional geochemical changes and thermal cracking, resulted in the production of a mixture of hydrocarbons, including gases such as methane, ethane, propane, and butane. The fossil fuels have been preserved in their anoxic environments for geological periods and are nowadays used as the main sources of energy.

The formation of methane occurs in sediments and in special habitats as the rumen and the rotting wet heartwood of trees. In the microbial food chain, involved in anoxic carbon transformation, the interspecies hydrogen transfer is an important feature. Since sulphate is a more advantageous electron acceptor for thermodynamic reasons, dissimilatory sulphate reduction prevails in marine sediments which usually have high levels of sulphate. Methanogenesis, on the other hand, plays a major role in freshwater sediments.

The fossil fuels which have been preserved under anoxic conditions are partly degraded in an aerobic environment. While lignites and coals are resistant to microbial degradation, most components of crude oil are readily attacked by a variety of organisms. The crude oil represents an extremely heterogeneous mixture of substrates containing up to 200 different hydrocarbons. Oil-degrading microorganisms are ubiquitous in nature. Many bacteria (*Pseudomonas, Micrococcus, Corynebacterium, Mycobacterium*), yeasts (*Candida, Torulopsis, Pichia*), and filamentous fungi (*Cladosporium resinae*) readily degrade n-alkanes (C_{11} to C_{19}). Highly recalcitrant are the multiple ring systems which, in nature, remain stable for long periods. Such compounds cannot readily be utilized as sources of carbon and energy, but are usually degraded through co-metabolism.

The ubiquitous occurrence of hydrocarbon-degrading microorganisms is related to the fact that hydrocarbons are continuously synthesized. They are constituents of the wax-like substances covering plant leaves, and, therefore, are not only fossils of the primary production of the marine algae of ancient geological periods but also occur as secondary metabolites that presently are produced in large quantities.

Oil-degraders in soils and waters have considerable ecological importance in view of the increasing numbers of oil spillages. Since all types of microbial activities depend on the presence of water, oil decomposition occurs near the oil–water interface. While oil degradation is a desirable process in spillages, it may be unwanted on other occasions. Economically important losses are caused by microbial deterioration of oil–water emulsions used for lubrication of machine tools. Serious problems may arise from growth of moulds (e.g. *Cladosporium resinae*) in aircraft fuel and storage tanks. The development of mycelial mass in the water–oil interface may result in plugging of the fuel lines and cause power loss of the engines.

In the set of hydrocarbons, methane has an exceptional position, as already explained in the preceding chapter. Only a restricted number of bacteria are capable of oxidizing methane and of using this C_1 compound as the carbon and energy source. The methanotrophic bacteria oxidize methane by means of a methane-oxygenase and generate reducing power for energy production by oxidation of methane to CO_2 via methanol, formaldehyde, and formate. The intermediate formaldehyde is incorporated into the cell either by the ribulose-5-phosphate or by the serine pathway.

Obligate methanotrophs are members of the genera *Methylomonas, Methylococcus, Methylosinus*, and *Methanomonas*. These organisms also possess the ability to fix elemental nitrogen. Obligate C_1-metabolism is also known in bacteria which are incapable of methane oxidation but which utilize methanol or methylamines. In addition, there are great numbers of bacteria and yeasts that are classified as facultative methylotrophs. These organisms are capable of utilizing C_1-compounds (except methane) and also have the ability to oxidize substrates containing C—C bonds. The latter group includes several yeasts and bacteria of the genera *Arthrobacter, Pseudomonas, Bacillus, Hyphomicrobium, Methylobacterium.*

The nitrogen cycle
General aspects of nitrogen cycling

Apart from carbon and water, nitrogen is the nutrient that is required in greatest quantities. It is a key constituent of all living cells and occurs in several oxidation states, R—NH_2, NH_3, NH_4^+, N_2, N_2O, NO, NO_2^-, NO_3^-. The main forms of nitrogen in the biosphere are N_2, NH_3, R—NH_2, and NO_3^-. While the atmosphere contains large amounts of chemically unreactive N_2, the lithosphere and particularly the oceans have a relatively low nitrogen content. In the cycling of nitrogen (Fig. 8.8), non-biological transformations have but little importance. Through lightning discharges and photochemical reactions only small amounts of N_2 are converted into NH_3. Biological transformations are of fundamental importance because some reactions are exclusively performed by microorganisms. On a global basis, nitrogen of the biosphere is distributed as follows:

N in the atmosphere	$3\ 800\ 000 \times 10^9$ t
N in the plant biomass (on land)	12×10^9 t
N in dead organic matter (on land)	300×10^9 t
N in the plant biomass (in oceans)	0.3×10^9 t
N in dead organic matter (in oceans)	550×10^9 t.

Although the atmosphere is the main reservoir of nitrogen, only a few per cent of the primary production depend on fixation of N_2. The majority of biomass production is based on NH_4^+ and NO_3^-. The reservoir of inorganic N (NH_4^+, NO_2^-, NO_3^-) has been estimated to be in the range of 2×10^{11} t.

The central compound of the nitrogen cycle is NH_4^+, the product of protein and amino-acid degradation from dead plants, animals, and microorganisms. In biological materials, N exists almost exclusively in the reduced form (R—NH_2), and by ammonification it is released as NH_3 (NH_4^+). In this process, immobilized N is converted into mobile N which is used as nitrogen source by plants and microorganisms. Ammonification has been estimated to amount to 3×10^{10} t/yr. Free NH_4^+ which is not incorporated into biomass, is subject to nitrification, a process leading to

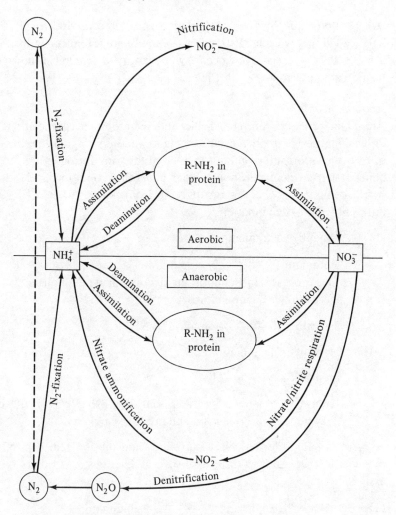

Fig. 8.8 The nitrogen cycle (biological reactions)

the production of NO_3^-. Bacterial nitrification by chemolithoautotrophic nitrifiers requires aerobic conditions. Many plants and microorganisms have the capacity of utilizing nitrate in a process known as assimilatory nitrate reduction. Under anaerobic conditions, a variety of micro-organisms make use of dissimilatory nitrate reduction. This process, also known as denitrification (cp. Fig. 2.9), leads to losses of gaseous nitrogen (N_2, N_2O). In denitrification, nitrate is used as the terminal e-acceptor; it is an alternative to O_2 respiration. The loss of gaseous nitrogen by denitrification is balanced by N_2 fixation. It has been estimated that about

2×10^8 t N/yr are involved. N_2 fixation is, therefore, vital for a well-balanced global N cycle. Estimations of the biological nitrogen fixation are 2×10^8 t N/yr (land and ocean) while industrial (chemical) nitrogen fixation amounts to 0.4×10^8 t N/yr.

Ammonification
Ammonia released during aerobic and anaerobic decomposition of organic matter is rapidly recycled by plants and microorganisms. Losses of NH_3 by vaporization amount to 15% of the total nitrogen loss, 85% being lost from denitrification. Under anaerobic conditions, NH_4^+ is a stable compound. The release of NH_4^+ from amino acids occurs by different types of deamination:

(1)   Oxidative deamination:

glutamate $\xrightarrow{\text{glutamate-DH}}$ 2-oxoglutarate
This process is most important in amino-acid metabolism.

(2)   Desaturative deamination:

aspartic acid $\xrightarrow{\text{aspartase}}$ fumarate + NH_3

(3)   Hydrolytic deamination:

urea $\xrightarrow{\text{urease}}$ NH_3 + CO_2

Urease is repressed by NH_4^+, but also exists as constitutive enzyme, e.g. in *Proteus sp.* and in *Sporosarcina ureae*.

At neutral pH, little free NH_3 is present, and the ionized form NH_4^+ prevails. Microorganisms dispose of several reactions for primary NH_4^+ assimilation:

(1) NH_4^+ + 2-oxoglutarate $\xrightarrow{\text{glutamate-DH}}$ glutamate

(2) NH_4^+ + pyruvate $\xrightarrow{\text{alanine-DH}}$ alanine

(3) NH_4^+ + glutamate $\xrightarrow[\text{ATP}]{\text{glutamine synthetase}}$ glutamine

Glutamine synthetase has a high affinity to NH_4^+ and operates at extremely low NH_4^+ concentrations (less than 1 mM).

The major process in the assimilation of NH_4^+ produced during N_2 fixation is the glutamine synthetase–GOGAT pathway. GOGAT is glutamine: α-oxoglutarate aminotransferase; the enzyme catalyses the amination of oxoglutarate to glutamic acid.

glutamine + 2-oxoglutarate $\xrightarrow{\text{GOGAT}}$ 2 glutamic acid

Nitrification

Nitrification is the aerobic process in which ammonia is oxidized to nitrite, and nitrite to nitrate, by the chemolithotrophic nitrifying bacteria. The process occurs in two stages.

(1)   Ammonia is oxidized to nitrite via hydroxylamine. The stoichiometry is

$$NH_4^+ + 1\tfrac{1}{2}O_2 \rightarrow NO_2^- + 2H^+ + H_2O + 276 \text{ kJ } (-\Delta G_0'/\text{mol})$$

(2)   For oxidation of nitrite to nitrate the stoichiometry is

$$NO_2^- + \tfrac{1}{2}O_2 \rightarrow NO_3^- + 73 \text{ kJ } (-\Delta G_0'/\text{mol})$$

Nitrification is a strictly aerobic process and does not occur at redox values lower than $+200$ mV (E_0'). The optimum of nitrification occurs at neutral or slightly alkaline conditions (pH 7–8). Since nitrate, the end product in the two-step reaction, is highly soluble and easily leached from soils after rainfall, the process is agriculturally disadvantageous. Therefore, attempts have been made to counteract nitrification by use of inhibitors of ammonia oxidation. A compound specifically inhibiting the oxidation of NH_4^+ is, for instance, 'N-serve' (2-chloro-6-trichloromethyl pyridine). In contrast to nitrate, the positively charged NH_4^+ ions are strongly adsorbed to the negatively charged clay minerals, and thus are prevented from leaching.

The organisms involved in nitrification represent two separate groups of bacteria. They are obligate chemolithoautotrophs obtaining carbon from CO_2 and energy from oxidation of the reduced nitrogenous compounds. Until recently, nitrification was mainly thought to be contributed by the bacterial species *Nitrosomonas europaea* and *Nitrobacter winogradskyi*. It is now known that a variety of other species are involved in nitrification. Oxidation of NH_4^+ to NO_2^- is performed by members of the genera *Nitrosomonas, Nitrosospira, Nitrosolobus, Nitrosovibrio,* and *Nitrosococcus*, while members of the genera *Nitrobacter, Nitrospina,* and *Nitrococcus* participate in the oxidation of NO_2^- to NO_3^-. High concentrations of NH_4^+ inhibit nitrite oxidation. By reducing the concentration of NH_4^+, the first-step nitrifiers thus favour the development of the second-step nitrifiers. The conversion of ammonium to nitrate is connected with acidification causing higher solubility of minerals.

•The nitrifiers are slow-growing organisms. Generation times under optimum conditions in the laboratory are in the range of several hours, while, in soils, generation times of several days have been established. Slow growth and low growth yields (per mole of substrate) are characteristic of the nitrifiers, and also of some other chemolithotrophs. While in *Escherichia coli*, for the synthesis of 1 g dry mass (biomass), 2 g of glucose are required, *Nitrosomonas* has to oxidize 30 g of NH_3 for production of the same amount of biomass. The low growth yield is related to the relatively low amount of energy generated during oxidation of the reduced inorganic substrates, and to the high energy requirement for the generation of reducing power. For thermodynamic reasons, the +uction of NAD^+ by direct coupling to the e-donor NH_4^+ or NO_2^- is not possible, because the redox potential (E_0') of $NAD^+/NADH$ is -320 mV, but that of NH_4^+/NH_2OH $+899$ mV, and that of NO_2^-/NO_3^- $+420$ mV. During substrate oxidation, the electrons enter the respiratory chain at the levels of cyt c or cyt a. Consequently, only one site is available for an oxidative phosphorylation, leading to a relatively low gain of energy. In addition, a large part of the available energy has to be used for the generation of reducing power (NADH) required for CO_2 fixation, in an ATP-dependent process of reversed electron transport. The nitrifiers, therefore, live in a tense energy situation, which is mirrored by the long generation time and the low growth yield.

Ammonia oxidation is best at high pH values, because the enzyme involved in the initial oxidation step appears to prefer the non-ionized NH_3. The mixed-functional oxygenase requires molecular O_2, one O-atom going into NH_2OH. In the second step which is catalysed by hydroxylamine-oxidoreductase and leads to nitrite, the electrons are coupled to cyt a_1, resulting in the generation of ATP.

The concentration of nitrifying bacteria in soil, in general, is between 10^3 and 10^5 cells/g soil. In environments with high NH_4^+ contents like sludge, concentrations increase up to 10^7–10^8 bacteria/g of substrate. Until recently, nitrification was exclusively attributed to the activity of chemolithoautotrophic bacteria. It is now well established that also a number of nonlithotrophic bacteria and fungi have the capability of oxidizing NH_4^+. In contrast to the autotrophic nitrification, this heterotrophic process appears not to be connected with microbial growth. It is probably related to co-oxidation. The rate of nitrification by heterotrophs is much less than by the chemolithotrophic nitrifiers. Although the amount of nitrate production by heterotrophic nitrification is negligible, the process explains nitrate production in acidic soils where growth of lithotrophic nitrifiers is inhibited.

Denitrification

Denitrification refers to the conversion of NO_3^- (or NO_2^-) into dinitrogen (N_2) and/or gaseous oxides of nitrogen (NO, N_2O) by bacterial nitrate respiration (Fig. 2.9). The process occurs under anoxic conditions and is performed by essentially aerobic bacteria. Nitrate serves as an alternative e-acceptor in the absence of molecular O_2. Denitrification has attracted much interest for several reasons. (1) Loss of fertilizer nitrogen means a decreased efficiency of fertilization. (2) By release in addition to N_2 of NO and N_2O into the atmosphere, denitrification is involved in reactions that may cause destruction of the ozone layer. (3) Denitrification is the mechanism which balances dinitrogen fixation in the global N cycle. (4) Potential application of the process in the removal of nitrogen from waste materials (waste water) with high nitrate concentrations.

Nitrate reduction is performed by many bacteria, fungi, and by all plants assimilating nitrate as the nitrogen source. In this process, which occurs under both aerobic and anaerobic conditions, NO_3^- is reduced to NH_3. Contrary to assimilatory nitrate reduction, respiratory (dissimilatory) nitrate reduction is only known in bacteria. NO_3^- is reduced via NO_2^- and NO to N_2O and N_2. By using NO_3^- as an electron sink, the bacteria perform nitrate respiration which serves to generate energy, as does O_2 respiration. The denitrifying bacteria dispose of a respiratory chain in which reduction of NO_3^- to NO_2^- is coupled to cyt b. Compared to the electron transport chain involving O_2, that of the denitrifying bacteria is shorter and, therefore, leads to the generation of only 2 ATP. Growth with nitrate, consequently, is less efficient than growth with O_2.

The reduction of NO_3^- to NO_2^- is catalysed by a dissimilatory nitrate reductase, an Mo- and Fe-containing enzyme which is repressed by O_2 and derepressed by anaerobic conditions. The enzyme differs from assimilatory nitrate reductase, which is NH_3-repressed. Dissimilatory reduction of NO_3^- follows two routes (Fig. 2.9). (1) Reduction to N_2 via NO and N_2O; it is still open to question whether or not NO is an intermediate. (2) Reduction to NO_2^-. The first route, known as denitrification (or nitrate respiration), only occurs in aerobic bacteria. So far, no obligate anaerobic denitrifiers have been detected. Some specialized bacteria not only grow with NO_3^-, but also with NO_2^-, or even with N_2O as the terminal e-acceptor. Obviously, dissimilatory NO_2^- reductase and N_2O reductase can be coupled to the electron transport chain and thus allow the generation of energy. Representative bacteria producing N_2 or N_2O are found in the genera *Bacillus, Pseudomonas, Hyphomicrobium, Spirillum, Moraxella,* and *Thiobacillus* (*T. denitrificans*). Also nitrifying bacteria have recently been shown to be capable of producing N_2O. The second route of anaerobic nitrate reduction leads to nitrite or ammonia. It occurs in a great number of genera, including *Enterobacter, Escherichia, Bacillus, Micrococcus, Mycobacterium, Staphylococcus,*

Vibrio and *Clostridium*. In this type of nitrate respiration, only the first step (NO_3^- to NO_2^-) is coupled to the electron transport chain and allows energy generation. Nitrite is then reduced, in a process known as nitrate ammonification, to NH_3, which is excreted into the medium. The reduction of NO_2^- to NH_3 is used by many bacteria during fermentation and, therefore, is also known as 'fermentative nitrite reduction'. This process explains why the concentration of $^{15}NH_4^+$ (from $^{15}NO_3^-$) is higher in sediments than in soil.

Since dissimilatory nitrate reduction is an essentially anaerobic process, it is largely governed in soil by the water regime (water potential) that determines the levels of redox potential and the oxygen supply. There is a strong denitrification in waterlogged soils where O_2 diffusion is limited. Under optimum denitrification conditions, 15% of the nitrate is released in the form of gaseous N-products. Even in well-drained soils, denitrification occurs because of the presence of anaerobic water-filled microhabitats. Wherever the redox potential drops below +200 mV, utilization of O_2 as the terminal e-acceptor is limited, and denitrification is initiated. Most denitrification occurs between 10° and 40°C, little below 5°C. It has been estimated that, on a yearly basis, about 10% of the total carbon oxidized in soils is matabolized via NO_3^- respiration.

The numerically dominating denitrifying bacteria are members of the *Alcaligenes* group of the pseudomonads; *P. fluorescens* biotype II appears to be most common.

Apart from pO_2 governing repression or derepression of nitrate reductase, denitrification is influenced by a variety of other factors. By accumulation of NO_2^-, denitrification is inhibited. Also certain heavy metals have been shown to impair denitrification, in particular cadmium (50 $\mu g/ml$). At low pH values, the denitrifying ability of soils is generally depressed.

The release of nitrous oxides into the atmosphere is of global significance because of its possible role in the destruction of the ozone layer in the upper atmosphere, which protects the earth from excessive UV radiation. Levels of atmospheric N_2O range from 0.2 to 0.5 ppm, and the greatest part of it appears to originate from biological reactions. N_2O production prevails under slightly aerobic conditions and is increased at lower pH and at high NO_3^- concentrations. With ample supply of organic energy material, complete denitrification to N_2 is favoured. The ratio of N_2O/N_2 has been intensively studied; it has been hypothesized that increased use of N fertilizers will increase the amount of N_2O released during denitrification, thus promoting the destruction of the stratospheric ozone layer which protects the earth from the harmful effects of the sun. There is much evidence that, fortunately enough, much of the N_2O produced by denitrification is reduced to N_2, before it escapes into the atmosphere. Nevertheless, the concentration of NO_3^- in soils has an important bearing on the relative amounts of N_2O and N_2. It is generally agreed that a complex interaction of factors such as substrate (nitrate) concentration, pH, temperature, and oxygen tension (related to the soil water potential) determines the extent of denitrification and the ratio of N_2 to N_2O and NO, respectively. In most field studies, N_2O was found to constitute less than 10% of the total gas evolved. Higher levels of N_2O production were usually found under conditions of extremely high nitrate concentrations and readily available organic matter. Vegetation and fertilization, therefore, promote denitrification.

In addition to the deleterious effects caused by increased N_2O production due to high NO_3^- concentrations, the accumulation of nitrate in soils and waters has also some other unwanted effects. High nitrate concentrations in drinking water or food (e.g. spinach) can provoke a disease in man and animals known as 'methemoglobinaemia'. In the gastrointestinal tract, NO_3^- is reduced to NO_2^- by the action of microorganisms. When NO_2^- enters the blood stream, hemoglobin is converted into methemoglobin. Since O_2 is firmly and (irreversibly) bound to this molecule, the O_2 transport by the erythrocytes is impaired, thus causing cyanosis. The disease is usually restricted to children under six months because, at this age, denitrifying bacteria pass through the stomach unaffected and get admitted to the intestines. In older children and adults, the bacteria are killed by stomach acids, and NO_3^- ions are absorbed before reduction to NO_2^- occurs. Nitrite intoxication has also been identified in cattle after feeding them plant materials with excessive NO_3^- concentration (as sometimes induced by overfertilization, in particular with slurry). Further concern exists with respect to the possibility of the formation of carcinogenic nitrosamines in the organism by chemical condensation of nitrite and secondary amines.

Dinitrogen fixation
Only prokaryotes are capable of dinitrogen fixation. The transfer of atmospheric N_2 into organic matter by terrestrial and aquatic microorganisms balances the losses of nitrogen due to denitrification. The physiology and biochemistry of N_2-fixation have already been discussed in chapter 2 (Fig. 2.17), some dinitrogen-fixing bacteria have been described in Chapter 3, and the symbiotic associations with N_2-fixing microorganisms have been treated in Chapter 7.

The beneficial effects of root nodules for nitrogen nutrition of leguminous plants were first demonstrated by Hellriegel (1886–1888). That the root nodules harbour bacteria had already been observed by Frank (1879). The first isolation of an anaerobic, free-living, N_2-fixing bacterium (*Clostridium pasteurianum*) was achieved by Winogradsky (in the 1890s), and in 1901 Beijerinck isolated the aerobic N_2-fixing *Azotobacter chroococcum*.

It has been estimated that, on a global basis, 85% of N_2-fixation on earth is of biological origin, while 15% is fixed by industrial processes. The total fixation amounts to 276×10^6 t/yr. About 140×10^6 t/yr are fixed on land, 100×10^6 t in the oceans, and 36×10^6 t by industrial fixation (N-fertilizer production). Major contributions on land are due to N_2-fixation in legumes (35×10^6 t), rice-paddies (4×10^6 t), grasslands (45×10^6 t), and forests (40×10^6 t). The agronomic efficiency is highest in legumes; for tropical clover, N_2-fixation of up to 900 kg N/ha $\times$ yr has been reported. In legumes the average value has been estimated between 100 and 300 kg N/ha $\times$ yr. In the alder tree (*Alnus*), the N_2-fixing efficiency is of the same order.

The symbiotic association between roots of tropical grasses (e.g. *Paspalum notatum*) and N_2-fixing *Azotobacter paspali* has been found to be more effective than the non-specific associations between plant roots and azospirillae in certain tropical and semitropical crops and forage grasses (e.g. *Brachiaris digitaria, Andropogon*). Organisms involved in rhizosphere N_2-fixation are *Azospirillum lipoferum* and *A. brasilense*. The agronomic significance of the azospirillae as N-suppliers is still a matter of debate and remains to be established.

N_2-fixation by the symbiotic cyanobacterium *Anabaena azollae* in *Azolla* amounts up to 125 kg N/ha $\times$ yr, and also free-living cyanobacteria in rice fields fix considerable amounts (30 to 50 kg N/ha $\times$ yr). Compared to the symbiotic N_2-fixing bacteria, the free-living forms (e.g. *Azotobacter, Clostridium*) contribute only minor amounts ranging from 1 to 3 kg N/ha $\times$ yr.

The main N_2-fixing bacteria occurring as free-living organisms or in symbiotic association are listed below.

(1) Free-living N_2-fixing bacteria
Aerobic: *Azotobacter*, CH_4-oxidizing methylotrophs, cyanobacteria.
Microaerophilic: *Azospirillum, Rhizobium.*
Facultative anaerobic: *Enterobacter, Klebsiella.*
Anaerobic: *Clostridium*, phototrophs, *Desulfovibrio.*

(2) N_2-fixing bacteria living in symbiotic association

Nodules: *Rhizobium* in legumes, *Frankia* in alder.

Rhizosphere: *Azospirillum, Azotobacter paspali, Klebsiella.*

Nitrogen fixation in the field is influenced by a variety of factors, including soil moisture, temperature, and availability of organic materials. The process also underlies seasonal variation.

As photosynthetic organisms with the ability of fixing N_2 under aerobic conditions, the cyanobacteria are pioneers on volcanic soils and occur in habitats of extremely low nutrient content. Free-living cyanobacteria under certain conditions show mass development in 'blooms' developing in freshwater lakes and oceans. *Anabaena azollae* in association with the aquatic fern *Azolla* functions as 'biological manure' in rice paddies. Cyanobacteria, associated with fungi in lichens, represent the main nutritional source available to tundra ruminants.

Biological nitrogen fixation has attracted much interest because of its economic importance to agriculture. In order to achieve high-yield crops, necessary for nourishing the increasing mankind, attempts are being made to improve N_2-fixation in the associations between plants and bacteria. They are directed towards improving the *Rhizobium*-legume symbiosis, and towards establishing efficient associations of plant roots and N_2-fixing bacteria in the rhizosphere. The expectations, in particular with respect to the non-symbiotic associations, must not be overestimated in view of the energy requirements in N_2-fixation. For reduction of 1 molecule of N_2, 18 to 24 molecules of ATP and 6 electrons (reducing power) are required. Consequently, intensive N_2-fixation in the rhizosphere is only feasible under the provision that large amounts of organic compounds are made available to the bacteria by root exudation. An additional prerequisite is the successful competition of the N_2-fixing bacteria with other rhizosphere organisms.

A speculative attempt at exploitation of biological nitrogen fixation is the transfer of *nif*-genes from bacteria into plants by genetic engineering. On the grounds of present biotechnology, an increase in food production, in particular with respect to proteins, will more likely be achieved by the mass production of SCP (single cell protein) by methylotrophic bacteria grown on methanol as a cheap and abundant substrate.

The sulphur cycle

Sulphur is an essential element of the living cell and constitutes about 1% of the dry matter. It occurs mainly in the form of S-containing amino acids (cysteine, homocysteine, cystine, methionine) and S-contain-

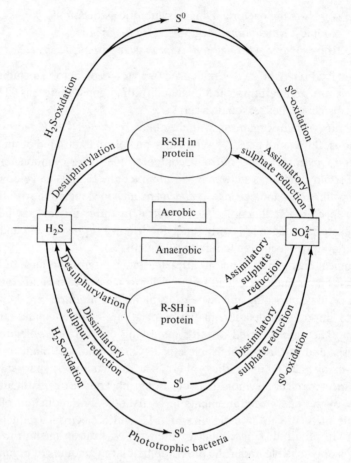

Fig. 8.9 The sulphur cycle (biological reactions)

ing growth factors (thiamin, biotin, lipoic acid). Sulphur compounds involved in the sulphur cycle are hydrogen sulphide, elemental sulphur, thiosulphate, sulphite, and sulphate (Fig. 8.9). The most common forms are H_2S (redox state $-II$), S^0 (redox state 0), and SO_4^{2-} (redox state $+VI$). Some conversions are performed only by prokaryotes. Most micro-organisms and green plants are capable of using sulphate as the sole source of sulphur, while animals depend on the supply of reduced sulphur.

The living biomass on land contains 25 to 40×10^8 t of S; 35 to 60×10^8 t are contained in the dead organic matter. In the oceans, the living and the dead biomass comprise only a fraction of sulphur compared to that on land, corresponding to the smaller total biomass in aquatic habitats. The greatest reservoir of sulphur in the biosphere is the sulphate in the oceans, which is estimated to amount to 14×10^{14} t. In the marine environments the average sulphate concentration is 28 mM. Hence, for oxidation of organic matter in the oceans, more sulphate than oxygen is available. Up to 50% of the organic C in aquatic environments is, therefore, mineralized by anaerobic sulphate respiration.

The major part of sulphur in the lithosphere consists of sulphate and iron sulphide (FeS); the latter can be oxidized to sulphate both biologically and chemically. In most habitats sulphate is available to plants and microorganisms and is assimilated through assimilatory sulphate reduction. This process results in the production of sulphydryl compounds (R—SH) that become part of the biomass. The reduction of sulphate proceeds from SO_4^{2-} (stepwise to APS (adenosine-5-phosphosulphate), to PAPS (3'-phosphoadenosine-5'-phosphosulphate), to SO_3^{2-}, and to S^{2-}. The first step, the activation of SO_4^{2-} to APS, requires ATP (cp. Fig. 2.10).

Sulphur is released from dead organic matter as H_2S by a process called desulphurylation (or desulphuration). Most H_2S is produced biologically by sulphate reduction. At neutral pH, H_2S dissociates according to

$$H_2S \rightarrow H^+ + HS^-.$$

At high pH, S^{2-} dominates according to

$$H_2S \rightarrow 2H^+ + S^{2-}$$

and under acidic conditions, H_2S is the major sulphur species. While HS^- and S^{2-} are water-soluble, H_2S volatilizes. Also at neutral pH, some H_2S is released in the form of gas because of the equilibrium between HS^- and H_2S. The active form of sulphur used by S-oxidizing bacteria is HS^-. Anaerobic generation of H_2S by dissimilatory sulphate reduction (Fig. 2.10) is, in its initial step, comparable to assimilatory sulphate reduction. Intermediates are thiosulphate and tetrathionate. During dissimilatory sulphate reduction (sulphate respiration), the electrons from organic substrates (or H_2) are transferred to APS, and the reductive process is coupled to oxidative phosphorylation. The H_2S present in the atmosphere, originates both from microbiological processes and from volcanic activities. In the air, it is converted into SO_2 and SO_3 which re-enter the lithosphere with rain water. SO_2 resulting from volcanic activities and industrial pollution likewise is converted into sulphate. The cycling of sulphur between lithosphere and atmosphere is an important factor in the overall sulphur budget.

H_2S is used as an energy source of aerobic chemolithoautotrophic thiobacilli, and also of *Beggiatoa, Thiothrix,* and *Thiovolum.* Under anaerobic conditions, H_2S is used as an electron donor by the phototrophic bacteria. Some phototrophs that oxidize H_2S deposit S^0 in their cells as an intermediate. The storage is influenced by the external concentration of H_2S. At low concentration or absence of H_2S, oxidation proceeds to sulphate. Intracellular S^0 deposition is characteristic for *Chromatium,* while some other phototrophs (e.g. *Ectothiorhodospira* and *Chlorobium*) deposit S^0 extracellularly.

Bacteria capable of desulfurication are members of the genera *Desulfovibrio, Desulfotomaculum,* and several recently described anaerobic sulphur bacteria (*Desulfomonas, Desulfobacter, Desulfococcus, Deşulfonema, Desulfosarcina*). They occur in soil and sediments and metabolize organic acids, ethanol, higher fatty acids and hydrogen. While the classical sulphate reducers perform an incomplete oxidation and accumulate acetate, many of the newly discovered forms are capable of complete oxidation of organic matter. The concentration of desulphurizing bacteria in soils is usually less than 10^3 cells/g of soil, whereas in sediments the concentration may amount to 10^7 cells/g of sediment. In soils, the sulphate reducers become active under waterlogged conditions, particularly in swampy areas. The critical factor in dissimilatory sulphate reduction is the redox potential (E_0') which must be below zero mV.

In many marine sediments, the rate of dissimilatory sulphate reduction is limited by the low concentration of carbon compounds. Marine pollution leading to an increase in organic matter also causes an increase in H_2S production. This is a potentially detrimental process because of the toxic effects of higher concentrations of H_2S. There is, in natural habitats, a competition for the electron donors available between sulphate reducers and methanogens. In the presence of high concentrations of sulphate, dissimilatory sulphate reduction is favoured, provided that appropriate electron donors are available from the fermentative degradation of organic compounds. At low sulphate concentration, methane production prevails. The situation is obvious in sediments of lakes with low sulphate concentration and in marine sediments with usually high sulphate concentration. The black appearance characteristic for anaerobic sediments results from the formation of FeS, due to H_2S production from SO_4^{2-} in the presence of Fe^{2+}. While desulphurication usually refers to reduction of sulphate to H_2S, bacteria also exist that reduce free elemental sulphur to H_2S. The best studied example is *Desulfuromonas acetoxidans* which lives in an associative symbiosis with green phototrophs that, on their part, oxidize the produced H_2S to elemental sulphur, and thus regenerate the terminal electron acceptor required by the S^0 reducer.

Dissimilatory sulphate reduction plays an economically important role in the anaerobic corrosion of iron. Under anaerobic conditions metallic iron is oxidized according to

$$4 \text{ Fe} + 8 \text{ H}^+ \rightarrow 4 \text{ Fe}^{2+} + 4 \text{ H}_2 \text{ ('anaerobic polarization')}$$

The H_2 produced normally protects the iron from further oxidation. However, in the presence of sulphate and desulphurizing bacteria, a cathodic depolarization is induced resulting in further Fe-oxidation. The reduction of SO_4^{2-} (with H_2) follows the equation

$$4 \text{ H}_2 + SO_4^{2-} \rightarrow H_2S + 2 \text{ H}_2O + 2OH^-$$

In the presence of H_2S and OH^-, the Fe^{2+} is converted into FeS and $Fe(OH)_2$ according to

$$4 \text{ Fe}^{2+} + H_2S + 2 \text{ OH}^- + 4 \text{ H}_2O \rightarrow FeS + 3 \text{ Fe (OH)}_2 + 6 \text{ H}^+$$

The sum of the three equations describes the conversion of metallic iron into FeS and $Fe(OH)_2$, i.e.

$$4 \text{ Fe} + SO_4^{2-} + 2 \text{ H}_2O + 2 \text{ H}^+ \rightarrow FeS + 3 \text{ Fe(OH)}_2.$$

Sulphate-reducing bacteria, capable of using H_2 produced during anaerobic polarization of iron, cause considerable damage to offshore iron constructions or pipelines in waters containing high concentrations of sulphate.

As a result of dissimilatory sulphate reduction, biogenic sulphide mineral deposits have been formed during geological periods. They occur as stratified layers, such as are known in sulphide ore deposits (Katanga, Zaire), or in Kupferschiefer (Germany). Sulphate contains two stable isotopes of sulphur, ^{32}S (*c.* 95%) and ^{34}S (*c.* 4%). The sulphate-reducing bacteria show a preference for the lighter ^{32}S isotope. Consequently, by biological discrimination against the heavy isotope, the biogenic sulphide contains a smaller portion of ^{34}S compared to the initial sulphate used for dissimilatory sulphate reduction. The same discrimination applies to the oxidation of H_2S to S^0 by phototrophs, resulting in S^0 deposition. By the technique of isotope fractionation, the biological origin of natural sulphur deposits has been proved. In sulphide mineral deposits of volcanic or hydrothermal origin the isotope ratio differs from that of biogenic deposits.

Reduced sulphur compounds, mainly H_2S, are oxidized by a variety of aerobic and anaerobic microorganisms. Among the aerobic and micro-aerophilic bacteria, the chemolithotrophs include the thiobacilli, *Beggiatoa*, and the archaebacterium *Sulfolobus acidocaldarius* that occupies a geothermal ecological niche. Most thiobacilli, generating energy through the oxidation of reduced S-compounds such as HS^-, S^{2-}, S^0, and $S_2O_3^{2-}$, are obligate chemolithoautotrophs that depend on CO_2 fixation. Some are also capable of utilizing organic carbon compounds. The majority are strict aerobes, a few, such as *Thiobacillus denitrificans*, have the ability to reduce nitrate under anaerobic conditions (nitrate respiration). *Thiobacillus thiooxidans* produces considerable amounts of sulphuric acid, is particularly adapted to pH values below 2, and even tolerates $pH = 0$. The capacity of the thiobacilli for acidification has been exploited in the agricultural practice by addition of elemental S^0 to alkaline soils. By the activity of the thiobacilli sulphuric acid is produced, and the pH is lowered. In S^0 oxidation, the bacteria attach to the sulphur crystals. The sulphur oxidation is described by the following reaction

$$S^0 + 2\,O_2 + H_2 \rightarrow SO_4^{2-} + 2\,H^+.$$

For thermodynamic reasons, the H_2S (or S^0) oxidizing bacteria cannot directly reduce NAD^+. The redox potential (E_0') for $NAD^+/NADH$ is -320 mV; for S^0/HS^- it is -270 mV, and for SO_4^{2-}/HSO_4^- it is -220 mV. NAD^+ is reduced through a reversed electron transport, which requires ATP generation during the oxidation of the reduced inorganic substrate. Since much energy is required for CO_2 fixation, the growth yields in the chemolithoautotrophs are relatively low.

Oxidation of H_2S to H_2SO_4 by thiobacilli may cause problems in biodeterioration. Sulphur present in limestone is known to cause gradual decay of limestone buildings and monuments due to oxidation under humid conditions. Acid-induced deterioration may become apparent in any place where air (oxygen) and reduced S-compounds are present. Thiobacilli are also involved in aerobic metal corrosion. They enhance an essentially electrochemical process. Metallic Fe is solubilized producing cations according to

$$Fe \rightarrow Fe^{2+} + 2\,e$$

At the site of electron accumulation (cathode), the electrons react with O_2 according to

$$O_2 + 2\,e + 2\,H^+ \rightarrow 2\,OH^-$$

The OH^- radicals react with the metal cations and produce Fe deposits.

Oxidation of Fe^{2+} by *Thiobacillus ferrooxidans* is also effected according to the following reaction

$$4\ Fe^{2+} + 4\ H^+ + O_2 \rightarrow 4\ Fe^{3+} + 2\ H_2O$$

This organism is capable of generating energy through oxidation of both reduced sulphur and iron compounds. Iron and sulphur oxidation thus are closely related processes.

The oxidation of reduced sulphur compounds under anaerobic conditions is essential for the life of the anoxic phototrophs, using H_2S, S^0, or $S_2O_3^{2-}$ as electron donors for the production of reducing power (NADH) necessary for CO_2-fixation. Organisms involved are the Chromatiaceae, Chlorobiaceae, Rhodospirillaceae, and *Chloroflexus*. They occur in regions, where H_2S and light are available under anoxic conditions.

Apart from the aerobic chemolithotrophs and the anaerobic phototrophs, there exist in nature also aerobic chemoorganotrophs capable of oxidizing reduced S compounds. The biochemistry of this process has not yet been studied in detail.

The phosphorus cycle

Phosphorus is a vital element to all macro- and microorganisms. In the biosphere, phosphorus exists almost exclusively as phosphate (PO_4^{3-}), i.e. in the form of organic orthophosphate esters. Phosphorus occurs in nucleic acids, phospholipids, and in adenylates such as ATP. In substrate-level and electron transport phosphorylation, inorganic phosphate is bound to ADP leading to the production of ATP. The participation in energy-conversion makes P an essential component in any metabolic process. In the lithosphere, P is most common as apatite [3 $Ca_3(PO_4)_2 \times Ca(FeCl)_2$] and as fluorapatite [$Ca_5F(PO_4)_3$]. Hydroxylapatite [$Ca_5(OH)(PO_4)_3$] is a component of the bones of animals. The atmosphere normally does not contain phosphorus because common gaseous forms of P do not exist, contrary to several other vital elements such as C, O, H, N, and S. In soils, phosphorus may be present up to the order of magnitude of 1 g per kg of soil. Only a small fraction of that amount, usually less than 5%, is available to the organisms in a soluble form; the greater part includes insoluble inorganic phosphates and organic P-complexes such as inositol phosphate. In aquatic environments, the total P concentration is extremely small as compared to soil. Water usually does not contain more than 0.01 to 0.07 mg P per litre.

Because of the insolubility of the major phosphorus compounds, P is often the biologically limiting factor. Only primary phosphates (e.g.

NaH_2PO_4) are highly soluble in water. The secondary and tertiary phosphates have increasingly lower solubilities. Pyrophosphates readily hydrolyse to orthophosphate and then become nutritionally available. The dissolved phosphate in soils and waters is available to plants and microorganisms and is actively cycled. Availability is restricted by precipitation of phosphate with calcium and magnesium ions at neutral to alkaline pH, and with iron and aluminium at neutral to acid pH. Under acid conditions, phosphate is liberated; calcium phosphate, however, is much less soluble than calcium carbonate. IronIII phosphate is extremely insoluble. By H_2S-producing microorganisms some of the iron is removed as FeS; this process brings back to solution a part of the precipitated phosphate. Many microorganisms are capable of solubilizing phosphate, in particular calcium phosphate. This is usually achieved by the production of organic acids, or by the production of nitric and sulphuric acid with nitrifiers and thiobacilli, respectively. Mobilization of insoluble iron(III) phosphates is also known by microbial reduction of iron(III) ions to iron(II) ions under anaerobic conditions. Because of their phosphate solubilizing capacity, some microorganisms are even capable of utilizing apatite as the sole source of phosphorus.

Cycling of phosphorus occurs between inorganic and organic forms. The key processes are represented by the decay of organic matter and by the dissolution of inorganic phosphorus. By solubilization of phosphate from inappropriate inorganic or organic forms of phosphate, microorganisms play an important role in phosphorus cycling. During the transfer from inorganic to organic bound phosphate, and from immobilized insoluble phosphorus to a mobile and more soluble form, the oxidation/reduction status of phosphorus, contrary to other essential elements, remains unaltered. A change in valence has been reported in P transformation under anaerobic conditions. Some bacteria are capable of reducing phosphate (PO_4^{3-}; valency +5) to phosphite (PO_3^{3-}; valency +3) and hypophosphate (PO_2^{3-}; valency +1). Such reactions, however, are quantitatively small, compared to the phosphate cycling.

In most soils, soluble phosphates are present only in small concentrations limiting plant growth. Microbial mobilization of phosphates, therefore, is an important factor in plant nutrition. Phosphorus uptake by plants is also impaired by the low diffusion coefficient of phosphate. In order to improve the phosphorus supply, many plants have entered into a symbiosis with mycorrhiza fungi (vesicular-arbuscular mycorrhiza) that are capable to exploit the low concentration of phosphorus around the roots.

Transformations of other ions
Iron and manganese

Iron is abundant as iron(II) and ferric iron(III) ions in the lithosphere of the earth, but only a small portion is involved in biogeochemical cycling. In cellular metabolism, iron is required for biosynthesis of iron–sulphur-proteins and cytochromes involved in electron transport processes. Iron is also known to act as a cofactor of aconitase. Iron is not only an essential element of cellular constituents, but also plays an important role in lithotrophic bacteria. Under acidic conditions, where non-biological autoxidation does not occur, Fe^{2+} is oxidized by the chemolithotrophic *Thiobacillus ferrooxidans*. This organism is common in acid mine waters containing FeS, and tolerates pH 2.5. Oxidation of Fe^{2+} by the strict aerobes occurs according to the equation

$$4 \, Fe^{2+} + 4 \, H^+ + O_2 \rightarrow 4 \, Fe^{3+} + 2 \, H_2O$$

Iron and manganese have several properties in common. Both elements form insoluble hydroxides. Fe^{2+} is oxidized to Fe^{3+}, Mn^{2+} to Mn^{4+}. In the presence of Fe^{2+} or Mn^{2+}, many microorganisms deposit Fe^{3+} or Mn^{4+} oxides or hydroxides. In addition to *T. ferrooxidans*, the thermophilic *Sulfolobus acidocaldarius* and *Sulfobacillus thermosulfoxidans*, as well as *Leptospirillum ferrooxidans*, *Metallogenium*, *Gallionella*, *Leptothrix*, and *Siderocapsa* are capable of iron oxidation. True lithotrophic oxidation has only been shown for *T. ferrooxidans*, and only for iron , not also for manganese.

Fe^{2+} and Mn^{2+} are also more readily oxidized chemically; Fe^{2+} is unstable in neutral and alkaline habitats and at redox potentials above E_0' +200 mV. Thus, changes in the oxidation state may be caused by redox and pH alterations induced by microorganisms, but do not depend on direct metabolic reactions.

Many bacteria (e.g. *Bacillus, Pseudomonas, Arthrobacter*) and fungi (e.g. *Aspergillus, Fusarium, Cephalosporium*) possess the ability to precipitate oxides and hydroxides of iron and manganese from organometal complexes. Deposition of iron or manganese hydroxides in slime capsules is known in *Hyphomicrobium* and *Pedomicrobium*.

At low pO_2, some organisms can use Fe^{3+} as an electron sink forming Fe^{2+}. By formation of Fe^{2+} in water-logged soils, a greenish-grey colour develops characteristic for gleyed soils. Involved in iron reduction are mainly bacilli and pseudomonads. While Fe^{3+} prevails in aerobic habitats, Fe^{2+} accumulates in anaerobic environments. In the presence of H_2S,

Fe^{2+} is rendered insoluble by the formation of FeS. In many freshwater habitats, *Gallionella, Sphaerotilus* and related organisms produce iron hydroxide $(Fe(OH)_3)$ precipitates.

It has been shown that the occurrence of deep-sea manganese nodules is associated with bacterial activities. Mn^{4+} reducers are found in marine sediments and at the site of manganese nodules. These ferromanganese concretions contain 20–40% Mn, up to 50% Fe, and 1–2% Ni and Co. Particularly because of the two latter elements, the 'manganese nodules' are challenging objects for deep-sea mining.

Calcium

Calcium has a variety of vital functions both in macro- and micro-organisms. In the spore-forming bacteria, it is necessary for the production of endospores containing calcium dipicolinate. Calcium ions influence membrane permeability and are also involved in the movement of flagella.

In the biosphere and lithosphere, calcium mainly occurs in the form of calcium carbonate in sedimentary deposits. Cycling of calcium involves soluble and insoluble salts. While $Ca(HCO_3)_2$ has a high solubility, $CaCO_3$ is much less soluble. In aquatic environments, calcium is present as $Ca(HCO_3)_2$, $CaCO_3$ or $CaSO_4$. The equilibrium in oceans between calcium hydrogencarbonate and calcium carbonate is the main pH buffer:

$$Ca(HCO_3)_2 \rightleftharpoons CaCO_3 + H_2O + CO_2$$

Removal of CO_2 by photosynthetic organisms causes carbonate precipitation. Huge amounts of $CaCO_3$ have been, and are, deposited by the marine phytoplankton. The calcium carbonate incrustation of corals is the result of the activity of algal symbionts. Carbonate precipitation is also known in foraminifera (rhizopods) mediated by endosymbiotic algae. In the presence of $CaSO_4$, and under anaerobic conditions, sulphate-reducing bacteria cause precipitation of $CaCO_3$ according to

$$CaSO_4 + 8\,[H] + CO_2 \rightarrow CaCO_3 + 3\,H_2O + H_2S$$

Apart from biological activities, formation of limestone during past geological eras probably has also originated from expulsion of CO_2 in tropical waters that were saturated with calcium bicarbonate due to temperature increase.

In nature, calcium is often associated with phosphorus, e.g. in the apatites. Insoluble calcium phosphates are produced according to the reaction

$$3 \, Ca^{2+} + 2 \, PO_4^{3-} \rightarrow Ca_3(PO_4)_2.$$

As discussed earlier, insoluble calcium phosphates can be solubilized by organic or inorganic acids produced by microorganisms.

Silicon and other elements
After oxygen, silicon is the most abundant element in the earth's crust. The major component is silicon dioxide (SiO_2). Some microorganisms have a silicon requirement. They possess the ability of acquiring otherwise insoluble silicon materials and produce cell walls (shells) of a siliceous nature. The main groups of silicon-utilizing microorganisms are the diatoms, silicoflagellates, and radiolaria.

Cycling between soluble and insoluble forms of silicon is mainly performed by diatoms. The soluble form in terrestrial and aquatic environments is $Si(OH)_4$; the insoluble silicates are based on SiO_2. By SiO_2 precipitation, the diatoms, during geological periods, have produced huge amounts of 'diatomaceous earth'. The diatomite ('Kieselgur') is largely composed of fossil diatoms and is used in a number of industrial processes. Large deposits of diatomite are commercially mined. It is known from geological studies that, after the appearance of silicon utilizing microorganisms, the concentration in the world's oceans of dissolved silicon decreased considerably. Large quantities of silicon have been immobilized in this way. The accumulation of silicon precipitates demonstrates the profound effect which biological processes may exert on element cycling. A variety of microorganisms, in particular fungi and bacteria, are capable of decomposing silicates on rock surfaces by the production of acids. Fungi attacking silicate minerals usually produce gluconic acid.

Other elements, both metals and metalloids, likewise undergo microbial transformations. In particular, arsenic (As), antimony (Sb), mercury (Hg), selenium (Se), cadmium (Cd), tin (Sn), and lead (Pb) are involved in such biological transformations. The reactions comprise oxidation, reduction, and methylation processes. Sb($+3$) is oxidized to Sb($+5$) by *Stibiobacter senarmontii*, a lithotrophic bacterium; As($+3$) to As($+5$) by pseudomonads. Oxidation of elemental selenium to selenite has recently been demonstrated in a strain of *Bacillus megaterium*. Reduction of oxidized forms of mercury and selenium has been shown to be performed by certain fungi and bacteria. Physiologically, these processes represent reductive detoxifications. The reductive capacity of salmonellae, in the presence of selenium, has been used to develop special media suitable for their selective isolation. A great number of fungi (*Aspergillus, Penicillium, Fusarium, Mucor,* etc.) and bacteria (*Pseudomonas, Aeromonas, Bacillus, Clostridium*) have been found to be capable of biological methylation. Methyl mercury (CH_3Hg^+) has attained a notorious reputation in connection with the Minimata disease in Japan. Intoxications in damp rooms decorated with wallpaper containing arsenical pigments could be traced back to the production from arsenic of volatile trimethyl arsine ($(CH_3)_3As$) by certain fungi (e.g. *Penicillium brevicaule*). Arsines are also produced from reduction of arsenate or arsenite by bacteria (*Pseudomonas, Alcaligenes*).

The role of microorganisms in the degradation of man-made compounds

As a consequence of industrialization and the use of organic chemicals in modern agriculture, millions of tons of synthetic compounds are dispersed throughout the biosphere. The major products comprise synthetic polymers, pesticides, and detergents. Many of these man-made compounds have chemical structures that are not encountered in nature. These so-called 'xenobiotics' often resist biodegradation and thus represent a problem of environmental concern. In order to avoid ecological damage, xenobiotic (persistent) chemicals should be prevented from entering the biosphere and accumulating to hazardous levels.

It is a well-established fact that all organic compounds including polymers synthesized by plants, animals, and microorganisms are decomposed in the process of mineralization of the organic matter. In contrast, a number of man-made (synthetic) compounds resist biodegradation. Certain xenobiotics may become partly or totally degraded by solely chemical or photochemical reactions. Non-biological breakdown of xenobiotic compounds may result in the production of intermediates that, on their part, are susceptible to microbial degradation. Persistence (recalcitrance) of synthetic chemicals must always be regarded in relation to the time scale. Some become degraded within a period of days or weeks, others resist degradation for months or years. If persistent chemicals exert toxic effects or possess carcinogenic or teratogenic properties for men and other animals, use of such compounds creates serious environmental problems. A classic example of a toxic recalcitrant chemical accumulating in the food chain is DDT, which, after recognition of its potentially hazardous role, has been banned in a number of countries. Although pesticides are usually applied in relatively low concentrations, they may become concentrated in organisms of higher trophic levels by a process known as bioaccumulation or biomagnification. An environmental chemical that is resistant to degradation may become concentrated at the top trophic level by a factor of between a thousand and a million. Consequently, bioaccumulation of potentially mutagenic, carcinogenic, or teratogenic compounds is a matter of particular environmental concern.

Resistance of man-made compounds to microbial breakdown may be related to a variety of factors. Although recalcitrance cannot be predicted with certainty from the chemical structure, there are some structural conditions known to be related to biodegradability. Branched carbon chains, multiple chlorine atoms in aliphatic compounds, presence of sulphonate or nitro groups, chlorine substitution in aromatic compounds, and condensed aromatic rings reduce biodegradability. The halocarbons are both chemically and biologically extremely stable. Saturated ring systems such as cyclohexane are less resistant than the corresponding aromatic analogues. Recalcitrance of a chemical may also be caused by lack of a transport system or lack of the necessary catabolic enzymes. Breakdown of certain compounds requires specific environmental conditions. Thus, the presence of molecular oxygen is a prerequisite for degradation of hydrocarbons and aromatic compounds. In bacteria, enzymes involved in the degradation of aromatic compounds are often coded by plasmids.

Many man-made organic molecules are subject to complete biodegradation by microorganisms that use the substrate as carbon and energy source and convert the compound into inorganic products. Complex and recalcitrant chemicals that do not readily serve as nutrients and apparently do not sustain growth, may none the less be degraded by a process termed cooxidation or cometabolism. Cometabolic transformation requires the presence of a utilizable carbon compound and does not reveal a recognizable benefit to the organism. The alteration may lead to increased recalcitrance or may facilitate subsequent microbial attack. In general, cometabolic transformations occur rather slowly. The physiological nature of cometabolic reactions is not yet fully understood; the ecological importance of this phenomenon, however, is obvious.

The evolution of new organisms and the production of new organic compounds lasted millions of years and was paralleled by the evolution of new microbial activities directed towards degradation of the newly available substances. The present-day rapid development of synthetic organic chemistry has created numerous chemicals similar to naturally occurring compounds that are readily degraded, but also new classes of chemicals not present in nature. Despite the given metabolic versatility of micro-organisms, certain synthetic molecules appear to resist microbial degradation.

The question, whether and, if at all, how fast microorganisms may evolve new mechanisms for the degradation of presently recalcitrant molecules, cannot yet be answered. The established persistence of a variety of compounds in soils and waters proves a lack in catabolic omnipotence of the microbial communities. Some molecules obviously are highly refractory to microbial degradation. This applies in particular to synthetic polymers such as polyethylene or polyvinyl chloride. The existence of recalcitrant molecules is a major challenge to the chemist who is called upon to replace recalcitrant compounds by biodegradable substances. In connection with this claim, the term 'soft chemicals' has been introduced. Among the chemicals that are very slowly or not degraded to a detectable degree, and therefore persist in nature for long periods, a number of pesticides and synthetic polymers are of major importance.

Pesticides

Modern agricultural production that aims at maximum crops does not only depend on mineral fertilization but also requires control of competing weeds, destructive insects, pathogenic fungi, and other pests of economic plants. For chemical pest control, more than a thousand pesticides are on the market. These include herbicides, insecticides, fungicides, nematocides, rodenticides, and others. The yearly production of pesticides amounts to several millions of tons.

Herbicides (Fig. 8.10) have been studied most intensively with respect to degradation and persistence in soil. Microbial decomposition is known for chlorophenoxyacetic acid derivatives (e.g. 2,4-D, 2,4,5-T, MCPA), urea derivatives (e.g. monuron), phenylcarbamates (e.g. IPC, CIPC), substituted triazines (e.g. atrazine) and bipyridylium compounds (e.g. paraquat). 2,4-D (dichlorophenoxyacetic acid) is degraded by micro-organisms within a period of several weeks. The speed of breakdown is influenced by temperature, moisture, pH, type of soil, and other environmental factors. More rapid destruction is observed near the surface as compared to depth. A variety of bacteria including *Achromobacter, Arthrobacter, Corynebacterium, Flavobacterium, Mycoplana,* and *Pseudomonas* have been reported to be involved in the degradation of this compound. Complete destruction of the molecule requires oxidation, cleavage of the aromatic ring, and subsequent dehalogenation. 2,4,5-T

(1) Chlorophenoxyacetic acid derivatives

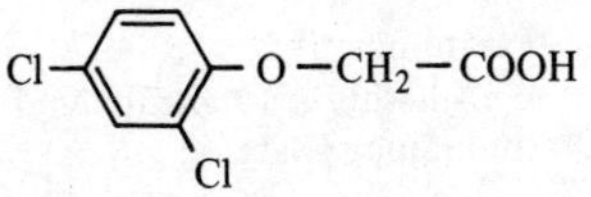

Cl—⟨benzene⟩—O—CH$_2$—COOH
Cl

2, 4-D
(2, 4-dichlorophenoxy) acetic acid

Cl
Cl—⟨benzene⟩—O—CH$_2$—COOH
Cl

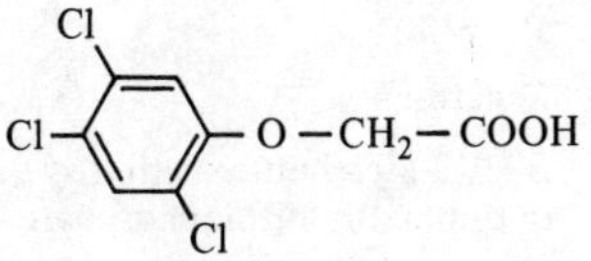

2, 4, 5-T
(2, 4, 5-trichlorophenoxy) acetic acid

CH$_3$
Cl—⟨benzene⟩—O—CH$_2$—COOH

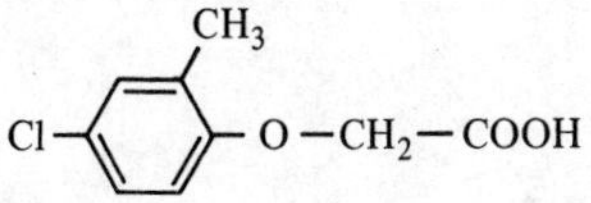

MCPA
4-chloro-2-methyl-phenoxyacetic acid

(2) Urea derivatives

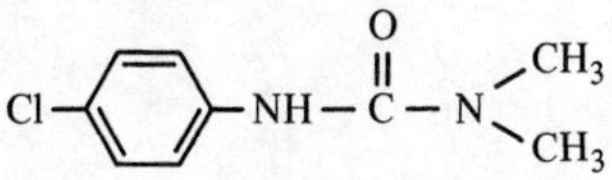

Cl—⟨benzene⟩—NH—$\overset{\overset{\text{O}}{\|}}{\text{C}}$—N$\overset{\diagup\text{CH}_3}{\diagdown\text{CH}_3}$

Monuron
3-(4-chlorophenyl)-1, 1-dimethylurea

(3) Phenylcarbamates

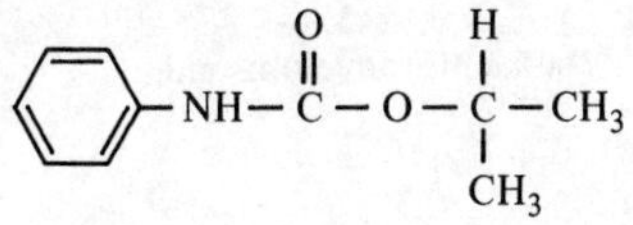

⟨benzene⟩—NH—$\overset{\overset{\text{O}}{\|}}{\text{C}}$—O—$\overset{\overset{\text{H}}{|}}{\underset{\underset{\text{CH}_3}{|}}{\text{C}}}$—CH$_3$

IPC
Isopropyl carbanilate

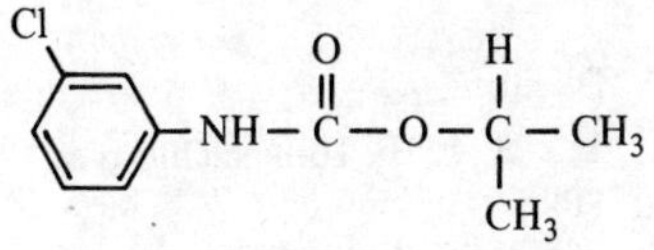

Cl
⟨benzene⟩—NH—$\overset{\overset{\text{O}}{\|}}{\text{C}}$—O—$\overset{\overset{\text{H}}{|}}{\underset{\underset{\text{CH}_3}{|}}{\text{C}}}$—CH$_3$

CIPC
Isopropyl *m*-chlorocarbanilate

(4) Triazines

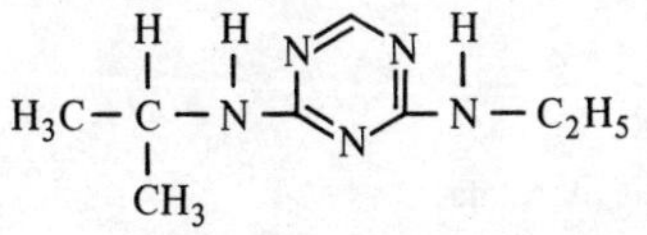

H$_3$C—$\overset{\overset{\text{H}}{|}}{\underset{\underset{\text{CH}_3}{|}}{\text{C}}}$—$\overset{\text{H}}{\text{N}}$—⟨triazine⟩—$\overset{\text{H}}{\text{N}}$—C$_2H_5$

Atrazine
2-chloro-4-ethylamino-
6-isopropylamino-triazine

(5) Bipyridylium compounds

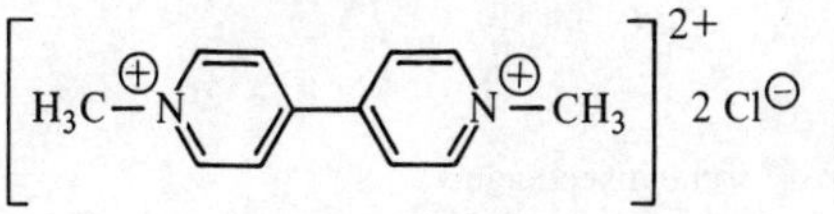

$\left[\text{H}_3\text{C}—\overset{\oplus}{\text{N}}⟨\text{pyridyl}⟩⟨\text{pyridyl}⟩\overset{\oplus}{\text{N}}—\text{CH}_3 \right]^{2+}$ 2 Cl$^{\ominus}$

Paraquat
1, 1-dimethyl-4, 4'-
bipyridinium dichloride

Fig. 8.10 Chemical structure of some herbicides

(1) Organophosphates

C$_2$H$_5$O$\backslash$
          $>$P—O—⟨benzene⟩—NO$_2$
C$_2$H$_5$O$/$

(with =S on top of P)

Parathion-ethyl

o, o-diethyl-*o*-(4 nitrophenyl)-thionophosphate

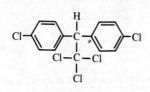

H$_3$CO$\backslash$ CH$_2$—COO—C$_2$H$_5$
          $>$P$\lessgtr$S |
H$_3$CO$/$ $\backslash$S—CH—COO—C$_2$H$_5$

Malathion

S-(1, 2-dicarbethoxyethyl)-*o, o*-dimethyldithiophosphate

(2) Organochlorine compounds

DDT

dichloro-diphenyl-trichloroethane

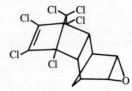

Lindan

γ-1, 2, 3, 4, 5, 6-hexachlorocyclohexane

Dieldrin

1, 2, 3, 4, 10, 10-hexachloro-6, 7-epoxy-1, 4, 4a, 5, 6, 7, 8, 8a-octahydro-endo, exo-1, 4

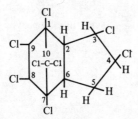

Chlordane

1, 3, 4, 7, 8, 9, 10-octachloro-tricyclo [5, 2, 1, 0] dec-8-en

Fig. 8.11 Chemical structure of some insecticides

(1) Dithiocarbamates

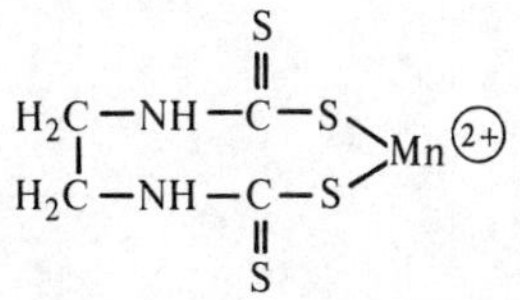

Maneb
mangan-ethylen-bis
(dithiocarbamate)

(2) Carboxamides

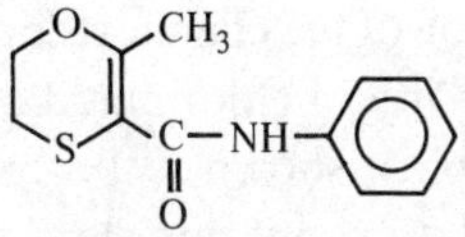

Carboxin
5, 6-dihydro-2-methyl-
N-phenyl-1, 4-oxathiin-
3-carboxamid

Fig. 8.12 Chemical structure of some fungicides

(trichlorophenoxyacetic acid) which formerly was regarded to be more resistant to microbial decomposition than 2,4-D, has later been shown to become rapidly degraded by *Pseudomonas cepacia*. Degradation of certain herbicides is also known to occur in plants, e.g. atrazine in *Zea mays*.

Insecticides (Fig. 8.11) mainly comprise organophosphates and organochlorine compounds. The first group includes parathion-ethyl and malathion, the second DDT and lindan. DDT has a chemical structure not encountered in biological materials, and, because of its low degradability, poses a serious ecological long-term problem (3–10 years persistence). Organophosphorus insecticides such as parathion and malathion are rapidly decomposed (within days or weeks). *Arthrobacter* sp. has been reported to use such compounds as the sole source of carbon and energy. Because of their carcinogenic potential, the formerly used dieldrin and chlordane have been banned, like DDT, in many countries.

Fungicides (Fig. 8.12) belonging to the chemical class of dithiocarbamates (maneb) and carboxamides (carboxin) are degraded by a variety of microorganisms.

Dioxin (Fig. 8.13) is a carcinogenic and teratogenic chemical that also occurs as a contaminant during the production of the herbicides 2,4-D and 2,4,5-T. Whether this notorious compound, the 'Seveso poison', is biodegradable, is still unknown.

Among the pesticides, the aliphatic acids and long-chain aliphatic acids are least resistant to biodegradation in soil, while chlorinated hydrocarbons are highly persistent. In general, recalcitrance is increased with the

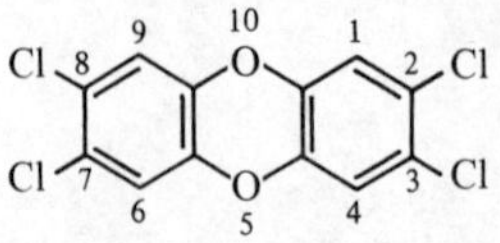

Cl 8 9 10 O 1 2 Cl
Cl 7 6 O 5 4 3 Cl

TCDD
Dioxin

2, 3, 7, 8-Tetrachlorobenzo-*p*-dioxin

Fig. 8.13 Chemical structure of dioxin

increase of chlorine atoms in the molecule. Resistance to biodegradation is also markedly influenced by the position of the chemical constituents on the benzene ring. Lack of biodegradability of chlorinated organic compounds under aerobic conditions has been shown to be caused by the chlorine substitutions that prevent oxidation and ring cleavage. According to recent findings, such compounds may become dechlorinated under anaerobic conditions. Ring cleavage occurs after reductive dechlorination. There are observations which indicate a rather rapid evolution and dissemination of degradative properties in bacterial populations with respect to the breakdown of chlorinated phenoxy herbicides. The occurrence of strains with new capabilities is often related to the presence of plasmids.

Although bacteria dominate in biotransformation of pesticides, fungi also participate in this process. The major groups involved in pesticide decomposition are *Achromobacter, Arthrobacter, Bacillus, Flavobacterium, Nocardia* (actinomycete), and *Aspergillus* (fungus). Compared to herbicides, less information is available on the destruction of insecticides and fungicides.

The interrelations between microorganisms and pesticides can be looked at from two angles. (1) The influence of microorganisms on pesticides, i.e. microbial degradation, and (2) the influence of the pesticides on non-target organisms. Although some effects of pesticides on non-target organisms have been reported, there is presently no indication that the application of pesticides at the recommended field rates causes permanent disturbance of the cycling of elements due to the inhibition of biochemical activities exerted by the soil microorganisms. Most biocides as used in agricultural practice do not pose a threat to microbiological activities in soil; they do not inhibit ammonifiers, nitrifiers, N_2-fixing bacteria, and other groups. Continued study and monitoring of new compounds, however, is necessary in order to avoid unforeseen effects on non-target organisms. Special attention has to be paid to the fungicides and fumigants, because such compounds are known to markedly affect both pathogenic and saprophytic fungi.

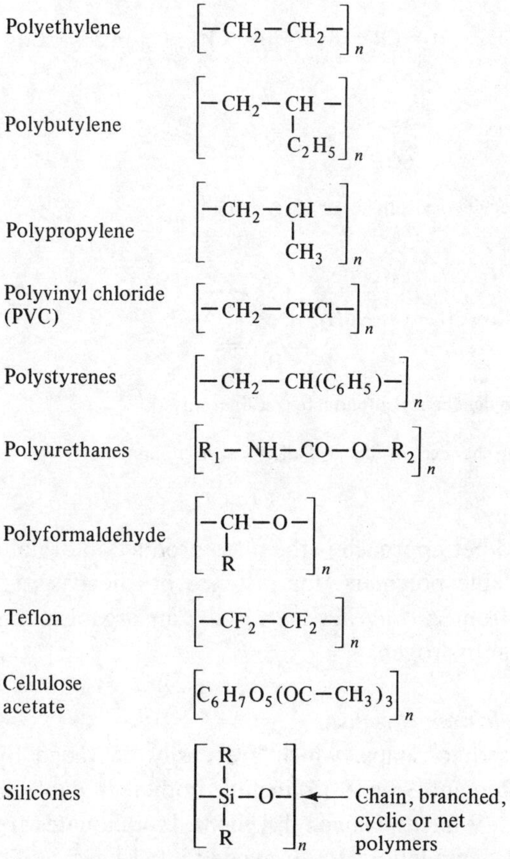

Polyethylene $\left[-CH_2-CH_2-\right]_n$

Polybutylene $\left[\begin{array}{c}-CH_2-CH- \\ | \\ C_2H_5\end{array}\right]_n$

Polypropylene $\left[\begin{array}{c}-CH_2-CH- \\ | \\ CH_3\end{array}\right]_n$

Polyvinyl chloride (PVC) $\left[-CH_2-CHCl-\right]_n$

Polystyrenes $\left[-CH_2-CH(C_6H_5)-\right]_n$

Polyurethanes $\left[R_1-NH-CO-O-R_2\right]_n$

Polyformaldehyde $\left[\begin{array}{c}-CH-O- \\ | \\ R\end{array}\right]_n$

Teflon $\left[-CF_2-CF_2-\right]_n$

Cellulose acetate $\left[C_6H_7O_5(OC-CH_3)_3\right]_n$

Silicones $\left[\begin{array}{c}R \\ | \\ -Si-O- \\ | \\ R\end{array}\right]_n$ ← Chain, branched, cyclic or net polymers

Fig. 8.14 The chemical basis of some synthetic polymers

Synthetic polymers

Synthetic polymers are used on a large scale for many purposes. Disposable goods, packaging materials, plastics, clothing, and many other items are fully or partially made of synthetic polymers. The most common products are polyethylene, polybutylene, polypropylene, polyvinyl chloride (PVC), polystyrene, polyurethane, polyformaldehyde, Nylon, Orlon, Teflon, cellulose acetate, and silicon resins (Fig. 8.14). A large number of these polymers are not degradable, and the huge masses that go into the municipal garbage are a major problem in refuse disposal. What is needed are biodegradable synthetic plastics that meet with the requirements for stability, but which also allow microbial degradation after simple chemical or physical treatment of the discarded materials. The production of polymers that after UV-irradiation become predisposed to biodegradation opens new perspectives for a solution of

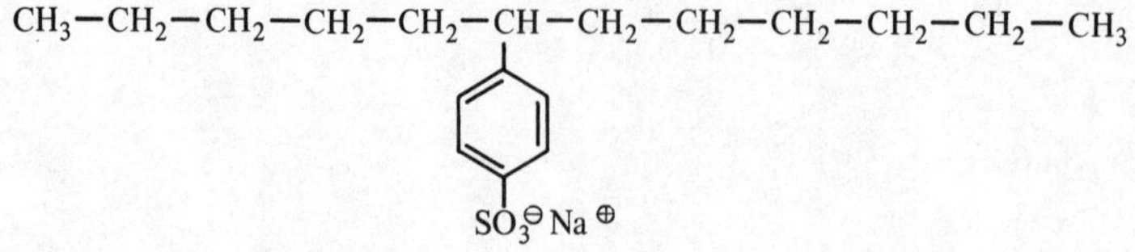

CH$_3$—CH$_2$—CH$_2$—CH$_2$—CH$_2$—CH—CH$_2$—CH$_2$—CH$_2$—CH$_2$—CH$_2$—CH$_3$

SO$_3^{\ominus}$ Na $^{\oplus}$

Dodecylbenzylsulphonate (degradable)

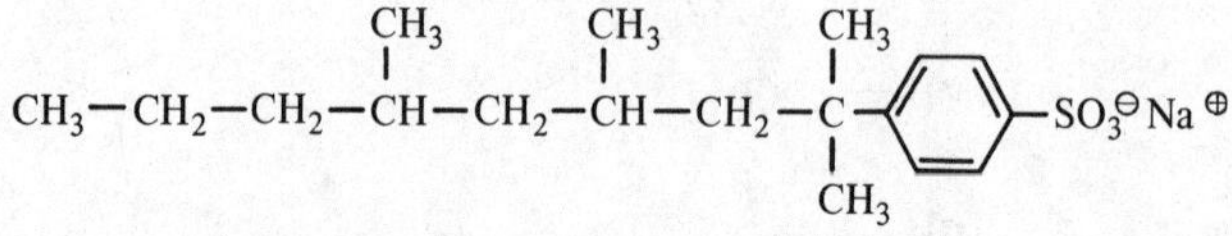

CH$_3$—CH$_2$—CH$_2$—CH—CH$_2$—CH—CH$_2$—C—⟨ ⟩—SO$_3^{\ominus}$ Na $^{\oplus}$

CH$_3$ CH$_3$ CH$_3$

CH$_3$

Tetrapropylenebenzylsulphonate (recalcitrant)

Fig. 8.15 The chemical structure of alkylbenzyl sulphonates

this problem. Another approach is the mass production of natural and, therefore, degradable polymers, for instance on the basis of poly-β-hydroxybutyrate from *Alcaligenes eutrophus*, an organism capable of oxidizing molecular hydrogen.

Other recalcitrant chemicals

As opposed to soaps, which are easily degraded by micro-organisms, the detergents (Fig. 8.15) include both degradable and recalcitrant compounds. While the linear alkyl benzyl sulphonates are susceptible to microbial degradation, the branched alkyl benzyl sulphonates resist decomposition. The so-called 'hard' detergents, which cause intensive foaming when entering waters, are now largely replaced by the so-called 'soft' detergents of the linear type. Members of the genera *Pseudomonas* and *Nocardia* are involved in the decomposition of detergents.

Simple aromatic hydrocarbons such as naphthalene, phenanthrene, and anthracene are easily degraded, while polycyclic aromatics, including benzo(a)pyrene and benzo(a)anthracene, are rather recalcitrant (Fig. 8.16).

Biodegradation under anaerobic conditions has been reported for a 'dangerous' substrate such as the explosive hexahydro-1,3,5-trinitro-1,3,5-triazine (RDX). This compound is microbiologically converted into a variety of products including hydrazines, formaldehyde and methanol.

Degradation of crude oil is of particular interest because of the huge amounts of oil production, and the relatively large quantities that indeliberately enter waters and soils. Oil tankers involved in accidents may cause

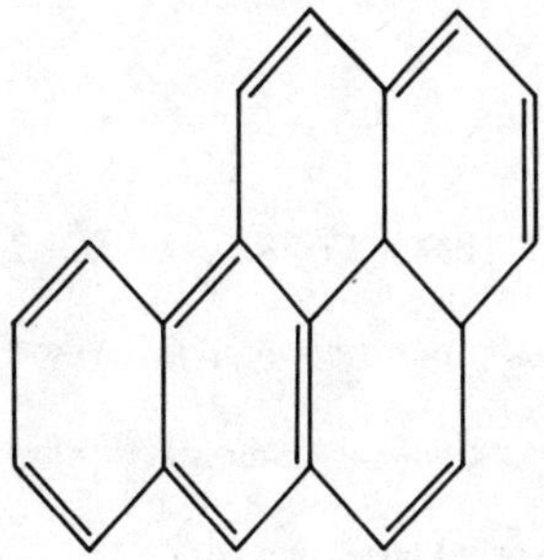

Benzo[a]pyrene: $C_{20}H_{12}$, carcinogenic

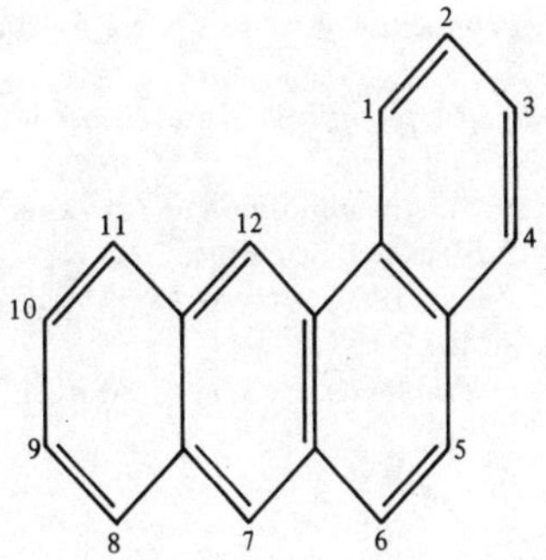

7, 12-dimethl-benzo[a]-anthracene and
7, 8, 12-trimethyl-benzo[a]-anthracene
are most carcinogenic

Benzo[a]anthracene: $C_{18}H_{12}$

Fig. 8.16 The chemical structure of some recalcitrant polycyclic aromatics

maritime disasters accompanied by the large-scale contamination of offshore sediments and beaches. The results of such events have drastically been demonstrated by several tanker accidents on the open sea that happened during the past few years. Crude oil is a mixture of aliphatic and aromatic hydrocarbons. While straight chain alkanes are easily degraded, the branched alkanes are more resistant. As already stated above, the aromatic hydrocarbons also have a low degradability. Their degradation depends on aerobic conditions and, therefore, does not occur in marine sediments. Microbial breakdown of oil spilled at sea is usually limited by the deficiencies in sea water of nitrogen and phosphorous. The various oil components, serving as carbon and energy source, can only be metabolized if the required minerals are available in appropriate concentration. A variety of microorganisms are capable of decomposing petroleum hydrocarbons, in particular pseudomonads, corynebacteria, mycobacteria, micrococci, and yeasts.

Further reading

Books

Bolin, B., Degens, E. T., Kempe, S. & Klepner, P. (1980). *The Global Carbon Cycle.* New York: John Wiley.
Bothe, H. & Trebst, A. (1981). *Biology of inorganic nitrogen and sulfur.* New York: Springer–Verlag.
Delwiche, C. C. (ed.) (1981). *Denitrification, nitrification and atmospheric nitrous oxide.* New York: John Wiley.
Ehrlich, H. L. (1980). *Geomicrobiology.* New York: Marcel Dekker.
Fenchel, T. & Blackburn, T. H. (1979). *Bacteria and Mineral Cycling.* London: Academic Press.
Kirk, T. K., Higuchi, T. & Chang, H.-M. (1980). *Lignin Biodegradation: Microbiology, Chemistry and Potential Applications*, vols. I and II. Boca Raton, Florida: CRC Press.
Leith, M. & Whittaker, R. M. (1977). *Primary Production in the Biosphere.* Berlin: Springer–Verlag.
Smith, O. L. (1982). *Soil Microbiology: A Model of Decomposition and Nutrient Cycling.* Boca Raton, Florida: CRC Press Inc.
Swift, M. J., Heal, D. W. & Anderson, J. M. (1979). *Decomposition in Terrestrial Ecosystems*, Studies in Ecology vol. 5. Oxford: Blackwell Scientific.
Trudinger, P. A., Walter, M. R. & Ralph, B. J. (eds) (1980). *Biogeochemistry of ancient and modern environments.* Berlin: Springer–Verlag.
Weinberg, E. G. (ed.) (1977). *Microorganisms and minerals.* New York: Marcel Dekker.

Articles
General aspects of microbial activities in nature

Burns, R. G. (1982). Enzyme activity in soil: location and a possible role in microbial ecology. *Soil Biology and Biochemistry*, **14**, 423–7.
Conrad, R. (1984). Atmospheric-biospheric exchanges. In *Current Perspectives in Microbial Ecology*, eds M. J. Klug & C. A. Reddy, pp. 461–7. Washington, D.C.: American Society for Microbiology.
Nozhernikova, A. N. & Yurganov, L. N. (1978). Microbiological aspects of regulating the carbon monoxide content in the earth's atmosphere. *Advances in Microbial Ecology*, **2**, 203–44.
Revelle, R. (1982). Carbon dioxide and world climate. *Scientific American*, **247**, 35–43.
Stewart, J. W. B. (1984). Interrelation of carbon, nitrogen, sulphur, and phosphorus cycles during decomposition processes in soil. In *Current Perspectives in Microbial Ecology*, eds. M. J. Klug & C. A. Reddy, pp. 442–6. Washington, D.C.: American Society for Microbiology.
Stout, J. D. (1981). The role of protozoa in nutrient cycling and energy flow. In *Advances in Microbial Ecology*, ed. M. Alexander, vol. 4, pp. 1–50. New York, London: Plenum Press.
Trevors, J. T. (1985). Hydrogen consumption in soil. *Plant and Soil*, **87**, 417–22.

Mineralization of organic matter and carbon cycling

Azam, F., Haider, K. & Malik, K. A. (1985). Transformation of ^{14}C labelled plant components in soil in relation to immobilization and remineralization of ^{15}N fertilizer. *Plant and Soil*, **86**, 15–25.

Berg, B. (1984). Decomposition of root litter and some factors regulating the process: Long-term root litter decomposition in a scots pine forest. *Soil Biology & Biochemistry*, **16**, 609–17.

Brunner, W. & Focht, D. D. (1984). Deterministic three-half-order kinetic model for microbial degradation of added carbon substrates in soil. *Applied and Environmental Microbiology*, **47**, 167–72.

Hayes, A. J. (1979). The microbiology of plant litter decomposition. *Science Progress, Oxford*, **66**, 25–42.

Hobbie, J. E. & Melillo, J. M. (1984). Role of microbes in global carbon cycling. In *Current Perspectives in Microbial Ecology*, eds M. J. Klug & C. A. Reddy, pp. 389–93. Washington, D.C.: American Society for Microbiology.

Jannasch, H. W. (1979). Microbial turnover of organic matter in the deep sea. *Bioscience*, **29**, 228–32.

Kilham, O. W. & Alexander, M. (1984). A basis for organic matter accumulation in soils under anaerobiosis. *Soil Science*, **137**, 419–27.

Ljungdahl, L. G. & Eriksson, K.-E. (1985). Ecology of microbial cellulose degradation. *Advances in Microbial Ecology*, **8**, 237–99.

O'Brien, B. J. (1984). Soil organic carbon fluxes and turnover rates estimated from radiocarbon enrichments. *Soil Biology and Biochemistry*, **16**, 115–20.

Reddy, C. A. (1984). Physiology and biochemistry of lignin degradation. In *Current Perspectives in Microbial Ecology*, eds. M. J. Klug & C. A. Reddy, pp. 558–71. Washington, D.C.: American Society for Microbiology.

Rudd, J. W. M. & Taylor, C. D. (1980). Methane cycling in aquatic environments. In *Advances in Aquatic Microbiology*, vol. 2, eds M. R. Droop & H. W. Jannasch, pp. 77–150. London: Academic Press.

Schink, B. (1984). Microbial degradation of pectin in plants and aquatic environments. In *Current Perspectives in Microbial Ecology*, eds M. J. Klug & C. A. Reddy, pp. 580–7. Washington, D.C.: American Society for Microbiology.

Schink, B. (1985). Mechanism and kinetics of succinate and propionate degradation in anoxic freshwater sediments and sewage sludge. *Journal of General Microbiology*, **131**, 643–50.

Scow, K. M., Simkins, S. & Alexander, M. (1986). Kinetics of mineralization of organic compounds at low concentrations in soil. *Applied and Environmental Microbiology*, **51**, 1028–35.

Seiler, W. (1984). Contribution of biological processes to the global budget of CH_4 in the atmosphere. In *Current Perspectives in Microbial Ecology*, eds M. J. Klug & C. A. Reddy, pp. 468–77. Washington, D.C.: American Society for Microbiology.

Simkins, S., Mukherjee, R. & Alexander, M. (1986). Two approaches to modelling kinetics of biodegradation by growing cells and application of a two-compartment model for mineralization kinetics in sewage. *Applied and Environmental Microbiology*, **51**, 1153–60.

Strand, S. E. & Shippert, L. (1986). Oxidation of chloroform in an aerobic soil exposed to natural gas. *Applied and Environmental Microbiology*, **52**, 203–5.

Varadachari, C. & Ghosh, K. (1984). On humus formation. *Plant and Soil*, **77**, 305–13.

Microbial processes involved in nitrogen cycling

Aulakh, M. S., Rennie, D. A. & Paul, E. A. (1984). Acetylene and N-serve effects upon N_2O emissions from NH_4^+ and NO_3^- treated soils under aerobic and anaerobic conditions. *Soil Biology and Biochemistry*, **16**, 351–6.

Azhar, E. S., Vandenabeele, J. & Verstraete, W. (1986). Nitrification and organic nitrogen formation in soils. *Plant and Soil*, **94**, 383–99.

Azhar, E. S., Van Cleemput, O. & Verstraete, W. (1986). Nitrification mediated nitrogen immobilization in soils. *Plant and Soil*, **94**, 401–9.

Broadbent, F. E. (1986). Empirical modeling of soil nitrogen mineralization. *Soil Science*, **141**, 208–13.

Castignetti, D. & Hollocher, T. C. (1984). Heterotrophic nitrification among denitrifiers. *Applied and Environmental Microbiology*, **47**, 620–3.

Claus, G. & Kutzner, H. J. (1985). Denitrification of nitrate and nitric acid with methanol as carbon source. *Applied Microbiology and Biotechnology*, **22**, 378–81.

Colbourn, P. & Dowdell, R. J. (1984). Denitrification in field soils. *Plant and Soil*, **76**, 213–26.

Dart, P. J. (1986). Nitrogen fixation associated with non-legumes in agriculture. *Plant and Soil*, **90**, 303–34.

Focht, D. D. (1982). Denitrification. In *Experimental Microbial Ecology*, eds R. G. Burns & J. H. Slater, pp. 194–211. Oxford, London, Edinburgh, Boston, Melbourne: Blackwell Scientific Publications.

Focht, D. D. & Verstraete, W. (1977). Biochemical ecology of nitrification and denitrification. *Advances in Microbial Ecology*, **1**, 135–214.

Fogg, G. E. (1978). Nitrogen fixation in the oceans. *Ecological Bulletins (Stockholm)*, **26**, 11–9.

Goodbroad, L. L. & Keeney, D. R. (1984). Nitrous oxide production in aerobic soils under varying pH, temperature and water content. *Soil Biology & Biochemistry*, **16**, 39–43.

Hernandez, B. S. & Focht, D. D. (1984). Invalidity of the concept of slow growth and alkali production in cowpea rhizobia. *Applied and Environmental Microbiology*, **48**, 206–10.

House, G. J., Stinner, B. R., Crossley, D. A. jr. & Odum, E. P. (1984). Nitrogen cycling in conventional and no-tillage agro-ecosystems: Analysis of pathways and processes. *Journal of Applied Ecology*, **21**, 991–1012.

Jensen, E. S. (1986). Symbiotic N_2 fixation in pea and field bean estimated by ^{15}N fertilizer dilution in field experiments with barley as a reference crop. *Plant and Soil*, **92**, 3–13.

Jørgensen, K. S., Jensen, H. B. & Sørensen, J. (1984). Nitrous oxide production from nitrification and denitrification in marine sediment at low oxygen concentrations. *Canadian Journal of Microbiology*, **30**, 1073–8.

Koike, I., Nishio, T. & Hattori, A. (1984). Denitrification and nitrification in coastal and estuarine sediments. In *Current Perspectives in Microbial Ecology*, eds M. J. Klug & C. A. Reddy, pp. 454–9. Washington, D.C.: American Society for Microbiology.

Lindberg, T. & Granhall, U. (1986). Acetylene reduction in gnotobiotic cultures with rhizosphere bacteria and wheat. *Plant and Soil*, **92**, 171–80.

Nishio, T., Koike, I. & Hattori, A. (1983). Estimates of denitrification and nitrification in coastal and estuarine sediments. *Applied and Environmental Microbiology*, **45**, 444–50.

Parkin, T. B., Sexstone, A. J. & Tiedje, J. M. (1985). Adaptation of denitrifying populations to low soil pH. *Applied and Environment Microbiology*, **49**, 1053–6.

Postgate, J. R. & Hill, S. (1979). Nitrogen fixation. In *Microbial Ecology: A Conceptual Approach*, eds J. M. Lynch & N. J. Poole, pp. 191–213. Oxford, London, Edinburgh, Melbourne: Blackwell Scientific Publications.

Poth, M. & Focht, D. D. (1985). [15]N kinetic analysis of N_2O production by *Nitrosomonas europaea*: an examination of nitrifier denitrification. *Applied and Environmental Microbiology*, **49**, 1134–41.

Prosser, J. I. & Cox, D. J. (1982). Nitrification. In *Experimental Microbial Ecology*, eds R. G. Burns & J. H. Slater, pp. 178–93. Oxford, London, Edinburgh, Boston, Melbourne: Blackwell Scientific Publications.

Rashid, G. H. & Schaefer, R. (1986). Denitrification studies in a temperate forest catena soil. *Plant and Soil*, **93**, 367–72.

Rosswall, T. (1982). Microbiological regulation of the biogeochemical nitrogen cycle. *Plant and Soil*, **67**, 15–34.

Rosswall, T. & Paustian, K. (1984). Cycling of nitrogen in modern agricultural systems. *Plant and Soil*, **76**, 3–21.

Smith, D. W. (1982). Nitrogen fixation. In *Experimental Microbial Ecology*, eds R. G. Burns & J. H. Slater, pp. 212–20. Oxford, London, Edinburgh, Boston, Melbourne: Blackwell Scientific Publications.

Stewart, W. D. P., Preston, T., Peterson, H. G. & Christofi, N. (1982). Nitrogen cycling in eutrophic freshwaters. *Philosophical Transactions of the Royal Society of London (ser. B)*, **296**, 491–509.

Stout, J. D. & Bawden, A. D. (1984). Rates and pathways of mineral nitrogen transformation in a soil from pasture. *Soil Biology and Biochemistry*, **16**, 127–31.

Tiedje, J. M., Sexstone, A. J., Myrold, D. D. & Robinson, J. A. (1982). Denitrification: Ecological niches, competition and survival. *Antonie van Leeuwenhoek*, **48**, 569–83.

Trevors, J. T. (1985). The influence of oxygen concentrations on denitrification in soil. *Applied Microbiology and Biotechnology*, **23**, 152–5.

Weathers, P. J. (1984). N_2O evolution by green algae. *Applied and Environmental Microbiology*, **48**, 1251–3.

Cycling and transformation of other elements

Bremner, J. M. & Steele, C. G. (1978). Role of microorganisms in the atmospheric sulfur cycle. *Advances in Microbial Ecology*, **2**, 155–201.

Burdige, D. J. & Nealson, K. H. (1986). Chemical and microbiological studies of sulfide-mediated manganese reduction. *Geomicrobiology Journal*, **4**, 361–88.

Cheng, C.-N. & Focht, D. D. (1979). Production of arsine and methylarsines in soil and in culture. *Applied and Environmental Microbiology*, **38**, 494–8.

Danielli, H. M. C. & Edington, M. A. (1983/84). Bacterial calcification in limestone caves. *Geomicrobiology Journal*, **3**, 1–16.

Ghiorse, W. C. (1984). Bacterial transformations of manganese in wetland environments. In *Current Perspectives in Microbial Ecology*, eds M. J. Klug & C. A. Reddy, pp. 615–22. Washington, D.C.: American Society for Microbiology.

Ghiorse, W. C. (1984). Biology of iron- and manganese-depositing bacteria. *Annual Review of Microbiology*, **38**, 515–50.

Goldhaber, M. B. & Kaplan, I. R. (1974). The sulfur cycle. In *The Sea*, vol. 5, ed. E. D. Goldberg, pp. 569–655. New York: John Wiley.

Hamilton, W. A. (1985). Sulphate-reducing bacteria and anaerobic corrosion. *Annual Review of Microbiology*, **39**, 195–217.

Isa, Z., Grusenmeyer, S. & Verstraete, W. (1986). Sulfate reduction relative to methane production in high-rate anaerobic digestion: Microbiological aspects. *Applied and Environmental Microbiology*, **51**, 580–7.

Iverson, W. P. & Olson, G. J. (1984). Anaerobic corrosion of iron and steel: a novel mechanism. In *Current Perspectives in Microbial Ecology*, eds M. J. Klug & C. A. Reddy, pp. 623–7. Washington, D.C.: American Society for Microbiology.

Jenneman, G. E., McInerney, M. J. & Knapp, R. M. (1986). Effect of nitrate on biogenic sulfide production. *Applied and Environmental Microbiology*, **51**, 1205–11.

Jones, J. G. (1986). Iron transformations by freshwater bacteria. *Advances in Microbial Ecology*, **9**, 149–86.

Jones, J. G., Gardener, S. & Simon, B. M. (1983). Bacterial reduction of ferric iron in a stratified eutrophic lake. *Journal of General Microbiology*, **129**, 131–9.

Kelly, W. J. & Reanney, D. C. (1984). Mercury resistance among soil bacteria: ecology and transferability of genes encoding resistance. *Soil Biology and Biochemistry*, **16**, 1–8.

Lyalikova, N. N. & Lebedeva, E. V. (1984). Bacterial oxidation of molybdenum in ore deposits. *Geomicrobiology Journal*, 3, 307–18,

Molla, M. A. Z., Chowdhury, A. A., Islam, A. & Hogue, S. (1984). Microbial mineralization of organic phosphate in soil. *Plant and Soil*, 78, 393–9.

Monticello, D. J. & Finnerty, W. R. (1985). Microbial desulfurization of fossil fuels. *Annual Review of Microbiology*, 39, 371–89.

Sarathchandra, S. U. & Watkinson, J. H. (1981). Oxidation of elemental selenium to selenite by *Bacillus megaterium*. *Science (Wash.)*, 211, 600–1.

Summers, A. O. & Silver, S. (1978). Microbial transformations of metals. *Annual Review of Microbiology*, 32, 637–72.

Stewart, J. W. B. & McKercher, R. B. (1982). Phosphorous cycle. In *Experimental Microbial Ecology*, eds R. G. Burns & J. H. Slater, pp. 221–38. Oxford, London, Edinburgh, Boston, Melbourne: Blackwell Scientific Publications.

Tate, K. R. (1984). The biological transformation of P in soil. *Plant and Soil*, 76, 245–56.

Wang, H.-K. & Wood, J. M. (1984). Bioaccumulation of nickel by algae. *Environmental Science & Technology*, 18, 106–9.

Biodegradation of man-made chemicals

Alexander, M. (1979). Recalcitrant molecules, fallible micro-organisms. In *Microbial Ecology: A Conceptual Approach*, eds J. M. Lynch & N. J. Poole, pp. 246–53. Oxford, London, Edinburgh, Melbourne: Blackwell Scientific Publications.

Alexander, M. (1981). Biodegradation of chemicals of environmental concern. *Science*, 211, 132–8.

Anderson, J. P. E. (1984). Herbicide degradation in soil: Influence of microbial biomass. *Soil Biology and Biochemistry*, 16, 483–9.

Aslanzadeh, J. & Hedrick, H. G. (1985). Search for mirex-degrading soil microorganisms. *Soil Science*, 139, 369–74.

Atlas, R. M. (1981). Microbial degradation of petroleum hydrocarbons: an environmental perspective. *Microbiological Reviews*, 45, 180–209.

Bauer, J. E. & Capone, D. G. (1985). Degradation and mineralization of the polycyclic aromatic hydrocarbons anthracene and naphthalene in intertidal marine sediments. *Applied and Environmental Microbiology*, 50, 81–90.

Baxter, R. M. & Sutherland, D. A. (1984). Biochemical and photochemical processes in the degradation of chlorinated biphenyls. *Environmental Science & Technology*, 18, 608–10.

Bossert, I., Kachel, W. M. & Bartha, R. (1984). Fate of hydrocarbons during oily sludge disposal in soil. *Applied and Environmental Microbiology*, 47, 763–7.

Brown, E. J., Pignatello, J. J., Martinson, M. M. & Crawford, R. L. (1986). Pentachlorophenol degradation: a pure bacterial culture and an epilithic microbial consortium. *Applied and Environmental Microbiology*, 52, 92–7.

Brunner, W., Sutherland, F. H. & Focht, D. D. (1985). Enhanced biodegradation of polychlorinated biphenyls in soil by analog enrichment and bacterial inoculation. *Journal of Environmental Quality*, 14, 324–8.

Bull, A. T. (1980). Biodegradation: some attitudes and strategies of microorganisms and microbiologists. In *Contemporary Microbial Ecology*, eds. D. C. Ellwood, J. N. Hedger, M. J. Latham, J. M. Lynch & J. H. Slater, pp. 107–36. London: Academic Press.

Chatterjee, D. K., Kilbane, J. J. & Chakrabarty, A. M. (1982). Biodegradation of 2,4,5-trichlorophenoxyacetic acid in soil by a pure culture of *Pseudomonas cepacia*. *Applied and Environmental Microbiology*, 44, 514–16.

Dwyer, D. F., Krumme, M. L., Boyd, S. A. & Tiedje, J. M. (1986). Kinetics of phenol biodegradation by an immobilized methanogenic consortium. *Applied and Environmental Microbiology*, 52, 345–51.

Eriksson, K.-E. & Kolar, M.-C. (1985). Microbial degradation of chlorolignins. *Environmental Science & Technology*, **19**, 1086–8,

Focht, D. D. & Brunner, W. (1985). Kinetics of biphenyl and polychlorinated biphenyl metabolism in soil. *Applied and Environmental Microbiology*, **50**, 1058–63.

Gauger, W. K., MacDonald, J. M., Adrian, N. R., Matthees, D. P. & Walgenbach, D. D. (1986). Characterization of a streptomycete growing on organophosphate and carbamate insecticides. *Archives of Environmental Contamination and Toxicology*, **15**, 137–41.

Goldstein, R. M., Mallory, L. M. & Alexander, M. (1985). Reasons for possible failure of inoculation to enhance biodegradation. *Applied and Environmental Microbiology*, **50**, 977–83.

Hankin, L. & Sawhney, B. L. (1984). Microbial degradation of polychlorinated biphenyls in soil. *Soil Science*, **137**, 401–7.

Ingham, E. R. & Coleman, D. C. (1984). Effects of streptomycin, cycloheximide, fungizone, captan, carbofuran, cygon, and PCNB on soil microorganisms. *Microbial Ecology*, **10**, 345–58.

Jones, S. H. & Alexander, M. (1986). Kinetics of mineralization of phenols in lake water. *Applied and Environmental Microbiology*, **51**, 891–7.

Kaplan, D. V. & Kaplan, A. M. (1985). Biodegradation on N-nitrosodimethylamine in aqueous and soil systems. *Applied and Environmental Microbiology*, **50**, 1077–86.

Kleopfer, R. D., Easley, D. M., Haas, B. B. jr, Deihl, T. G., Jackson, D. E. & Wurrey, C. J. (1985). Anaerobic degradation of trichloroethylene in soil. *Environmental Science & Technology*, **19**, 277–80.

Knackmuss, H.-J. (1981). Degradation of halogenated and sulfonated hydrocarbons. In *Microbial Degradation of Xenobiotics and Recalcitrant Compounds*, eds T. Leisinger, A. M. Cook, R. Hütter & J. Nüesch, pp. 190–212. London: Academic Press.

Knackmuss, H.-J. (1984). Biochemistry and practical implications of organohalide degradation. In *Current Perspectives in Microbial Ecology*, eds M. J. Klug & C. A. Reddy, pp. 687–93. Washington, D.C.: American Society for Microbiology.

Larson, R. J. (1984). Kinetic and ecological approaches for predicting biodegradation rates of xenobiotic organic chemicals in natural ecosystems. In *Current Perspectives in Microbial Ecology*, eds M. J. Klug & C. A. Reddy, pp. 677–86. Washington, D.C.: American Society for Microbiology.

Latorre, J., Reineke, W. & Knackmuss, H.-J. (1984). Microbial metabolism of chloroanilines: enhanced evolution by natural genetic exchange. *Archives of Microbiology*, **140**, 159–65.

Nelson, L. M., Yaron, B. & Nye, P. H. (1982). Biologically induced hydrolysis of parathion in soil: kinetics and modelling. *Soil Biology and Biochemistry*, **14**, 223–7.

Novick, N. J. & Alexander, M. (1985). Cometabolism of low concentrations of propachlor, alachlor, and cycloate in sewage and lake water. *Applied and Environmental Microbiology*, **49**, 737–43.

Ou, L.-T. (1984). 2,4-D degradation and 2,4-D degrading microorganisms in soils. *Soil Science*, **137**, 100–7.

Rubio, M. A., Engesser, K.-H. & Knackmuss, H.-J. (1986). Microbial metabolism of chlorosalicylates: effect of prolonged subcultivation on constructed strains. *Archives of Microbiology*, **145**, 123–5.

Sahm, H., Brunner, M. & Schoberth, S. M. (1986). Anaerobic degradation of halogenated aromatic compounds. *Microbial Ecology*, **12**, 147–53.

Schmidt, E., Hellwig, M. & Knackmuss, H.-J. (1983). Degradation of chlorophenols by a defined mixed microbial community. *Applied and Environmental Microbiology*, **46**, 1038–44.

Shaler, T. A. & Klecka, G. M. (1986). Effects of dissolved oxygen concentration on

268   *Activities of ecological significance*

biodegradation of 2,4-dichlorophenoxyacetic acid. *Applied and Environmental Microbiology*, **51**, 950–5.

Shelton, D. R. & Tiedje, J. M. (1984). General method for determining anaerobic biodegradation potential. *Applied and Environmental Microbiology*, **47**, 850–7.

Shelton, D. R. & Tiedje, J. M. (1984). Isolation and partial characterization of bacteria in an anaerobic consortium that mineralizes 3-chlorobenzoic acid. *Applied and Environmental Microbiology*, **48**, 840–8.

Shelton, D. R., Boyd, S. A. & Tiedje, J. M. (1984). Anaerobic biodegradation of phthalic acid esters in sludge. *Environmental Science & Technology*, **18**, 93–7.

Spain, J. C., Van Veld, P. A., Monti, C. A., Pritchard, P. H. & Cripe, C. R. (1984). Comparison of *p*-Nitrophenol biodegradation in field and laboratory test systems. *Applied and Environmental Microbiology*, **48**, 944–50.

Thomas, J. M., Yordy, J. R., Amador, J. A. & Alexander, M. (1986). Rates of dissolution and biodegradation of water-insoluble organic compounds. *Applied and Environmental Microbiology*, **52**, 290–6.

9

Methods used for the study of microorganisms in their natural environments: A guide to pertinent literature

Microorganisms have mainly been studied as pure cultures of individual species under laboratory conditions, and our present knowledge of the biology of bacteria, fungi and other microorganisms is largely based on the investigation of axenic cultures. The many methods used for the study of pure cultures have been described in books, manuals, reviews, and numerous original papers. All aspects of microbiological methodology, in particular with reference to bacteriology and mycology, have been covered in a series of books edited by Norris, J. R. and Ribbons, D. W., entitled *Methods in Microbiology*, published by Academic Press (London). Vol. 1 appeared in 1969, Vol. 18 in 1985. A comprehensive manual dealing with the methods used to study bacteria is the *Manual of Methods for General Bacteriology*, edited by Gerhardt, P., Murray, R. G. E., Costilow, R. N., Nester, E. W., Wood, W. A., Krieg, N. R., and Phillips, G. B., published in 1981 by the American Society of Microbiology (Washington DC). This manual deals with the microscopic, cultural and analytical techniques used to isolate, cultivate and characterize bacteria, and contains the manifold methods to study morphology, physiology, metabolism, and genetics. It also includes chapters on sterilization of media and equipment, on preservation of microorganisms and on laboratory safety. A detailed description of the methods developed for enrichment, isolation, and identification of the various groups of prokaryotic microorganisms is given in *The Prokaryotes*, a two volume handbook on habitats, isolation, and identification of bacteria, edited by Starr, M. P., Stolp, H., Trueper, H. G., Balows, A., and Schlegel, H. G., published in 1981 by Springer–Verlag (Berlin Heidelberg).

In ecological research, the autecological approach, as usually applied to the laboratory study of microbial species, has been extended to synecology. The synecological studies focus on distribution and abundance of microorganisms in their natural habitats and are directed towards the elucidation of how the microbial activities are influenced by abiotic factors and by interactions with other organisms. The aims of the synecological approach, therefore, require additional techniques for the quantification of microbial processes as they occur in nature. In order to characterize microorganisms with respect to morphology, physiological properties, and biochemical activities, laboratory studies are unrenounceable. For ecological studies, however, it is of fundamental importance to get additional information on numbers and distribution of microorganisms, and to determine their activities as displayed in their natural environments. There are available a variety of methods adapted to the specific needs and aspects of microbial ecology. The following two books deal exclusively with this subject:

(1)   Parkinson, D., Gray, T. R. G., Williams, S. T. (eds) (1971). *Methods for studying the ecology of soil microorganisms.* IBP Handbook No. 19. Oxford: Blackwell.
(2)   Rosswall, T. (ed.) (1973, 3rd edn 1976). *Modern methods in the study of microbial ecology.* Bulletin No. 17 of the Ecological Research Committee of NFR. Stockholm: Editorial Service/ NFR.

Since more recent summarizing publications on the methods in microbial ecology are not available, some additional information and a list of pertinent literature will be given in this Chapter. It may be mentioned in passing that ecological methodology has also received some input from space biology. The interest in detecting extraterrestrial life requires extremely sensitive methods that allow recognition of low biological activities.

The study of microorganisms present in complex habitats such as soils, waters, and sediments follows two principally different lines. (1) Disruption of a soil sample permits isolation of the various organisms, and subsequent study of their morphology, nutritional requirements, physiological properties, and metabolic activities in pure culture. This conventional approach also allows enumeration of the microorganisms within the limits determined by the applied technique. (2) Non-disruptive methods aim at the direct study of distinct microorganisms with regard to their location and their physiological performance *in situ*. It must be considered, however, that the second approach necessarily can only be an approximation because any technique applied to the soil necessarily involves some sort of disturbance.

In ecological studies, the sampling procedures play an important role, and many special techniques have been developed for taking samples from soil, waters, air, tissues, foods, etc. The procedures must be adapted to the particular purpose. Not only the size of the sample, but also the variability, reproducibility, and statistical analysis of sampling have to be considered. A multiplicity of samplers has been developed in marine microbiology, including special containers for deep-sea sampling of barophilic organisms.

When studying microorganisms in their natural habitats, the main questions of ecological relevance refer to (a) types, numbers, and distribution, (b) microbial biomass, and (c) growth rates and activities. These data must be related to the lapse of time, and the factors governing the environmental conditions.

Types, numbers, and distribution of microorganisms

For the evaluation of types, numbers, and distribution of microorganisms, both direct and indirect methods are applied. The direct methods comprise light and electron microscopy, including staining, epifluorescence, and immunofluorescence. Algae and protozoa can directly be classified by microscopy, and also studied with respect to enumeration and distribution. With bacteria and fungi, direct microscopical observation *in situ* is possible, but provides only limited information. Considerable progress has been achieved by the introduction of the fluorescent antibody technique which permits specific microorganisms to be identified in their natural environments. Distribution of microorganisms can be studied by direct (microscopical) methods and by the indirect buried slide technique. For the study of bacteria and fungi, the indirect methods involving isolation, cultivation, identification, and enumeration have much more importance than the direct methods. The most common techniques for isolation and enumeration of bacteria and fungi are (a) plating with solid or semisolid media (usually agar; also gelatin, or silica gel), and (b) MPN-technique with liquid media. The MPN(Most Probable Number)-technique is a procedure of dilution to extinction. The sample is diluted until the cell density becomes so low that transfers turn out to be sterile and growth or metabolism does not appear in the tubes. This technique is especially useful for the enumeration of specific metabolic groups of both aerobes and anaerobes, e.g. nitrifiers and methanogens. The pour plate method does not give the total number of all microorganisms present in the sample because of the technical difficulties of obtaining a homogeneous suspension and because of the selective pressure of the media. With soil samples, the number of bacteria is usually underestimated, while the number of fungi is often over-emphasized due to heavy sporulation (production of conidia). Isolation and enumeration of bacteria in waters is easier than in soils because of the greater homogeneity of the substrate. In sediments, however, the problems are the same as in soils. Direct counts in water samples are commonly 100 to 1000 times greater than viable counts. This discrepancy is partially due to the presence of non-viable bacteria and also due to the fact that a given substrate used for plating is selective and does not allow growth of all organisms present. Isolation of bacteria following enrichment is especially useful in ecological studies. This technique allows isolation of organisms that are rare in the community and would be overgrown by the dominating flora in direct isolation procedures. Techniques for enrichment of distinct organisms have been developed for both batch culture and continuous culture.

Further reading

Books and Articles

Bakken, L. B. (1985). Separation and purification of bacteria from soil. *Applied and Environmental Microbiology*, **49**, 1482–7.

Bone, T. L. & Balkwill, D. L. (1986). Improved flotation technique for microscopy of *in situ* soil and sediment microorganisms. *Applied and Environmental Microbiology*, **51**, 462–8.

Brock, T. D. (1984). How sensitive is the light microscope for observation on microorganisms in natural habitats? *Microbial Ecology*, **10**, 297–300.

Clarke, K. R. & Joint, I. R. (1986). Methodology for estimating numbers of free-living and attached bacteria in estuarine water. *Applied and Environmental Microbiology*, **51**, 1110–20.

Hobbie, J. E., Daley, R. J. & Jasper, S. (1977). Use of nuclepore filters for counting bacteria by fluorescence microscopy. *Applied and Environmental Microbiology*, **33**, 1225–8.

Jones, J. G. (1979). A guide to methods for estimating microbial numbers and biomass in fresh waters. *Freshwater Biological Association*, publication 39, Ambleside: England.

Kauri, T. (1980). Rapid multipoint method for quantification of various physiological groups of bacteria in soil. *Soil Biology and Biochemistry*, **12**, 125–30.

Larsson, K., Wenbull, C. & Cronberg, G. (1978). Comparison of light and electron microscopic determinations of the number of bacteria and algae in lake water. *Applied and Environmental Microbiology*, **35**, 397–404.

Lundgren, B. (1981). Fluorescein diacetate as a stain of metabolically active bacteria in soil. *Oikos*, **36**, 17–22.

MacDonald, R. M. (1986). Sampling soil microfloras: Problems in estimating concentration and activity of suspensions of mixed populations of soil microorganisms. *Soil Biology and Biochemistry*, **18**, 411–16.

Mormak, D. A. & Casida, L. E. jr (1985). Study of *Bacillus subtilis* endospores in soil by use of a modified endospore stain. *Applied and Environmental Microbiology*, **49**, 1356–60.

Nikitin, D. I. (1973). Direct electron microscopic techniques for the observation of microorganisms in soil. *Bulletins from the Ecological Research Committee Stockholm*, **17**, 85–91.

Okereke, G. U. (1984). Possible use of N_2O in MPN tubes for enumeration of denitrifiers. *Plant and Soil*, **80**, 295–6.

Ramsay, A. J. (1984). Extraction of bacteria from soil: efficiency of shaking or ultrasonication is indicated by direct counts and autoradiography. *Soil Biology and Biochemistry*, **16**, 475–81.

Reed, W. M. & Dugan, P. R. (1978). Distribution of *Methylomonas methanica* and *Methylosinus trichosporium* in Cleveland Harbor as determined by an indirect fluorescent antibody-membrane filter technique. *Applied and Environmental Microbiology*, **35**, 422–30.

Schmidt, E. L. (1974). Quantitative autecological study of microorganisms in soil by immunofluorescence. *Soil Science*, **118**, 141–9.

Sieracki, M. E., Johnson, P. W. & Sieburth, J. M. (1985). Detection, enumeration, and sizing of planktonic bacteria by image-analyzed epifluorescence microscopy. *Applied and Environmental Microbiology*, **49**, 799–810.

Szwerinski, H., Gaiser, S. & Bardtke, D. (1985). Immunofluorescence for the quantitative determination of nitrifying bacteria: interference of the test in biofilm reactors. *Applied Microbiology and Biotechnology*, **21**, 125–8.

Trolldenier, G. (1973). The use of fluorescence microscopy for soil micro-organisms. *Bulletins from the Ecological Research Committee*, **17**, 53–9.

Van Vuurde, J. W. L. & Elenbaas, P. F. M. (1978). Use of fluorochromes for direct observation of microorganisms associated with wheat roots. *Canadian Journal of Microbiology*, **24**, 1272–5.

Watson, S. W., Novitsky, T. J., Quinby, H. L. & Valois, F. W. (1977). Determination of bacterial number and biomass in the marine environment. *Applied and Environmental Microbiology*, **33**, 940–6.

Wilson, J. M., Trinick, M. J. & Parker, C. A. (1983). The identification of vesicular-arbuscular mycorrhizal fungi using immunofluorescence. *Soil Biology and Biochemistry*, **15**, 439–45.

Zviagintzev, D. G., Dmitriyev, E. A. & Kozhevn, P. A. (1978). Studies of soil microorganisms by luminescent microscopy. *Mikrobiologiya*, **47**, 1091–6.

Microbial biomass

The importance of microorganisms in ecosystems with respect to their role in the cycling of bioelements has led to an increased interest in the estimation of the microbial biomass. Direct estimation by microscopic monitoring of size and number of microorganisms is only applicable to some specific morphological groups but cannot be applied to the determination of the total microbial biomass. Calculations based on indirect cell counts (plating, MPN) and measurements of cell volumes likewise have only limited value. For quantification of the biomass in complex substrates, several methods have been developed. The ATP assay and the chloroform fumigation technique have become generally accepted. Because of the more or less constant proportion of ATP in cellular materials, its amount is related to the biomass. It has been shown that microbial biomass carbon is between 0.5% and 4.5% of the total organic carbon. The amount of ATP in biomass carbon is around 8 mg ATP/g biomass carbon; hence, the ratio of biomass C:ATP arrives at 125 (1000:8). Because of the fluctuations of ATP concentration related to the physiological state of the cell, the ATP values are not strictly correlated with biomass. The advantage of this assay despite the physiologically conditioned variations is its extreme sensitivity. Amounts of 10^{-14} g ATP can be determined with the bioluminescence test (luciferin–luciferase reaction).

The chloroform fumigation technique for biomass measurement is based on the idea that microorganisms in soil killed by chloroform vapour treatment represent dead microbial biomass that subsequently is metabolized (mineralized) by all sorts of microorganisms introduced into the treated soil by addition of untreated soil. The released CO_2 is directly correlated with the microbial biomass. CO_2 production in the standardized assay is followed for ten days. This simple, rapid and objective assay is the most direct estimation of the actual biomass. By combining the biomass assay with respiratory values it has been found that at 22 °C a substrate-induced maximum respiratory rate of 1 ml CO_2/hour corresponds to about 40 mg of microbial biomass carbon present in the soil.

In agricultural, forest, and grassland soils, fungi make up 75% of the biomass, while bacteria amount to 25%. In principle, estimation of bacterial biomass alone is also possible by analysing the muramic acid or diaminopimelic acid concentration in soil.

Further reading

Books and articles
ATP assay for biomass estimation

Ahmed, M., Oades, J. M. & Ladd, J. N. (1982). Determination of ATP in soil: Effects of soil treatments. *Soil Biology and Biochemistry*, **14**, 273–9.

Brookes, P. C., Tate, K. R. & Jenkinson, D. S. (1983). The adenylate energy charge of the soil microbial biomass. *Soil Biology and Biochemistry*, **15**, 9–16,

Fairbanks, B. C., Woods, L. E., Bryant, R. J., Elliott, E. T., Cole, C. V. & Coleman, D. C. (1984). Limitations of ATP estimates of microbial biomass. *Soil Biology and Biochemistry*, **16**, 549–58.

Karl, D. M. (1980). Cellular nucleotide measurements and applications in microbial ecology. *Microbiological Reviews*, **44**, 739–96.

Kucnerowicz, F., Van der Werf, R. & Verstraete, W. (1982). Estimation of microbial ATP in waters and soils. *Antonie van Leeuwenhoek*, **48**, 522–3.

Oades, J. M. & Jenkinson, D. S. (1979). Adenosine triphosphate content of the soil microbial biomass. *Soil Biology and Biochemistry*, **11**, 201–4.

Sparling, G. P. & Eiland, F. (1983). A comparison of methods for measuring ATP and microbial biomass in soils. *Soil Biology and Biochemistry*, **15**, 227–9.

Sparling, G. P., Speir, T. W. & Whale, K. N. (1986). Changes in microbial biomass C, ATP content, soil phospho-monoesterase and phospho-diesterase activity following air-drying of soils. *Soil Biology and Biochemistry*, **18**, 363–70.

Tate, K. R. & Jenkinson, D. S. (1982). Adenosine triphosphate measurement in soil: An improved method. *Soil Biology and Biochemistry*, **14**, 331–5.

Trevors, J. T. (1985). A comparison of three methods for determining ATP biomass in agricultural soil. *Systematic and Applied Microbiology*, **6**, 107–9.

Webster, J. J., Hampton, G. J. & Leach, F. R. (1984). ATP in soil: a new extractant and extraction procedure. *Soil Biology and Biochemistry*, **16**, 335–42.

Other methods for biomass estimation

Anderson, J. P. E. & Domsch, K. H. (1978). Mineralization of bacteria and fungi in chloroform-fumigated soils. *Soil Biology and Biochemistry*, **10**, 207–13.

Anderson, J. P. E. & Domsch, K. H. (1978). A physiological method for the quantitative measurement of microbial biomass in soils. *Soil Biology and Biochemistry*, **10**, 215–21.

Atlas, R. M. (1982). Enumeration and estimation of microbial biomass. In *Experimental Microbial Ecology*, eds. R. G. Burns & J. H. Slater, pp. 84–104. Oxford, London, Edinburgh, Boston, Melbourne: Blackwell Scientific Publications.

Bjørnsen, P. K. (1986). Automatic determination of bacterioplankton biomass by image analysis. *Applied and Environmental Microbiology*, **51**, 1199–204.

Bratbak, G. (1985). Bacterial biovolume and biomass estimations. *Applied and Environmental Microbiology*, **49**, 1488–93.

Bratbak, G. & Dundas, I. (1984). Bacterial dry matter content and biomass estimations. *Applied and Environmental Microbiology*, **48**, 755–7.

Brock, T. D. & Pedros-Alio, C. (1982). Assessing biomass and production of bacteria in eutrophic Lake Mendota, Wisconsin. *Applied and Environmental Microbiology*, **44**, 203–18.

Domsch, K. H., Beck, Th., Anderson, J. P. E., Söderström, B., Parkinson, D. & Trolldenier, G. (1979). A comparison of methods for soil microbial population and biomass studies. *Zeitschrift für Pflanzenernährung und Bodenkunde*, **142**, 520–33.

Durska, G. & Kaszubiak, H. (1980). Occurrence of α, ε-diaminopimelic acid in soil. I. The content of α, ε-diaminopimelic acid in different soils. *Polish Ecological Studies*, **6**, 189–93.

Durska, G. & Kaszubiak, H. (1980). Occurrence of α, ε-diaminopimelic acid in soil. II. Usefulness of α, ε-diaminopimelic acid determination for calculations of the microbial biomass. *Polish Ecological Studies*, **6**, 195–9.

Fazio, S. D., Mayberry, W. R. & White, D. C. (1979). Muramic acid assay in sediments. *Applied and Environmental Microbiology*, **38**, 349–50.

Findlay, R. H., Moriarty, D. J. W. & White, D. C. (1983). Improved method of determining muramic acid from environmental samples. *Geomicrobiology Journal*, **3**, 135–50.

Jenkinson, D. S. (1976). The effects of biocidal treatments on metabolism in soil. IV. The decomposition of fumigated organisms in soil. *Soil Biology and Biochemistry*, **8**, 203–8.

Jenkinson, D. S. & Ladd, J. N. (1981). Microbial biomass in soil: measurement and turnover. In *Soil Biochemistry*, vol. 5, eds E. A. Paul & J. N. Ladd, pp. 415–71. New York: Marcel Dekker.

Jenkinson, D. S. & Powlson, D. S. (1976). The effects of biocidal treatments on metabolism in soil. I. Fumigation with chloroform. *Soil Biology and Biochemistry*, **8**, 167–77.

Jenkinson, D. S. & Powlson, D. S. (1976). The effects of biocidal treatments on metabolism in soil. V. A method for measuring soil biomass. *Soil Biology and Biochemistry*, **8**, 209–13.

Lynch, J. M. & Panting, L. M. (1981). Measurement of the microbial biomass in intact cores of soil. *Microbial Ecology*, **7**, 229–34.

Mimura, T. & Romano, J.-C. (1985). Muramic acid measurements for bacterial investigations in marine environments by high-pressure liquid chromatography. *Applied and Environmental Microbiology*, **50**, 229–37.

Nannipieri, P. (1984). Microbial biomass and activity measurements in soil: ecological significance. In *Current Perspectives in Microbial Ecology*, eds. M. J. Klug & C. A. Reddy, pp. 515–21. Washington, D.C.: American Society for Microbiology.

Nannipieri, P., Ciardi, C., Badalucco, L. & Casella, S. (1986). A method to determine soil DNA and RNA. *Soil Biology and Biochemistry*, **18**, 275–81.

Paul, E. A. & Voroney, R. P. (1984). Field interpretation of microbial biomass activity measurements. In *Current Perspectives in Microbial Ecology*, eds M. J. Klug & C. A. Reddy, pp. 509–14. Washington, D.C.: American Society for Microbiology.

Ross, D. J. & Tate, K. R. (1984). Microbial biomass in soil: effects of some experimental variables on biochemical estimations. *Soil Biology and Biochemistry*, **16**, 161–7.

Shen, S. M., Pruden, G. & Jenkinson, D. S. (1984). Mineralization and immobilization of nitrogen in fumigated soil and the measurement of microbial biomass nitrogen. *Soil Biology and Biochemistry*, **16**, 437–44.

Sparling, G. P. (1981). Microcalorimetry and other methods to assess biomass and activity in soil. *Soil Biology and Biochemistry*, **13**, 93–8.

Growth rates and activities

In order to understand microbial life in complex systems such as soil, it is not only necessary to know the types of organisms, their numbers and distribution, the total biomass and the proportions of the various groups, but it also requires detailed knowledge of growth, reproduction and metabolic activities. The overall activity is usually evaluated by measurement of O_2 uptake, or CO_2 evolution, or enzyme activities.

For measurement of O_2 uptake (aerobic respiration) in soil electrolytic respirometry is a well-suited technique. It is based on the replacement of O_2, at concurrent absorption of CO_2, in a closed system containing the substrate with the respiring organisms. The respiration rate is directly correlated with the rate of electrolysis, which can be monitored. Variations in gas volume within the respiration chamber (respirometer), due to changes in atmospheric air pressure, have to be compensated. The method is applicable to sieved unamended and amended soil and also to undisturbed soil cores. Sensitivity in electrolytic respirometry is better than 1 μl O_2 per hour and g soil. With special methods simultaneous measurement of O_2 consumption, production of CO_2 and other metabolic compounds (e.g. ethylene from acetylene by N_2-fixing bacteria) is possible.

A method that distinguishes between biological and chemical activities is based on the O_2 uptake rate-temperature relationship. Biological reactions show a temperature optimum and do not occur at elevated nonbiological temperatures, whereas chemical reactions increase with temperature beyond the range of biological reactions.

Radiorespirometry has a multiplicity of applications. It is generally used for monitoring metabolism of microorganisms in soil, namely microbial degradation of ^{14}C-labelled compounds and measurement of the metabolically evolved $^{14}CO_2$. This rapid and highly sensitive method has also been applied in devices for extraterrestrial life detection.

Exposure of a soil sample to $^{14}CO_2$ allows for measurement of microbial $^{14}CO_2$ incorporation. Several methods have been proposed to remove the non-biologically adsorbed $^{14}CO_2$ and to convert the ^{14}C-labelled biomass fraction into $^{14}CO_2$, which is then trapped and quantified by scintillation counting. This method allows for quantification of the primary productivity *in situ*.

The overall activity of microorganisms in soil can also be determined by measuring the activity of the electron transport system (ETS) by means of reduction of triphenyltetrazolium chloride (or other tetrazolium salts). The colourless oxidized form is reduced to coloured formazan, which can be extracted and quantified. Comparative studies on the estimation of dehydrogenase activity and respiration in soil have revealed that the correlation between O_2 uptake and formazan formation is poor. The technique is more useful for studying microbial activity at the micro-sites in soil. According to expectation it has been found that the biologically active sites are primarily localized on, and around, organic debris.

The test for the biochemical oxygen demand (BOD) is widely used for measuring the decomposable organic material especially in waters. BOD_5 (a test during 5 days at 20 °C) is a standard pollution monitoring tool. Special electrodes (BOD sensors) have been developed that allow estimation of BOD within 15 minutes.

Another method for measuring microbial activity in soil is microcalorimetry. All microbial processes are accompanied by heat evolution. Although some technical problems have still to be solved for wider application, the method is a useful tool for quantitative registration of biological processes in soil. Microcalorimetric values have been shown to correlate well with respiration.

A great number of methods have been introduced for the measurement of specific processes in the field. N_2-fixation and denitrification are considered here as examples. The acetylene reduction test has become a standard procedure for measuring nitrogenase activity. The assay has also been applied to *in situ* studies. It has become obvious, however, that the operational and interpretative problems are greater than in *in vitro* studies with pure cultures. Determination of N_2-fixation in natural environments has also been performed with techniques using the isotope ^{15}N. Several methods are available for the study of denitrification. By addition of C_2H_2 to a denitrifying system, reduction of N_2O (to N_2) is inhibited, and nitrate and nitrite are stoichiometrically reduced to N_2O

without a change in the rate of nitrate reduction. Besides chromatographic techniques, denitrification has also been studied with methods
using ^{13}N-labelled nitrate or ^{15}N-labelled compounds in field experiments.

Further reading

Books and articles
Staining techniques

Chrzanowski, T. H., Crotty, R. D., Hubbard, J. G. & Welch, R. P. (1984). Applicability of the fluorescein diacetate method of detecting active bacteria in freshwater. *Microbial Ecology*, **10**, 179–85.
Ingham, E. R. & Klein, D. A. (1984). Soil fungi: relationships between hyphal activity and staining with fluorescein diacetate. *Soil Biology and Biochemistry*, **16**, 273–8.
Schnürer, J. & Rosswall, T. (1982). Fluorescein diacetate hydrolysis as a measure of total microbial activity in soil and litter. *Applied and Environmental Microbiology*, **43**, 1256–61.

Respirometry

Coveney, M. F. & Wetzel, R. G. (1984). Improved double-vial radiorespirometric technique for mineralization of ^{14}C-labeled substrates. *Applied and Environmental Microbiology*, **47**, 1154–7.
Larson, R. J. & Perry, R. L. (1981). Use of the electrolytic respirometer to measure biodegradation in natural waters. *Water Research*, **15**, 697–702
McKinley, V. L., Federle, T. W. & Vestal, J. R. (1983). Improvements in and environmental applications of doublevial radiorespirometry for the study of microbial mineralization. *Applied and Environmental Microbiology*, **45**, 255–9.
Pazout, J. & Vancura, V. (1981). Simultaneous measurement of ethylene and CO_2 production and of O_2 consumption in soil and pure microbial cultures. *Plant and Soil*, **62**, 107–15.

Radiotracer methods

Atlas, R. M. & Hubbard, J. S. (1974). Applicability of radiotracer methods of measuring $^{14}CO_2$ assimilation for determining microbial activity in soil including a new *in situ* method. *Microbial Ecology*, **1**, 145–63.
Hubbard, J. S., Hobby, G. L., Horowitz, N. H., Geiger, P. J. & Morelli, F. A. (1970). Measurement of $^{14}CO_2$ assimilation in soils: An experiment for biological exploration of Mars. *Applied Microbiology*, **19**, 32–8.
Karube, I., Matsunaga, T., Mitsuda, S. & Suzuki, S. (1977). Microbial electrode BOD sensors. *Biotechnology and Bioengineering*, **19**, 1535–47.
Smith, D. W., Fliermans, C. B. & Brock, T. D. (1972). Technique for measuring $^{14}CO_2$ uptake by soil microorganisms *in situ*. *Applied Microbiology*, **23**, 595–600.

Calorimetry

Konno, T. (1976). Calorimetric application on measurements of activity of soil microorganisms. *Netsu*, **3**, 148–51.

Ljungholm, K., Noren, B. & Wadsö, I. (1979). Microcalorimetric observations of microbial activity in normal and acidified soils. *Oikos*, **33**, 24–30.
Ljungholm, K., Noren, B., Skold, R. & Wadsö, I. (1979). Use of microcalorimetry for the characterization of microbial activity in soil. *Oikos*, **33**, 15–23.

Enzyme Activities

Benefield, C. B., Howard, P. J. A. & Howard, D. M. (1977). The estimation of dehydrogenase activity in soil. *Soil Biology and Biochemistry*, **9**, 67–70.
Casida, L. E., jr (1977). Microbial metabolic activity in soil as measured by dehydrogenase determinations. *Applied and Environmental Microbiology*, **34**, 630–6.
Trevors, J. T. (1984). Electron transport system activity in soil, sediment, and pure cultures. *CRC Critical Reviews in Microbiology*, **11**, 83–100.
Trevors, J. T. (1984). Effect of substrate concentration, inorganic nitrogen, O_2 concentration, temperature and pH on dehydrogenase activity in soil. *Plant and Soil*, **77**, 285–93.
Trevors, J. T. (1984). Dehydrogenase activity in soil: a comparison between the INT and TTC assay. *Soil Biology and Biochemistry*, **16**, 673–4.
Trevors, J. T. (1984). Rapid gas chromatographic method to measure H_2O_2 oxidoreductase (catalase) activity in soil. *Soil Biology and Biochemistry*, **16**, 525–6.
Trevors, J. T., Mayfield, C. I. & Inniss, W. E. (1982). Measurement of electron transport system (ETS) activity in soil. *Microbial Ecology*, **8**, 163–8.
Wada, H., Saito, M. & Takai, Y. (1978). Effectiveness of tetrazolium salts in microbial ecological studies in submerged soil. *Soil Science and Plant Nutrition*, **24**, 349–56.

Estimation of N_2-fixation

Broadbent, F. E., Nakashima, T. & Chang, G. Y. (1982). Estimation of nitrogen fixation by isotope dilution in field and greenhouse experiments. *Agronomy Journal*, **74**, 625–8.
Chalk, P. M., Douglas, L. A. & Buchanan, S. A. (1983). Use of ^{15}N enrichment of soil mineralizable N as a reference for isotope dilution measurements of biologically fixed nitrogen. *Canadian Journal of Microbiology*, **29**, 1046–52.
Danso, S. K. A. (1986). Review: Estimation of N_2-fixation by isotope dilution: an appraisal of techniques involving ^{15}N enrichment and their application – comments. *Soil Biology and Biochemistry*, **3**, 243–4.
Edmeades, D. C. & Goh, K. M. (1979). The use of the ^{15}N-dilution technique for field measurements of symbiotic nitrogen fixation. *Communications in Soil Science and Plant Analysis*, **10**, 513–20.
Englund, B. & Meyerson, H. (1974). *In situ* measurement of nitrogen fixation at low temperatures. *Oikos*, **25**, 283–7.
Giller, K. E., Wani, S. P. & Day, J. M. (1986). Use of isotope dilution to measure nitrogen fixation associated with the roots of sorghum and millet genotypes. *Plant and Soil*, **90**, 255–63.
Knowles, R. (1981). The measurement of nitrogen fixation. In *Current Perspectives in Nitrogen Fixation*, eds A. H. Gibson & W. E. Newton, pp. 327–33. Canberra: Australian Academy of Science.
Lethbridge, G., Davidson, M. S. & Sparling, G. P. (1982). Critical evaluation of the acetylene reduction test for estimating the activity of nitrogen-fixing bacteria associated with the roots of wheat and barley. *Soil Biology and Biochemistry*, **14**, 27–35.
Martensson, A. M. & Ljunggren, H. D. (1984). A comparison between the acetylene reduction method, the isotope dilution method and the total nitrogen difference method

for measuring nitrogen fixation in lucerne (*Medicago sativa* L.). *Plant and Soil*, **81**, 177–84.

Wada, E., Imaizumi, R., Kabaya, Y., Yasuda, T., Kanamori, T., Saito, G. & Nishimune, A. (1986). Estimation of symbiotically fixed nitrogen in field grown soybeans: an application of natural $^{15}N/^{14}N$ abundance and a low level ^{15}N-tracer technique. *Plant and Soil*, **93**, 269–86.

Estimation of ammonification and denitrification

Alef, K. & Kleiner, D. (1986). Arginine ammonification, a simple method to estimate microbial activity potentials in soils. *Soil Biology and Biochemistry*, **18**, 233–5.

Hallmark, S. L. & Terry, R. E. (1985). Field measurement of denitrification in irrigated soils. *Soil Science*, **140**, 35–44.

Jenneman, G. E., Montgomery, A. D. & McInerney, M. J. (1986). Method for detection of microorganisms that produce gaseous nitrogen oxides. *Applied and Environmental Microbiology*, **51**, 776–80.

Lippold, H., Foerster, I., Hagemann, O. & Matzel, W. (1981). Messung der Denitrifizierung auf Grünland mit Hilfe der Gaschromatographie und der ^{15}N-Technik (Measuring Denitrification on Grassland by Means of Gas Chromatography and ^{15}N-Technique). *Archiv für Acker- und Pflanzenbau und Bodenkunde*, **25**, 79–86.

Parkin, T. B., Kaspar, H. F., Sexstone, A. J. & Tiedje, J. M. (1984). A gas-flow soil core method to measure field denitrification rates. *Soil Biology and Biochemistry*, **16**, 323–30.

Rolston, D. E. & Broadbent, F. E. (1977). Field measurement of denitrification. *Environmental Protection Technology Series, EPA*, 600/2–77–233, 91.

Stout, J. D. & More, R. D. (1980). The measurement of denitrification in soil, using $^{13}NO_3$. In: *Biogeochemistry of ancient and modern environments*, eds P. A. Trudinger, M. R. Walter & B. J. Ralph, pp. 293–8. Berlin: Springer–Verlag.

Yoshinari, T. & Knowles, R. (1976). Acetylene inhibition of nitrous oxide reduction by denitrifying bacteria. *Biochemical and Biophysical Research Communications*, **69**, 705–10.

Yoshinari, T., Hynes, R. & Knowles, R. (1977). Acetylene inhibition of nitrous oxide reduction and measurement of denitrification and nitrogen fixation in soil. *Soil Biology and Biochemistry*, **9**, 177–83.

Other methods for measuring microbial activities

Darrah, P. R. & Harris, P. J. (1986). A fluorimetric method for measuring the activity of soil enzymes. *Plant and Soil*, **92**, 81–8.

Hunt, H. W., Cole, C. V. & Elliott, E. T. (1985). Models for growth of bacteria inoculated into sterilized soil. *Soil Science*, **139**, 156–65.

Isbister, J. D., Shippen, R. S. & Caplan, J. (1980). A new method for monitoring cellulose and starch degradation in soils. *Bulletin of Environmental Contamination Toxicology*, **24**, 570–4.

Karl, D. M. & Bossard, P. (1985). Measurement of microbial nucleic acid synthesis and specific growth rate by $^{32}PO_4$ and ^3H adenine: field comparison. *Applied and Environmental Microbiology*, **50**, 706–9.

Nannipieri, P., Johnson, R. L. & Paul, E. A. (1978). Criteria for measurement of microbial growth and activity in soil. *Soil Biology and Biochemistry*, **10**, 233–9.

Paris, D. F. & Rogers, J. E. (1986). Kinetic concepts for measuring microbial rate constants: Effects of nutrients on rate constants. *Applied and Environmental Microbiology*, **51**, 221–5.

Pollard, P. C. & Moriarty, D. J. W. (1984). Validity of the tritiated thymidine method for growth rates: measurement of isotope dilution synthesis. *Applied and Environmental Microbiology*, **48**, 1076–83.

Radmer, R. J. & Kok, B. (1979). Rate–temperature curves as an unambiguous indicator of biological activity in soil. *Applied and Environmental Microbiology*, **38**, 224–8.

Revsbech, N. P. & Jørgensen, B. B. (1986). Microelectrodes: their use in microbial ecology. *Advances in Microbial Ecology*, **9**, 293–352.

Staley, J. T. (1985). Measurement of *in situ* activities of nonphotosynthetic microorganisms in aquatic and terrestrial habitats. *Annual Review of Microbiology*, **39**, 321–46.

Epilogue

The final goal of microbial ecology is to increase scientific knowledge for a better understanding of microbial life in nature. Further progress in the elucidation of the complex processes will depend largely on the development of potent methods for ecological field studies, on the cooperation of microbiologists working in different habitat-oriented fields, and on interdisciplinary research beyond the borders of microbiology. The still existing gap between micro- and macroecology must be overcome.

Research in microbial ecology is not only of academic interest but also contributes to the solution of practical problems. Microorganisms may themselves cause unwanted effects or lessen the detrimental effects originating from human perturbations. Examples of undesired microbial activities are the accumulation of nitrate in ground water due to nitrification as a consequence of excessive fertilization, or the anaerobic corrosion of iron, or the spoilage of food, or the role of microorganisms as pathogens. Desired activities are, for instance, the degradation of xenobiotics such as pesticides and synthetic polymers, or the removal of heavy metals from industrial effluents by means of microorganisms.

The persistence of xenobiotic compounds is a great challenge to the microbial ecologist. Many organic chemicals dispersed in nature are recalcitrant or fully resistant to microbial degradation. The accumulation in the environment of toxic, mutagenic, or carcinogenic compounds and metabolites is a hazard to the health of man and animal. In principle, the unwanted effects related to the use of pesticides, herbicides and other xenobiotics can be eliminated by either suspending their use or changing over to ecologically less harmful compounds. The latter possibility has been successfully practised with the introduction of degradable surfactants. Whether the spontaneous evolution of new degradative capabilities from the existing microflora or the 'construction' of microorganisms with new abilities by genetic engineering will contribute to solve the serious long-term problems of persisting organic compounds, is still a matter of speculation and debate. In view of the fact that microorganisms are involved in many processes related to environmental quality, one can predict that microbial ecology will gain increasing societal importance and attract growing numbers of students.

Index

ADP, *see* Adenosine-5'-diphosphate
AMP, *see* Adenosine-5'-monophosphate
APS, *see* Adenosine-5'-phosphosulphate
ATP, *see* Adenosine-5'-triphosphate
Abundance of microorganisms
  aquatic environments 132, 133
  extreme environments 137
  terrestrial environments 123,124
Acetaldehyde 36
Acetate
  acetic acid bacteria 80
  assimilation by microalgae 13
  methanogenesis 104
  oxidation 40
  product of fermentation 40, Fig. 2.13
  rumen 202, Fig. 7.4
  sulphate-reducing bacteria 33, 83, 244
Acetobacter
  A. aceti 80
  A. xylinum 156
Acetogenic bacteria 34
Acetoin Fig. 2.13
Acetone, product in fermentation 34, 40,
  Fig. 2.13
Acetyl-CoA 36, 40, Figs. 2.14, 2.15
Acetylene 192
  reduction test 45, 277
N-Acetylglucosamine 6, Figs. 2.2, 8.7
Acetyl-methyl carbinol 89
N-Acetylmuramic acid 6, 274, Fig. 2.2
Acetylphosphate 36
Acheloplasma 104
Achromatium 51, 68, 86
  A. oxaliferum 11
Achromobacter 254, 258
Acid bogs 142
Acid-fast stain, mycobacteria 102
Acid mine waters 138, 249
Acidic rain 142, 143
Acidaminococcus 97
Acidophilic organisms 165
  habitats 143
Acinetobacter 95, 123
Aconitase 249
cis-Aconitate Fig. 2.15

Acrasin 155
Acrasiomycetes 107
Actinobacillus 93
Actinomyces 199, 206, 227
  A. bovis 102
Actinomycetes 102, 103, 221, 227
Acyl-AMP 44
Adansonian principle 14
Adaptation 180
  capacity of 5
  to low nutrient conditions 144
Adenosine-5'-phosphosulphate 243
  reductase Fig. 2.10
Adenosine-5'-diphosphate 26, Fig. 2.4
  in enzyme regulation 49
Adenosine-5'-monophosphate 26, Fig. 2.4
  in enzyme regulation 49
Adenosine-5'-triphosphate
  anabolism and catabolism 26
  carrier of biological energy 25
  chemical structure Fig. 2.4
  denitrification 237
  energy charge 26
  enzyme regulation 49
  estimation of biomass 273
  generation of 26, 31, Fig. 2.7
  nitrogen fixation 45
  oxidative phosphorylation 27, 29
  photophosphorylation 27
  proton motive force 31
  respiration 29
  substrate level phosphorylation 26, 29
  sulphurylase Fig. 2.10
Adenylate energy charge (EC) 26
Adhesion 12, 80, 120, 156, 207
Aedes 174
Aeration 166
Aerobacter aerogenes,
  minimum water potential Fig. 5.2
Aerobes, obligate 22
Aerobic respiration 22, 29, 31, Fig. 2.8
Aerococcus 152
Aeromonas 252
  A. salmonicida 92
Aerotaxis 155

Aerotolerance 23, 55
Agar
  decomposition 68, 70
  media 52, 56
  pour plate method 271
Agaricus bisporus 158
Aggressines 208
Agrobacterium 123, 143, 152, 197
  A. tumefaciens 81, 197
  A. rhizogenes 197
Air
  -born microbes 174
  dispersal of pathogens 124
  numbers of microorganisms in 173
Akinetes 61
Alanine
  dehydrogenase 234
  in murein Fig. 2.2
Alcaligenes 82, 83, 123, 136, 238, 252
  A. eutrophus 260
Aldolase 37
Algae
  blooms 50, 134
  cell wall 153
  classification 108
  eutrophication 134
  freshwater 108
  marine 108
  mats 167
  microalgae 12, 13, 107–9
  planktonic 109
  soil 108, 124
  symbiotic associations 107, 108
  unicellular 108
Alimentary tract 94, 102
Alkalophic organisms 143, 165
Alkanes 227, 230, 261
  oxidation 22
Alkylbenzyl sulphonates 260
  chemical structure Fig. 8.15
Alnus glutinosa 103
Allochthonous microflora 115, 173, 199
Alysiella 68
  habitat 69
Amanita 193
Ambrosia beetle 202
Amensalism 188
Amino acids
  growth factor 17
  osmoregulation 139
  protein synthesis 43
Aminoacyl-AMP 44
Ammonification 187, 216, 232, 234
Ammonium
  assimilation 216
  chemolithotrophic oxidation 84

inhibitors of oxidation 235
monooxygenase 236
nitrogen cycle Fig. 8.8
nitrogen source 18, 99, 232
oxidation 236
product of nitrogen fixation 45
repression of nitrogenase 45
Amoebae 109, 185, 206
Amphidinium 203
Amylose, structure 223, Fig. 8.4
Anabaena 63, Fig. 3.1
  A. azollae 46, 197, 240
Anabaenopsis arnoldii 143
Anabolism 25, 26
  energy consuming processes 42–4
Anaerobes
  facultative 23, 166
  intestinal tract 166
  obligate 22, 166
  rumen 201
  techniques for cultivation 24
Anaerobic respiration
  see carbonate respiration
  see fumarate respiration
  see nitrate respiration
  see sulphate respiration
  see sulphur respiration
Anaplerotic reactions 42, 167
Anemochoric dispersal 174
Animals, interactions with
    microorganisms 198–209
Anopheles 174
Anoxic (anoxygenic) photosynthesis 6, 18,
    27, 64, 135
Antagonistic
  relationships 187
  effects 188
Antagonisms, among microorganisms
    187–90
Antarctic 141
Antibiosis 188
Antibiotics 188, 199
  production by streptomycetes 103
  resistance to 89, 180
Antibodies 209
Antigens 209
  O, H, Vi 90
Antonie van Leeuwenhoek 4
Appendages
  attachment 156
  cellular 12, 120
Aquatic environments (habitats) 129–37
  temperature fluctuation 165
Arabinose, chemical structure Fig. 8.3
Archaebacteria 4, 12, 15, 104–6, 139
  cell wall 7

Archaebacteria
    lipids 10, 139
    representatives 10, 85
Aquaspirillum 77
Ardisia crispa 191
Arginine-dihydrolase 14
Aridisols 118
Armadillo 103
Aromatic compounds, degradation 101,
    253
Aromatic hydrocarbons 260
Arthrobacter 101, 232, 249, 254
    A. glacialis 123
    resistance to desiccation 153
    soil 123
Arthrobotrys 205
Ascidia 67, 203
Ascomycetes 106, 107, 193, 197, 224
Ascospores 107
Aspartase 234
Aspergillus 124, 227, 249, 252, 258
    A. fumigatus 140
    A. glaucus Fig. 5.1
    A. niger 107
    A. oryzae 223
Assimilatory nitrate reduction 18, 216,
    233, 237
Assimilatory sulphate reduction 18, 243,
    Fig. 8.9
Association, metabolic 184, 185
Astasia longa 108
Asterionella 107
Asticcacaulis 71
    buoyancy 73
Atmospheric conditions, influencing
    growth 166, 167
ATP-synthase 29, Fig. 2.7
Atrazine 254
    chemical structure Fig. 8.10
Attachment
    rhizobia to root hairs 196
    to surfaces 71, 156–8
Autecology 172
Autochthonous microflora 101, 115, 123,
    173, 198
Autolysis 19
Autotrophy 18, 19
Auxotrophy 19, 43
a_w-value, *see* Water activity
Axial fibrils 75, 154, Fig. 3.4
Axenic culture 49, 177
Azide 45
Azoferredoxin 44, Fig. 2.17
Azolla 197
Azomonas
    A. agilis 81
    A. insignis 81

Azospirillum 24, 192
    A. brasilense 240
    A. lipoferum 77, 80, 240
Azotobacter 24, 53, 80, 154, 240
    A. chroococcum 11, 240
    A. paspali 81, 240
    A. vinelandii 81
    enrichment 178

Babesia 110
Bacillariophyceae (diatoms) 108
Bacillus 99, 100, 141, 143, 153, 206, 227,
    237, 249, 258
    B. acidocaldarius 143
    B. anthracis 99, 207
    B. cereus 99
    B. cereus var. mycoides Fig. 5.2
    B. coagulans 163
    B. macerans 223
    B. megaterium 99,. 251, Fig. 5.2
    B. pasteurii 99
    B. polymyxa 99, 224
    B. popilliae 100
    B. psychrophilus 99, 141
    B. stearothermophilus 99, 163, Fig. 5.2
    B. subtilis 99, Fig. 5.2
    B. thuringiensis 100
    enrichment 54
    denitrification 83
    thermophilic 141
    minimum water potential Fig. 5.1
Bacteria
    acetic acid 80
    acetogenic 34
    archaebacteria 104–6
    budding 71–4
    cell wall-deficient 104
    CO-oxidizing 82
    coryneform 101, 102
    cyanobacteria 61–4
    endospore forming 99–101
    gliding 68–70
    green sulphur 64, 135
    halophilic 138, 139
    hydrogen oxidizing 82
    hydrogen sulphide oxidizing 185, 244
    iron–sulphur 73, 141
    lactic acid 98
    magnetotactic 155
    methane oxidizing 82, 227, 231
    methanogenic 10, 104, 105
    methylotrophic 82, 135, 216, 241
    nitrifying 85, 235, 236
    nitrogen-fixing 80, 81
    phototrophic 18, 27, 64–8
    phytopathogenic 191, 197, 198
    prosthecate 71–4

purple sulphur 64–7
sheathed 70, 71
spirilla 77
spirochetes 75–7
sporeforming 99–101
sulphate reducing 33, 83, 185, 243
sulphur reducing 83, 244
thermophilic 140–2
Bacterial chromosome 6
Bacterial diseases of animals
  anthrax 100
  bovine pleuropneumonia 104
  bronchitis 93
  brucellosis 87, 207
  erysipelas, swine 98
  fowl cholera 93
  furunculosis (fish) 92
  glanders 79
  listeriosis 98
  lumpy jaw 102
  melioidosis 79
  meningitis 93
  pseudotuberculosis 91
  respiratory disease 87
  tetanus 100
  tuberculosis 102
  tularemia 88
Bacterial diseases of men
  anthrax 99
  arthritis 91, 98
  bacteriaemia 90, 96, 207
  botulism 100
  bronchitis 93
  brucellosis 87, 207
  cholera 92
  conjunctivitis 79, 206
  cystitis 96
  diarrhea 89, 91, 92, 96
  diphtheria 10, 101, 208
  donovanosis 94
  dysentery 91
  endocarditis 79, 90, 96, 98, 100
  enteritis 91
  enterocolitis 91
  epidemic typhoid fever 103
  erysipeloid 98
  gas gangrene 100
  gonorrhea 95
  ileitis 91
  legionellosis (legionnaires' disease) 88, 206
  leprosy 103, 175
  leptospirosis 77
  listeriosis 98
  Malta fever 87
  melioidosis 79
  meningitis 79, 93, 95

  otitis 79
  pinta disease 77
  plague 91
  pneumonia 79, 90, 205, 207
  psittacosis 104, 206
  rabbit fever 88
  rat-bite fever 94
  relapsing fever 77
  rheumatic fever 97
  septicemia 91
  syphilis 77, 205
  tetanus 100
  trachoma 104, 206
  tuberculosis 102, 205
  tularemia 88
  typhoid fever 90
  vaginitis 79
  Weil's disease 77
  whooping cough 87
  yaws 77
  yersiniosis 91
Bacterial diseases of plants
  alfalfa wilt 101
  blights 80
  cankers 80
  crown gall 197
  fasciation 101
  fire blight 92, 175
  foliar diseases 80
  hairy-root disease 197
  hyperplasias 80
  potato ring rot 101
  potato scab 103
  rots, wet, soft 80, 197
  wild fire (tobacco) 175
  wilts 80
Bacterial features, of taxonomic value 14
Bacterial fermentations 34–7
Bacterial luminescence 12, 136, 203
Bacterial nutrition 16, 18, 19
Bacterial photosynthesis 6, 10, 18, 27, 64, 135, 168
Bacterial species 13, 15
Bacterial viruses 9, 89, 190
Bacteriochlorophylls 27, 64, 168
  spectral absorption 168
Bacteriocin 91
Bacteriophaeophytin 27
Bacteriophage 89, 190
Bacteriorhodopsin 105
Bacteroides 23, 89, 94, 200
  B. amylophilus 201
  B. pneumosintes 11
  B. ruminicola 201
  B. succinogenes 94, 201, 222
Bacteroids, in nodules 195, Fig. 7.3
Bactoderma 142

Baeocytes 63
Balantidium coli 110
Barophilic, barotolerant organisms 145
Bartonella 206
Basidiomycetes 106, 107, 175, 186, 197,
    206, 221
  brown rot 225
  mycorrhiza 193
  white rot 224
Basidiospores 107
Batch culture 19
Bdellovibrio 11, 22, 78
  bdelloplast Fig. 7.1
  development cycle 78, 189, Fig. 7.1
  habitats 78
  metabolism 190
  motility 174
  phylogenetic relationship 78
  Y_{ATP} 78, 190
Beggiatoa 68, 86, 154, 246
  association with
    Spirochaeta plictabilis 76
  metabolism 69, 244
Behaviour of microorganisms 154–8
Beijerinck 52, 240
Beijerinckia 81
Beneckea 92, 136
  B. paraphaemolytica 92
Benthos 132
Benzo(a)anthracene 260, Fig. 8.16
Benzo(a)pyrene 260, Fig. 8.16
Bergey's *Manual of Determinative
    Bacteriology* 14
Bergey's *Manual of Systematic
    Bacteriology* 14
Bicarbonates 218, 250
Bifidobacterium 102
  B. bifidum 50, 89, 102, 176
Binary fission 11, 19
Bioaccumulation 253
Biocoenosis 115
Biodegradation, *see* decomposition,
    degradation
Bioelements, microbial cells 16
Biogeochemical cycles 215–52
Biogeochemistry 220
Biological control, insects 100
Biological oxygen demand (BOD) 228,
    277
Bioluminescence, *see* luminescence
Biomass, microbial
  ATP in 273
  composition 16
  decomposition 215
  procedures for determination 273
  in soils 124, 220
Biosphere 215

Biosynthesis 43
  of cellular materials 16
  of monomers 25
  of polymers 25
Biotope 172
Biotype, biovar 15
1,3-Bisphosphoglycerate 36, Figs. 2.11,
    2.12
Black Sea 130
Blastobacter 73
Blastocaulis–Planctomyces 51, 73
Blooms
  of algae 50, 74, 109, 134
  of cyanobacteria 63, 134, 241
Blue-green algae, *see* Cyanobacteria
Bordetella 87, 206
  B. parapertussis 87
  B. pertussis 87
  B. bronchiseptica 87
Boletus 193
Borrelia 56, 75, 76, 206
  B. recurrentis 77
Botrytis 227
  B. cinerea 223
Brachyarcus 51, 79
  B. thiophilus 79
Branhamella 95
Brevibacterium 123
  B. linens 101
Brucella 87, 206, 207
  B. abortus 87
  B. melitensis 87
  B. suis 87
  CO_2 requirement 167
  infectious abortion 87
Budding and/or appendaged bacteria 71–4
Buoyancy 132, 135, 155, 156
Buried slide technique 271
Butanol, product in fermentation 36, 40,
    Fig. 2.13
2,3-Butanediol, product in fermentation
    36, Fig. 2.13
2,3-Butylene glycol 89
Butyrate, product in fermentation 36, 40,
    Fig. 2.13
  sulphate reduction 83
Butyrivibrio 23, 94
  B. fibrisolvens 201, 222
Butyrylphosphate 36

C_1-compounds, utilization 4, 82, 231
^{14}C-compounds 226
  use in carbon transformations 220
CIPC (Isopropyl-*m*-chlorocarbanilate) 254
  chemical structure Fig. 8.10
CO (carbon monoxide), oxidation by
    bacteria 82

CO_2 (carbon dioxide)
  aquatic habitats 129
  atmosphere 166, 217
  concentration in air 167, 215
  electron acceptor 23, 104
  requirement for growth 95, 167
CO_2-fixation
  autotrophic 17, 31, 43, 167, 246, Fig. 2.6
  cyanobacteria 63
  energy requirements 43
  heterotrophic 17
Cabbage clubroot 107
Calcium
  endopore 250
  metabolism 250
  occurrence 250
  transformations 250, 251
Calcium carbonate, precipitation 250
Caldariella acidophila 141
Calothrix 63
Calvin cycle 167, Fig. 2.6
  chemolithoautotrophs 31, 84
  key enzymes 43
  photoautotrophs 27
Calymmatobacterium granulomatis 94
Campylobacter 77
  C. fecalis 78
  C. fetus 77
  C. sputorum 78
  infectious abortion 78
Candida 231
  C. albicans 227
Capsules 12, 100, 207
Carbonates 218, 250
Carbonate respiration 32, 33, Fig. 2.8
Carbon dioxide, *see* CO_2
Carbon monoxide-oxidizing bacteria 82
Carbon cycle 217–32, Fig. 8.1
  anaerobic environments 215
  general aspects 217–20
Carbonic acid 129
Carboxin 257
  chemical structure Fig. 8.12
Carboxydobacteria 82
Cardiobacterium hominis 94
Carnivores 122, Fig. 4.3
β-Carotene 61
Carotenoids 27, 167, 219
Caryophanon latum 99
Catabolism 12, 25, 42
  catabolic enzymes 46
  energy yielding reactions 24–42
  glucose Fig. 2.12
  metabolic pathways 25, 37–41, Fig. 2.12
Catabolite repression 46
Catalase 14, 37, 96, 167
Cathodic depolarization 245

Caulobacter 71, 136, 145, 152, 174
  development cycle 72, Fig. 3.3
  habitats 72, 142, 157
Caulococcus 74
Cell, microbial
  chemical composition 16
  structure 6, 152–4
Cell wall
  algae 153
  bacteria 6, 7
  composition 6, 15
  fungi 12, 153
  Mycoplasma 153
  yeasts 153
Cell wall-deficient bacteria 104, 153
Cellobiose 76, 202, 221
Cellulase 76, 202
  in fungi 221
Cellulomonas 101, 123, 221
Cellulose
  decomposing bacteria 115, 120
  degradation 68, 70, 76, 94, 103, 185, 200, 202, 220, 221
  fungus cell wall 106
  plant cell wall 7
  rumen 200, 222
  structure Fig. 8.2
Cellulose acetate 259, Fig. 8.14
Cephalosporium 124, 221, 249
Ceratium 203
Chaetomium 221
Chemical oxygen demand (COD) 228
Chemocline 134, 217, Fig. 4.4
Chemolithoautotrophy
  concept 68
  obligate 246
Chemolithoheterotrophy 84
Chemolithotrophic bacteria 11, 82
  CO_2 fixation 11, 17, 43, 84
  habitats 85
  heterotrophic growth 85
  obligate 84–7
  substrates 84
Chemoorganotrophs 17, 19, 29, 177
Chemostat 20, 178
  enrichment 53, 145
Chemotaxis 154
Chemotrophs 18
Chemotype 90
Chemovar 15
Chicken embryos 103
Chinons 31
Chitin
  animal residues 226
  decomposition 68, 70, 103, 227
  fungi 7, 106, 227
  structure 226, Fig. 8.7

Chlamydia 51, 206
  C. psittaci 103, 206
  C. trachomatis 103, 206
  survival in soil 125
Chloramphenicol 10, 103
Chlordane 257
  chemical structure Fig. 8.11
Chlorobiaceae 64, 247
  enrichment 53, 179
Chlorobium 64, 185, 244
  C. limicola Fig. 3.2
Chloroflexaceae 64
Chloroflexus 27, 64, 68, 247
  C. aurantiacus 67, 141
Chloroform fumigation technique 274
Chlorogloeopsis 64
Chlorophyceae 108
Chlorophylls 10, 12, 167
  cyanobacteria 61
  Prochloron 67
Chloroplast
  molluscs 203
  symbiont theory 9, 16, 183
Chromatiaceae 64, 247
  enrichment 179
Chromatium 15, 185, 244
  C. okenii 64, 67, 178, Fig. 3.2
  C. vinosum 178
  C. weissei 178
Chromobacterium
  C. libidum 92
  C. violaceum 92
Chromosome
  eukaryotes 6
  prokaryotes 6
Chrysophyceae 109
Chytridiomycetes 106, 197
Chytrids 133
Ciliates 109, 110, 186
Ciliphora, *see* Ciliates
Citrate (citric acid)
  formation 40, 117, Figs. 2.15, 2.19
  synthase 40, Fig. 2.15
  utilization 89
Citrobacter 89, 91
Cladosporium 124, 227
  C. resinae 231
Clams 203
Classification of microorganisms 13–15
Clays
  adsorption of NH_4^+ ions 235
  effects on survival of microorganisms
    125
  types 117
Clone 49
Clonothrix 70
Closed system 19

Clostridia 228
  fermentations 37, 223
  N_2-fixation 80, 100
  oxygen sensitivity 100
  soil 123
Clostridium
  C. aceticum 34
  C. acetobutylicum 23, 100
  C. botulinum 100, 208, Fig. 5.2
  C. butylicum 100, 184
  C. cellobioparum 222
  C. histolyticum 208
  C. lochheadii 201
  C. pasteurianum 240
  C. perfringens 23, 100, 208
  C. septicum 100
  C. sporogenes 23
  C. tetani 23, 115, 208
  enrichment 54
  nitrate respiration 32
Cnidospora 110
Coagulase 96, 208
Coal, origin 230
Coctosoma scutellatum 204
Coelenterates 203
Coenzyme A 40
Coenzyme M 10
Coenzyme Q Fig. 2.7
Coliform bacteria, serotypes 89
Collagenase 208
Colonization, by microorganisms 124, 128,
    145, 157, 175, 176, 207
  barriers 176
  lava fields 176
  soil particles Fig. 4.2
Co-metabolism 231, 253
Commensalism 186
Communities 115, 172
Compatible solutes 139
Competition 178, 187
Conidia 102, 107
Conidiospores 124
Coniferyl alcohol, structure 224, Fig. 8.6
Consumers, in carbon cycle Fig. 8.1
Continuous culture 20, 53
Copepods 135
Coral reefs 63
Corrosion of metals 157
  aerobic 245
  anaerobic 246
Corynebacterium 123, 152, 197, 204, 206,
    227, 231, 254
  C. autotrophicum 80
  C. diphtheriae 101, 208
  C. fascians 101
  C. insidiosum 101
  C. sepedonicum 101

Coryneform bacteria 82, 101, 102
    abundance in soil 123
    habitats 101, 199
Coumaryl alcohol 224
    structure Fig. 8.6
Coxiella burnetii 125, 206
Crenothrix 70
    C. polyspora 157
Cristispira 75
    C. pectinis 11
    symbiosis with Mollusca 76
Crustaceans 131
Cryptococcus vishniacii 141
Cultivar 15
Cultivation of microorganisms 54–6
Culture methods 50
Curtobacterium 101
Cyanellae 186
Cyanide 45
Cyanidium caldarius 143
Cyanobacteria 4, 10, 11, 15, 27, 61–4, 124,
    185, 240, Fig. 3.1
    blooms 63, 134, 241
    epiphytic association 63
    features 61
    gas vacuoles 61
    growth rate 177
    habitats 11, 63, 143
    heterocysts 61, 80, 196
    lichens 63, 186
    N₂ fixation 61, 63, 240
    oxic photosynthesis 18, 61
    phycobionts 11
    primary production 63
    taxonomy 61
Cyanophora 186
Cycling of biolements 132, 215–52
    carbon 217–32
    nitrogen 232–41
    oxygen 215
    phosphorus 247, 248
    sulphur 241–7
Cylindrospermum 63
Cystobacter fuscus 70
Cysts 11, 81, 153, 154
    properties 153
Cytochromes 14, 31, 237, Fig. 2.7
Cytophaga 68, 141, 157, 221, 227
    C. columnaris 70
Cytoplasmic inclusions 11, 14
Cytoplasmic membrane 29

DDT 257
    chemical structure Fig. 8.11
Deamination 187
    types 234
Death phase 19

Decomposition
    plant biomass 122, 175
    role in ecosystem Fig. 4.3
Deep sea microorganisms 141, 145
Degradation
    alkanes 22
    aromatic compounds 22
    cellulose 120
    chitin 120
    compounds resistant to 219
    fossil fuels 229–32
    lignin 224
    man-made compounds 242–61
    organic matter 220–9
    pesticides 254–8
    recalcitrant chemicals 120, 260, 261
    synthetic polymers 259, 260
Denitrification 14, 23, 32, 83, 105, 135,
    192, 233, 236–9, Figs. 2.9, 8.8
    bacteria 82, 83, 238
    gaseous products 32, 192, 233
    nitrogen cycle Fig. 8.8
Dental caries 97, 199
Dental plaques 93, 95, 156
Dermocarpa 63, Fig. 3.1
Derxia 81
    D. gummosa 81
Desiccation, resistance to 70, 101, 153,
    162, 186
Desulfobacter 33, 83, 244
Desulfococcus 33, 83, 244
Desulfomonas 83, 244
Desulfonema 33, 83, 244
Desulfosarcina 33, 83, 244
Desulfotomaculum 33, 83, 99, 153, 244
    D. acetoxidans 33, 83
    D. ruminis 201
Desulfovibrio 33, 69, 83, 185, 240, 244
    D. desulfuricans var. aestuarii 83
    D. salexigens 83
Desulfurococcus 104, 106
Desulfuromonas acetoxidans 33, 84, 185,
    244
Detergents 219, 252, 260, Fig. 8.15
Detritus 215
    food chain 122
    particles 157
    terrestrial 220
Development cycle
    Bdellovibrio 78, 189, Fig. 7.1
    Caulobacter 72, Fig. 3.3
    fungi 12
    myxobacteria 69
Dextran, from saccharose 97
Diaminopimelic acid 274, Fig. 2.2
Diatomite 251
Diatoms 7, 107, 108, 131, 143, 220, 251

Diauxic growth 46
2,4-D, Dichlorophenoxyacetic acid 254
  chemical structure Fig. 8.10
Dideoxyhexoses 90
Dieldrin 257
  chemical structure Fig. 8.11
Diffusion 165
Dihydrolipoic dehydrogenase Fig. 2.14
Dihydrolipoic transacetylase Fig. 2.14
Dihydroxyacetone phosphate 37, Figs.
  2.11, 2.12
Dilution rate 53
Dimethylether 82
Dinitrogen fixation, *see* Nitrogen fixation
Dinoflagellates 108, 203, 220
Dinophyceae 108
Dioxin 257
  chemical structure Fig. 8.13
1,1-Diphenylethylene 80, 95
Dipicolinic acid 102, 153, 250
Diplomonas 23
Disease
  carriers 95, 96
  foodborn 89
  nosocomial 89, 90, 91, 209
  transmission 88, 90, 91, 174
  zoonotic 87
  see Bacterial diseases
Dispersal of microorganisms 114, 174, 175
Dissimilatory nitrate reductase 237
Dissimilatory nitrate reduction
  see Denitrification and Nitrate
    ammonification
Dissimilatory sulphate reduction 23, 32,
  83, 185, 243, Fig. 2.10
  competition with methanogens 244
  sulphur cycle Fig. 8.9
Dissimilatory sulphur reduction 83, 244,
  Fig. 2.8
  sulphur cycle Fig. 8.9
Distribution, microorganisms 176
  aquatic environment 132–6
  geographical 175
  terrestrial environment 123–5
  ubiquitous 5
Division rate 20
DNA 6, 15
  base composition 77
  section of a molecule Fig. 2.1
Dominance 187
Doubling time, *see* Generation time
Drinking water 174
  nitrate concentration 239
Dunaliella 138
  D. salina 105
  D. viridis 139

Earthworms 122
Ebert 90
Ecological amplitude 176
Ecological niche 51, 52, 84, 86, 116, 172,
  176, 204, 246
Ecosystems 124, 126, 130, 172
  aquatic 129–37
  extreme 137–45
  terrestrial 116–29
Ectomycorrhiza 193, Fig. 7.2
Ectoparasites 205
Ectosymbiosis 182, 200
Ectothiorhodospira 64, 67, 143, 244
  E. halochloris 67
  E. halophila 67
  E. mobilis Fig. 3.2
Edwardsiella 91
Effectors, of enzymes 49
Electron acceptors 22, 23, 32, Fig. 2.8
Electron donors 4, 11, 31
Electron microscopy 51, 71
Electron transport
  chain 29, Fig. 2.7
  cyclic 27
  phosphorylation 23, 34, 40, 243
  reversed 27, 236
Embden–Meyerhof–Parnas (EMP)
  pathway, *see* Fructose-1,6-
  bisphosphate pathway
Endogone 194
Endomycorrhiza 193, Fig. 7.2
Endoparasites 205
Endospores 11
  germination 153
  resistance 99, 153
Endospore-forming bacteria 11, 99–101
Endosymbionts 203
  transmittance 204
Endosymbiosis 182, 185
Endotoxins 87, 90, 95, 208
End-product inhibition 49, Fig. 2.18
End-product repression 46
Energy 6, 34, 36
  conservation 31
  consuming processes 42–4
  growth yield coefficient 22
  yielding processes 24–42
Energy charge (EC) 26
Energy flow Fig. 4.3
  aquatic ecosystems 131, 132
  terrestrial ecosystems 120–3
Energy parasites 103, 207
Energy sources 24, 122
Enrichment culture 51, 52, 53, 92, 178, 219
Entamoeba 23
  E. histolytica 110

Enteric bacteria, nitrate respiration 32
Enterobacter 80, 89, 237, 240
  E. aerogenes 89
  E. agglomerans 90
  E. cloacae 90
Enterobacteria 88–92, 158
  differentiation 89
  metabolism 88
Enterotoxin 89, 92, 96
Entner–Doudoroff pathway, *see*
    2-Keto-3-deoxy-6-phosphogluconate
Environments 115
  aquatic 129–37
  extreme 137–45
  hypersaline 63
  terrestrial 116–29
  unsuitable for life 138
Enzymes 14, 17, 44, 46, 47, 99
Epifluorescence 271
Epilimnion 134, Fig. 4.4
Epilithic microorganisms 132, 157
Epiphytes 69, 73, 157, 167
Epiphyton 132
Epizoon 132
Erosion 117
Erwinia 197
  E. amylovora 92, 115, 175
  E. carotovora 92, 223
  E. herbicola 92, 191
Erysipelothrix, *E. rhusiopathiae* 98
Erythritol 87, 207
Erythrose-phosphate 39
Escherichia coli
  DNA molecule 6
  growth rate 177
  growth yield 236
  indicator of fecal contamination 89, 200
  minimum water potential Fig. 5.2
  opportunistic pathogen 89
  taxonomy 15
Estuary 67, 114, 229
Ethanol
  formation in fermentation 40, 92, Fig.
    2.13
  sulphate reduction 83
Eubacteria 4, 11, 12, 15
Eubacterium 101, 200
  E. cellulosolvens 201
Euglena gracilis 108
Euglenophyceae 108
Eukaryotic microorganisms 4, 7, 12, 13,
  15, 106–10
Euphotic zone 63, 129, 131, 220
Eutrophic waters, bacterial concentration
  135
Evolution, prokaryotes 4,

Exospores 153
Exotoxin 208
Extreme environments 5, 114, 115
  hydrostatic pressure 145
  lack of nutrients 144, 145
  pH 142–4
  salinity 67
  temperature 140–2
  water potential 160
Extremophiles 137

FAD/FADH, *see* Flavin adenine
    dinucleotide
FMN, *see* Flavin mononucleotide
Fatty acids 176, 199, 227
  growth factor 104
  rumen Fig. 7.4
  sulphate reduction 83
Faeces 94, 199, 200
Feedback inhibition, *see* End-product
    inhibition
Fermentations 34–7, Fig. 2.13
  products 14, 36, 40
Ferredoxin 37, 45, Fig. 2.17
Filaments 9, 12, 61
Filtration 51
Fimbriae 119, 156, 157, 207
Fischerella 63, Fig. 3.1
Fixation
  carbon dioxide 43
  dinitrogen 44–6
Flagella 9, 12, 154
Flagellates 185, 202
Flavin adenine dinucleotide 31, 40
Flavin mononucleotide 31, 203, Fig. 2.7
Flavobacterium 88, 93, 123, 132, 136, 141,
  143, 191, 227, 254, 258
Flavodoxin 45
Flavoproteins 24, 29
Flexibacter 70, 88
Flexibacteria 64, 68
Flexibility, microbial 152, 153, 180
Fluorescence microscopy 173
Fluorescent antibody technique 271
Focal infection 207
Food chain 122, 229, Fig. 4.3
Food poisoning 90, 96
Food web 122
Foraminiferae 109, 203
  cell wall 153
Formaldehyde 82
Forma specialis 15
Formate, formic acid 104
  fermentation product 36, 40, 88, Fig.
    2.13
  -hydrogen-lyase 36

Fossil fuels 217
  degradation 229–32
  preservation 230
Francisella tularensis 88
Frank 240
Frankia 102, 196, 240
Freshwater ecosystems 114
Freeze-drying 56
Fructans 223
Fructosanes, in rumen 200
Fructose-6-phosphate 43, Figs. 2.12, 2.19
Fructose-1,6-bisphosphate pathway 36,
    37, 92, Figs. 2.12, 2.19
Fruiting bodies
  fungi 12, 106
  myxobacteria 69
Fumarate
  formation 234
  respiration 34, Fig. 2.8
  TCC Fig. 2.15
Fumarase Fig. 2.15
Fungi 12, 106, 107, 143, 189, 224
  aquatic 133
  biomass in soil 122
  cell wall 153
  classification 12
  domesticated 202
  endosymbiotic 182
  growth rate 177
  nematode-trapping 205
  predatory 206
  water potential 162
  xerophytic Fig. 5.1
Fungi imperfecti 106, 124, 133, 175, 186,
    193, 221
Fungicides 257, Fig. 8.12
Fusarium 221, 227, 249, 252
  F. heterosporum 163
  F. roseum 162
Fusobacterium 23, 94, 199, 200
  F. necroforum 94
  F. nucleatum 94
  F. polymorphum 163

G + C mol% 15, 77, 96, 99
Gaffky 90
Galactose Fig. 8.3
Galacturonic acid Fig. 8.5
Gall formation (*A. tumefaciens*) 81
Gallionella 71, 249, 250
Gametes 12
Gas vacuoles
  bacteria 79
  cyanobacteria 155
Gasteromycetes 193
Gastrointestinal tract 87
  nitrate reduction 239

Gene transfer 16, 180
Generation time 20, 136
  E. coli 5, 19
  Nitrobacter 85
Genetic
  code 25
  material 6
Genospecies 13
Genotypic adaptation 180
Geosmin 102
Geotrichum candidum 140
Gliding 154
  bacteria 68–70
  cyanobacteria 11
  diatoms 108
  microalgae 12
Gliocladium 221
Gloeobacter 62
Gloeocapsa 62, 141
Glucanases 221
Gluconobacter 79
  G. oxydans 80
Glucose
  metabolism 37, 43, Fig. 2.12
  structure Fig. 8.3
β-Glucosidase 46, 221
Glucose-phosphate 44
Glucuronic acid, chemical structure Fig.
    8.3
Glutamate
  dehydrogenase 144, 234
  synthase 45
Glutamic acid Fig. 2.2
Glutamine: α-oxoglutarate
    aminotransferase (GOGAT) 234
Glutamine synthetase 45, 145, 234
Glyceollin 198
Glyceraldehyde phosphate 37, 39
Glycerol 145
  compatible solute 162
Glyceraldehyde phosphate 36, Figs. 2.6,
    2.11
  dehydrogenase Figs. 2.11, 2.12
Glycocalyx, role in infectious disease 156,
    207
Glycogen 61
Glycolysis 36
Gnotobiotic animals 198
Gonidia 69
Gonococcus 152
Gonyaulax
  G. polyedra 108
  G. tamarensis 108
Gradients
  as habitats 127–9
  stratified lake 137
Gramicidin 99

Green algae 108
  growth rate 177
  in lichens 186
Green sulphur bacteria 64, 135
  syntrophic association 33, 244
Ground water 173, 174
Growth
  aerobic 22
  anaerobic 22, 23
  batch culture 19, 20
  cardinal g. temperatures Fig. 5.3
  continuous culture 20
  exponential 177
  g. factor requirements 17, 55, 77, 104, 176
  at gradients 136, 137
  influence of environmental factors 158–68
  minimum water potential 160
  parameters 20–2
  phases 19
  physiology 19–24
  photoheterotrophic 61
  rates 20, 177, 178, 219
  water activity 158
  yield 22, 236
Guanine + cytosine ratio in DNA, *see* G + C mol%

Habitats, *see* Environments
Haem 31
Haemine ring 31
Haemophilus 206
  H. aphrophilus 93
  H. influenzae 18, 93
  H. segnis 93
Hafnia, *H. alvei* 90
Halobacteria 105, 133, 155
  bacteriorhodopsin 29, 105, 139
  extreme 10, 138, 166
  generation of ATP 29, 139
  habitats 105, 139
  photosynthetic 139
  purple membrane 29, 105
  water potential 160, Fig. 5.1
Halobacterium 12, 138, Fig. 5.2
  H. cutirubrum 139
  H. holobium 29
  H. salinarium 139
Halocarbons 253
Halococcus 12, 138, Fig. 5.2
  H. morrhuae 139
Halophiles, *see* Halobacteria
Hansenula 227
Haptophyceae 109
Haustoria 182, 186
H-donor, *see* Hydrogen donor

Heavy metals 238
Hellriegel 240
Hemicelluloses 122, 222, 223
  components Fig. 8.3
Herbicides 254, Fig. 8.10
Herbivores 122, 220, Fig. 4.3
Heterocysts 11, 61, 63, 145, 153
Heterotrophy 18, 19
Heterotrophic CO_2-fixation 17
Histisols 118
Holdfast 71, 120, 145
Holomictic lake 134
Homotaxis 155
Horizons, in soil 117, 188, Fig. 4.1
Hormogonia 61
Humic substances 118, 128, 219, 226
Humicola 221
  H. languinosa 140
Hyaluronidase 208
Hybridization 15
Hydra 203
Hydrocarbons
  degradation (breakdown) 82, 103, 253
  oxidizing bacteria 82
  production 227, 231
  surface films 136
  utilization 82
Hydrochoric dispersal 174
Hydrogen
  electrode 167
  electron donor 18, 27, 64, 82, 104
  formation in fermentation 37, 82
  formation in N_2-fixation 45
  methanogens 104
  oxidation 84
  oxidizing bacteria 82
  peroxide 37
  production 36, 37, 82
  rumen 105
  sulphate reduction 83, 105
  utilizing bacteria 104
Hydrogen ion concentration (pH), *see* pH
Hydrogenase 37, 82
Hydrogen sulphide
  chemolithotrophic oxidation 84, 85, Fig. 8.9
  electron donor 27, 64, 130, 185, 244
  heterotrophic oxidation 86
  oxidizing bacteria 185, 244
  phototrophic oxidation Fig. 8.9
  production 83, 89, 130, 135, 228
  products of oxidation 86
  sources 243
  toxic effects 244
Hydrostatic pressure 131, 135, 138, 145
Hydrostatic pressure potential 159
Hydroxylamine 235

p-Hydroxyphenylpropane Fig. 8.6
Hypersensitivity reaction 198
Hyphae 12, 106
Hyphomicrobium 71, 136, 232, 237, 249
    development cycle Fig. 3.3
Hyphomonas 73
Hyphomycetes 206
Hypolimnion 67, 134, 155, Fig. 4.4
Hypomyces hippomoeae 202

IPC (Isopropyl carbanilate) 254
    chemical structure Fig. 8.10
Ichthyophthirius multiphiliis 110
Identification 13, 56
Illite 117
Immunoglobulin 198, 209
Immunity 209
Immunofluorescence 271
Indigenous microflora, *see* Autochthonous
    microflora
Indole 14
Inositol phosphate 247
Insecticides 257, Fig. 8.11
Insects
    degradation of cellulose 202
    endosymbionts of 203, 204
    symbiosis 116, 202
Interactions
    classification 182–4
    microbe–microbe 184–90
    microorganisms–animals 198–209
    microorganisms–plants 191–8
Intercalary cells 11, 62
Interfaces 127, 136, 137
Interspecies hydrogen transfer 105, 184,
    202, 230
Intestinal
    flora 102, 176, 200
    tract 68, 76, 89, 98, 110, 182, 198
Intertidal zones 63, 67
Intracytoplasmic membranes 14
Iron
    springs 69
    sulphur bacteria 73, 141
    sulphur proteins 31, 249, Fig. 2.7
    transformations 249, 250
Isocitrate dehydrogenase Fig. 2.15
Isolation, microorganisms 49–54
    direct 51, 52
    following enrichment 52–4, 272
    selective 251
Isoleucine 49, Fig. 2.18
Isoprenoids 230

Kaolinite 117
KDPG-pathway, *see* 2-Keto-3-deoxy-6-
    phospho-gluconate pathway

Keratin decomposition 70, 227
Keratinomyces 227
2-Keto-3-deoxy-6-phospho-gluconate
    pathway 37, 49, 92, Fig. 2.12
Klebsiella 80, 89, 240
    K. aerogenes 90
    K. pneumoniae 90
Koch, Robert 99
Krebs cycle, *see* Tricarboxylic acid cycle
Kurthia 101
Kusnezovia 74

L-forms 87
Labyrinthulales 107
Lachnospira 94
    L. multiparus 201
Lactate
    fermentation product 30, 40, 96, Fig.
        2.13
    sulphate reduction 83
    utilization 95
Lactic acid bacteria
    growth factor requirements 17
    metabolism 98
Lactobacillus 98, 152, 199
    L. acidophilus 98
    L. brevis 98
    L. bulgaricus 98
    L. casei 98
    L. fermentum 98
    L. lactis 98
    L. plantarum 98
    L. viridescens Fig. 5.2
Lactose 89
Lag phase 19
Lake 114, 172
    amictic 134
    eutrophic 63, 134
    holomictic 134
    meromictic 134
    oligotrophic 134, 228
    saline 63
    stratification 67, 133, 136, 163, Fig. 4.4
Lamprocystis 67
Lampropedia 152
    L. hyalina 96
Leaching 141, 143
Leaf flora 191
Lectins 157, 196
Leghaemoglobin 81, 195
Legionella pneumophila 88, 206
Legumes (leguminous plants), amount of
    N_2-fixation 240
Leptospira 76, 206
    L. icterohaemorrhagiae 77
Leptospires 75, 76
    motility 77

Leptospirillum ferrooxidans 249
Leptothrix 70, 249
  L. ochracea 71, 157
Leptotricha, *L. buccalis* 94
Leucocidins 207
Leuconostoc, *L. mesenteroides* 97
Leucosporidium, *L. antarcticum* 142
Leucothrix 68, 69
  L. mucor 152, 157
Lichens 182
  epiphytic associations 11
  mycosymbionts 186
  phycosymbionts 63, 186
Lieskeela 70
Light
  distribution of phototrophs 130
  enrichment of phototrophs 54
  photooxidation 168
Lignin
  building blocks 224, 225, Fig. 8.6
  component of biomass 122, 224
  biodegradation 120, 219, 224
  structure 224
Lignocellulose 226
Lindan 257
  chemical structure Fig. 8.11
Lipoate Fig. 2.14
Lipids 7, 10
Lipopolysaccharides 7, 90, 208
Lipoproteins 7
Listeria 206
  L. monocytogenes 98
Lithosphere 116, 117
Lithotrophic bacteria, *see*
  Chemolithotrophic bacteria
Litter, *see* Detritus
Log phase 19
Luciferin/Luciferase 203
Luciferous (luminous, luminescent)
  bacteria 92, 115, 136, 203
Luminescence 12, 108, 136, 203
Lyngbya 63
Lyophilization 56
Lysine Fig. 2.2
Lysine-decarboxylase 14
Lysis of bacteria
  by Bdellovibrio 190
  by myxobacteria 70
Lysobacter 70
Lysozyme 176

MCPA (4-chloro-2-methyl-phenoxyacetic
  acid) 254
  chemical structure Fig. 8.10
Macroelements 16
Macrohabitats 126, 127
Macromonas 86

Magnetic crystals 115
Magnetotaxis 155
Malaria 110, 174
Malate, dehydrogenase 42, Fig. 2.15
Malathion 257
  chemical structure Fig. 8.11
Maneb 257
  chemical structure Fig. 8.12
Manganese
  buoyancy 155
  deep-sea nodules 250
  oxidation 74
  transformations 249, 250
Mannose, chemical structure Fig. 8.3
Matric potential (ψ_m) 119, 159, 162
Media (assay, complex, differential,
  liquid, maintenance, selective, solid,
  synthetic) 54–6
Megasphaera 23, 97
Meiosis 6
Meromictic lake 134
Mesophilic microorganisms 140, 163, Fig.
  5.3
Metabiosis 184
Metabolic associations 184–7
Metabolism 24–49
  chemotrophs 29–37
  regulation of 46–9
  phototrophs 27–9
Metal leaching 141, 143
Metal transformations 251
Metalimnion 134
Metallogenium 71, 155, 249
Metchnikoff 73
Methane
  formation 104, 187, 227
  monooxygenase 82, 231
  oxidation 17, 82, 187, 227, 229
  oxidizing bacteria 82, 227, 231
  rumen 202
Methanobacterium 12, 23, 104, 141
  M. bryantii 105
  M. omelianskii 105, 184
  M. ruminantium 202
Methanobrevibacter 104
Methanococcus 12, 23, 104
  M. vanniellii 17
Methanogenesis
  in freshwater sediments 230
  in marine habitats 130
  in nature 105
  inhibition by sulphate reduction 105
Methanogenic bacteria
  characteristics 104
  hydrogen consumption 84
  N_2 fixation 44
  O_2 intolerance 24
  occurrence 105, 115, 228

Methanogenium 104
Methanogens, *see* Methanogenic bacteria
Methanol
    oxidation 73, 82
    product in fermentation 36
    substrate for methanogenesis 104
Methanolotrophs 82
Methanomicrobium 12, 104
Methanomonas 227, 231
Methanosarcina 12, 23, 104
Methanospirillum 23, 104
Methanotrophs, *see* Methane oxidizing
    bacteria
Methemoglobinaemia 239
Methionine 10
Methods for the study of growth rates and
    activities 276–8
    microbial biomass 273, 274
    types, numbers, distribution 271, 272
Methyl-red reaction 89
Methylamine 82, 104
Methylation, biological 252
Methylobacterium 232
Methylococcus 141, 227, 231
Methylomonas 231
Methylosinus 227, 231
    M. trichosporium 80, 153
Methylotrophic bacteria 44, 82, 135, 216,
    241
Methylotrophs, *see* Methylotrophic
    bacteria
Microaerophilic bacteria 22
Microalgae *see* Algae
Microbe–animal interactions 198–209
Microbe–microbe interactions 184–90
Microbe–plant interactions 191–8
Microcalorimetry 277
Micrococci 199
Micrococcus 95, 136, 206, 231, 237
    M. cryophilus 141
    M. luteus 95
    M. lysodeicticus Fig. 5.2
    M. varians 95
Microcolonies 50, 123, 126, 182
Microcyclus 78, 142
Microecosystem, *see* Microhabitat
Microelements 16
Microenvironment, *see* Microhabitat
Microhabitat 126, 127, 182, 238
Micromanipulator 50
Microorganisms
    in extreme environments 137–45
    at extreme hydrostatic pressure 145
    at extreme pH values 142–4
    at extreme temperatures 140–2
    at low nutrient concentration 144, 145
    at low water potential 138, 139

Microscilla 70
Microzones 125
Mineralization 79, 215, 217
Minimata disease 252
Mitochondria 6
    generation of energy 29
    symbiont theory 9, 183
Mitosis 6
Mixed culture 185
Molar yield coefficient (Y_m) 22
Molluscs 76, 203
Molybdenum 81
Molybdoferredoxin Fig. 2.17
Montmorillonite 117, 128
Monuron 254
    chemical structure Fig. 8.10
Moraxella 95, 237
Morganella 91
Morphovar 15
Most probable number (MPN) procedure
    271
Motility 11, 12, 68–70, 108, 154, 155, 174
Mucor 252
    M. mucedo 107
    M. pusillus 140
    M. ramanianus 184
Mucosa 176
Mud 67, 109, 229
Murein 6, 11, 153, Fig. 2.2
Mutation 50, 180
Mutants 177, 179, 209
Mycelium 12, 106
Mycetomes 204
Mycobiont 186
Mycobacteria 82, 199
Mycobacterium 206, 227, 231, 237
    M. bovis 102
    M. leprae 51, 102, 175
    M. tuberculosis 102, 205
Mycolic acids 102
Mycoplana 254
Mycoplasma 153, 197, 206
    M. mycoides 104
Mycoplasmas 18, 104
Mycorrhizae 192–4, Fig. 7.2
    effect on plant growth 194
    phosphorus uptake 194, 248
    in soil 124
    vesicular–arbuscular 194
Myxamoebae 155
Myxobacteria 152, 153, 154
    fruiting 69
    gliding 68
    habitats 70
Myxococcus fulvus 70
Myxomycetes 107
Myxomycota 107

Myxospores 69, 153

N₂-fixation, *see* Nitrogen fixation
N₂O, *see* Nitrous oxide
NAD/NADH, *see* Nicotinamide adenine dinucleotide
NADP/NADPH, *see* Nicotinamide adenine dinucleotide phosphate
NADH: Ferredoxin oxidoreductase 37
N-Acetylglucosamine 6, 176, Fig. 2.2
N-Acetylmuramic acid 6, Fig. 2.2
Nanoplankton 109
Natural selection 177–80
Neisseria 95, 206
  N. gonorrhoeae 95, 156, 163
  N. meningitidis 95
  CO₂ requirement 167
Nematoctonus 205
Nematodes 205
Neurotoxin 100, 208
Neuston 132, 136
Neutralism 198
Neutrophilic organisms 165
Nevskia 74
Niche, *see* Ecological niche
Nicotinamide adenine dinucleotide 26, 27, 31, 36, 40, 246, Fig. 2.5
Nicotinamide adenine dinucleotide phosphate Fig. 2.5
Nicotine 101
Nif-genes 45, 241
Nitrate
  ammonification 238, Figs. 2.9, 8.8
  assimilatory reduction 18, 216, 233, 237
  dissimilatory reduction *see* Denitrification
  leaching into ground water 235
  nitrogen cycle Fig. 8.8
  nitrogen source 232
  production by nitrification 84
  reductase 32
  terminal e⁻ acceptor 77, 233
Nitrate respiration, *see* Denitrification
Nitrification 187, 232
  autotrophic 235, 236
  heterotrophic 236
  nitrogen cycle 216, Fig. 8.8
Nitrifying bacteria (nitrifiers) 19, 85, 124, 235, 248
  concentration in soil 236
  enrichment 178
  generation time 235
  reversed electron transport 236
Nitrite
  intoxication 239
  oxidation 84
  reductase 32, 238

Nitrobacter 176
  N. winogradskyi 85, 235
Nitrococcus 85, 235
Nitrogen
  in cellular components 18
  global cycle 45, 232, Fig. 8.8
  liquid n for preservation 56
  molecular, in N cycle Fig. 8.8
Nitrogen cycle 45, 79, Fig. 8.8
  ammonification 216, 234
  denitrification 236–9
  general aspects 232–4
  nitrification 235, 236
  nitrogen fixation 239–41
Nitrogen fixing bacteria 44, 80, 81, 90, 124, Fig. 2.17
  free living 44, 46, 80
  symbionts 44, 46, 80, 103, 194, 241
Nitrogen fixation 11, 14, 18, 239–41
  acetylene reduction test 45
  global N cycle 234, 240, Fig. 8.8
  lichens 81
  organisms capable of 44, 46, 63, 77, 80
  plasmid involvement 45
  process 44, Fig. 2.17
  rhizobia 46, 81, 194–6
  rhizosphere associations 77
  symbiotic associations 200
Nitrogenase 44, Fig. 2.17
  measurement of activity 277
  oxygen sensitivity 45, 80, 196
Nitrosamines 239
Nitrosococcus 85, 235
Nitrosolobus 85, 235
Nitrosomonas 176
  N. europaea 85, 235
  growth yield 236
Nitrosospira 85, 235
Nitrospina 85, 235
Nitrous oxide (N₂O) 45, 192, 239, Fig. 2.9
  reductase 237
Nocardia 82, 101, 102, 123, 204, 227, 258, 260
Noctiluca 203
Nomenspecies 13
Non-sulphur purple bacteria 27, 67
Nosocomial infections 89, 90, 91, 209
Nostoc 63
Nucleic acids 15, 16, 17
Nucleoid 6
Nucleoside-monophosphates 44
Nucleotide sequence 15
Nucleus 6
Nutrition 16–19
  mixotrophic 84
Nutritional
  requirements 14, 15, 16–18, 51, 54
  types 14, 18, 19

Obligately symbiotic bacteria 103, 104
Oceanospirillum 77
Oceans 63, 129
  nitrogen concentration 228
  temperature 129
Oil, crude
  composition 230
  degradation 231, 260
  origin 230
  spillage 231
Oligonucleotide base sequence,
    16S rRNA 10
Oligotrophic waters, bacterial
    concentration 135
Oligotrophy 144, 145
Oomycetes 107, 133, 206
Oral cavity 69, 76, 94, 95, 97, 101, 102
Organic acids and weathering 117
Organic matter
  decomposition 187, 218–29
  in sea water 131
Ornithine, in peptidoglycan 101
Oscillatoria 63, Fig. 3.1
  O. rubescens 63
Osmoregulation 139
Osmotic conditions, influencing growth
    165, 166
Osmotic fragility 166
Osmotic shock 152
Osmotolerance 139, 166
Oxalacetate 40, 42, 167, Fig. 2.15
Oxalic acid 117
Oxalosuccinate Fig. 2.15
Oxic (oxygenic) photosynthesis 6, 18, 61
Oxidation–reduction potential 216, 228
  anaerobic bacteria 56
  influence on growth 167
Oxidation–reduction reactions 11
Oxidative phosphorylation, *see* Electron
    transport phosphorylation
Oxisols 118
Oxocarotenoids 61
2-Oxoglutarate 42, 145, 234
  dehydrogenase Fig. 2.15
Oxygen
  dependence on 6
  diffusion coefficient in water 127
  as electron acceptor 22
  gradients of 128
  methane oxidation 229
  molecular 22
  radicals 37
  reduced partial pressure 54
  respiration 23
  sensitivity of nitrogenase 167
  singlet state 168
  solubility in water 23, 130, 166, 228
  synthesis of fatty acids 22
  tolerance 23, 55
  toxicity 24, 37, 55, 100
Oxygen–hydrogen reaction 29
Ozone layer of atmosphere 237, 238

PAPS, *see* 3′-Phosphoadenosine-5′-
    phosphosulphate
PEP *see* Phospho-enol pyruvate
pH values
  extreme 142–4
  gradients 144
  range of 165
PHB *see* Poly-β-hydroxybutyric acid
Palaeomicrobiology 220
Paracoccus denitrificans 183
Paramecium 110, 203
Paraquat 254
  chemical structure Fig. 8.10
Parasites
  facultative, obligate 183
  of men and animals 110, 205–9
  necrotrophic 205
  obligate intracellular 103, 206
  of plants 197, 198
Parasitism 183
Parasporal body 100
Parathion-ethyl 257
  chemical structure Fig. 8.11
Paspalum notatum 81
Pasteurella 88, 93, 206
  P. enterocolitica 93
  P. haemolytica 93
  P. multocida 93
  P. novocid 93
  P. pestis 93, 207
  P. pseudotuberculosis 93
  P. tularensis 93
Pasteur effect 49
Pasteuria 73
Pathogens
  in compromised patients 209
  dispersal through the air 174
  of fishes 68, 92
  of men and animals 75–9, 87–104, 204–9
  obligate 51, 206
  opportunistic 79, 89, 90, 92, 97, 197, 199
  of plants 80, 101, 103, 197, 198
  reservoirs 77
  soil-born 80
  transmission 174, 175
Pathovar 15
Pathways 37–42
Peats 117, 229
Pectin
  degradation 68, 70, 95, 202, 223
  structure Fig. 8.5

Pectolytic enzymes 224
Pediculus humanus, transmission of
  Borrelia 77
Pediococcus 97
Pedomicrobium 249
Pelodictyon 64, 67, 152
  P. clathratiforme Fig. 3.2
Pelonema 69
Pelonemataceae 69
Pelosigma 79
Penicillium 124, 221, 252
  P. brevicaule 252
  P. notatum 107
Pentachloronitrobenzene 52
Pentose phosphate pathway 37, 39, Fig.
  2.12
Peptidoglycan, *see* Murein
Peptococcus 23, 97
Peptostreptococcus 97, 200
  P. elsdenii 201
Peridinium 203
Periphyton 132
Periplasmic space 78
Permeases 165
Peronospora tabacina 174
Peronosporales 197
Peroxidases 24
Persistence, of xenobiotics 254
Pesticides 219, 252
  microbial degradation 254–8
Phagocytosis 99, 207, 209
Phagovar 15
Phenon 14
Phenotypic adaptation 180
Phenylcarbamates 254
Phormidium 63
Phosphatases 128
Phosphate 248
3'-Phosphoadenosine-5'-phosphosulphate
  243
Phospho-enol pyruvate 36, 42, 167, Figs.
  2.12, 2.19
Phosphofructokinase, regulation 49, Fig.
  2.19
6-Phosphogluconate Fig. 2.12
3-Phosphoglycerate 36, 43, Figs. 2.6, 2.11
Phospholipase 208
5-Phosphoribosyl-1-pyrophosphate 44,
  Fig. 2.16
Phosphoribulokinase 43, 49
Phosphorus 216, 247, 248
Photoassimilation 11, 13, 64
Photoautotrophs 27
Photobacterium 92, 203
Photolithotrophs 19
Photooxidation 168
Photosensitizers 168

Photosynthesis
  algae 12
  anoxic (anoxygenic) 6, 18, 27, 64, 135
  bacteria 27, 168
  cyanobacteria 10
  oxic (oxygenic) 6, 18, 61
Phototaxis 154
Phototrophic bacteria 16, 18, 27, 64–8,
  240, Fig. 3.2
  CO_2 fixation 17, 43
  electron donors 244
  enrichment Fig. 6.1
  growth rates 177
  habitats 67
  N_2 fixation 80, 240
  primary production 67, 135
  types 27, 64
Phototrophy
  electron donors 64, 244
  photoheterotrophic growth 11
  photophosphorylation 27
Phragmidiothrix 70
Phycobiliproteins 61
Phycobiont 11, 63, 108
Phycobilins 167
Phycomycetes 106, 175
Phyllosphere 182, 191
Phytoalexins 198
Phytoflagellates 109
Phytopathogenic bacteria, *see* Plant
  pathogens
Phytopathogenic fungi 175
Phytophthora
  P. drechsleri 163
  P. infestans 107, 175
  P. megasperma 198
Phytoplankton 108, 131, 132
Phytotoxins 192
Phytridium 189
Pichia 231
Pigments 14
Pili 106, 120, 156
Pilobolus 174
Pinocytosis 109
Pioneer microorganisms 175, 241
Planctomyces 71, 142
Plankton *see* Phytoplankton
Planococcus, *P. citreus* 96
Plant diseases 80, 92, 101, 104, 107, 197,
  198
Plant litter 120
Plant pathogens 125, 191, 197, 198
Plasmids 6, 45, 81, 155, 197, 253
Plasmodiophora brassicae 107
Plasmodiophorales 107
Plasmodium 110, 174
Plasmopara viticola 107, 175

Platyhelminths 203
Plectonema 63
  P. nostocorum 138
Plesiomonas 92
Pleurocapsa 63
Polar regions 141
Pollution 67, 136, 243
Polyaromatics 120
Polycyclic aromatics 260
Polyethylene 254
Poly-β-hydroxybutyric acid 154
  as degradable polymer 260
Polymyxin 99
Polynucleotides 43, 44
Polyols 139, 186
Polypeptide 47
Polyphenols 219
Polyphosphates 154
Polysaccharides 43, 90
  dental plaques 97, 199
  involved in adhesion 80, 120
Polybutylene 259, Fig. 8.14
Polyethylene 259, Fig. 8.14
Polyformaldehyde 259, Fig. 8.14
Polymers
  degradation of synthetic 259
  synthetic 219, 252, Fig. 8.14
Polypropylene 259, Fig. 8.14
Polystyrenes 259, Fig. 8.14
Polyurethanes 259, Fig. 8.14
Polyvinyl chloride (PVC) 254, 259, Fig.
  8.14
Populations 172–80
  change of 53, 180, 187
  growth 20, 177
  mixed 53, 185
Pore diameter and water potential 19
Porphyrins 18, 230
Precursors 25, 43
Predation 93, 177, 183, 205
Predators 13, 109, 205
Preservation of microorganisms 55, 56
Primary production 120, 215, 220
  algae 13, 108
  in C cycle Fig. 8.1
  degradation 120
  in food chain Fig. 4.3
  global net p.p. 220
  green plants 37
  limiting factors 131
  measurement 277
  in oceans 129
  phototrophic and chemolithotrophic
    bacteria 67, 215
  rates 131
Pristanes 230
Proactinomycetes 103

Prochloron 67, 183
  P. didemni 67
Prodigiosin 168
Progenote 10, 15
Prokaryotes, *see* Prokaryotic
    microorganisms
Prokaryotic microorganisms 4, 10–12,
  61–106
  chemotrophic 68–106
  evolution 10
  morphology 5
  phototrophic 61–8
  physiological versatility 5
2-Propanol, product in fermentation 36
Propionate
  product in fermentation 40, Fig. 2.13
  substrate of sulphate-reducing bacteria
    83
Propionibacterium 199
  P. acnes 101
  P. freudenreichii 101
Prosthecae 12, 71
Prosthecate bacteria 71–4, 132, 142
Prosthecobacter 73
Proteins
  amino acid sequence 16
  in N cycle Fig. 8.8
  in S cycle Fig. 8.9
  synthesis 43
Proteases, adsorption to soil particles 128
Proteus
  P. mirabilis 91
  P. vulgaris 91
  survival in soil 125
Protochloroplast 183
Protomitochondrion 183
Proton motive force 31
Prototrophs 9
Protozoa 13, 110, 124, 135, 189
  biomass in soil 122
  in food chain Fig. 4.3
  growth rate 177
  habitats 109
  rumen 23
  symbiotic relationships 109, 185, 186,
    202
Providencia 91
  survival in soil 125
Pseudomonads 17, 80, 158, 191
  habitats 79, 123
  KDPG pathway 40, Fig. 2.12
  nitrate respiration 32, 83
  versatility 17, 79
Pseudomonas 79, 82, 132, 136, 141, 197,
  206, 227, 231, 232, 237, 249, 252, 254,
  260
  P. aeruginosa 79, 115, 125

P. carboxydovorans 82
P. caryophylli 80
P. cepacia 254
P. fluorescens 238, Fig. 5.2
P. gazotropha 82
P. gladioli 80
P. mallei 79
P. marginalis 80
P. pseudomallei 79
P. solanacearum 80, 125
P. syringae 80
P. tabaci 175
P. tolaasii 158
Pseudomurein 7
Psychrophilic microorganisms 132, 140, 142, 163, Fig. 5.3
Puccinia graminis 174, 197
Pure culture 49–51
Purines, as growth factor 17
Purple (sulphur) bacteria 53, 64, 135, Fig. 6.1
Purple (non-sulphur) bacteria 64, Fig. 6.1
Purple membrane 29, 105
Pyocyanin 168
Pyridine nucleotides (NAD, NADP), *see* Nicotinamide adenine dinucleotide; Nicotinamide adenine dinucleotide phosphate
Pyrimidines, as growth factor 17
Pyrococcus furiosus 141, Fig. 5.3
Pyrodictium occultum 141, Fig. 5.3
Pyrophosphates 248
Pyruvate
    dehydrogenase multienzyme complex 40, Fig. 2.14
    in fermentations 36, 40, Figs. 2.12, 2.13

Radiation 167, 168
Radiation energy 120
Radiolarians 108, 110, 203
Radiorespirometry 276
Raphidonema nivale 141
Recalcitrance, *see* Persistence
Red tides 108
Red water fever 110
Redox potential, *see* Oxidation–reduction potential
Refuse disposal 259
Regulation
    enzyme activity 46, 48
    enzyme synthesis 46
    feedback inhibition 49, Fig. 2.18
    of metabolism 46–9
    of threonine deaminase 49, Fig. 2.18
    of phosphofructokinase Fig. 2.19

Relative humidity 158
Repression
    catabolite r. 46
    end-product r. 46
Reservoirs of pathogens 87, 88, 91, 93, 94, 103
Resistance
    of endospores 153
    to pathogens 209
    to temperature 178
Respiration 6, 18
    aerobic 22, 29, 37, 216
    anaerobic 32, 37, 83, 84, Fig. 2.8
    chemoorganotrophs 29
    chemolithotrophs 31
    under water stress 162
Respiration rate, specific 5
Respiratory chain 25, 29, 167
    components 29, 31
Respiratory tract, diseases 87, 88, 91
Respirometry 276
Resting structures 153, 173
Rhizobia 46, 82, 115, 194
    attachment to root hairs 157
    host specificity 81
    legume symbiosis Fig. 7.3
    survival in soil 125
Rhizobium 32, 240
    R. japonicum 125
    R. leguminosarum 194
    R. lupini 194
Rhizoctonia 221
Rhizophydium 189
    R. planktonicum 106
Rhizoplane 81, 124
Rhizopus nigricans 107
Rhizosphere 117, 124, 182, 191, 192
    denitrifying bacteria 83
    microflora 192
    N_2-fixing bacteria 77, 241
Rhodocyclus purpureus 64
Rhodomicrobium 71
    R. vanniellii 64
Rhodophyceae 108
Rhodopseudomonas 15, 64, 71
    R. sphaeroides Fig. 3.2
    R. viridis 180
Rhodospirillaceae 64, 247
    selective enrichment 180
Rhodospirillum 64
    R. rubrum 179, 180, Fig. 3.2
Rhodotorula 133
    R. rubra 184
Ribose-5-phosphate 44
    activation Fig. 2.16
Ribosomal RNA, nucleotide sequencing 15, 16

Ribosomes
  in chloroplasts and mitochondria 9, 183
  structure 6
Ribulose bisphosphate-cycle, *see* Calvin
  cycle
Ribulose-1,5-bisphosphate 43, Fig. 2.6
Ribulosebisphosphate carboxylase 31, 43,
  Fig. 2.6
Ribulose-5-phosphate 39, Fig. 2.12
Ribulose monophosphate cycle, in C_1
  metabolism 82, 231
RuMP-pathway, *see* Ribulose
  monophosphate-cycle
Rice paddies 68
  N_2-fixation 197, 240
Rickettsia 51, 88, 174, 197, 206
  R. prowazekii 103, 206
  natural hosts 206
Rigidity of microorganisms 11, 152, 153
RNA hybridization with DNA 15
  nucleotide sequences 183
  ribosomal 15, 16
Rodents, reservoir of pathogens 77
Roots
  exudates 117
  hairs 194
  nodulation of legumes 194, 195, Fig. 7.3
Root nodules 240
  by Frankia 103, 196
  H_2 production 82
  in legumes 194-6
  in nonlegumes 196
Rumen
  as ecosystem 200, Fig. 7.4
  products of fermentation 202, 221
  protozoa 109
  symbiosis 182, Fig. 7.4
Rumen bacteria 95, 98, 101, 105, 157, 201,
  223
  fatty acids requirement 18
Ruminococcus 23, 97
  R. albus 201, 222
  R. flavefaciens 201, 222
Rusts 107, 197

S-value 14
S_{AB}-value 15
Saccharomyces
  cerevisiae 92, 107
  rouxii 139
Saccharose, laevan production 223
Salinity 138, 166
Salmonella 206
  S. enteritidis 90
  S. paratyphi 90
  S. typhi 90, 183
  S. typhimurium 90, 162, Fig. 5.2

minimum water potential Fig. 5.2
  survival in soil 125
  survival in water 175
Salt evaporation pond 63
Salt lakes 160
Salt marshes 67
Salt tolerance 178
Sampling procedures 271
Saprolegnia 107
Sarcina 152
  S. ureae 99
Sarcomastigophora 109
Sclerotina borealis 141
Sediments 137, 229
  dissimilatory sulphate reduction 83
  estuarine 130
  freshwater 105, 134
  marine 135
Selection 50, 177-9
Selective advantage 53, 178, 187, 188
Selective media 51
Selenomonas 23, 94
  S. ruminantium 201
Seliberia 71, 74
  S. carboxydohydrogena 82
Serine pathway 82, 231
Serotypes, in Salmonella 89
Serovar 15
Serratia marcescens 89, 91
Shape, microorganisms 5, 152
Sheathed bacteria 12, 61, 70, 71
  attachment 156
Shigella 206
  S. dysenteriae 91
  survival in soil 125
Siderocapsa 249
Silage 98
Silicon
  as limiting factor 131
  precipitation 251
  transformations 251, 252
  utilizing microorganisms 251
Silicones 259, Fig. 8.14
Simonsiella 68
  habitat 69
Sinapyl alcohol 224
  structure Fig. 8.6
Single cell protein (SCP) 241
Singlet state oxygen 168
Size
  eukaryotic cells 5
  microorganisms 4, 5, 11, 152
  prokaryotic cells 5, 14
Skin
  human flora 199
  infection 98
  as microbial habitat 96

Sleeping sickness 174, 175
Slime moulds 13, 107, 109, 155
Smuts 107, 197
Soda lakes 143
Soil
  aggregates 120
  biomass in 122
  composition and structure 116–18
  habitat of microorganisms 123, 126
  horizons Fig. 4.1
  numbers of microorganisms 173
  organic contents 117
Soil microflora
  autochthonous 101, 102
  microbial populations 173
Soil particles 123
  classification 127
  microbial colonization of Fig. 4.2
Soil profile 117, Fig. 4.1
Solubility, oxygen in water 130
Solute (osmotic) potential 159
Solutes 158
  compatible 180, 186
Sorbitol 46
Sorption of microorganisms 119
Species
  concept in bacteriology 13
  diversity 137
Sphaerocytophaga 70
Sphaerotheca morsuvae 175
Sphaerotilus 152, 250
  S. natans 70, 71, 135, 157
Spirillum 77, 82, 141, 185, 237
  S. minus 77
  S. serpens 190
  minimum water potential Fig. 5.2
Spirochaeta 75, 206
  S. halophila 76
  S. plicatilis 76
Spirochetes 75–7, 153, 185
  cell morphology Fig. 3.4
Spiromonas 79
Spiroplasma 104
Spirulina 63
  S. platensis 143
Spongilla 203
Spore-forming bacteria 99–101
  enrichment 54
Spores 153, 178
  algal 12
  bacterial 99
  dormancy 99
  fungal 12
  survival 125
Sporocytophaga 70, 221, 223
Sporolactobacillus 99
  S. inulinus 100

Sporosarcina 153
  S. ureae 100
Sporozoa 186
Springs
  acid hot s. 86, 106
  alkaline hot s. 67
  hot s. 63, 115, 141
Stalked bacteria 74
  phototrophs 64
Staphylococcus 152, 206, 207, 237
  S. albus 96, Fig. 5.2
  S. aureus 96, Fig. 5.2
  S. epidermidis 96
Starch 223
Static culture 19
Stationary phase 19
Stella 71
Stentor 110
Sterilization 50, 51, 99
Sterol requirement 104
Stibiobacter senarmontii 251
Stigmatella erecta 70
Storage materials 153, 154
Stratification 136, 137
Streptobacillus moniliformis 94
Streptococcus 152, 199, 206, 207
  S. bovis 201
  S. mutans 97, 156, 199
  S. pneumoniae 209
  S. pyogenes 97, 156, 207
  S. salivarius 156, 199, 207
Streptokinase 208
Streptomyces 123, 197, 227
  S. scabies 103
Streptomycetes 103
Streptomycin 103
Substrate affinity 53, 144, 178, 188
Substrate-level phosphorylation 23, 36,
  Fig. 2.11
Succession, microbial
  allogenic 176
  autogenic 176
Succinate 34, 42
  tricarboxylic acid cycle 40, Fig. 2.15
Succinivibrio 23, 94
Succinomonas 94
  S. amylolytica 201
Succinyl-CoA Fig. 2.15
Sucrose, polysaccharides 97
Sugar phosphate 43
Sulfobacillus thermosulfoxidans 249
Sulfolobus 12, 85
  S. acidocaldarius 86, 140, 143, 246, 249,
  Fig. 5.3
Sulphate
  in marine environments 130, 135, 243

Sulphate – *continued*
  reducing bacteria 83–5, 124, 135, 185
  as terminal electron acceptor 83
Sulphate reduction
  assimilatory 18, 243
  dissimilatory 23, 32, 83, 104, 130, 135,
    229, 230
  electron donors for 83
Sulphate respiration, *see* Dissimilatory
  sulphate reduction
Sulphide, biogenic deposits 245
Sulphite, chemolithotrophic oxidation 64
Sulphite reductase Fig. 2.10
Sulphur
  anaerobic, *see* respiration 33
  in biosphere 242
  in cellular components 18
  in growth factors 242
  isotope fractionation 83, 245
  natural deposits 83, 86, 245
  oxidation 84, 246
  reducing bacteria 84
  as storage material 154, 244
Sulphur cycle 86, 216, 241–7, Fig. 8.9
Sulphur purple bacteria 27, 64
Sulphur respiration, *see* Dissimilatory
  sulphur reduction
Sulphureta 87
Superoxide anion radical (O_2^-) 24
Superoxide dismutase 24, 37, 167
Surfaces
  attachment to 199, 207
  as habitats 127, 128, 199
Surface films 136
Surface to volume ratio 5
Survival of microorganisms
  in aquatic environment 132–6
  influence of humidity 162
  mechanisms 124, 153
  pathogens 125
  in terrestrial environment 124–6
Swarm cell
  Bdellovibrio 98
  Caulobacter 72, Fig. 3.3
  Hyphomicrobium 73, Fig. 3.3
  myxobacteria 69
Symbionts of
  animals 107, 136, 200–4
  plants 192–7
Symbiosis of microorganisms
  cyclic 204
  definition, types of 182
  with insects 116, 202
  legume–Rhizobium 194–6, Fig. 7.3
  rumen 200, Fig. 7.4
Synchytrium endobioticum 107

Synechococcus 62, 63, Fig. 3.1
  S. lividus 64, 141
Synecology 172
Synthetic polymers Fig. 8.14
  microbial degradation 259–60
Syntrophic associations 33, 84, 184
Systematics 13

TCC, *see* Tricarboxylic acid cycle
TC-loop, in archaebacteria 10
Tactic responses 154, 155
Taxon 13, 56
Taxonomy 13–16
Taxospecies 13
Teflon 259, Fig. 8.14
Teichoic acids Fig. 2.3
  in cell wall 7, 96
Teliospores 198
Temperature
  cardinal growth ts. 163, Fig. 5.3
  extreme 140, 142
  freezing t. 177
  range of 140, 163–5
  selective factor in enrichment 54
Termites 202
Terrestrial environments 116–29
Tetracyclins 103
Tetradecanal 203
Thallus 12
Thermal stress 165
Thermoacidophilic bacteria 10
Thermoactinomyces 141, 153
  T. vulgaris 102
Thermocline 67, 134, Fig. 4.4
Thermophiles, *see* Thermophilic
  microorganisms
Thermophilic microorganisms 85, 140,
  Fig. 5.3
  acidophilic 143, 163
Thermophily 140
Thermoplasma 12, 104
  T. acidophilum 106, 143, 144
Thermus aquaticus 140, 142, Fig. 5.3
  fatty acid pattern 142
Thiamin pyrophosphate Fig. 2.14
Thiobacilli 85–7, 143, 244, 248
  biodeterioration 246
  as chemolithoautotrophs 85, 244
  habitats 86, 141
Thiobacillus
  T. acidophilus 86
  T. denitrificans 85, 178, 237, 246
  T. ferrooxidans 86, 143, 249
  T. intermedius 86
  T. neapolitanus 85
  T. novellus 85

T. thermophilica 143
T. thiooxidans 86, 138, 246, 247
T. thioparus 85
Thiobacterium 86
Thiodendron, *T. latens* 73
Thiodictyon 67
Thiopedia, *T. rosea* Fig. 3.2
Thioploca 86
Thiomicrospira 86
Thiospira 86
Thiospirillum jenense 64, Fig. 3.2
Thiosulphate 84
Thiotrix 69, 86, 152, 244
  T. nivea 157
  T. trichogenes 69
Thiovolum 51, 244
  T. majus 11
Thraustochytridiales 133
Threonine deaminase 49
  regulation Fig. 2.18
Thylakoid membrane 27, 61
Tissue culture 103, 206
Torulopsis 133, 227, 231
Toxins 100, 176, 205, 208
Toxothrix 69
Trace elements 17
Transaldolases 39
Transcription 47
Transformations
  calcium 250, 251
  iron, manganese 249, 250
  silicon 251
Transketolases 39
Transport 165
Treponema 75, 76, 206
  T. carateum 77
  T. dentium 199
  T. pallidum 11, 175, 205
  T. pertenue 77
Treponemes 51, 76, 177
Tricarboxylic acid cycle 40, Fig. 2.15
Trichinella spiralis 23
2,4,5-T, Trichlorophenoxyacetic acid 254
  chemical structure Fig. 8.10
Trichoderma 221
Trichodesmium 63
Tricholoma 193
Trichomes 11, 61, 99
Trichomonas 23
Trichophyton 227
Triphenyltetrazolium chloride 277
Trophic levels 122
Truncatella 221
Trypanosoma 109
  T. gambiense 174, 175
Tsetse fly 174

Tundra ruminants 241
Turbidostat 20

Ubichinon 27, 31
Ultrafreezing 56
Upwell areas 144, 217
Urea decomposition 100
Urease 89
  adsorption to soil particles 128
Uredinales 107
Ustilaginales 107

Vectors, in dispersal of disease 174
Veillonella 97
  V. alcalescens 199, 201
Verticillium 221
  V. alboatrum 52
  V. dahliae 163
Vesicular–arbuscular (VA) mycorrhiza 194
Vibrio 88, 132, 141, 206, 237
  V. cholerae 92, 156, 175
  V. costilocus Fig. 5.2
  V. marinus 141
Violacein 92, 168
Viroids 10
Virulence 208
Viruses 9
Vitamins
  assay 17
  as growth factors 17, 55, 185
Vorticella 110

Warburg–Dickens–Horecker pathway, *see*
  Pentose phosphate pathway
Wart disease of potato 107
Waste water 173
Water activity (a_w) 158
Water blooms 11
Water fern 46
Water film, on soil particles 162
Water potential (ψ)
  concept 119
  definition 159
  minimum w.p. for growth 160, Figs. 5.1,
    5.2
Water regime 158–63
Water stress 160
Weathering, role of microorganisms in 117
Winogradsky 50, 52, 68, 240
  column 179, Fig. 6.1
Wood decay 225
Wright–Burri closure 56

Xanthobacter autotrophicus 24
Xanthomonadin 80

Xanthomonas 79, 197
  X. campestris 125
  X. citri 80
  X. malvacearum 80
Xanthophyceae 109
Xenobiotic chemicals 252, 260, 261
Xeromyces bisporus 139, Fig. 5.1
Xerotolerance 139
Xylans 200
  components of 222, Fig. 8.3
Xylaria 224
Xylose, chemical structure Fig. 8.3

Yeasts 23, 153, 199
  osmophilic 187
Yellow fever 174

Yersinia 206
  Y. enterocolitica 91
  Y. pestis 91
  Y. pseudotuberculosis 91
Yoghurt 98

Zoochlorellae 108, 203
Zoochoric dispersal 174
Zoogloea 79
  Z. ramigera 80
Zooplankton 131
Zoospores 107, 174
Zygomycetes 107, 174, 194
Zygospore 107
Zymogenous flora 115
Zymomonas mobilis 92